MEN IN
FEMINISM

MEN IN FEMINISM

EDITED BY
Alice Jardine &
Paul Smith

ROUTLEDGE   NEW YORK AND LONDON

First published in 1987 by Methuen, Inc.
Reprinted in 1989 by
Routledge, as imprint of
Routledge, Chapman and Hall, Inc.
29 West 35th Street
New York, NY 10001

Published in Great Britain by
Routledge
11 New Fetter Lane
London EC4P 4EE

Copyright © 1987 by Methuen, Inc.

All rights reserved. No part of this book may be reprinted
or reproduced or utilized in any form or by any electronic,
mechanical or other means, now known or hereafter
invented, including photocopying and recording, or in any
information storage or retrieval system, without permission
in writing from the publishers.

Library of Congress in Publication Data
    Men in feminism.

        Includes index.
        1. Feminism.   2. Men—Psychology.   3. Sex role.
I. Jardine, Alice.   II. Smith, Paul.
HQ1154.M439   1987   305.4'2   86-33195
ISBN 0-416-01591-3
ISBN 0-415-90251-7

British Library Cataloguing in Publication Data

Men in feminism.
    1. Feminism
    I. Jardine, Alice A.   II. Smith, Paul
    305.4'2   HQ1154

    ISBN 0-416-01591-3
    ISBN 0-415-90251-7

Printed in the U.S.A.

Contents

Introduction

This book has its most immediate beginnings in two sessions conducted at the Modern Language Association meetings in Washington, D.C., December 1984. Sponsored by the Society for Critical Exchange (SCE) at the instigation of James Sosnoski, SCE's director, these sessions were organized by Paul Smith and were intended to produce a dialogue between male and female academics around the question of "Men in Feminism." This project has many beginnings, of course, but was most directly dictated by a couple of specific circumstances.

First, the two editors and another contributor, Rosi Braidotti, were engaged in a correspondence about an article by Smith, "A Question of Feminine Identity."[1] Discussion of that article directly involved consideration of the fact that the current work of a considerable number of male intellectuals in the humanities is consciously employing and deploying feminist thought and feminist theory. Some of this correspondence will be found in Alice Jardine's essay in this volume, while its more general effect was to have helped suggest the topic for the MLA sessions.

At about the same time, Smith was guest-editing an issue of *The Dalhousie Review* which was to include Stephen Heath's "Male Feminism," which begins this volume. That text was made available before the MLA to all seven session participants, as were drafts of papers by Ross and Smith. The first of the two sessions then consisted of papers by Ross, Smith, and Heath while the second session consisted of "responses" by Mayne, Weed, Jardine, and Kamuf; all are included here. The title of the sessions—provocative not just for its general topic, but perhaps even more for its use of the word "in"—was the product of conversations between Smith and Kamuf, and Smith and Sosnoski.

The dialogue that was begun at the MLA sessions provoked a certain amount of interest and even caused some little controversy. Several people who had heard the papers suggested that they be edited into a book along with other contributions. Smith was originally reluctant to do this work and asked Jardine if she would be interested in taking on such a task. Jardine agreed on the condition that the book be coedited. Once that was agreed upon we began to draw up a list of possible contributors.

At first we both felt, in our different ways, that the question of "men in feminism" was a relatively unpromising one. It seemed in a very real sense elitist and narrow, of interest only within the often somewhat insulated corridors of academia. One indication of this was the fact that we had trouble locating intellectuals, who, having shown interest in the question, would offer, for instance, a gay or a black perspective on the problem. It became clear almost immediately that this is largely a reflection of a serious institutional problem and that most (though, finally, not all) of our contributors would be straight, white academics. We mention this here, not to excuse ourselves or the book, but rather to point out what we still recognize as one of the major limitations of the topic.

However, at the same time we realized that the question was important in other ways. Even within the relatively narrow confines of academia political stuggles occur, have effects, and can be instructive. We recognized, because of the strength of both the positive and negative reactions we got when talking to colleagues about the project, that we had touched upon a struggle to which not much overt attention had hitherto been given. And, as we think many of our contributors demonstrate, thinking about "men in feminism" brings up questions and problems which go right to the heart of feminist theory.

In general, we wanted those issues and questions to be addressed as it were conversationally; that is, we have tried to continue the MLA dialogue here between roughly equal numbers of men and women. Many of the papers included here are related in that they respond to each other at some level. Unfortunately, it was not possible to ensure that all the contributors had access even to the MLA papers, but it seems nonetheless that common referents and common issues run through many of the contributions.

While recognizing some of the limitations of our project, we thought it productive finally that the issue of "men in feminism" be addressed and considered within the context of contemporary feminist theory. Our final editorial decisions about inclusion and exclusion in this volume have not been based upon strict agreement, pluralism, synthesis, comprehensiveness, balance, or any of the usual abstract terms of antho-logic. Rather, we have attempted to foreground the heterogeneity, to leave apparent the rough edges of this always impassioned debate. Most importantly, we hope that the dialogue that we begin here will continue, and that this book will be useful to anyone who, in any way at all, would want to support the theoretical and practical efforts of feminism.

Acknowledgments

This project would not have been undertaken at all without the initial energy, enthusiasm, and encouragement of James Sosnoski and the Society for Critical Exchange.

The editors would like to thank Elizabeth Weed and the Pembroke Center at Brown University for helping in several crucial ways in the preparation of this volume.

We thank Elaine Showalter for permission to reprint her "Critical Cross-dressing: Male Feminists and the Woman of the Year"; the editor of *The Dalhousie Review* for permission to reprint a shorter version of Stephen Heath's "Male Feminism"; and the editors of *subjects/objects* for permission to reprint "Women in the Beehive: A Seminar with Jacques Derrida." Denis Donoghue's "A Criticism of One's Own" is reprinted by permission of *The New Republic*, © 1986, The New Republic, Inc.

We also thank Stephen Pogue for permission to use his painting, "The Other," on the jacket.

Alice Jardine would like to thank Rosi Braidotti, Jane Gallop, Anne Menke, Nancy Miller, and Naomi Schor for their willingness to embark upon endless discussions about men in/and/or feminism.

Paul Smith would like to thank all the students and friends (not necessarily different categories) in his feminist classes at Wesleyan University and Miami University over the last four years, many of whom have helped him develop an optimism which is perhaps not sufficiently apparent in this book but which is real just the same.

1.
Male Feminism

STEPHEN HEATH

Men's relation to feminism is an impossible one. This is not said sadly nor angrily (though sadness and anger are both known and common reactions) but politically. Men have a necessary relation to feminism—the point after all is that it should change them too, that it involves learning new ways of being women *and men* against and as an end to the reality of women's oppression—and that relation is also necessarily one of a certain exclusion—the point after all is that this is a matter *for women*, that it is their voices and actions that must determine the change and redefinition. Their voices and actions, not ours: no matter how "sincere," "sympathetic" or whatever, we are always also in a male position which brings with it all the implications of domination and appropriation, everything precisely that is being challenged, that has to be altered. Women are the subjects of feminism, its initiators, its makers, its force; the move and the join from being a woman to being a feminist is the grasp of that subjecthood. Men are the objects, part of the analysis, agents of the structure to be transformed, representatives in, carriers of the patriarchal mode; and my desire to be a subject there too in feminism—to be a feminist—is then only also the last feint in the long history of *their* colonization. Which does not mean, of course not, that I can do nothing in my life, that no actions are open to me, that I cannot respond to and change for feminism (that would be a variant on the usual justification for the status quo, men are men and that's that); it just means that I have to realize nevertheless—and this is an effort not a platitude—that I am not where they are and that I cannot pretend to be (though men do, colonizing, as they always have done), which is the impossibility of my, men's, relation.

Nothing in the above is intended to suggest a kind of criterion of immediacy. Women are not feminists by virtue of the fact alone of being women: feminism is a social-political reality, a struggle, a commitment, women *become* feminists. Simply, the negotiation between lived experience and feminism is for them direct, feminism includes that experience as its material and its energy, producing a knowledge of it for action, for change. The contradictions that may exist between, say, a woman's experience in her family in the defined roles of wife and housewife and mother which may be felt by her as the authentic terms of her being, where she is really "herself," and the perspectives feminism will give on that experience, those defined roles, on her position as a woman, are what feminism is about, what it looks at, works from, involves, allowing the move and join from woman to feminist. For a man the negotiation is blocked, doubly contradictory: his experience is her oppression, and at the end of whatever negotiation he might make he can only always also confront the fact that feminism starts from there. To refuse the confrontation, to ignore, repress, forget, slide over, project onto "other men" that fact, is for a man to refuse feminism, not to listen to what it says to him as a man, imagining to his satisfaction a possible relation instead of the difficult, contradictory, self-critical, painful, impossible one that men must, for now, really live.

"I am tired of men arguing amongst themselves as to who is the most feminist, frustrated by an object feminism becoming the stakes in a displaced rivalry between men because of a refusal by men to examine the structure of the relations between themselves," Claire Pajaczkowska.[1] There we have an expression of anger from a feminist, tiredness and frustration. And I accept that. But how? At a distance? Of course I think that *I* never have argued about being "the most feminist," others, not me. Yet I can hardly stay at that distance, self-assured, as if I do then, exactly, feminism *is* an object, something I *can* simply position myself in relation to, like some academic study. But then again, if I take it up into me, into my life, calling into question the assumptions of the position of myself (as opposed to just "taking it up" like Sanskrit or Deconstruction), how do I develop a reflection on it, how do I think and talk and write about—*with*—feminism without falling back into the male argument, without producing another version of the object feminism up for grabs, "the stakes"?

Pajaczkowska suggests an answer, by examining the structure of the relations between men, me in those relations. She says this, in fact, in an article on pornography, a response to two pieces by men on that topic; which reminds me of a remark by another feminist, B. Ruby Rich, again in an article on pornography, to the effect that if "the legions of feminist men" wanted to do something useful, "a proper subject," they could "undertake the analysis that can tell us why men like porn (not, piously, why this or that exceptional man does *not*)."[2]

Pornography and the relations between men and liking pornography . . . That pornography *is* a relation between men, nothing to do with a relation to women except by a process of phallic conversion that sets them as the terms of male exchange, is now an established part of radical critical awareness; the analysis has been made many times. Which still leaves theoretical-political *issues*: even if a typical reality of pornography can be recognized, is pornography only that, are there distinctions to be made, different kinds? is all pornography violent and offensive? are there connections between pornography and sexual liberation that are important, progressive? are men's and women's pleasures in sexual imagery bound up with or separate— separable—from pornographic representations and how? are pornographic images for male arousal necessarily the reproduction of domination? what should be done about pornography and how? is it in itself a central target for action or does it deflect from the needed critique of and challenge to the violent sexual objectification of women running through the whole range of cultural forms that are socially accepted as non-pornographic? All these and more are issues that have been, are being debated by women, by feminists (for an argued account, from which I have borrowed here, I refer to the relevant chapter of Elizabeth Wilson's *What Is To Be Done About Violence Against Women?*[3]).

My immediate concern though is male feminism. I once wrote, quoting a phrase coined by Robin Morgan and used in women-against-pornography movements: "'Pornography is the theory and rape the practice'—learning to understand the truth of that statement—and to understand it personally, with respect to one's own life—is a political-ethical necessity."[4] I believe that, for men: if men do not grasp that in themselves, then I think that the social structure of sexual oppression is still abstract for them and that feminism is beyond them, out there, just an object again. This is not, obviously, to say that feminism is merely about pornography, only that pornography in our societies, the capitalized circulation of images of sexual-commodity women, is one good crystallization of that social structure, that oppression (there are many others), whether or not those images are ostensibly violent or ostensibly not. "Pornography is the theory and rape the practice" says it exactly; and if, a reproach that is made, this is a crude position, and reading the feminist debate round the issues mentioned above does make the question complex, difficult, it must still be said that starting from it is necessary for men—do we want to be *subtle* about it, more prevarication, more defensiveness?

One way of grasping the structure of the relations between men is, indeed, with respect to pornography in these terms: what complicity of masculinity does pornography involve me in? Whether or not *I* have anything to do with it is in this context irrelevant (no need for personal piousness); it has to do with me, inescapably, not just because I live in its society but because too, which is what that means, pornography is this society's running commentary on the sexual for me, the final image I can have (how do I dissociate myself from that image and don't I in the very fact of dissociation recognize its involvement of me, in me?). And it runs into theory as well. For Freud after all, in the last years of his long life's work of the elaboration of psychoanalysis, "the repudiation of femininity must surely be a biological fact, part of the great riddle of sex."[5] Edged through by "femininity," object and limit, explanation and enigma, psychoanalysis turns round and round again to its difficulties, all its insights and its blindnesses coming down into Freud's ultimate weariness, the gloom of understanding, "the repudiation of femininity." Pornography in its typical contemporary reality knows nothing but that: it gives a "female sexuality" that fits and reassures the repudiation, the representation of her confirmed and confirming—woman as phallic, the same in a masculine sexual economy, and woman as passive, feminine, the exact and separate other half, the opposite sex, that that economy requires, allaying the fear of the non-identity of maleness, that men might really be feminine and passive too ("masculine" and "feminine," those concepts that Freud rejects as "of no use" in psychology but that he continues to use, filling them with "active" and "passive," and that he finds with the psychical "bedrock" of every male or female individual: men fear passivity, women envy the penis, femininity repudiated). Pornography is developed to be about "men together," in every sense of the term: all the figures in its system are male, masculinity from start to finish; its consumption defines a community of men; its aim is my identity as defined maleness, *me* together, untouched by real relations of sexual difference that include me in the fact of difference, in a sexuality that is heterogeneous, problematic, unstable, the process of my individual history, not just one sex, one's sex, the given heterosexual.

What can then be asked, I think, coming back to theory, coming back to male feminism, is whether that sexual system, that togetherness, is not always in danger of being replayed: contemporary theory as the rebonding of men round "the feminine" (what exactly is happening when Derrida proclaims his wish to write "as (a) woman" and all those deconstructing academics excel themselves for the time of a book or an article in woman's non-place, knowing as "*she* knows" that "there is no truth"?[6]), male feminism as getting hold again—for the last time?—of the question of "the woman" (are we sure that we are *so* far from the general cultural fascination with woman and "liberation" and the sexual, from all its modes of recuperation?). Pajaczkowska's tiredness and frustration can go alongside and as a counterbalance to Freud's weariness: the repudiation of femininity and an object feminism, feminism as an expression of women that becomes an object for me, another way of retrieving her, very nicely, as mine, another view of the old enigma, woman again. Is it possible to wonder whether there is not in male feminism, men's relation to feminism, always potentially a pornographic effect?

Which is said in difficulty, in recognition of something of the contradictions that there must be in this social reality for men who try
to be with feminism. Society, Freud insisted, was rooted in male homosexual love, it was this which was compatible with group ties;
women laid the foundations of civilization by the claims of their love
which are then also its disturbance, an opposition of women little
capable of instinctual sublimation, a sexual threat; so that society
stands on the bond of men, repressed homosexuality, maintained in
its patriarchal forms on the absolute distinction of the sexes, men as
men, one and then the other, she as the difference, the projected
"dark continent," man's unknown. Recently, Rosalind Coward has
stressed that it is in reality "men's bodies, men's sexuality which is
the true 'dark continent' of this society."[7] The risk of men's relation
to feminism is that it stay a male affair, an argument round women
that masks again its male stakes, that refuses again as women are
projected back into the safeguard of our identity the real problem,
the real point at which change must come, exactly ourselves, the end
of "masculinity"—which, of course, is the end of "woman" too.

"What do men know about women's martyrdoms?", wrote Thackeray in 1848 in his novel *Vanity Fair*: "We should go mad had we to
endure the hundredth part of those daily pains which are meekly
borne by many women. Ceaseless slavery meeting with no reward;
constant gentleness and kindness met by cruelty as constant; love,
labour, patience, watchfulness, without even so much as the acknowledgement of a good word; all this, how many of them have to
bear in quiet, and appear abroad with cheerful faces as if they felt
nothing. Tender slaves that they are, they must needs be hypocrites
and weak."[8]
Thackeray is sympathetic *and* patronizing *and* caught up in all the
attitudes that help to make the situation of women he describes.
Women are exploited but that exploitation is also their nature; they
are tender slaves, that is what makes them women. All the terms that
Thackeray uses—gentleness, kindness, love, labour, patience, watchfulness—are women's qualities, the fact of their true womanhood,
and the situation described is the context in which those qualities are
brought out; so that what is at stake is not change but recognition—
the acknowledgement of a good word, the due reward for the ceaseless slavery. Sincerely, Thackeray is locked into his perception of
"women's martyrdoms": women's lot is cruel and he is alongside
them to express the cruelty; martyrdom is the very condition of saints
and he is there to celebrate saintliness, reconfirming that lot.
We can see this easily now, looking back at the past, men as well
as women. But how much of male feminism today may not also be

analysable as a similar gesture of sympathy-reconfirmation? Can men
see that? Suspicion of sympathy: *why, how* am *I* sympathetic?

Barthes one day in conversation: "you study what you desire or
what you fear." In any formal sense I haven't studied feminism or
feminist issues (is formal study anyway the point?) but I have read
and thought about and written in relation to it and them, written on
matters that are matters with which feminism is concerned—sexual
difference, the contemporary construction of sexuality, the imaging
and representation of men and women. Desire? Fear? Both? The questions are difficult to avoid. Writing after all is always an imaging and
representation of myself, the passage of a certain desire: it takes a
stance and asks for me to be seen in this or that way, even if I cannot
control—master—its effects, how you will read me. Of course, there
are conventions and genres of the elimination of desire, my writing
as the voice of truth, reason, science, which is then the imaging and
representation of an institutionalized mastery, my desire for that, that
as my "fitness." To respond to feminism is to forgo mastery: "the
personal is political" tells me also that I cannot refuse to analyze my
desire, that the impersonal safety of authority can no longer be mine.
Is that then where the fear enters and connects? Feminism makes
things unsafe for men, unsettles assumed positions, undoes given
identities. Hence so often the violence of the reactions, that is clear.
But hence too perhaps, less clear, elements in the relations men make
with feminism, their sympathy. If I can move close to feminism, it
may be that I can regain something of a male/female security, get back
something of an identity. Do I write from desire-fear, to say simply
in the last analysis "love me," accept me at least as "modestly, ingloriously marginal"? Which was indeed Barthes's definition of *the
lover* today.

Desire and fear at any rate could serve as something of a genealogical probe for male feminism, somewhere from which to think about
this or that manifestation and its implications. To think about, which
does not mean to reduce to but merely to remember *as well* the sexual
strategies of discourse, the subjectivity of the production of knowledge. One could, for example, think about Lacan and his work in this
way, giving a different perspective to those of the accounts by followers and propagators. From the initial encounter with the woman,
the enigma of her (in the 1930s, curiously coincidental with the beginnings of Freud's "return" to "femininity," "the dark continent,"
Lacan confronts female paranoia, the Papin sisters and Aimée, the
subject of his thesis) through to the *Encore* seminar and beyond (Lacan
in the 1970s devoting himself explicitly to "what Freud expressly left
aside, the *Was will das Weib?*, the *What does woman want?*"[9]), we have
what? The question, the woman, her non-existence, her not-allness,

a pleasure—*jouissance*—proper to her, supplementary, beyond the phallus, related to God . . . and an address and a self-address in and out of all this which is at once provocative, Lacan putting feminists right, ah the phallus, and identificationary, Lacan a better woman and in love with him and herself, talking about love itself a *jouissance* and psychoanalysis nothing else but that anyway . . . "When it comes down to it," announced Lacan on one occasion to his seminar audience, "I am a perfect hysteric, that is to say, without symptoms, except from time to time mistakes in gender," having given an example of taking "Miss"—*Mademoiselle*—for masculine.[10] The male analyst understands the woman and speaks in her place, is the perfection of the hysteric, no symptoms, save only the mistakes in gender, the misidentifications indeed, running in and out of her from *his* position, miss-taken but perfect—fear, desire, the love letter as regrounding of authority.

(And where does that leave the woman Lacanian analyst? In his place too? Exactly?)

When the Lacanian analyst sees young people on nude-bathing beaches, what does she know? "They [the young people] want to go all the way to the end, but there is no end, other than castration and death."[11] Naively, I understand death as an end, a final reality, but *castration*? The fact of sexual reproduction is also the fact of death, the continuation of the species at the cost of the individual who is transient, mortal. To say which, however, is not to say castration, castration as end, another final reality. There are lots of things one might grasp on nude beaches, and depending on their location: for instance, the beaches in the South of France which this analyst most likely has in mind raise questions to do with the treatment and place of the old (why "young people"?), with racial inequality (how many of France's "immigrant" population are to be seen?), with the whole economic definition of the body, the sexual. But *castration*?

"It's extraordinary," commented Juliet Mitchell in an interview recently, "what happens when you get rid of the centrality of the concept of the phallus. I mean, you get rid of the unconscious, get rid of sexuality, get rid of the original psychoanalytic point."[12] Just as on the beach we confront castration, so we cannot think without the centrality of the concept of the phallus—to do so would be to "get rid of" the unconscious and sexuality. These latter are bound up with difference and division and language in the individual, the excess of the individual over the simple sexual function of species reproduction, the movement of desire that that excess constitutes in our particular histories as speaking beings. For psychoanalysis, which indeed opens up for understanding this scene of the unconscious and sexuality, the phallus, the penis sublime as symbol, is *the* mark of division

and difference, the ur-signifier, the ultimate and initial point of meaning, closing the unconscious and sexuality round it. And from there
the scenario is everywhere played out, down to the young people on
the beach, no other end, it's extraordinary . . .

What can I say to that? Apart from, in the crudest psychoanalytic
response, *nothing*, since to say anything to it is merely an indication
of my resistance, defence, denial, since the phallus and castration
give the very structure from where I can speak at all. I can say and
try to show that what is being described by psychoanalysis with the
phallus and castration and all the other accompanying terms fits a
specific social-historical definition and production of men, women,
sexuality. I can say and try to show that the fact of division, the
unconscious and the sexual is not by definition dependent on the
primacy of the phallus, locked immutably in the same old fixed scenario (joining the whole debate on psychoanalysis and historical understanding to which Juliet Mitchell herself has contributed so much).
The theoretical work is valuable and perhaps I can help in it. But what
can I say from day to day, teaching, talking, just generally around?
I find myself in fact continually defending and criticizing Freud and
Lacan, psychoanalysis in their terms, rejecting and needing its descriptions, those terms. Which is where it is true that castration is the
end, the final reality of this peculiar split, the original point to which
it all comes down and from which, getting rid of the centrality of the
concept of the phallus, it all has to be rethought, relived.

But then these are pious words and perhaps this is another way
of saying the impossibility of men's relation to feminism. It is as
though psychoanalysis is there as a kind of necessary impasse today,
full of truth about the construction of our subjectivity, about the realization of the sexual identity of men and women, and full of an
historical and social censorship, the foregone conclusion of the centrality of the concept of the phallus. The use of the truth against the
censorship by women is one thing, but men after all *are* that truth,
they can hardly simply use it against the censorship they today define
and represent. I think of another analyst, close to and distant from
Lacan, saying once: "Imagine that it were a woman who had invented
the unconscious . . . certainly she would not have invented that unconscious. Impossible, absolutely impossible."[13] Yes and no? No
doubt she would not have, but the unconscious that Freud invented
he also found, found these particular structures and the phallus with
them. Freud gets Dora right and she him, which is where the protest,
the use, the critique, the reinvention begin, as they only can, from
her.

Feminism is a subject for women who are, precisely, its subjects,
the people who make it; it is their affair. Feminism is also a subject

for men, what it is about obviously concerns them; they have to learn to make it their affair, to carry it through into our lives. Feminism speaks to me, not principally nor equally but *too*, to me too: the definitions and images and stories and laws and institutions oppressive of women that it challenges, ends, involve me since not only will I find myself playing some part in their reproduction but I too am caught up in them, given as "man" in their reflection, confined in that place which is then presented as "mine." I have written about this, written about matters of feminism, for example in the book *The Sexual Fix* quoted above about the current construction of sexuality for men and women or in an essay entitled "Difference" about psychoanalysis and sexual difference.[14] But I do not at all think, even less claim, that these are feminist writings; it is just that they depend on learning from feminism. This is, I believe, the most any man can do today: to learn and so to try to write or talk or act in response to feminism, and so to try not in any way to be anti-feminist, supportive of the old oppressive structures. Any more, any notion of writing a feminist book or being a feminist, is a myth, a male imaginary with the reality of appropriation and domination right behind. But who am I to say this? But still, can't I say that this seems to me how we should see it, part of the ethics of sexual difference today?

Then I think of a counter-example, a bit of *evidence*. Isn't John Stuart Mill's *The Subjection of Women* evidently a feminist book? No doubt. Here is a book written by a man that was clearly progressive and important for feminism, part of its history, Mill's intervention into the debate over the equality of the sexes widely recognized by women in the late nineteenth-century and subsequently as "an enormous advantage to the whole women's movement."[15] No doubt. But *historically*. Today the history has changed, feminism has grown and advanced, there is no place in that way for a Mill.

And anyway Mill did not set out to write a feminist book, "just" a book about the situation and rights of women. And anyway recognition of his book's very positive and effective contribution need not avoid the possibility of a negative aspect, Mill's work depending on his male authority and perhaps hiding the work of the women around him on whose actions and analyses he depended at the same time that his book would encourage them. And anyway, the point of this here, the *preoccupation* with acting, speaking, writing "feminist," as opposed to the *fact* for women of being feminist, is male contemporary, observable now in certain groups of men (intellectuals, radicals): something to do with being right, correct, finding the authority of identity (and vice versa).

It happens often enough in meetings and discussions in which issues concerning feminism are involved and at which women are

largely present that one hears a man preface what he wants to say
with "I live with a radical feminist" or "I have talked about this with
a lot of radical women" or some other, similar statement. What follows is then usually some objection, the expression of some effectively
reactionary, very male-sexist position. This is a version, of course, of
the some-of-my-best-friends-are ploy, as such not specific to debates
about women and feminism, found also in, say, those about race,
about racism.

What interests me, though, is that some of us have learnt not to
say such things, have learnt that we cannot guarantee our position
in that way, that *just because* the personal is political it cannot be used
to shore up some purity of being—some rightness—for me. The personal as political means that I cannot simply refer to the personal as
my identity, that I have to think that identity through in the social
terms it carries at its center, as an *identity*: however many feminist
women I know, it is not going to remove me from the structures of
sexism, absolve me from the facts of male positioning, domination
and so on. The oppression of women is not personal, it is social and
I am involved in it as a person in this society; there is no personal
guarantee against that. Though this is not to say that I am powerless
to renegotiate my identity against those structures, that positioning—
that after all has been the work of women in feminism, opposing the
given terms for them, renegotiating *their* identity.

Where then am I when I hear "I live with etc."? Somewhere else.
I know better. Do I? And really somewhere else? The problem is still
one of guarantees: to believe I am somewhere else and know better
is still to appeal to a personal distinction and to suggest an authorization. But what could this latter be? It is not, another version of the
personal guarantee, that women's discourse is secured as feminist by
the fact of their being women (there are reactionary and anti-feminist
women) but that the relation between discourse and experience is
politically negotiable by women in respect of the reality of their position as objects of oppression, inequality, sexism. Unable to make
that negotiation, I am caught in the double bind of a position and a
discourse that will always also be today a reflection of domination,
social maleness. Whenever I know, precisely I don't, and I have to
accept a certain insecurity, the end of authority and authorization, to
live a difficult and contradictory process of renegotiation in which *I*
can never be assured (no matter what reassurance—the guarantees—
I might try to claim). I have to beware too of turning this into some
kind of existential tragedy (the tough-time-men-now-have on which
popular magazines are always running stories); it's just a political
fact, no more, no less.

One can also add to the "I live with etc." gesture the frequently
observed ambition of men to be more radical, the most radical in

feminism. Once again the more, the most, guarantees, proves correctness. Except, of course, that it doesn't; the extreme simply wipes out the experience it purports to represent (as men have always ordinarily done). So that "radical" in what preceded ought to have been in inverted commas, since this "radical" is literally reaction, male reaction, against the new reality of women and feminism that exactly it refuses in the very moment it speaks for it, for them.

In a lecture given a few years ago to the—shortlived—Cambridge Alternative English Faculty (the lecture subsequently became part of a chapter of his *Walter Benjamin or Towards a Revolutionary Criticism*), Terry Eagleton, after having reviewed some of the issues for a Marxist aesthetics and listed "the major Marxist Aestheticians of the century to date" from Lukács to himself, turned to "feminist criticism" as "a paradigm" for "a 'revolutionary literary criticism,'" entering as he did so the following "reservation": "Feminist criticism is still notably underdeveloped, and much of it so far has been empiricist, unsubtle and theoretically thin."[16] I think there was a little *frisson* in the audience, something rather daring had been said, and also some unexpressed rage.

"Reservation" is an interesting word in this context: the stance of the securely judging voice, commending and caveating; the indication of the containing place assigned, feminist criticism sent back to its reservation; and then, coming round to the voice again, the confirmation of the stance, this voice reserving its rights as it enters the reservation, seeing feminist criticism within the limits of its place. And in fact, "feminist literary theory" as sighted by Eagleton is exactly a theoretical problem from the outside, the onlooker's worry about specificity and autonomy, about whether the people on the reservation have anything very much to say for themselves theoretically, depending as they do on other "general theories" ("most notably, Marxism, semiotics and psychoanalysis"): "There is, then, a theoretical problem about the meaning of an autonomous 'feminist literary theory' of any developed kind." Not that there isn't also a political problem, that of the "'radical-feminist' problematic," the "jealous defence of feminist 'autonomy'—*separatism*, in fact" which is "a scandal that any revolutionary, man or woman, must surely denounce." Feminism is found lacking in autonomy in theory, which is its failing (note the doubting quote marks, "'feminist literary theory'"), but when you get autonomy in practice it is another kind of failing, a real scandal (and the quote marks shift their position and attack, "feminist 'autonomy'").

Might not all this be completely irrelevant? Suppose we abandoned the judgment of autonomy, specificity and so on, stopped worrying about feminist theory in those terms, recognized it as strongly unreserved, not much bothered about where it might fit in some overall theoretical spectacle. Theory, we know, has its etymological roots in spectacle, the Greek *theoria* with its indications of sight and contemplation, and women have long been the point of its spectacular exclusion, at best a voice-off (as with the "woman from Mantinea, called Diotima" to whom Socrates appeals in *The Symposium* for his major speech on love[17]). Perhaps theory, not the theoretical but *theory* with all its reservations, is today a male move, an argument from men, their self-preserve, the dominant reservation (Irigaray has been saying and showing this in her work, to be greeted again and again with cries of "irrationalism," another scandal[18]). And then what are men doing when they shift their gaze from theory to practice, a less controllable spectacle, and inveigh in their theory-books against "'radical feminism'" (more quote marks), against that "feminist 'autonomy'" which any revolutionary woman, he says, must surely denounce? Isn't feminism now exactly about women's autonomy and isn't the definition of the terms of that autonomy exactly an issue for women? Is it helpful, appropriate, feminist for men to stand in judgment of feminism and its theoretical work and its political debates, brandishing an assumed standard of autonomy in the one hand and its foregone dismissal in the other?

None of this is written to be cleverer than or superior to Terry Eagleton (to whom, as my teacher, I anyway owe so much), even if in the reflection of writing I cannot—do not know how to—avoid that male image, the image of bettering, of asserting superiority. Given theory and reservations, Eagleton's "theoretically thin" is probably right; he thinks it is. I think the contrary, that if we step outside the bounds of theory and reservations, stop waiting to see "what a 'feminist literary theory' as such might mean" (why are we waiting to see and should women wait too?), we shall find a range of work by feminists (Irigaray and Spivak and Bovenschen and Coward and . . ., though the point is not to produce an imitation of Eagleton's list of "major Marxist aestheticians") which can only make the judgment of "theoretically thin" appear as a gesture of reaction and resistance (*who* cares if this work doesn't fit some decided image of what should be "a 'feminist literary theory' as such"?). Eagleton knows all this better than I do, but then he takes his position and I take mine; and in that movement I feel once again the difficulties, the conflict, the impossibilities of men's relation to feminism.

I experience embarrassment—a kind of critical unease—at writings by men on female sexuality: how can they, how can *he* still presume . . .? But then I think of the reverse, women writing on male sexuality, Kate Millett in *Sexual Politics*, for example, or all the work on pornography by Andrea Dworkin, Angela Carter, Susan Griffin and so many others. That they know, that *she* knows something essential about male sexuality seems to me evident; I learn from them. So, reversing again, men can write on female sexuality and women can learn too.

I hesitate, the embarrassment. All this reversing would be fine were it not that the two sides are neither equal nor symmetrical, are simply *not* the same. And this can be seen in the very idea of female sexuality, its construction as an object, something to write about. Take Freud: an essay entitled "Female Sexuality" but not one entitled "Male Sexuality," a chapter in the *New Introductory Lectures* on "Femininity" but not one on "Masculinity." Of course, Freud everywhere writes about men and sexuality, about the male sexual, but that is the norm, the point of departure, and as such at least unproblematic, not in question, not *the* question. When women around Freud write on female sexuality (Andreas-Salomé, Bonaparte, Deutsch, Horney . . .), often challengingly, they too are caught up in that question, his, and so contained nevertheless, as still by Lacan, still waiting contemptuously for women to come out with something of interest: "since the time we've been begging them, begging them on our knees—I mentioned previously women analysts—to try to tell us, well, not a word! never been able to get anything out of them."[19] He's right, they can't say anything interesting. How could they when the point is this *question*, which is always beyond whatever they might be able to say as the very fact of their being: they *are* the question. Female sexuality here is male sexuality, the male position and problem: woman as *my* other, she as the defining limit—the *jouissance au-delà*, as Lacanians put it—of my horizon as man.

In the overall system of sexuality that is tightened to perfection in the nineteenth century and that still today determines so powerfully in so many ways the facts of our lives, male sexuality is repetition, female sexuality is query (darkness, riddle, enigma, problem, etc.). Of the former one can say nothing inasmuch as there is nothing to say beyond a few technical descriptions and a couple of moral injunctions or routine celebrations; men are men, there is no metaphysical agitation. Of the latter one can say nothing either inasmuch as women as woman are the difference in the system so that there is everything to say; she is too much, a whole difficulty of knowing, which is where female sexuality becomes the object, the topic, the title of the paper or the chapter or the book. We are in a long history from the nineteenth century through to today in which the self-evidence of sex (man, woman, the sexual act, reproduction) begins to weaken, in which "sexuality" is the term of the recognition of everything that "sex," "one's sex," "the two sexes" do not say, those notions unable to tell us very much about sexual identity, about masculinity and femininity, about being a man, being a woman. Hence the tightening of the system, the definitions and redefinitions, the worried construction of "female sexuality," all that writing; hence the constant return of sexuality to sex, to a phallic identity of man and woman, the sexual fix.

In a way, then, female sexuality is a bad question from a rotten history; *and* a necessary one, for women against that history, disturbing its monolithic fiction (I pick up a feminist anthology, *Desire: The Politics of Sexuality*, not a single piece is called "Female Sexuality" or "Femininity," as though here the exploration of sexuality for women has already gone elsewhere to that construction[20]). While "male sexuality" is a good question from a rotten history that could not pose it; an inevitable question for women, for Millett, for the writers on pornography, for those on rape, domestic violence, all the other matters of oppression. Instead of begging on our knees for women to go on silently proving their phallic otherness, we can listen to what they are effectively saying about *us*, about male sexuality, about the male operation of the sexual in our societies.

This is not to suggest that men might not have, ought not to have, something significant and real and unoppressive to say about women and sexuality: men's experience after all is part of many women's sexuality and men can know things in different ways, just as women can of men's sexuality. For the present though, in our societies, in our sexual history, I doubt in fact that men, that we, can. There is no equality, no symmetry, and so there can be no reversing: it is for women now to reclaim and redefine the terrain of sexuality, for us to learn from them. Which explains the unease, my opening embarrassment.

At a meeting of the Lacan School a woman analyst says this: "The nature of femininity is to be cause of man's desire and, as corollary, not to be able to be recognized other than by a man is the nature of femininity. I know that the MLF [Women's Liberation Movement] will be super-angry but I'll carry on . . ."[21]

Whether or not feminists will be "super-angry" (my rendering of the here trivializing *furax*, a kid's slang version of *furieux*, "furious") will presumably depend on the stress given "femininity." If it is a matter of femininity as the constructed image of women, the image in which they are recognized and held as women, then what is being said is a truism: man's desire is set in relation to that construction of femininity which women are made to match and which thus exists precisely by virtue of its recognition by men. In that sense indeed, it really does take a man to know a woman, since she in this femininity is his knowledge, his image, the height of his imagination—"a real woman." If it is a matter of something else, of femininity in connection with the reality and experience of women, being a woman, then what is being said might well give rise to anger, to political critique, to feminism.

Perhaps it is almost that "feminine" and "femininity" should be scrapped, their use abandoned; they come too loaded with the image, the construction, the monolithic male definition of the "qualities" of women-woman. But not "masculine" and "masculinity," which *can* be used each time to name the elements of a system that assures male domination. The "feminine" produced within that system is a male malady, fully masculine: *he* is sick from women, hence his endless attempts to confirm *her* as illness (the whole nineteenth-century coupling of women and sickness, "for her own good"). "Femininity": the woman you want, the woman you fear; "masculinity": exactly the same.

Sometimes the sexologists ask us to consider and remember the terms of ownership in sexual exchange: "Did you know that while it is true that anatomically a penis belongs to the man, his erection belongs to a woman?"[22]

Just about everything could be taken apart in that self-assured—Did you know?—sentence, from its hesitant grammatical logic (so that we might read the erection as belonging *anatomically* to a woman) to its instant heterosexuality (why can't the erection belong to him or to another man or, come to that, to no one at all in particular?). But my interest here is in the notion of belonging. Since I take it that it isn't a question of belonging anatomically for a woman, in what sense *does* his erection "belong"? The flourished big deal for women in these ownership stakes, his erection belongs to her, is, of course, the reverse, is the reality of the same old story, *she* belongs to the erection: if there is an erection, then there must be "a woman," she is its natural consequence, she's going to have to be around belonging—what, after all, does woman want? Somewhere at the far end of the sexologists' happy sentence is the philosophy of rape: his erection *belongs* to a woman, so she *must* want it and *ought* to get it, etc.

Perhaps there are different ways of thinking about belonging. Thus Michèle Montrelay: "In the sexual act, the penis plunges into a 'feminine' *jouissance* of which one no longer knows to whom it belongs."[23] I am not sure about the "one" there used to cover both men and women (is the experience of no longer knowing the same for a woman as for a man?) and "the sexual act" is again heterosexual (how does the question of belonging carry over—should it?—to relations between men, between women?) but, that said, I can recognize what she describes as true, *possibly* true (this is a *version* of the sexual act). Montrelay also writes of a man as "son of his mother, and as such participating in her femininity." And I can recognize again what she is saying, despite the difficulties with "femininity," can grasp it as

experience, her way of talking about the instability, the breakdown
of the phallic identities on which the discourse of belonging depends
(note how the sexologists make everything turn on penis and
erection).

Belonging is a male problem in our existing system of man and
woman, "masculinity' and 'femininity"; it is the obsession of my identity as a man, getting things straight, knowing where I am and what
I have and where she is and what she hasn't. Look at D. H. Lawrence,
pioneer-philosopher and preacher-professor of the system: all that
mulling over the sexual act, maleness and femaleness, keeping man
and woman pure, bringing one into the singularity of one's male self
through that act and the necessary passivity of the belonging woman
claiming his erection as her object. Of course, we've made progress,
look at any book or film, *Rich and Famous* for example, a film that
acknowledges Lawrence as "a sexual test pilot waiting to dive": Chris
(Hart Bochner), a young male *Rolling Stone* journalist, "I don't like
girls of my age, they're always looking out for their orgasm"; Liz
(Jacqueline Bisset), an older woman novelist, "So?"; Chris, "They
should be looking out for ours." Another big deal, belonging again,
she *with me*. Of course, some of us have made more progress, look
at . . . At what exactly? Have we? What is the relation between men
and feminism and the sexual and belonging yet again? To what extent
do men use feminism for the assurance of an identity, now asking
to belong as a way of at least ensuring their rightness, a position that
gets her with me once more?

I can recognize what Montrelay describes, what she is saying, but
she starts from the other side to the sexologists who themselves start
from my side, the male assumption. She is utopian, about the confusion and disappearance of sides, no more belonging; they are realistic, within the reality of a system they repeat and thus support,
a system of belonging. Male feminism is between the two, the im-
possibleness yet again: itself a long way off and itself very near to
the reality of today which feminism precisely opposes for change.

"What does woman want?", said Freud, hardly jesting, and stayed
too readily with the old answers—to be a man (penis envy), to be a
woman (vaginal orgasm, a baby to make up for the penis she lacks)—
and the old discomfiture—"the riddle of the nature of femininity"
against which throughout history "people have knocked their
heads." Freud wasn't alone with that question, he just happens to
have given it its most famous and powerful formulation (and part of
the power depends on the very real advance that psychoanalysis
makes nevertheless in the exploration and understanding of sexuality, the complex individual history of sex and gender and identity).
The problem of "woman" was the great nineteenth-century thing,

exactly in proportion as women became a problem, as they challenged, that is, their established institution and oppression as "woman," "womanhood," the sweetly serving Queens that Ruskin defensively celebrates in _Sesame and Lilies_ (defensively because of the challenge, "We hear of the mission and of the rights of Woman . . ."). Baudelaire knew how to answer the question: "Woman is in heat and she wants to be fucked"; Freud knew from psychoanalysis that he didn't really know, hence the return to the enigma, the worry of the question. Which worry is anyway there in the very fact of the question, Baudelaire is as defensive as Ruskin, and the contempt and hatred increase in time to women's ideas of and demands for emancipation, self-definition, reaching a height in the early years of the twentieth century—they can be read, for instance, in T. S. Eliot's early poetry or in Otto Weininger's _Sex and Character_ (Freud interrupts— he says "I cannot interrupt"—his discussion of Little Hans to comment on the castration complex as both "the deepest unconscious root of anti-Semitism," a Jew having "something cut off his penis," and the strong "unconscious root for the sense of superiority over woman," Weininger's book being then cited as an instance of this connection, this dual hostility; perhaps he might later have cited Eliot's poetry too, whose anti-Semitic elements have often been noted).

We now know another question, have learnt to move from "What does woman want?" to "What do women want?" And we know, in theory at least, that it is not for us to answer but to listen. Yet the new question is not so distant from the old one, from an "a" to an "e" is a long way and not so far. We know that there is no essence-woman (but should we know that, is that a refusal of something, of real difference to which we are then comfortably blind?) and we know that the plural is important, living women in the plural, not fitting our images and decrees of "femininity" and "masculinity" (but should we know that, shouldn't we know too that the plural is a singular force, the women's _movement_?). We know so much . . . But in all this women are still the thing, what we have and hold in the question; maybe for as long as _we_ ask the question, think like that, it's too easy, too easy to _know_, maybe we're missing the point that the question has been taken away from us, maybe if we really listened that's what we'd hear, the end of _our_ question, of our _question_.

Here's a better question for us, its particular reference is to "male critics" and "feminist criticism" but those terms could be appropriately extended to "males" and "feminism": "Why is it that male critics in search of a cause find in feminist criticism their last hope?" Because . . . women have been men's problem, the question; and the historical reality of literature and theory over the last hundred and fifty years has been crucially bound up with that, a problematic of sexuality and

sexual identity in which the pressure of women's struggles against
the given definitions and representations has produced men's concern with that question and provided men today with a terrain which
they can progressively and reappropriatingly occupy, a cause and a
last hope. Because . . . the effects of feminism in academic institutions
with the development of women's studies and an awareness generally
of the need to consider women and their representation have led to
a situation where "things to do with women" are tolerated (up to a
point, and with differences, of course, from particular institution to
particular institution and then from department to department), if
not accepted, as an area of interest, of possible study, with men thus
able to make radical gestures at little cost, quite within the limits that
the academy has already extended and reset. In that sense (I stress
in that sense), feminism (but feminism has now come down to an
"interest," an "area") is easy for white males in our Western universities, can readily be part of their profession; issues of class and
race are much more difficult and much more absent (absent here
meaning simply not recognized within the academic limits, remaining
unspeakable and unspoken). As far as male critics are concerned,
indeed, the meshing in the academy of some feminist criticism with
French theory, deconstruction et al, has greatly helped, especially in
the United States: I can do post-structuralism, Derrideanism, Lacan-
ianism, and feminism in a guaranteed "radical" cocktail, theory till
the cows come home, or don't. Not that that flip way of putting it
should let *me* out of criticism: after all, I participate in some of this
too, am close to it; and however apart from it I may feel and believe
myself to be, I cannot afford not also always to recognize the com-
plicities that carry through against the apartness I try to maintain.
Because . . . men have a social-sexual stake in feminism, in involving
themselves with it. I don't want to imply that their relation to feminism is reducible merely and inevitably to a social-sexual strategy,
an "interest" of that kind, but we might as well admit that in the
existing circumstances that relation cannot be magically free of the
given terms of male/female positioning, of the general relations of
men to women. Because . . . But all this is just my own paraphrase
and realization of the answer suggested already by Gayatri Spivak
when she asked the initial question: "Perhaps because, unlike the
race and class situations, where academic people are not likely to get
much of a hearing, the women's struggle is one they can support
'from the inside'. Feminism in its academic inceptions is accessible
and subject to correction by authoritative men."[24]

Barthes: "What is difficult is not to liberate sexuality according to
some more or less libertarian project, it is to disengage it from mean-

ing, including from the transgression of meaning"; Tillie Olsen: let's ask "the question of the place, proportion, *actual* importance of sexuality in our (now) longer-lived, more various, woman lives" (and I think we could add men into that question too, woman and man lives, even if it is then also asked differently) (and I think we can recognize in both Barthes and Olsen the Western and class elements—*whose* lives are longer-lived and more various, *who* can afford to talk of sexuality in this way?).[25]

There is a strange spiral of effects and retro-effects round "sexuality" in relation to which we live (a limited "we"). The development of a conception and understanding of sexuality, its extension of the sexual away from a mere perception of "the sexual act" (the perception that is Marx's, for example, even as his daughter Eleanor is translating a major document in the history of the pressure of that extension, Flaubert's *Madame Bovary*), *is* liberating, our lives have changed; at the same time that (and here Marx's terms are right) sexuality has become a commodity definition, the fetish of sexual exchange, with a hyper-objectification of women in a circuit of "pleasure" maintained by everything from sexology to advertising, what was and is liberating closed down into the ideological orders of "liberation." Sexuality, we now understand, is bound up with language and representation, the history of an individual's construction of identity in meaning, is a complex matter and movement of desire; and then again, our societies have produced sexuality as *the* meaning, including the meaning of feminism (thus equivalent to and contained within "sexual liberation"), as a kind of natural-essence bedrock, what it's all about, where we really are; which brings us back to a new version of "the sexual act," equal opportunities, orgasm rewards, men and women, rich and famous . . . Sexual politics? Simple. *We know what it means.* Hence Barthes, the need to disengage sexuality from its meaning; hence Olsen, the need to question its place.

It is to psychoanalysis that we largely owe the conception and understanding of sexuality (psychoanalysis that began with Freud at a crucial moment of sexual concern, of challenge to the terms of the existing relations between men and women, women's protest against them; a moment that also saw the beginnings of sexology in the work of such as Krafft-Ebing and Havelock Ellis). "The great enigma of the biological fact of the duality of the sexes," yes, but Freud hears, finds, learns an articulation of the sexual as sexuality in the process of the construction of the human subject, a difficult and precarious psychical reality. The key point of this articulation is, of course, the unconscious: "the reality of the unconscious is sexual," says Lacan, but that sexual is not anchored in the body as its simple reflection or expression; the unconscious is "discordant," it takes over and marks out

the body, defines my sexuality which is thus not a pre-given content
but, precisely, a process, a history.

Finally, however, it is not quite that easy. If the psychoanalyst's
sexuality is not that of sexology and "the sexual act" ("This is not its
terrain," as Lacan insists[26]), it cannot be simply disconnected from
the sexual, the duality of the sexes, Freud's enigma, male and female.
Anatomy isn't destiny but neither is it just irrelevant, as Freud kept
trying to say and wondering at and stumbling over, as Lacan with
his determining phallus and castration somewhere knows, no matter
how symbolically sublimated those references are supposed to be.
Psychoanalysis indeed, part of its intense value, is exactly bound up
with all the problems of the relationships, overlaps and breaks between the sexual as male and female for sexual reproduction and the
individual's history as a speaking human being, given a definition as
a man or a woman, produced in a particular patterning of "masculinity," "femininity," unconscious desire. The *Three Essays on the Theory of Sexuality* are a problematic story about the developing match
and mismatch of the sexual and sexuality from infancy to adulthood;
the case histories, Dora and the Rat Man, the Wolf Man and Schreber
(Little Hans is too programmed to fit the norm, the child was painfully
too little to have demonstrated how much more was at stake than
the decreed scenario), are stories—novels—of the multiple, complex,
heterogeneous mix-up of sexuality, sexual identity.

One of the most interesting things in Freud is that he recognizes
sexual difference, and to start with between men and women. Pre-
Freud (I simplify, one can find exceptions, premonitions, bits and
pieces of awareness), women were women, different to men, of
course, potentially troubling, needing control, but women, woman,
you *knew* that. With Freud, the recognition, they really aren't the
same, they've gone out of the image of their mere identity as difference (she reflects my identity by the difference I know her to be as
woman, my woman, my picture) and the disturbance is substantial,
extensive (I too am disturbed, no longer identical with myself, as-
suredly man). The unconscious ruins everything and the sexuality
then understood liberates women from the sexual: they are precisely
not just the woman, organs, reproduction, biology. Freud begins
again on those ruins the question of difference, the sexual-sexuality,
men's and women's histories, noting, for example, that we must give
up "any expectation of a parallelism between male and female sexual
development," recording his impression that "a man's love and a
woman's are a phase apart psychologically."[27] Freud ends complementarity, the one for the other, the Adam and Eve syndrome, she
made for him, "two halves purely," as John Updike puts it in a novel
entitled . . . *Marry Me.*

In Lacan this becomes the continual emphasis that there is no sexual relation, this indeed being the bedrock reality of analysis: "the real, the only one to motivate the outcome of analytic discourse, the real that there is no sexual relation."[28] Who would relate to who? The individual human subject caught up in meanings, representations, the movement of his or her desire is not to be brought down to *one* in an act of relation to some other one: the division, the excess, the unconscious runs through and across him or her; that I am one, finished, fixed, here and now simply present, one of a couple, is myth, imaginary. "The only person with whom one wants to sleep is one's mother."[29] I think the formulation is typically reductive (as so often in psychoanalysis it cannot allow for change, specific differentiations: to want to sleep with anyone is really to want to sleep with one's mother, the only person) but what it gets at is that relation is problematic, that one is never only "one," belonging shot through by longing, the reality of one's construction from division.

There is no *sexual* relation because there are never two *sexes* but one and the other on both sides of the "relation" (whether man and woman, woman and woman, man and man). One is always in my or yourself one and the other, or rather, in Lacan's writing, one and the Other, the symbolic as cause of the subject's identity-in-division, the chain of signifiers in which *I* take place. Relation, the idea of relation, depends on an imaginary other who will complement me as one, make up for the fact of division, stop the loss of identity. Women have been powerfully represented and held as "woman" to be this other and then, the pressure of the reality of women, feared and hated and attacked as the imaginary other of "woman" fails and his identity is questioned—at which point she finds herself carried over into the realm of the Other, projected as an enigmatic radical alienness, the back of beyond, and then made up all over again, with talk of her mystery, her ineffable *jouissance*, her closeness to the position of God and so on.

Two things interest me in all this: first, that the division in which everyone, men and women, is inscribed as "one" and the process of desire thus initiated do not express "man" or "woman" (part of what Freud says gropingly and conventionally when he makes libido "masculine," not sex-expressive, and what the Lacanians follow when they insist that desire cannot be sexualized); second, that the division of everyone is also the difference, the out-of-phaseness, of male and female, man and woman. Psychoanalysis has a classic way of tying these two things together: the phallus, castration, different positions of male and female children in the Oedipus Complex, etc. Which may have its specific historical plausibility, its function as specific historical explanation given a particular social organization of the relations between men and women. But feminists have for long understood that the universalized primacy of the phallus in psychoanalysis, the phallus as aboriginal signifier, can only be maintained by fiat (it just *is*, there is nothing else to say), that, on psychoanalysis's own terms, exactly because the man's fright of castration at the sight of the female genital claimed by Freud is constructed from the paternal threat of castration recognized in the Oedipal moment, posing the problem of having or not-having, then the phallus cannot sustain the whole of sexual difference and sexuality, that the crucial matter of the relation to the maternal body, her sameness and difference and the articulations of that for the boy and the girl, is crucial, outside of any notion of the *pre*-Oedipal which just runs everything back from the phallus and relics off—Freud's buried civilization—the maternal as *before* and can then only see interest in it as regressive, exactly where you would expect women to be and where men shouldn't.

What has all this got to do with male feminism? Perhaps that men need to work out this not-simply-Oedipal complex of division, difference, that they need to think through politically—sexual politics—sameness and difference and otherness (there's something extremely conventional about just assuming that women are defining their difference, that that's the way in which we are going to acknowledge their presence, again), that we should take seriously at last the "hetero" in heterosexuality, which means the heterogeneity in us, on us, through us, and also take seriously the "sexuality," which means, I think, giving up, precisely, heterosexuality, that oppressive representation of the sexual as act, complementarity, two sexes, coupling.

Difference as social and ideological limitation, the term of patriarchy: her difference gives the identity of the male position, she different is his reality, man and woman, "the opposite sex," everything in place.

Difference as political opportunity, she asserts, gains, realizes her difference, breaks the "his" and "her" identity, its imposition, women away from men, out of their place.

Difference as desire: no difference, only differences, no one and other, no his-her, man-woman, nor hetero-homo (another difference definition drawn up from the man-woman norm), a new sociality, deferring places, in that sense a utopia.

But *whose* desire?

There is a lot about psychoanalysis in these notes. I think, as so often, of Barthes: "The monument of psychoanalysis must be traversed—not bypassed—like the fine thoroughfares of a very large city, across which we can play, dream, etc.: a fiction." And of Laura Mulvey: "Psychoanalytic theory is . . . appropriated here as a political weapon." And of Juliet Mitchell introducing in 1984 a piece written ten years earlier with "then I was still hoping it would prove possible to use psychoanalysis as an incipient science of the ideology of patriarchy—of how we come to live ourselves as feminine or masculine within patriarchal societies."[30]

A fiction to be gone through, a political weapon to be appropriated as such, an analysis of patriarchal positioning in our lives as masculine or feminine (*perhaps*, "then I was still hoping . . ."). I can use these three gestures to define psychoanalysis here, its use. The critique of the phallocentrism of psychoanalysis (Freudian, Lacanian) is now easy in many ways (which does not mean unnecessary) but the understanding that psychoanalysis produces remains nevertheless; the questions of subjectivity, of "masculinity" and "femininity," of sexual difference and identity in the individual's history remain to be worked through all the same: from within patriarchy the terms of patriarchy are analyzed *and* reproduced *and* then more than that, the remaining understanding and questions. Which doesn't make for a simple, cut and dry relation to psychoanalysis (hence, I think, the difficulties and shifts and problems of Mitchell's work, these being a real part of its value, precisely): fiction, political weapon, incipient science of the ideology of patriarchy (the "incipient" is important) . . . Feminism is the necessary lever on psychoanalysis today, the dialectical pressure that forces it into truth (it always was, in Freud: the Dora case-history is an obvious text for this, strikingly read as such in many recent feminist accounts). Not that this resolves the argument as to "whether there is a radical potential for feminism in Freudian psychoanalysis"[31] but it does indicate that the argument is important, that it is, indeed, a radical argument, that psychoanalysis is already political for feminism, and productively so ("it came into the arena of discussion in response to the internal needs of feminist debate"[32]).

How one would say that and follow it through would be different according to context. Mine immediately was British feminism—all my references here were to that, Mulvey and Mitchell and then, in the paragraph above, the Editorial Board of *Feminist Review* and Jacqueline Rose. Things would be different if one's context was French, for example, with the reality of a very influential cultural establishment of psychoanalysis insistently reproducing versions of mastery and discipleship and anti-feminism which have sometimes been played out by women against other women (the "Psychanalyse et Politique" group and its publishing outlet "Des Femmes" registering the French phrase for "Women's Liberation Movement" as its trademark and taking legal action to prevent other women using it). All of which, indeed, should be brought back into and made part of the British argument too so that, say, Lacanian theory *and practice* are examined (has anyone ever even commented on Jeanne Favret-Saada's moving account of her resignation from the Lacan School?[33]). It is difficult and contradictory to use psychoanalysis and doubtless that is reflected here, in the movement of these notes.

I started this note from Barthes, Mulvey, Mitchell: two feminists, one male . . . what? Individualist perhaps: "I believe now that the only effective marginalism is individualism."[34] But one of the things men learn from feminism is that women have had enough of being marginal, marginalized: patriarchal society is about marginalization, keeping women out or on the edges of its economy, its institutions, its decisions. To change things, moreover, involves not individualism but collective action, women together, what feminism is about. Of course, Barthes added that "individualism" would have to be understood in new ways, "more radical, more enigmatic" (but then "enigmatic" is not a happy choice either). This was in the last interview he gave, four days before his death, entitled by the magazine in which it appeared "The Crisis of Desire."

Is the position of men to feminism marginal, an individualism? I think it is, and *at best*, despite the difficulties of the terms; not meaning by that to exclude shared actions and relations, simply saying that feminism has decentered men, something else they must learn, and that that means that there is no simple position, only a shifting marginalism, a new individualism in the sense that collective identity of men is no longer available (no longer available once you listen and respond to feminism). This, again, is not tragic (not to be lived as loss, along the "if-only-I-were-a-woman-I-would-have-an-authentic-identity" lines), just a fact of life (of life politically, listening and responding to feminism). And perhaps we can come back to psychoanalysis here. I can think of any number of feminist women in Britain who are directly involved in psychoanalysis but no men. Obviously I don't mean that there are no men in psychoanalysis, only that the political-personal commitment to analysis, here where I live and work, seems common for women, rare for men. A reflection on male feminism should probably recognize that, this not to conclude that feminism should lead men into psychoanalysis but to move to consideration of whether and how the radical potential of psychoanalysis for feminism, the argument about that at least, actually involves men. Perhaps psychoanalysis with its exploration of subjectivity, its problematization of identity, can offer an individualism, away from the certainties of our representations of man and masculinity, that men too readily resist, refuse. The fiction to be gone through can tell a different story of ourselves, politically appropriate if we want to analyze and change the patriarchal positioning central to our lives.

In a graduate class at Yale concerned with Richardson's *Clarissa* a male student remarks affirmatively that of course he cannot conceive of anyone other than as "a full human subject"—"what else could one be?" The female teacher answers simply, "well, you can be a victim." It is like a little scenario of the center and the margin. What is difficult for men aware of feminism is not to imagine equality for women but to realize the inequality of their own position: the first is abstract and does not take me out of my position (naturally women should be equal with me); the second is concrete and comes down to the fact that my equality is the masking term for their oppression (women are not equal with me and the struggle is not for *that* equality).

Do I write male? What does that mean? We have learnt—from semiotics, psychoanalysis, deconstruction, the whole modern textual theory—not to confuse the sex of the author with the sexuality and sexual positioning inscribed in a text. There is no simple relation of direct expression between myself as male or myself as female and the discourse, writing, text I produce, this production involving me in the whole mesh of discursive orders of language, all the available forms and constructions with their particular positions, their particular terms of representation, all the defined senses of "masculine" and "feminine" (and in which I am anyway caught up from the start, given as "man" or "woman").

But this cannot be allowed to end those initial questions, however much I might want to push responsibility away into a world of conventions and forms, inscriptions of position, into all that world of textuality of which we are invited to be the playfully deconstructing prisoners. I must recognize the facts of those forms and conventions and their implications in my position as a man in this society, a position which my writing risks reinscribing, confirming, prolonging. Just as women are not bound by the dominant discursive orders which nevertheless socially define them and against which, from which, beyond which their new reality has to be made, articulated, brought into being. Hence no doubt the strong emphasis from women on women's writing, female discourse, writing the body and so on, theoretically dubious (from the perspective of male theory?) with its potential essentialism (a kind of immediate expressive unity of woman, the female) and politically strong (elaborating a reality of women speaking and writing out as women). For men, though, exactly because of the fundamental asymmetry that holds between them and women (their domination), there can be no equivalent: men's writing, male discourse, will simply be the same again; there is no politically progressive project that can work through that idea (unless perhaps in and from areas of gay men's experience, in a literature for that). "Telling the truth about one's body: a necessary freeing subject for the woman writer," says Tillie Olsen.[35] What seems unlikely is that that sentence could also be written for the male writer.

The truth about men and their bodies *for the moment* is merely re-
petitive (this has to be put without any suggestion of some inverse
romanticization of women and their bodies): the régime of the same,
the eternal problem of the phallus, etc. (with its celebrants from Lawrence on, through Miller and Mailer on into the present day). Taking
men's bodies away from the existing representation and its oppressive
effects will have to follow women's writing anew of themselves: for
today, telling the truth about the male body as freeing subject is utopia, about the female body *actuality*.

So there I am between a male writing as oppression and a male
writing as utopia, and still I am, here and now as you read this page,
a male writing. All I can do is pose each time the question of the
sexual positioning of my discourse, of my relations to and in it, my
definition as man, and then through it to the practice and reality of
men and women, their relations in the world. To do this, not to elide
the question, to give up the image of neutrality, is not not to write
male, not to run continually into terms of oppression, but it is, at
least, to grasp writing as an involvement in an ethics of sexual difference, which is a start today towards another male writing.

A woman reading is not the same as reading as a woman. In a
long history women have been trained not to read as women, to
repeat and conform to male readings, male tradition, a particular recognition of the canon of literature ("canon" with its strange appro-
priateness, ecclesiastical law and phallic weapon). Which is not to
say that they have simply repeated, simply conformed, that there has
not been misreading, other reading, in revolt, refusal; domination,
after all, implies an edge of resistance, the elsewhere of what it seeks
to hold down. And, of course, the dominant order has also in that
long history decreed and tolerated set areas for reading as a woman,
women's reading—the novel in late eighteenth-century England, the
Hollywood "woman's film" of the 1940s, there are many examples.
Such areas are safe and unsafe: clearly defined and "trivial" and at
the same time a little uncertain just because women are there with
their readings (hence the period attacks on novel-reading and its dangers, hence, differently, from the other side, the reoccupation of the
"woman's film" by feminist film theorists today).

Reading as a woman is a place given, the available positions,
"women's" genres, styles, and so on, or an alternative project, a
struggle to be won, all the pressures of women re-reading, of feminist
criticism. "A woman writing as a woman," Peggy Kamuf pointed
out, involves a split: the repetition of the seemingly identical
"woman" in fact breaks the assumption of identity, "making room
for a slight shift, spacing out the differential meaning which has always been at work in the single term."[36] The same goes for "a woman

reading as a woman." To read _as_ is to make the move of the construction of an identity in which the diverse, heterogeneous relations
of experience are gathered up in a certain way, a certain form. A
woman reading is different from reading as a woman which, in turn,
is not necessarily the same as reading as a feminist. Except that one
can see the necessity in reverse: reading as a feminist involves reading
as a woman (it involves a knowledge of what it is to be a woman
both negatively, the assigned place of oppression, and positively, the
force of the struggle against oppression) which includes a woman
reading (reading as a woman takes up a woman's experience). Putting
this necessary reversibility in these terms is then doubtless open to
theoretical debate. Since sex is not immediate identity, since reading
as a woman is construction, where is the necessary link between
reading as a woman and being a woman? Since feminism is a social-
political awareness of the oppression of women and a movement to
end it, where is the necessary link between identity as a woman and
being a feminist? Or, to put it another way, this circuit cuts out men.

A man reading is never now not the same as reading as a man. In
a long history men have been trained simply to read, they have the
acquired neutrality of domination, theirs is the security of indifference—it is women who are different, the special case. Reading as a
man is not a project, it is the point of departure; which is why, say,
for male modernist writers seeking an avant-garde dislocation of
forms, a recasting of given identity into multiplicity, writing differently has seemed to be naturally definable as writing feminine, as
moving across into a woman's place (Joyce provides an obvious instance, his two great novels ending in "female" monologue or po-
lylogue, Molly Bloom, Anna Livia). It is a point of departure which
cannot be merely thrown off, forgotten. We can learn to read as
women and we can learn to read as feminists; that is, we can learn
women's readings, feminist readings, we can make connections that
we never made before, come back critically on our point of departure.
Yet we must recognize too that we are that point of departure, not
in the sense that that is our identity, that we are just that (we are a
history, a process that is unfinished), but in the sense that that is
nevertheless where we are at, in this society that is our position. It
would be nice to forget one is a man (and I am more prone to this
fantasy than most) but we can't, we have to assume what being a
man means. So the circuit of reading, the reversibility described
above, cannot include us as it includes women, though we can go
along with it, perhaps.

I think one has politically to accept the contradictions (not be put
off by charges of theoretical impurity, incorrectness). The relation of
sex to identity is not immediate, we are constructed as gendered individuals in a complex psycho-social history; "male" and "female,"

"masculinity" and "femininity" are positions, places, terms of identification; we are unfinished, sexually heterogeneous, however much
the orders of heterosexual law constrain and define; woman and man
do not exist only men and women with all the shared experience that
race and class can cut across much more decisively at many points,
in many situations. *And* the relation of sex to identity is direct and
powerful; men and women exist in radical separation, in difference
that is produced as the ground of oppression; the shared experience
is cut across by sexual difference, which sexual difference also cuts
across race and class; the women's movement, in other words, is a
reality.

Thus when Elaine Showalter warns against overstating "the essentialist dilemma of defining the *woman* reader, when in most cases
what is implied and intended is a *feminist* reader. Reading as a feminist, I hasten to add, is not unproblematic; but it has the important
aspect of offering male readers a way to produce feminist criticism
that avoids female impersonation. The way into feminist criticism,
for the male theorist, must involve a confrontation with what might
be implied by reading as a man, and with a questioning or surrender
of paternal privileges"[37], I feel this is right; and I also feel that, has-
tening to add, she does run too quickly over the problematic nature
of the idea of a man reading as a feminist. Male feminism is not just
different from feminism (how ludicrous it would be to say "female
feminism"), it is a contradiction in terms. Or, at the very least, it is
always also that. There *is* a female impersonation in a man reading
as a feminist, whatever else there might be too. To think otherwise
is to abstract the personal (and that much modern theory is keen on
such abstraction says something politically about that theory): reading
as a feminist and reading as a woman and a woman reading are bound
up together, there is no bypassing one of the stages. I think Showalter
also says this when she talks of the development by feminist critics
of "theories proved on our pulses" and repeats a warning that "feminist techniques could be copied and lifted out of their personal and
political contexts."

I like the poems of Adrienne Rich, she says things exactly; and the
titles of her collections to start with: *The Will to Change, Diving into
the Wreck, The Dream of a Common Language, A Wild Patience Has Taken
Me This Far . . .*[38]

What does it, can it mean for me to say that I like them? One poem
is called "Trying to Talk with a Man" (*DW*, 3) but a common language
is a dream: at times perhaps for anyone, man or woman, "each /
speaker of the so-called common language feels / the ice-floe split,
the drift apart / as if powerless" (*CL*, 16); certainly from woman to
man, her rage no longer contained in "the ordinary pact / of men &

women" (*DW*, 50), now focused in "a world masculinity made / unfit for women or men" (*DW*, 36). A world that is unfit for women or men but where women are absent and elsewhere: "*Could you imagine a world of women only,* / the interviewer asked. *Can you imagine* / *a world where women are absent.* (He believed / he was joking). Yet I have to imagine / at one and the same moment, both. Because / I live in both" (*CL*, 61). Unfit for women or men but where men own the streets, "when did we ever choose / to see our bodies strung / in bondage and crucifixion across the exhausted air" (*WP*, 3), where "no-man's-land does not exist" (*WP*, 4): "A man's world. But finished" (*DW*, 8). So where am I reading these poems? As a woman? (When all of them, this writing, tell me in their "rage," their "wild patience," their "making for the open," that I am not). As a feminist? (When all of them, this writing, tell me stories, images, scenes, reactions, words that leave me no position, no place from which I could avoid by some identification or impersonation their reality, their politics; and "What we're after / is not that clear to me, if politics / is an unworthy name" *WP*, 49). As a version of "The phantom of the man-who-would-understand, / the lost brother, the twin" (*CL*, 62)? (When the poet continues "for him did we leave our mothers, / deny our sisters, over and over?"). Maybe the task of male critics is just to read (forget the "as") and learn silence: "Silence can be a plan / rigorously executed / the blueprint to a life / It is a presence / it has a history a form / Do not confuse it / with any kind of absence" (*CL*, 17). But a silence broken by these poems, theirs not ours, "these words, these whispers, conversations / from which time after time the truth breaks moist and green" (*CL*, 20).

Perhaps (the mode of these notes is "perhaps"), perhaps male feminism should involve a fundamental *admiration*. The word, yes, is old-fashioned, is tangled up with ideas of love and courtship (the heroine's "admirers" in this or that classic novel), is eminently deconstructible as the original senses are teased out and we find the notion of considering with astonishment and stupefaction moving into that of contemplating with reverence and esteem and gratified pleasure (one can feel psychoanalysis, the uncanny, just round the corner). But still, *admiration*, in the sense in which Irigaray has recently brought it back, thinking precisely of an ethics of sexual difference. She gets at it by rereading Descartes who in *Les Passions de l'Ame* makes admiration the first of all the passions, the "sudden surprise" of the new and the different that precedes objectification of the other as this or that quality, this or that characteristic. Or as Irigaray explains it: "What has never existed between the sexes. Admiration keeping the two sexes unsubstitutable in the fact of their difference. Main-

taining a free and engaging space between them, a possibility of separation and alliance."[39]

Admiration as utopia, what has never existed between the sexes;
so how to open this space of a radical sexual difference that is not
the old difference (psychoanalytic theory too readily turns admiration
to the immobility of castration, a supposed male astonishment, the
fright that Freud thinks no man is spared "at the sight of a female
genital," a male fixation, what Descartes describes as the body "mo-
tionless as a statue," stopped rigid in single perception: "astonishment is an excess of admiration that can never be other than bad"[40])?
The question brings us back to the impossible relation of men to feminism, that relation only as a possible future, and to the recognition
of male feminism as today a contradiction in terms, but then necessary
as that, necessary for men to live as such. Perhaps in the end all one
can say, indicating the core reality of male feminism, is what Irigaray
says as so many others have said, part of the political consciousness
of feminism: "I will never be in a man's place, a man will never be
in mine. Whatever the possible identifications, one will never exactly
occupy the place of the other—they are irreducible the one to the
other."[41] Perhaps men could learn to realize that, no sadness, no
anger, just an acceptance of the irreducible, something like Irigaray's
admiration.

More pious words? Of course. I take Irigaray and use her writing
to end mine, and with a word, "admiration," as though that could
do anything, could resolve any of the difficulties, any of the doubts
I feel as I read over what I have written. But perhaps "admiration"
can say that too, that there is no ending, that *I* cannot resolve. And
then I think that I wrote most of this in a hospital ward for women,
the majority of them elderly, watching my mother for hours and days.
There is every conventional reason not to mention that here and no
real reason why I shouldn't. It had something to do with admiration
and is at least a possibly real ending.

1984

I think now, at a distance, that such an ending has too many problems just to be left without comment, is not enough. I knew it then,
it can be felt in the writing, even while I could anyway only end like
that, falling off into silence and leaving the piece apparently held in
an attitude of awed contemplation. The reference to my mother, to
writing in hospital, is real but it is also an emotional location of the
piece as legitimation, not that far from the kind of personal guarantee
of which I am earlier critical. The final paragraph says something true
at the same time that its truth cannot be turned into an end without

some loss of truth, of the critical, political truth with which "Male Feminism"—and male feminism—is concerned.

The wider point here can be made by considering the use of Irigaray, the appearance of the notion of "admiration." I do not want to go back on this (on the contrary); simply, it has difficulties which were, wrongly, left aside. Again, what Irigaray says is true, yet when I quote it, use it, produce it in conclusion, I finish up with a false unity, a fetishizing elision—look, her! For difference and contradiction, I substitute silence, admiration as that; hence the last paragraph, nothing more to say.

"I will never be in a man's place, a man will never be in mine. Whatever the possible identifications, one will never exactly occupy the place of the other—they are irreducible the one to the other." Yes, but the irreducibility can quickly become not difference and contradiction but a gulf, as though between two species, and the implications of men in feminism—feminism which has to include men, their transformation, in its project—are cut short: just admiration, as of an object, the awed contemplation. The autonomy of feminism is converted into its separateness and the necessary acknowledgment by men of the former becomes my drift into fixation with the latter.

It is significant in this context that feminism itself is envisaged in the piece in a way which can tend to suggest it as a unified field, masking the various positions and movements and struggles that are its reality. My concern in the first instance was to write about feminism as the overall fact of the recognition and understanding by women of their oppression and their determination to act against it. From the perspective of the consideration of male feminism (only from that perspective) the alternatives within feminism, the different feminisms, seemed to me at the time secondary; the aim was to explore something of what is at stake in men's coming to terms with that fact of recognition, understanding, determination for change, with the whole process of women changing things for themselves and for us— a process which is plural and heterogeneous, not singular and homogeneous, but which is still nevertheless perceivable as this overall fact, feminism.

The other side of that perception, though, is the structure of being "outside," the outsideness that admiration in part enacts, self-exclusion as value, an authentic male response (the reverse extreme to the "more radical, most radical" gesture discussed in the piece). Running feminisms into feminism allows—goes with—a gender-defined object, feminism as women and women's. Which is right and wrong: right because feminism is gender-defined, and necessarily and crucially so; wrong because that gender definition is also problematic, is a debate within feminism about feminism that "feminism" covers over (in its general social currency moreover "feminism" has been taken over as the term for a new psychology of women, their reductive and controlling identification in the aftermath of a women's liberation movement now, hopefully, past). Which is right and wrong too for men specifically, for thinking about male feminism: right because feminism for us must involve awareness of *a* separateness, precisely that acknowledgment of women's autonomy, of *them*; wrong because that autonomy is not to be translated into exclusion, albeit in the deferential form this takes in the piece, but is rather to be seen as the very basis of our participation, where we start from, knowing one is a man, what that means.

It was with the consequences of this knowledge we gain from feminism that "Male Feminism" was concerned. Its problems, brought up in the ending, are then those of the relations of such a knowledge to feminist practice—*what does feminism mean for men?* is abstracted too far from *what is feminism?* The insistence in the piece on the political-ethical reality of feminism for men, for me-as-a-man (an insistence which I belive to be important and needed, against the appropriative displacement of feminism into a set of ideas for a theoretical argument or a known politics, against men just assuming it is there for them to "go into," to have "positions" in, all the ways in which we avoid bringing it back questioningly onto ourselves) runs the risk of turning into a personal essentialism, outsider and object, ethics separating from politics as *I* stop in silence (admiration, contemplation, deference are the signs of this in the piece, the negative turn of the positive emphases from which they emerge). It is not that I would want now to change what I wrote, only that I need here to have drawn attention to the problems.[42]

1986

2.
Men in Feminism: Men and Feminist Theory[1]

PAUL SMITH

"Men in Feminism": the title for these two sessions and for which I have to take some large part of responsibility, has turned out to be at least provocative, perhaps offensive, at any rate troublesome for the participants. The provocation, the offence, the trouble that men now are for feminism is no longer—at least in the academy where most of us here reside—simply a matter of men's being the object or *cause* of feminism (men's fault, feminism's cause; men as agents of that which feminism seeks to change). Men, some men, now—and perhaps by way of repeating an age-old habit—are entering feminism, actively penetrating it (whatever "it" might be, either before or after this intervention), for a variety of motives and in a variety of modes, fashions. That penetration is often looked upon with suspicion: it can be understood as yet another interruption, a more or less illegal act of breaking and entering, entering and breaking, for which these men must finally be held to account. Perhaps the question that needs to be asked, then, by these men, with them, for them, is to what extent their irruption (penetration and interruption) is justified? is it of any political use to feminism? to what extent is it wanted?

Within the American academy (feminisms outside the academy and outside of America are something I'd want to talk about; but for now, speaking from where we are, in the American academy at a particular juncture) there seems now to be a material split, a breach between women's studies (its programs and institutions) and feminist theory (with its more marginal programs and institutions). If it can be assumed for now—though I'm sure people will have disagreements—that women's studies has been relatively well integrated into the institutional and disciplinary structures of the academy, then the area known as feminist theory (that is, the area concerned with post-structuralist and deconstructionist theorizing) might come to be seen as the bearer of whatever further political promise feminism offers in the academy.

It is, of course, not altogether clear that this area of feminist theory is not being recuperated, institutionalized, disciplined, in its turn. There are discernible within that area of academic activity networks of power, hierarchies, reputations, a whole politics amongst the women who are feminist theorists; these networks already become formally consonant with the existing institutional apparatus. Indeed, the set of relations involved there is perhaps only quantitatively different from what's already in place; qualitatively, things are rather similar.

This may be nothing more than an indication that poststructuralist feminist theory is just one strand amongst the many others which today constitute the more widespread presence of what we call "theory" in the humanities. Feminist theory of this sort—and however "feminist" it may be, and howsoever "feminist" is construed—does not exist outside the academy and, more specifically, is in many ways not easily separable from the general "theory" that has worked its way into studies in the humanities over the last ten or twenty years.[2]

This theory, as feminist theory itself has taught us to know, is implicated fully into the phallocracy: it helps invent, legitimate, and reproduce the male order. This is as much true by etymological accident (the sight, the objectifying clarity of *theoria*) as it is empirically true (we can currently celebrate the presence of theorists in the universities, and we know that they're settling themselves ever more nicely and enjoying the fruits of a certain tenure). And, for overdetermined reasons, men still seem able to sing to that institutional tune as well as the *parvenues*.

But that's the point, feminist theory will tell us; that's why "feminist theory" is different from "theory." It's exactly because theory is phallocentric that feminist theory can be effective. If, as "theory" tells us, women are taken by the masculine order to be the other, the very point of difference, women's theory is necessarily subversive of that order and thus of the very structures it works within. So, it is said, the aim of feminist theory's critique is to "see" theory ("see" as in a poker game), and see theory change its spots. If this is indeed the intendment of feminist theory, then men, biological men, are necessarily a problem. Men are in a sense the bearers or supports of the phallocratic habit.

Yet feminist theory wants to indict the very structures which it knows uphold masculinity and femininity. Feminist theory broadly speaking sees ("through" phallocentric theory) that male-centered social and psychical structures place biological men as enforcing agents for those structures. At the same time these structures place women as the other, in a different relation, in a place which is not a place—women always *for* those structures but never really *in* them. Feminist theory shows, then, that women are oppressed/hidden/repressed/marginalized by those structures but at the same time privileged to escape them or be displaced by them.

I sketch out—crudely and in ways which are maybe arguable—this essential paradox in order to ask a brace of questions. Can men, male theorists, understand this theoretical and academic position in feminist theory? And can they thence be of any political use to feminist theory?

In one sense, I think, they can understand it. As the everyday practitioners of fetishism, they shouldn't be too much put out of joint by this paradoxical view of women as being both there and not there, both "for" the structures and also disavowed by them. The basic "there/not there" formation of masculine, fetishistic *stances* in relation to women is repeated even in the most well-meaning male. Indeed, even the possible disposition of men in relation to feminism which Luce Irigaray describes and recommends (that is, the one which Stephen Heath adopts in his essay "Male Feminism")—the role of "admirer"—seems to me almost another endorsement of fetishism.

There's another, more prosaic way in which men can (and, I think, do) understand this double ascription of women: that is, in so far as it's a *theoretical* ascription. The intellectual task of understanding feminist theory is not a problem since feminist theory is situated within the array of poststructuralist discourses with which many of us are now perhaps over-familiar. Feminist theory is, in this sense, understandable; it's also understandable how and why it exists; and one hopes to be understanding when it advances its claims. The problem is perhaps not one of understanding per se.

What the problems actually are for men in feminism, and what problems feminist theorists have with men in feminism is not going to be easy to utter, either here or elsewhere. But one question which needs to be considered, I think, is the normative, even legalistic aspect of feminist theory itself, and the ensuing culpability of the male breaker and enterer. The question—in any context—of who is allowed to say or do what, to whom and about whom, is ultimately a legal question: it can be raised only where any given discourse is forming or has formed a mode of pragmatic legislation, when it is legalizing itself, defining its outside, naming potential and actual transgressors. Any discourse will desire to be its own space; it needs to think of itself as *sui generis*; it must exclude. Let me stress that I think this to be the case with any discourse—it's not a question here of impugning feminism on these grounds any more or less than Marxism, Reaganism, or whatever. Feminist theory has its exclusive mechanisms—it excludes particular people, it excludes other feminist discourses, it establishes ways of checking credentials, it coins and controls a vocabulary, and so on. Here, as everywhere, the important thing for the transgressor to know is, not just the sentence, but the reason for the law's existence: for the greater good, or to advance special interests?

So far as men are concerned, then; so far as they, supposed "homomorphs" of that which feminism challenges, break into that discourse as it formalizes itself; as they learn to understand it and follow its guidelines; what could be required or expected of them? I've already suggested that men can understand feminist theory and that the problems are elsewhere. This was the message I myself received recently. In response to my article, "A Question of Feminine Identity," Alice Jardine asked this in relation to men in feminism:

> What is it that keeps them from speaking and writing of themselves, of their own positionality in the contemporary discursive field? I am not, of course, talking here about becoming "personal," just of knowing what they already know—that no one speaks or writes suspended between heaven and earth.

Further on she says:

> Most difficult of all is that these *few* men, our allies, have learned their lessons well. The actual content of their writing is rarely incorrect per se. It is almost as if they have learned a new vocabulary perfectly, but have not paid enough attention to syntax or intonation.

These comments—addressed to a certain context, to be sure, but of wider concern just the same—detained me for a long while as I wrote this paper. Indeed, they still detain me. So, perhaps it would be useful, without becoming too "personal," to unpack some of my reaction to them.

It would be disingenuous to try to claim that my primary reaction was not rather defensive, or that this defensiveness ran as a strand through any number of other moments of response—annoyed, resigned, argumentative, submissive, and so on. But generally, Alice's statements appeared to me as a familiar, though kindly, representation of the sort of suspicion which female feminists often have of male feminists; thus they produced in me an overdetermined repetition of a fear—precisely, the fear of being excluded—and a desire to vindicate myself in relation to the other's demands. Even though Alice speaks of me and other men as allies, we're clearly not quite right as allies (or maybe not even the right allies); we're not able to do quite the right thing. Even the fact that I'm perceived as understanding feminist theory (I've learned by lessons well) proves "difficult" for this female feminist because, finally, I do not have the right intonation and syntax. I don't have the native accent; I'm an alien.

Of course, I can be an alien only in a system which perceives itself as having some definitional integrity which can be enforced or embodied as a correctness of speech or activity.

I might well be mistaking Alice's comments: I'm perhaps too quick to assume that they arise from a sense of the integrity of feminist discourse, similar to a kind of nationalism. This analogy might constitute an "incorrect" reading. Perhaps, rather, Alice's comments are making a more theoretical reference—more to my inability to speak authentically the mother tongue, the specificity of which is theoretically more available to women than to men. Perhaps the suggestion is that males who would be feminist need to undertake to write and speak as if they were women, to explore their relation to the imaginary, to mime the feminist theoretical effort of undermining the male economy by deploying the very excess which that economy has neglected.

If this last is the suggestion, it's a question that needs to be taken up, certainly. Perhaps we can assume that one of the initial problems for male feminism is that it has often tended to think of the revindication of the specificity of women's bodies, or of woman, as either a theoretical error or as at best a provisional and strategic gesture.[3] This tendency seems now to have been a gesture of refusal. One of its effects has been to absolve men feminists from the responsibility of speaking their own bodies. That responsibility clearly must be taken on, but the effort can perhaps be made only with the help of, or within, the apparatus of feminist theory. If feminist theory would claim that a man speaking or writing in feminism cannot or simply does not include his body, the first question might be to ask what are the signs that are being looked for. What does a male writing his imaginary actually produce? I am, I must confess, stumped by that question, the only answers at which I could guess seeming unlikely to be "correct."

On the one hand, we men might think that the writing of our imaginary would be exactly a pornography, the manifestation of our imaginary relation to the maternal body and nothing so much as a pure ambivalence, or an even more resilient fetishism. If the structures in which we are caught, in which our egos are constructed, are accurately described by theory and feminist theory, is our imaginary anything but a pornographic defence against the mother's body? Even though most social discourse currently at work is in a sense "about" our sexuality, it remains true that, as Irigaray and others have pointed out, we still have everything to say "about" our sexuality. But that doesn't mean that our fetishism will be combatted simply by our exhibiting it, putting it out as an exhibit for the court. If we are even to offer feminism (and ourselves) an answer to Ruby Rich's question, why it is that we like pornography so much, we're not going to do that by just producing it.

On the other hand, there's perhaps another answer, mooted from time to time in feminist theory. That is, men could write like a Genet, a Klossowski, a Jabès, a Joyce, a Blanchot, or like any other of the male authors whom feminist theory has at different moments authorized. Yet we know into what theoretical difficulties the champions of these supposedly perverse writers have been led, especially of late: an ahistorical and often irresponsible advancing of the claims of the avant-garde; the positing of some unspecified or inexplicable agency of sexual-revolutionary genius in such writers; great pseudo-biological schemas of innate bisexuality, and so on.[4]

Or, continuing in something like the same vein, we could do work like that of Roland Barthes, and proclaim that we're consistently undermining ourselves, marginalizing ourselves, deprivileging ourselves—only to land up like Barthes himself: all the more admired by the male academy and with an express loathing of sexual politics—indeed, of politics itself.

These are some of the impossible, incorrect and perhaps even incriminating answers to the questions which emerge for a man in trying to think through a relation to feminist theory—to work through, however crudely, the problems which seem to be the material effects of feminist theory on a man. It goes without saying that there is a lot of such work to be done, that it's crucial work, and that we've scarcely, if at all, begun it. But, for me at least, one of the difficulties of beginning is the sensation that it's impossible to say anything properly correct. There is always the probability of being incriminated, the continual likelihood of appearing provocative, offensive, and troublesome to the very people who have taught me to ask the questions, even at the very moment when I begin to grapple with the only theoretical language available.

These feelings, these fears, are in a large part the result of having to engage with a discourse whose laws I can never quite obey. I recognize that such a discourse has its reasons for treating me as a "homomorph," for not taking me quite seriously, for not taking me in. But as yet the final legislative decisions have not been handed down. Men still constitute a shadowy, unlegislatable area for feminist theory.

So long as this is still the case, so long as the edict has not been passed, it seems to me that it could still be useful to have men in feminism, men who are still, or as yet, neither outlaws or in-laws. Not those white academic "authoritative men" who Gayatri Spivak guesses might subject feminist work to correction as a result of their essentially male or phallocratic habits. Nor men who might simply learn the skills, the techniques, the competence (the intonation?) of feminist approaches in a kind of benevolent mimicry. Nor, certainly, those who would try to rival women in obeying what they see as the true word of feminism. Nor those who would by intimidation persuade women, in Elaine Showalter's words, to translate feminism's "findings . . . into the warp of their obscure critical languages" (p. 000).

Rather, there are academic men for whom feminism has been as integrally a part of their theoretical education as any other discourse, and who have both a lived and a theoretical sense of their own difference which has been instituted and inspissated by their "understanding" of feminist theory. These are the men who, by dint of their own histories and educations, have no choice but to work with feminism because its discourses are preeminently instructive in relation to issues which are simultaneously men's problems and feminism's cause. In the context of academic feminist theory these men might perhaps do something akin to what women do within theory more generally: that is, they can be there to help to subvert, unsettle and undermine the (seemingly rather fast to settle) laws of the discourse. Not, of course, to undermine feminism itself, but only a process of settling, solidifying. This they might do purely by virtue of existing in it as a difference. If it were ever needed, their difference might act as a reminder of the material fact of difference, the real consequences of which is feminism's material cause.

In case that sounds a trifle too deconstructionist, too dependent on the logic of continual deferral, I'd want to add that difference cannot, of course, be deferred forever, and nor can it be dealt with only at the textual and theoretical levels. Rather, difference is a material constituent of social life; it is real and has real effects; it is not purely academic and none of its effects will disappear with the establishment of a legalized set of discursive parameters. In other words, men can—perhaps, or at least—help the effort to forestall the academic institutionalization of feminism. They may be able to take an interrogative, but sympathetic role. Indeed, from the point of their impossible—provocative, offensive, troublesome—position in or near feminism, they might be able to help keep in view the referent which most of our current theory is all too eager to defer.

That referent is quite simply a political struggle of which feminism is a part. It may well be that the limit for men in feminist theory is also the limit of academic feminist theory itself. When poststructuralist feminist theory turns to construct its public sphere, or when it has done with codifying itself in the contested but limited sphere of the academic, the question might be no longer one of "men in feminist theory," or even of "men in feminism," but rather we'll really be able to talk about alliances between men and women feminists, about people engaged in a political struggle on many fronts. I'm far from sympathizing with the kind of sentiment expressed by Terry Eagleton recently, that theory and the oppressed are natural allies since theory has always been more acceptable to the ruled than the rulers. In American academia, poststructuralist theory—feminist or not—is by and large ingrown, with no public sphere to which to belong or through which to be effective. At the moment the heat generated in this kitchen around this question of men in feminism might well appear an indication of (even a compensation for) a rather narrowly conceived theoretical project.

3.
Men in Feminism: Men and Feminist Theory

STEPHEN HEATH

Thinking about this MLA session, I wrote an essay entitled "Male Feminism." Once written and sent out to the other participants, however, it became clear that it was not going to be possible for me to speak that essay here; its length alone would be prohibitive. The difficulty I had thus made for myself was only eased a few days ago when I received the paper that Paul Smith has just delivered, under the title of this session, "Men in Feminism: Men and Feminist Theory." It seemed to me at once that that paper valuably raised a number of questions and that starting from it and them there was something that I could try to say.[1]

One or two things struck me immediately in what Paul said, concerning feminist theory:

> Feminist theory . . . however "feminist" it may be, and howsoever "feminist" is construed, does not exist outside the academy.

And then:

> The intellectual task of understanding feminist theory is not a problem since feminist theory is situated within the array of post-structuralist discourses with which many of us are now perhaps over-familiar.

Reading those remarks, I remembered, apparently very different, Derrida a couple of years back beginning what I suppose is his most direct written engagement with feminism as follows:

> We will therefore not leave time to come back to what is behind us, nor to look attentively. We will only take a glimpse. (In

French to take a glimpse is to look into the spaces between things, *entre-voir*, that is, interview).[2]

For Paul, and for us in this session, his responsibility, "Men in Feminism" has a subtitle, "Men and Feminist Theory," and the problem is the "men and," not the "feminist theory" which is known, understandable, ranged "within the array of post-structuralist discourses with which we are now over-familiar," as such "not a problem." For Derrida, feminism seems not so clear—oddly enough given that he after all is the arch poststructuralist—but more a matter of spaces between things; and he is not going to look attentively, no array, "only take a glimpse," "*entre-voir*." That, of course, is the vocabulary of fetishism: the glimpse, the inter-*entre* view, the seen but not attentively, on the margin of disturbance. Freud's accounts of fetishism give us all the terms for this glimpsing-glancing seeing that does not stop to look, that turns away from the reality and leaves behind, off somewhere else. And, of course, fetishism was a major reference for Paul, but in a number of ways: from men as "the everyday practitioners of fetishism" to, in an earlier version, "feminists fetishising women" (but the question there is what is it that makes *us* need to see women, feminists liking women, talking about and finding terms for that, as fetishism?); and then also a fetishism of feminist theory which is seen to be not seen, perfectly framed in the academy outside of which it has no existence, perfectly understandable, no problem "of understanding per se." We go from the glimpse to the clearly seen, from lack of attention to sure understanding, but it is the same strategy of not seeing: Derrida glances off the reality, Paul constructs its replacement image, his "feminist theory," and then naturally enough fetishism becomes the necessary theoretical term, the mode of seeing and understanding. Who, after all, understands more than the fetishist? He understands *perfectly*, which is the problem or the normal state of functioning, depending on how you look at it; Freud stresses that the penis is "the normal prototype of fetishes" and the norm of sexual identity, "the primacy of the phallus,"[2] the way we are, men and women, so that there is no escape for and from "feminists fetishising women."

None of this is meant to be glibly "holier than thou," certainly not than Paul. It is simply that I think there is a problem, one of place (the fetishist must keep everything in his "its place"), that is quickly apparent as men, as we, approach feminism. I do not want to say that "where am I?" is a male question but I do think that men want very much to know *where they are* vis-à-vis feminism, that feminism can quickly be produced by them as a matter of their place (and so of its), and as a *theoretical* matter, especially in a context like this, this MLA session, where we can too easily make feminism *an approach*, which then gives *us* an approach, a handy object, some thing we can place ourselves in relation to, "feminist theory" as *topic* (exactly, our *topos*)—where can I stand?

The title of the session is first of all "Men in Feminism." To be in or out, that is the question we readily get ourselves into: gaining, obtaining, maintaining, sustaining, *fixing* a place, a position, ours. Derrida, though, speaks, writes a discourse of non-place, or rather challenges "a certain idea of the *locus* [*lieu*] and the place [*place*]"[3] and I said earlier that he seemed to want not to be too clear about feminism. But then he turns out to be very clear, even as he refuses to look attentively, only the fetish glimpse (which is why he *is* so clear): he writes reactively, against what he calls "'reactive' feminism" which he grants may have a certain historical necessity but which must not, obviously, be allowed to occupy the whole terrain, back with a vengeance to locus and place—where is mine going to be?:

> Can one not say, in Nietzsche's language, that there is a "reactive" feminism, and that a certain historical necessity often puts this form of feminism in power in today's organized struggles? Perhaps one should not so much combat it head on—other interests would be at stake in such a move—as prevent its occupying the entire terrain.[4]

"'Reactive' feminism" sounds like women's movement and struggle, in reaction—precisely—against oppression, against the sexual terms of existing social reality. Identifying it as such, as "'reactive' feminism," is the male vision; and from that identification it is then seen as "occupying the entire terrain," or about to . . . dangerously, a threat. Perhaps in the realm of theory I can counter the danger, at least hang on to a place, one at least of displacement, hisplacement, hang on in my writing over and above and slidingly under the identities, the realities "they" analyze and seek to change on the basis of that analysis, their "'reactive' feminism." Thus Derrida, dreaming of, feeling "the necessity for a choreographic text with polysexual signatures"[5] (not that this seem to stop him publishing his books with the one male name on their covers).

Paul is nowhere near saying any of this but then again in a way what he does say can find itself in the end not so distant after all, comes back to matters of place and legality and exclusion or inclusion, finishes in a series of ironic reversals in which men now occupy the dark continent, are the excluded other ("men still constitute a shadowy, unlegislatable area for feminist theory"), the remainder as "reminder," the "irreducible difference" (they "might act as a reminder of the *material* fact of difference"). Margin to reaction, reminder to feminist theory's law . . . men can "help to subvert, unsettle and

undermine the (seemingly rather fast to settle) laws of the discourse"
. . . the entire terrain, the fast settlement . . .

All representation, we know, is transferential. Representation is
at once an image given, an argument made and a deputation established, a construction of object, me and other. Representation, to put
it another way, includes my position, my desire and its vicissitudes.
The problem for men, "men in feminism," has little in my opinion
to do with feminist theory but much to do with the representation
of feminism for men. What does woman want? What does feminism
want? Perhaps I still cannot help asking such questions, the second
as our new version of the first, but perhaps I can also nevertheless
try to break out of their representations, learn to take them back to
where feminism turns them, *to me*, feminism as *everyday theory* for
me—quite different to my MLA-projected, academy-enclosed "feminist theory." So that the question then is not what does feminism-
woman-she want? Or, why am I excluded, losing ground, remain-
dered? Rather, it is what is feminism for me? Or, how do I change,
who am I if I listen and respond to feminism, if I understand with
its understanding?

This is not a theoretical question nor can it be answered theoretically; it is a practical-theoretical-political-ethical one (feminist issues
are surely by definition always that). Which is what the construction
"feminist theory" can quickly mask, easily becoming a male representation, a male *topic* (again in every sense of the word). The understanding of feminist theory, quite simply of feminism, *is* a huge
problem for men, for us, because it involves grasping the fact that it
is *not* another discourse (let alone in a poststructuralist array), not
another voice to be added, an approach to be remembered and catered
for, but that it radically affects and shifts everything and that that
radical shift is not negotiable—the old understanding—in such panic
terms as "occupying the entire terrain," is not translatable into a problem of "inclusion"/"exclusion." It is easy for me to say that—an image
of self-righteousness is quick to form, *I* know—but the point is to live
it, including *in* theory, in writing, teaching and so on.

This is where Paul's imagination of positions seems to be difficult,
what he envisages men might do ("what could be required or expected of them?"). Part of the difficulty is to do with "correctness,"
the problem men, we, can have, again, of protecting—of self-pro-
tecting—position. I want to be somewhere *securely*. Thinking through
feminist theory, Paul says he feels "that it's impossible to say anything
properly correct." Which in a way is odd because he also quotes Alice
Jardine on the writing of men, his included, as "rarely incorrect per
se." But then her point is that correctness is not the point: being
properly correct is purely theoretical, pure theory; the reality is different, is unceasing, contradictory, difficult, heterogeneous, impos-

sible, everyday. My problem as a man is not being properly correct—as Jardine suggests, men can be extremely good at that, staking out their right place—but acknowledging that my relation to feminism is not going to be some simple recognition (I recognize feminism and ask that it mirroringly recognize me), that it must change me beyond any position to fall back on, beyond any foregone security.

In the passage from which the "rarely incorrect per se" came, Jardine continued:

> It is almost as if they ["these *few* men, our allies"] have learned a new vocabulary perfectly, but have not paid enough attention to syntax or intonation.

What I like there is "intonation"; it reminds me of an essay by Dorothy Richardson, "About Punctuation," in which she remarks that "in the slow, attentive reading demanded by unpunctuated texts the faculty of hearing has its chance until the text *speaks* itself"[6] (it might be noted, the appropriate coincidence, that both Jardine and Richardson value attention, replying to Derrida's immediate decision "not to leave time . . . to look attentively"). Intonation and hearing can serve as terms for the kind of recognition feminism involves: women's voices, women's experience, women's *facts*; not just an object "feminist theory," not just that representation but, on the contrary, an *acuteness* of identity—reading, hearing, seeing, learning beyond the *given*, including the feminism men think they know.

We have to give up the worry of place and non-place to which we are prone, with the fear and the anger and the defensive projections and constructions that result. Intonation and hearing, a way of saying a different attention, not the deconstructive inattention of fixing on the spaces between, not the reaction of such theory. Richardson again: "In telling things, technical terms must be used; which never quite apply."[7] It is not that we, men, do not fit feminist theory, are not fitting for it, have to torment ourselves about that; it is simply that we have to give up the fit of theory, however "choreographic," that the technical terms we might find never quite apply, however perfectly we can get off a new vocabulary, that our relation to feminism is not to be eased, however much we may cast it into the terms of academy and institution. The hardest thing is that feminism is ordinary, everyday, and "a change of world."

But where does that leave us? What should we do? There is no ready answer (that would be an easing), we just have to learn. All I can say here and now in the MLA, in this context, is that we should probably start by trying to grasp *who we are as men*, asking that from feminism rather than wondering what "they" want from an assumed male us. We need to drop the academic masks, to pose at every moment the sexual determinations of the discourse we develop as we teach and write, to stop knowing as we do, as we want, as we impose—and could "men in feminism" today be anything but another strategy of that, of our imposition?

4.
Demonstrating Sexual Difference

ANDREW ROSS

"God didn't make mistakes, the newspapers did"

(Sutcliffe, the Yorkshire Ripper)

"It is not my fault that I cannot eat or rest," he replied. "I assure you it is through no settled design."

(Heathcliff, Wuthering Heights)

In preparing this paper, I thought about ways of demonstrating sexual difference through the use of a concrete example. Not that there seemed to be any alternative, since sexual difference can never be simply assumed, it must be demonstrated. What feminists have meant by this has nothing to do with the division between biological men and women, but rather with categories that cannot be predetermined, are never fixed, and are constantly being rearticulated under different representational conditions. Moreover, what emerges from political analysis of these categories never resolves much; whatever else it does, sexual difference raises troubling questions about any assumed relationship between natural asymmetries (anatomical differences) and social inequalities. These questions are nowhere more pertinent than in legal pleas of "diminished capacity," where criminal law is asked to ignore its otherwise clear-cut distinction between the realm of biological (or psychiatric) statements about a subject, and the realm of statements about the social state of subjects in relation to their intentions and motives. For example, the question of premenstrual tension as a "biological disorder" directly imparing a woman's social behavior has often been cited as a problem for the legal handling of cases of diminished capacity.[1] The particular case I want to consider here, however, involves a man (a man in feminism) for whom the plea of diminished capacity became an infamous landmark in the recent history of feminist responses to the law.

My examples are drawn from the case of Peter Sutcliffe, the Yorkshire Ripper, who, between 1975 and 1981, in what is called "Bronte country" in Northern England, was the killer and mutilator of at least thirteen women (some "prostitutes," others not), and the attacker of at least seven others who survived; who, during this time, was the object of the costliest, most extensive, and most obsessive manhunt in police history; and whose actions and moral liability were the subject of one of the most revealing court trials in modern British social history.[2]

Sutcliffe would never have been exposed to the public milieu of a juried trial if the judge at the initial hearings had not expressed his dissatisfaction over what he called a "conflict" between certain statements made earlier by Sutcliffe to the police, and others made later in the course of psychiatric investigation. Up to this point in the proceedings, it was generally assumed that the defense plea for diminished responsibility on Sutcliffe's behalf would be accepted, a plea which drew upon the testimony of four psychiatrists that the defendant was a paranoid schizophrenic: that he had manifested four of the eight classic symptoms of paranoid schizophrenia; in short, that he was not *bad*, but merely *mad*.

What was this "conflict" which made the judge change his mind? Was it a simple rhetorical discrepancy between two statements that occasioned the need for an Old Bailey trial which called into question so many institutional practices: the cavalier ethics of the police methods employed during the investigation; the unbridled checkbook journalism of the tabloid press; the prejudicial and persecutory imperatives of the legal system; the forensic validity of psychiatric opinion; the more general validity of a male working-class culture that produced, possessed, and, in some part, protected, Sutcliffe during his life of crime; and lastly, the various factional responses from the feminist ranks, ranging from those who claimed that all men were on trial along with Sutcliffe, to those who advanced the arguably more radical claim that it was a socially sanctioned system of fixing and legislating categories of sexual difference that was on trial?

The conflicting statements made by Sutcliffe are alarmingly simple, and yet their contradictions ran so deeply that they all but scuttled the plea for diminished responsibility. At the time of his arrest, he said that he "had the urge to kill any woman," a category, then, which includes *all women*. However, the statements produced in court to substantiate his schizophrenic condition claimed that he had acted in the service of a divine mission, guided by God's voice, with the specific intent only of killing *all prostitutes*. This latter mission, to kill all prostitutes, was *recognized*, notoriously, at all levels of interpretation, from that of the popular press to that of the professional lawyer, as a moral mission, and therefore less culpable than the asocial desire to kill "all women," a desire only recognized, perhaps, in the well-known slogans of radical or revolutionary feminists who construct the following syllogism: "Some men rape and kill women. All men are potential rapist-killers. Therefore all women are potential victims." In point of fact, the Sutcliffe affair reveals little we do not already know about the respective social and political fallibility of either of these points of view (which is to say that under different circumstances, one would be tempted to argue that the syllogism of radical feminism is just as "false," indeed, just as reactionary, as the other, puritanical persecution of a specific social class of women, in this case, prostitutes). What the Sutcliffe case does reveal, however, is a discrepancy, or "conflict" as the judge put it, that cuts across these points of view, a conflict which, finally, could only be resolved by manhandling the entire legal apparatus to the point of inducing a social catharsis of national dimensions: a conflict, which, I shall argue, ultimately suggests that there is no determinate or necessary relation between the domain of biological categories (all women, all men) and the domain of social categories which demonstrate sexual difference (prostitutes, non-prostitutes). Rather, two different realms of necessity come into conflict, and it is a man, Sutcliffe—a man, moreover, who is of two minds about what it is to be a man—who reveals the dangers of failing to distinguish between the natural and the sexual.

Firstly, it should be borne in mind how rigorously the distinction between "all women" and "all prostitutes" was reproduced at all the significant levels of social reaction to Sutcliffe. It was not until the first non-prostitute was killed (his fifth victim) that the police investigation assumed an identity of its own. A police statement announced that "an innocent young woman has been slaughtered. The next Ripper victim could be anyone's wife, daughter, or girlfriend." A police poster read: "The next victim may be innocent." A national media scare activated public opinion for the first time: "All women are now at risk." It was then and only then that the feminists of Northern England were mobilized, and the tradition of "Reclaim the Night" protest marches was begun. The same marks of difference were observed during the trial, when repeated references were made to the "blemished" or "disreputable" victims, as opposed to the "innocent" victims, implying, of course, that the former deserved to die while the "innocent" did not; the prosecutor declared of the victims that "some were prostitutes, but perhaps the saddest part of the case is that some were not." In spite of protests by the English Collective of Prostitutes and by feminists up and down the country, the distinction was upheld because it was recognized to be crucial to the prosecutor's case.

Perhaps this is hardly surprising in a legal system which obliges its officials to refer to particular women as "common prostitutes" as a matter of course during court proceedings: here, the legal term, "common," primarily denotes "universal" availability (as opposed to a "proper" individual, the property of one individual). It must be pointed out, however, that the law does not operate systematically under any criterion that recognizes the *universality* of a particular category of women. In other words, the same person can be judged a "common prostitute" for certain social purposes and under certain legal circumstances, a "woman" in others, and a non-sexually specific "individual" or "subject" in still others. (Indeed, it is precisely because the law does not operate universally upon specifically female subjects that it cannot recognize claims made on behalf of "all women"). Nonetheless, even though the law, potentially and theoretically, recognizes the difference of each individual, the *particular* social effect of Sutcliffe's trial was actually to reinstate the difference between two categories of women (prostitutes and non-prostitutes), to redefine a difference that Sutcliffe is perceived to have recognized in intent, but to have confused in deed and action. In killing the "innocent" along with the "guilty," Sutcliffe was thus, in a sense, "punished" for confusing theory and practice, for failing to observe the universal distinctions that ought to govern such categories.

Prostitutes, as a category, after all, are assumed to be universally recognizable. Not only are they themselves supposed to exhibit a visible difference, but an entire social history has been exclusively devoted to various attempts to *essentialize* or *naturalize* their difference, even to the extent of calling upon medical opinion to ground this difference in physiological evidence.[3] Of course, the dominant political aim of this history has been to sanction upper-class male vice while repressing shows of feminine sexuality, but that is hardly a "fact" that is available to popular consciousness. On the contrary, what passes into popular consciousness is the concept of a difference that is essential or universal (prostitutes and all other women), and it is that concept of universality which speaks through Sutcliffe's actions. In effect, his moral mission is to eliminate a social category of women *as if it were a natural category*. He was therefore perceived as having killed according to this conceptual universality, and his mission, incredibly enough, was recognized as a "natural" one for a respectable man to pursue. Of course, this category of women has no "natural" constituents; indeed, many of Sutcliffe's victims were not even full-time prostitutes, but rather women who temporarily turned to prostitution in order to stabilize a fluctuating family income (the law is particularly confused in the case of what police call good-time girls—"sometimes you pay, sometimes you don't"). Prostitutes, then, are not a sexual class, nor are they a specifically professional class. In Sutcliffe's case, nonetheless, the distinction between prostitutes and non-prostitutes had to be perceived as sufficiently universal for him to have "criminally" confused it. This, at least, was the assumption contained in the argument developed by the prosecution: in other words, that Sutcliffe's killings were "understandable" in terms of rational motivation. As Lucy Bland explains:

> the law presumes that normally we intend the consequences of our actions and that when an unlawful act has been committed, the accused's *motives* are irrelevant to his/her liability. However, in challenging a plea for diminished responsibility, the establishment of understandable motive and motivation acts as a means for the prosecution to demonstrate *rational* intention to kill, and thus the existence of *mens rea* ["guilty mind"].[4]

Notwithstanding that this argument assumed as "natural" Sutcliffe's aggression against women *tout court*, it suggested that his intended actions were somehow rationally directed in believing, whether correctly or not, that his victims were "all prostitutes." The defense case, dependent on psychiatric opinion, consequently failed because it could not argue on the grounds of "conscious" intent, and because it could not respond to the claims that Sutcliffe's crimes were also *sexual* in nature.

When the plea for diminished responsibility was dismissed, the specificity of Sutcliffe's case was dropped in favor of what feminists rightly interpreted as an assumed "normalization" of his actions on the prosecutor's part.[5] Even at that, however, it would seem reductive to claim that Sutcliffe had done his killing in the name of "all men." In fact, he was supposed to have killed in the name of all men and most women, that is, all women, except for prostitutes (even although both the prosecution and defense were wrong to concentrate attention on particular configurations of his own psychic history in order to suggest that he had killed for, or in the name of, only certain women: his wife and his mother). In effect, what emerges from Sutcliffe's case is much too complex to be reduced to essentialist claims about the status of "all men" and "all women." On the contrary, the lesson of Sutcliffe, and others like him, calls for a thorough cultural critique of the codes of necessity that depend upon those very concepts of universality supporting statements about "all women" and "all men," for such statements reproduce the very conceptual apparatus that makes Sutcliffes into killers.

But what of Sutcliffe himself as a man? And what is his God? For a large part of his legal culpability rests, finally, upon a logical problem not unworthy of scholastic wrangling. God could indeed have entrusted him with the mission of killing "all prostitutes," but God could not have inveighed against "all women." God, after all, is not responsible for *sexual difference*; God is, however, responsible for sexual or biological *division* (the creation of anatomical men and women), and so he could not want to undo his own work by destroying all women. In view of Sutcliffe's fateful "discrepancy" in this matter, and in view of the fact that his plea for diminished responsibility (i.e., divine guidance) is dismissed, we could say that it was in fact God's *plausibility* that was upheld by the verdict. For Sutcliffe, however, whose social venom issues from a different realm of necessity, it is God's *fallibility* that is at stake. For Sutcliffe, every woman he kills *must* be a prostitute—he said "God didn't make mistakes, the newspapers did" when they reported that he had murdered an "innocent" woman. And when asked in court whether this vengeful God did not invalidate the miraculous God of his Catholic childhood, he replied, perhaps tongue-in-cheek, perhaps not, that it seemed similar to the "contradiction between the Old Testament and the New."[6]

As the popular press pointed out at length and with somewhat ambivalent gusto, the man who said this was not the bachelor, loner, outcast, underprivileged wretch, or psychopath for whom the police had been searching for over five years. The Ripper turned out to be a good-looking man, soft-spoken and courteous, intelligent, with a loving family background, a religious education, a good job, a nice house, a pretty wife, and even a mistress—in short, the perfect, virile man, socially, sexually, and emotionally well-integrated. Born and bred in the shadow of steel mills and smokestacks, Sutcliffe possessed a drive towards bourgeois respectability that also put him in the thralldom of certain moral imperatives—hence his social mission of cleaning the streets, working for society and not against it. As an exterminating angel, a guardian of the respectable social order, it is Sutcliffe who is more "efficient" than the police, or at least he represents policing better than the police do, which, of course, is why they fail to recognize, let alone apprehend, him for so long, despite having interviewed him nine times in the course of their investigations. Sutcliffe kills according to, and not in contravention of, the logic of a system sustained by its "categorical" imperatives in matters of moral and sexual difference. But clearly not *all men* are "possessed" by these codes of necessity to the point of committing such base crimes. What, then, was revealed to be particular rather than universal about Sutcliffe?

Two very brief incidents were highlighted in the course of the trial. Sutcliffe's first encounter with a prostitute was a shambles. She mocked him for his show of physical impotency, pocketed the money he had given her, and sent him away without sexual "recompense." Somehow it is Sutcliffe, or rather his lack, which is forced to occupy the feminine position as an object of exchange. Thus feminized, he acts to redress the balance, for his subsequent killings all reclaim a woman's body as compensation for this personal debt that he has incurred in the sexual economy. Only the body is involved in this murderous exchange; there was sex in only one instance (which is not to say, however, that these are not sexual murders). So too, in another incident, is he feminized when he is *penetrated* by God's voice, issuing from a gravestone on a hill.[7] It is as much a social voice, berating him for his private lack of public virility. To respond to this charge, and to reaffirm his masculinity, he must act and kill *in the name of that voice*, a voice which articulates what "all men" are supposed to have in the way of socialized masculinity.

There are more details and other examples, but it is time to make a concluding point. Whether culpability for these terrible acts is attributed to Sutcliffe in particular, to male violence in general, or to social and legal codes shot through with patriarchal oppression, it is important to recognize that there is no more of a determinate relation between the physical level of Sutcliffe's "impotency" and his criminal behavior than there is between the social imperative of virility (which speaks to him from billboards and gravestones alike), and his motivation to kill. In fact, that there is no determinate relation at all between the "natural" and the "social" that is not mediated by the configurations of sexual difference which made for the notorious complexity of Sutcliffe's case. On the contrary, what I have suggested is that Sutcliffe's case reveals a gap, discrepancy, or conflict between the natural and the social, a discrepancy which is socially intolerable because it demonstrates configurations of sexual difference that are not anatomically supported. As I have argued, this discrepancy is something the law does actually recognize, and quite literally in this instance, since it is the judge's perception of this discrepancy that creates the need for a trial in the first place. In the course of recognizing Sutcliffe's sanity, however, while condemning the "insanity" of his crimes, the law tries to resolve the point of "conflict" it has isolated, and thereby reaffirms a logic of universals that holds sway in the realm of social action that produces the likes of Sutcliffe. In pointing this out, my intention is not in the least to absolve Sutcliffe of any share of his repugnant acts. Nor is it to absolve "all men" of their social potential for aggressing against women, although my argument implies that claims about the universality of male violence only serve, in the long run, to naturalize such phenomena. Rather, my intention is to help reveal the incriminating silence of an entire social logic bound over to the necessity of predicating men and women as fixed sexual categories.

5.
Men in Feminism: Odor di Uomo Or Compagnons de Route?*

ALICE JARDINE

The general title of these two sessions, "Men in Feminism," sent me scurrying for cover—in fact, between the covers of several dictionaries, our concrete records of patriarchal meaning. "*Men*" I didn't really need to look up in the clear-cut context of these two panels. "*In*" still hangs in the air as quite mysterious to me, if a bit less so since this morning's discussion: (why not men *as* feminists? for example). And then, looking up the word "feminism" led me to reflect on the very structure of this encounter: two sessions organized by a man, with women once again responding, reacting—as always, in the negative position, inevitably interjecting: "That's not quite it"— or "You're not there yet." What if the men had responded to the women? But it's even more complicated, for while looking at my dictionaries, I suddenly realized that we have here: three men who *are* British and four women—*in*—French. Hmmm, I thought.

Now, "feminism" is a nineteenth-century word. The French *Littré* indicates that in 1892, the word "feminism" was sometimes used to refer to a *man* exhibiting feminine characteristics. More precisely, it states: "feminism: a break in the development of a man around adolescence which gives him certain feminine attributes." And, unbelievably, one also finds: "Feminist: a man who is attracted to women"! Hmm, I thought again. And so what, at the other pole, does the

---

The following reflections would have been impossible without lengthy conversations between Rosi Braidotti and myself in August 1984, in Bacchereto, Italy—conversations leading directly to our co-authored (and unpublished) first response to Paul Smith: "Corps Ré(s)pondantes." I am also indebted to Françoise Laburie for her suggestive contributions to the debate. All quotations are from the original MLA presentations.

Oxford *English* Dictionary say? Very different. No mention of men, simply: (1846) "Femininism[sic]: the state of being feminine" or "a feminine or woman's word or expression" or (1851) "Feminism: The qualities of females . . . " We are clearly dealing with two different traditions, the French and the English. And since I have tried to deal with the French one elsewhere (in my book *Gynesis*), here I will concentrate solely on the Anglo-American context. Feminism: no mention of men; a woman's word.

Anglo-American academic male critics do seem to be very *into* feminism these days. Younger . . . older . . . gay . . . straight men. What is striking is that most of these Anglo-American men tend only to speak of "women" or "feminism" in order to speak about "something else"—some "larger issue"—and then "women" are either reduced to bodily parts, abstract wholes (*wh*), or are spoken only in relation to other men. Elaine Showalter's perceptive and indeed very funny article, "Critical Cross-Dressing" provides us with a cast of characters where this is especially so: for example, Wayne Booth emphasizes bodily parts in order to talk about "larger questions" of Interpretation, Bakhtin, and Rabelais; Robert Scholes meditates on the clitoris to talk about Semiotics; Jonathan Culler, taking the more abstract route, needs "woman" to talk about Deconstruction; and Terry Eagleton needs women to talk about Marxist Theory. There are some French *pre*-texts here, but these remain very Anglo-American texts.

But then, it seems quite unfair of me to single out and categorize in this way. Should we not be talking here rather about new discursive formations in the Foucaultian sense—formations producing very different feminist *effects*? Discursive formations which we will not try to *interpret* (what do they *really* mean?) but, rather, whose functions we must try to interpolate with regard to power, institutions, and the disciplines—heretofore of MAN?

Roughly—and everything I say here will be rough, very pragmatic—roughly, I think there are three groups of male critics in the academy today:

1) First, the Silent Majority: those who neither read nor take into account the enormous body of work produced by feminist intellectuals over the past twenty years. Some of them are our most eminent and supposedly radical critics. I won't mention any names . . .
2) Then there are those who plug in and out of feminism without changing anything in the overall itinerary of their theory or practice. Three discursive strategies are particularly evident here: a) what I call "authoritative" writing on women from guys who already have authority; b) men who express sympathy towards feminism and then turn around and pan women's books

in the *NYROB* and elsewhere; c) those who operate one of the
oldest male seductive strategies around: Divide and Conquer.
To women they say: I like *your* work, but not *hers*; or: feminist
theorists are smarter than women's studies advocates; or: only
feminists *outside* of the academy are *really* radical.
3) But then there is a third group—there are those men who
are really trying, really reading and changing. And they are the
ones I'm addressing today. Our allies—the three men on this
morning's panel, for example.

Bacchereto, Italy
12 August, 1984

My dear Rosi,

I have just finished reading Paul Smith's paper, "A Question of
Feminine Identity . . . "
What strikes me most generally is how complex the question of
untangling the *énonciation* from the *énoncé* becomes when it is a question of our male allies—the men who have taken the time and energy
to read much of the corpus informing our own work. A question of
untangling the dancer from the dance? Something like that. What are
the *mechanisms*, linguistic and otherwise, whereby these men are able
to evacuate questions of *their* sexuality, *their* subjectivity, *their* relationship to language from their sympathetic texts on "feminism," on
"woman," on "feminine identity"?
Most difficult of all is that these *few* men, our allies, have learned
their lessons well. The actual "content" of their writing is rarely incorrect per se. It is almost as if they have learned a new vocabulary
perfectly, but have not paid enough attention to syntax or intonation.
When they write of us—always of us—their bodies would seem to
know nothing of the new language they've learned . . .

Dearest Alice,

I hesitate.
The paper you sent me bears witness to the historical significance
of the emergence of women as speaking, writing, desiring subjects.
As a "sign of the times" I enjoyed it very much; I mean—here's an
aware, sensitive, concerned, intelligent man addressing one of the
key feminist questions: feminine identity! In the midst of the ideological backlash of the 1980s, should we not be grateful to have such
political and intellectual allies? Yet I hesitate . . .

What I've just shared with you are short excerpts from letters between myself and Rosi Braidotti—an English-speaking feminist theor-

ist working in Paris—letters in response to a particular paper by Paul Smith. But as Paul Smith pointed out this morning, while addressed to a particular text and context, the issues raised in this exchange are of general concern nonetheless.

What are some of these more general concerns from a feminist point of view?

1) As formulated by the Seminar on Feminist Literary Theory at Harvard, the first issue might be articulated by the question, "*Why Now?*" What is this "Bandwagon Effect" whereby, in the academy, men are jumping on the feminist theory bandwagon at a time when it is experiencing a certain success in the academy *and*—paradoxically—at a time when the larger political context in which we are living gets more reactionary for women and others every day? A political context which is, among other things, devalorizing the work all of us in this room do in a technocratic culture?

2) Is what we are witnessing the appropriation of a struggle, with men telling us how to be "more sophisticated" and warning us not to fall into theoretically "regressive" traps? From my point of view, this is sometimes awfully close to the imperialist gesture of telling the peoples of the so-called Third World to stop worrying about their agriculture and make computer chips—even though their people are starving . . .

Or maybe not, maybe it's not about appropriation at all. Maybe—as Samuel Beckett puts it—it's just the fault of the pronouns: she/he/us/them. The inevitable struggle over discursive and political territories that has always surfaced historically for radical movements: can blacks trust whites? Can Third World women trust Western bourgeois feminists? Can women trust men?

3) Third issue: What is it about these men's texts that irritates so many feminists? Is it that we are being legalistic and exclusive as Paul Smith suggested this morning? Or is it maybe that what for many of us has been, above all, a private struggle has only very recently gone public, and we feel threatened by men's rather easy transformation of our private struggles into public exchange? Maybe. But perhaps we are also irritated by the prescription and reduction of complexity that has so far governed so much of men's interventions into feminism . . .

Alice: "Rosi, how long before it becomes no longer a question but an *answer*, a prescription about how women *should* go about what they're doing, saying, and writing . . . There is then a kind of streamlining of feminism—a suppression of the diversity and disagreement within the movement itself . . . "

Rosi: "Yes, in our work we've all tried to come to terms with the complexity of these issues . . . don't you think we could ask our male allies to respect this complexity and try to cope with it themselves?"

Or maybe what irritates us is simply the a-historicism of much of men's work on feminism. As Rosi again puts it: "it's easier for any man to forget the historical *fact* that is the oppression of women: it's one of their favorite blind spots."

Finally, in thinking about this irritation with men's interventions into feminism thus far, we could get more micropolitical: are we not irritated simply by their professional when not professorial tone so often sandwiched between sharp critiques of one woman writer after another? By their tendency to descend into pathos and apology as soon as they're threatened?—a definite *Odor di Uomo*. . . . By their general discursive strategies which indicate that they've heard our *demands* but haven't adequately read our work?

Rosi: "It just goes to prove, Alice, that our struggles are far from being over—in fact, they are just beginning for real . . . "

Struggle. The *inscription* of struggle. When the members of the same feminist theory group mentioned above tried to articulate how we can recognize a feminist text—whether written by a man or a woman—it was this that was found to be necessary. The *inscription of struggle*—even of *pain* . . .

Why then would men want to be *in* feminism if it's about struggle? What do men want to be in—in pain?

The three papers we heard this morning vary in their inscriptive response to this question. All were in their own way important and all deserve our close attention. Andrew Ross's paper, "Demonstrating Sexual Difference," focused on how the conflation of natural and sociosexual categories is actually what *leads* to phenomena like the Yorkshire Ripper in England. His point is well taken: biological categories do not equal social ones. Feminists have been saying nothing else for years. But this now rather familiar argument against "essentialism" does not go further; for example, it cannot work with and through what I find to be one of the most thought-provoking statements of recent date by a feminist theorist: Gayatri Spivak's suggestion (echoing Heath) that women today may *have* to take "the risk of essence" in order to think really differently. I'm afraid that the signs of struggle, suffering, and pain in Ross's and the Ripper's "demonstration" are elsewhere—they're *buried*, literally and in history.

Paul Smith's paper strikes me as more helpful. There is a struggle there—and it is signalled by his *questions*. There are *statements* I personally have a lot of trouble with, some of which were discussed this morning: for example, that "women's studies has been relatively well integrated into [. . .] the academy." I'd like to know where this is so—in a time of massive budget cuts, marginalization, and ideological pats on the head. Nor do I think that "feminist theory . . . does not exist outside of the academy," nor that it is "not separable from the general 'theory' that has worked its way into studies in the humanities over the last ten or twenty years." But disagreements about these statements aside, Smith's questions are genuine enough. For example, Smith suggests that men can *understand* feminism—that the problem lies elsewhere: "if feminist theory would claim that a man speaking or writing in feminism cannot or simply does not include his body, the first question might be to ask what are the signs that are being looked for? What does a male writing his imaginary actually produce?"

Smith's questions are important, indeed central. It is troubling, therefore, when he goes on to block the kind of work he'd have to do to begin to address them. He finally assumes that men who thought through their bodies would only be able to do what they did *before* feminist theory. Smith therefore posits men's function in feminism only as "a reminder of the material fact of difference, the real consequences of which is feminism's material cause." While I find this an intriguing strategy, it is also a familiar one. Reminding us, judging, scolding us by their *presence*. End of Struggle. Odor di Uomo.

I must admit that I found Stephen Heath's paper (the one circulated to us a few weeks ago as well as his remarks this morning) the most inscriptive of struggle—a struggle with the "impossible relationship of men to feminism." I stopped at.length over his insights and questions: "Is it possible to wonder whether there is not in male feminism, men's relation to feminism, always potentially a pornographic effect? Do I write from desire-fear, to say simply in the last analysis 'love me'? But what can I say from day to day, teaching, talking, just generally around?" Heath wants men to *learn* from feminism, to try to be as feminist *as possible*. He, too, argues against essentialism, and against male writers who would not leave us our space, while worrying about *their* place. But two reflections near the end of Heath's original paper (one of which he re-articulated this morning) seem self-defeating: first, he doubts that men could tell the truth about their bodies; and second, he valorizes "admiration" by men of feminist theory . . . He recognizes the problems with that stance, but poses "admiration" nonetheless as an ad-hoc posture for feminist men . . .

Feminist men. Male feminism. Is this but an exercise in oxymorons? or perhaps a promising utopian vision? I think that depends on what men want. What do men want? Assuming, at the very least, that they want to be *in* feminism . . .

And what do feminists want? If you will forgive me my directness, we do not want you to *mimic* us, to become the same as us; we don't want your pathos or your guilt; and we don't even want your admiration (even if it's nice to get it once in a while). What we want, I would even say what we need, is your *work*. We need you to get down to serious work. And like all serious work, that involves struggle and pain. As guide to that work, I would like to remind you of a sentence by Hélène Cixous—a sentence which, to my knowledge, has not been taken seriously by our allies at all: "Men still have everything to say about their own sexuality." *You still have everything to say about your sexuality*: that's a challenge, if it helps you to think of it that way. And, in closing, since none of the three men's papers today addressed that question, and, indeed, posited it as unanswerable, I would like to offer a short and pragmatic agenda for beginning this vast work which has yet to begin.

First, some general suggestions. I think that you—our male allies—should issue a moratorium on talking about feminism/women/femininity/female sexuality/feminine identity/etc. It is much easier to speak about women than to speak *as* a body-coded male—to imagine a new man. And secondly, I do not agree with Smith or Heath that to work through your male sexuality would only reproduce what's come before, reproduce the phallocentric imaginary. Not if you've really read and lived feminist work, which I think some of you have. Also, let me address Heath's question directly and, again, very pragmatically: what can you do as teachers, writers, and critics—everyday—just generally around? Well:

1) Echoing Heath, you can stop being sophisticated in theory and politically naïve in practice—for example, you can help stop the killing of women's books in reviews . . . Or stop your colleagues—when not yourself—from leaving them out, or simply dismissing them.
2) You could read women's writing—write on it and teach it. (By the way, at the risk of sounding like I'm granting Heath an honorary degree in feminist criticism, one of the few such efforts I have read with interest and great pleasure is Stephen Heath's "Dorothy Richardson and the Novel.")
3) You could sponsor women students (as long as we're going to remain in the institution).
4) You could recognize your debts to feminism in writing.
5) While doing so, you could watch out for the "shoulds" and "should-nots" and especially stop being so reductive. Please don't make a mythology—in the Barthesian sense—out of feminism.
6) You could critique your male colleagues on the issue of fem-

inism—although I warn you that this is likely to make you very unpopular.

7) And the most important, you yourselves could stop being *reactive* to feminism and start being *active* feminists—your cultural positionality as men allows you to!

And what about in the realm of theory? Here the list is endless. You have at least twenty years of feminist theory to take seriously. For example, at the most general level, you could take on—as men *after* feminism—some of the symbolic fields most addressed by feminist theory: for example, from cinematic theory, the symbolic hegemony of *vision* as organizing metaphor of patriarchal history; or men's relationship to technology, weapons, and war. Or Sports—what is going on in the male psyche with these bats and balls and nets?

In the deeper realms of psychoanalytic inquiry, . . . you have not even begun to think about your mothers. Nor have you rewritten your relationship to your fathers. For example, how would a male critic after feminism rewrite Harold Bloom's *Anxiety of Influence*?

What else? Well, there's men's relationship *after feminism*, to death, scopophilia, fetishism (we've had a beginning today), the penis and balls, erection, ejaculation (not to mention the phallus), madness, paranoia, homosexuality, blood, tactile pleasure, pleasure in general, *desire* (but, please, not with an anonymously universal capital D), voyeurism, etc. Now this *would* be talking your body, not talking *about* it. It is not essentialism; it is not metaphysics, and it is not/would not be representation. As Luce Irigaray put it, "The bodily in man is what metaphysics has never touched . . . "

On a more literary note, do theories of narrative structure in the male realm always have to be modeled upon traditional male desire: beginning, middle, end? What about problems of enunciation, voice, and silence? Can you think through the heterogeneity of the subject without putting the burden of the demised universal subject onto the female? And most important, when you're reading men's books, whether new or old, are you up to taking Nietzsche seriously?:

What has *the Man* not been able to talk about?
What is *the Man* hiding?
In what respect is *the Man* mistaken?

You see, you have all of your work before you, not behind you. We, as feminists, need your work. We don't need your Odor di Uomo. We need you as traveling *compagnons* into the twenty-first century.

6.
Walking the *Tightrope* of Feminism and Male Desire[1]

JUDITH MAYNE

At the Modern Language Association panels on "Men in Feminism" where several of the essays in this volume were presented initially, the term "feminism" was articulated primarily as a theoretical entity. Now it is certainly not the case that men have been absent from feminism: a decade or so ago, earnest discussion might have taken place in a women's studies classroom about the necessity to "educate" men, for instance, or men might have taken charge of day care to demonstrate their solidarity with the women's movement. "Men in feminism" is hardly a new formulation.

What distinguishes this particular forum is, precisely, the *theoretical* dimension. The negotiation of men's relation to feminism thus marks, perhaps, a new stage of theoretical sophistication within feminism. The relative merits of that theoretical sophistication might then be tested, as it were, by examining the relationship to feminism of a certain kind of man, equally theoretically sophisticated. The task of any theoretical project is to examine the working field of oppositions that constitute the scope of inquiry, in this case, feminist inquiry. Feminist theory is thus assessed in the essays by Stephen Heath, Paul Smith, and Andrew Ross. Stephen Heath describes man's "impossible relationship" to feminism as a sign, a symptom of feminist theory as a simultaneous investment in and distance from the persistent dualisms upon which our most fundamental, and problematic, notions of identity are based. Paul Smith situates the theoretical sophistication of feminism as a problem, the danger of a theory with a limited academic field of application: hence the familiar yet problematic fit between theory and practice defines his engagement with feminism. In Andrew Ross's discussion of the Yorkshire Ripper, the theoretical issue is most succinctly understood as a battle of opposing views. Ross's demonstration of the "danger of failing to distinguish between the natural and the sexual" collapses the distinction between the law and a certain kind of feminism which wants to speak in the name of "all women." Thus there are two theoretical protagonists in Ross's discussion, which correspond to the poles of "essentialism" and "anti-essentialism" (and their attendant implications of French and American allegiances) in current debates within feminism.

My purpose in this essay is to look at the theoretical agenda that frames these discussions of "men in feminism" from a perspective that is more appropriately described as a narrative vantage point than a theoretical one per se. The essays by Heath, Smith, and Ross to which the participants on the panel "Men in Feminism II" were asked to respond are theoretical texts, obviously; but they are, as well, narratives that possess a point-of-view (unified or otherwise) and that unfold (problematically or not) across a field of binary oppositions. The narrative to which I turn is of a distinctly different (but not unrelated) kind, for it is a commercial film defined throughout by the persona of an actor who would appear to have an antagonistic relationship at best to the issue of "men in feminism" that is of concern in this collection.

The film is *Tightrope* (1984), in which the image of Clint Eastwood as it has evolved over the years is pondered and interrogated. (Noting that the film was scripted and directed by Richard Tuggle, J. Hoberman speculates that *"Tightrope* is so personal that Eastwood couldn't sign it."[2]) In *Tightrope*, Clint Eastwood portrays a policeman, Wes Block, who is investigating a series of murders of women, all of them sex-related. *Tightrope* is a film obsessed with division, with separation, with the tension of opposition, most graphically portrayed in the spatial opposition between the Tenderloin district of New Orleans where many of the murders occur, and the suburban neighborhood where Block lives with his two daughters. (Block's ex-wife, glimpsed only briefly in the film, has left him and the family.)

The film is equally obsessed with sexual difference, and with the difference between two kinds of women, or more precisely, two kinds of females—sexual partners and daughters. Wes Block walks a tightrope in that the separation of the two worlds is fragile, and the narrative of *Tightrope* occupies the threshold space between the two realms. While the imagery of the film conveys the "tightrope" of the film's title, a brief discussion between Block and a woman in a courthouse makes clear that the tightrope upon which Block is poised is first and foremost a split within himself. The woman speculates as to the killer's motivations, and tells Block that "there's a darkness inside all of us . . . you, me, the man down the street. Some have it under control. The rest of us try to walk a tightrope between the two." The killer sought by Block is not out to get all women, or even all prostitutes (in any case, the film is unsure what the difference is). The killer is out to get Wes Block. He knows Block's fears and desires better than Block himself. Block's investigations lead him to sexual

liaisons with several prostitutes, where a fancy for bondage in hand-
cuffs becomes particularly evident. The murderer is an omnipresent
voyeur, and each woman with whom Block makes contact becomes
a victim of the killer. Block's double eventually transgresses the
boundary line separating the two worlds of the film, penetrating the
suburban house and assaulting Block's older daughter. Block's pursuit of the killer is an encounter with himself, with his own repressed—and some not-so-repressed—desires, until the final, inevitable showdown between the two men when the murderer is killed.

What makes *Tightrope* if not an exceptional film then at least an
interesting one is that this is a Clint Eastwood film "with a difference." *Tightrope* is a confessional film, and one to which a formula
invoked in some discussions of pornography is particularly appropriate: *Tightrope* is the theory, Dirty Harry the practice. And even
though *Tightrope* is not explicitly about pornography, but rather about
the network of relationships of which pornography is one expression,
and even though Clint Eastwood may not be one of the "legions of
feminist men," the film addresses more convincingly than many other
texts the question raised by B. Ruby Rich: "if the legions of feminist
men want to do something useful they could undertake the analysis
that can tell us why men like porn. . . . "[3]

As a self-reflexive Clint Eastwood film, *Tightrope* ponders questions
and connections that might be unspeakable in another kind of film—
between pleasure and danger, between heterosexual and homosexual
desire, between paternal affection and incest, between sexuality and
violence. More precisely, *Tightrope* problematizes the connections.
The connections take on a particularly interesting narrative configuration. For the obligatory romance transpires with a woman, Beryl
Thibodeaux (portrayed by Genevieve Bujold) who, as director of a
rape crisis center, is concerned about the status of the investigations,
and concerned in the name of "all women." It's worth pointing out
here how unusual this designation of a female lead is in the contemporary Hollywood cinema. If feminism has been mainstreamed into
Hollywood, it is usually in terms of female heroism, or the conflict
between love and career, and rarely in terms of a discourse or a perspective or a character that can be even remotely described as feminist. I mention this not in order to praise *Tightrope* as a progressive
film, but to ask what is served, within the narrative logic of this film,
by such an allusion to feminism. This is an allusion that transcends
the *Tootsie* school of feminist impersonation, for the representation
of Genevieve Bujold as a feminist emphasizes her initial separation
from the world occupied by Wes Block, a separation that is too profound to be bridged by a simple masquerade.

Tightrope is a love story of sorts, or more precisely, a heterosexual
romance, between a man and a woman for whom desire leads, in

however different ways, to connections between sexuality and violence. What Eastwood does in practice, Bujold ponders in theory. The connection between sexuality and violence is for Wes Block a symptom of the split between the two worlds of the film, and it is the function of Beryl Thibodeaux to heal that split. The feminist here is defined not only as the woman who defends female sexuality against male violence, but also as a figure who presumably comprehends the links between sexuality and violence.

If *Tightrope* is the theory and Dirty Harry the practice, then the links between sexuality and violence so central to *Tightrope* can be read in relation to the Dirty Harry films. In the first, *Dirty Harry* (1971), the narrative relies on an obsessive division of the world between the good and the evil. Harry Callahan pursues a killer who has raped a fourteen-year-old girl and buried her alive. The villain is unquestionably "other" in this film, an otherness emphasized by his hatred of, yet simultaneous identification with, gays. Early in the film, we see the killer attempt to shoot a gay man: that this hatred stems from his own sexual identity is suggested later, when Dirty Harry's first actual encounter with the killer in a park is immediately preceded by a come-on by a gay man named "Alice." In the logic of this film, Dirty Harry and the villain are of two entirely different worlds. The only characteristic shared by the two worlds is the complete absence of women. In *Magnum Force* (1973), Dirty Harry is still a lone force of law and order, but the police department, which in the first Dirty Harry film was portrayed as hopelessly bound up in excessive liberal concern for the rights of criminals, here is seen as corrupt in its own right. For the villians that are the object of Dirty Harry's search turn out to be four young policemen and a police official who are members of a vigilante group. The gay sexuality hinted at in *Dirty Harry* is present in *Magnum Force* as well; for as Harry's partner tells him, everyone in the department used to think the four young cops were "queer." Women are by and large excluded from the configuration of this film as well.

In *The Enforcer* (1976), Dirty Harry confronts affirmative action, and is forced to work with a female partner, portrayed by Tyne Daly. By some stretch of the imagination, she could be construed as a "positive image" in the sense that she turns out to be quite a good cop indeed— by saving Harry's life and losing her own. Here too, Harry makes a foray into a massage parlor (posing as "Larry Dickman"), which, although strictly in the line of business, could be seen as a prelude to Wes Block's journeys into the sex commerce in *Tightrope*.

The Dirty Harry film which is perhaps closest, thematically as well as chronologically, to *Tightrope* is *Sudden Impact* (1983), in which a woman artist (portrayed by Sondra Locke) systematically kills off a number of men, and one woman, who had gang-raped her and her sister some years before. Harry's investigation proves to be somewhat more complex than in the earlier Dirty Harry films, for the woman's decision to take the law into her own hands (one of the rapists was the son of the local sheriff, who prevented the criminals from paying for their crime) makes her an appropriate double for Dirty Harry. In *Sudden Impact*, the sexual relationship between the woman and Dirty Harry leads to the somewhat predictable conclusion that the woman may be guilty of the murders, but innocent of any crime. Her real crime—or disease—is man-hating, for which Dirty Harry provides the cure. Dirty Harry thus protects the woman in the name of a higher law.

When seen from the vantage point of *Tightrope*, two themes that circulate in the Dirty Harry series of films are particularly striking. The first is the strong suggestion of homosexuality, which seems to increase in direct proportion to the invisibility of women. It is almost as if the characters portrayed by Tyne Daly and Sondra Locke (in *The Enforcer* and *Sudden Impact* respectively) are significant in direct proportion to their ability to ward off the simultaneous attraction and repulsion of male homosexuality. In *Tightrope*, the killer leads Block on a sexual chase that includes a stop in a gay male bar and a rendezvous with a male prostitute. Block refuses the man, but when asked "How do you know you don't like it if you haven't tried it?" Block replies: "Maybe I have." Even in sarcasm, the suggestion of such a possibility loosens up the boundary lines between gay and straight so central to the Dirty Harry films.

Second is the simultaneous attraction and repulsion of women themselves. If women are virtually absent from the narrative configurations of *Dirty Harry* and *Magnum Force* as anything but cursory victims or imaginary reminders of the past (via brief reminders, for example, of Dirty Harry's deceased wife), the characters in *The Enforcer* and *Sudden Impact* are significant others. Tyne Daly, as Inspector Moore, is "plain" by Hollywood standards (and therefore "refreshing" by others); she wears sensible clothes and little make-up. What little sexual identity she has in the film is expressed in a telling scene with Harry when she refers to a building as "phallic" (Harry, somewhat confused, asks her if everything has a sexual connotation for her). As a somewhat detached observer of sexual symbolism, she anticipates Bujold's role in *Tightrope*. As artist Jennifer, Sondra Locke is like Harry in her single-minded pursuit of revenge, and the crossing of their paths keeps her hatred of a group of rapists from becoming a hatred of all men (and in any case, the designation of one woman as a member of the gang—occasionally referred to as a "dyke"—sets up an opposition between gay and straight women that is not transgressed).

Seen against the background of the Dirty Harry cycle, the narrative logic whereby feminism is "named" in *Tightrope* facilitates the open-ing-up of the space between opposing terms, the blurring of the boundaries between the realms of gay and straight, between desire and violence, between men and women, between good and evil. Like the female leads in *The Enforcer* and *Sudden Impact*, Bujold's character represents a kind of "otherness" with which Dirty Harry contends. But as a feminist, the Bujold character has something that the other female leads do not. For in *Tightrope*, feminism becomes a principle of law and order unavailable in the tightrope configuration of Wes Block's identity and identification with the killer. Tyne Daly becomes an acceptable partner by showing that she shares the same sense of law as Harry; and Sondra Locke is motivated by personal rage. As a feminist, then, the Bujold character kills the proverbial two birds with one stone: she is distinctly "other" than Block, yet she represents a set of social values which, however strange or foreign they might be to Block, are values to be contended with. Feminism as it is repre-sented in the film thus allows a reshuffling of the polarities of desire and violence.

However novel the role ascribed to the woman in *Tightrope* might be in the context of the Dirty Harry films, the function of Beryl Thi-bodeaux, when defined in this way, rings stereotypically true: woman as a principle of morality, the icon which, in a long history of Hol-lywood genres—the Western in particular comes to mind—allows the passage to resolution of one male identity crisis or another. But in the narrative of *Tightrope*, woman alone cannot function to this end: feminism is required. Put another way, the film needs to intro-duce a working opposition between "female" and "feminist."

All females—and again, one can't really say "woman" here, since the detective's own prepubescent daughters figure so centrally—are potential objects of the conflation of desire and violence, whereas the feminist observes the conflation from a theorist's point-of-view. *Tight-rope* appears to resolve quickly the distinction by having Block come to the rescue when the Bujold character is attacked by the killer. She defends herself—she teaches self-defense classes, after all—but it ap-pears as though she is about to be killed when Block arrives on the scene. This is the first woman Block has been able to "save."

If it appears as though the film introduces the distinction between "female" and "feminist" only to collapse it quickly into heterosexual formula, it is important to note that the rescue is not quite as clear-cut as my description might suggest. In an earlier scene, Wes Block is attacked by the killer and is saved only because one of his dogs (the only one spared, or missed, by the killer) comes to his rescue. And Thibodeaux does use every means imaginable to defend herself, from the techniques of self-defense to stabbing the villain with a pair of scissors (after all, it worked for Grace Kelly in *Dial M for Murder*).

Beryl Thibodeaux may well be rescued by a man, but the man himself was saved by a dog. Again, I point this out not in order to make claims for the "progressive" image of woman, or of male-female relations in this film, but rather to stress that the narrative resolutions are not as straightforward as they might initially seem, or as one might expect. Indeed, for all of the classic straightforwardness of the binary oppositions in *Tightrope*, the most distinctive overall tone of the film is confusion. To be sure, *Tightrope* has the proverbial happy ending, but virtually every step towards the resolution is marked by such uncertainty that it is not always clear what is being resolved. While Block tells the press that the murders are sex-related, and while several of the women are clearly identified as prostitutes, the circumstances are unclear in several instances. Nor is it made clear the extent to which sexual abuse is a part of the murders. The most devastating violation in the film is the assault on Block's daughter, yet an easily overlooked aside by a police inspector assures that no sexual assault occurred.

The very premise of *Tightrope* is a kind of confusion: Wes Block (once referred to as "Inspector Blocked" by Thibodeaux) doesn't know who he is, doesn't know how his desires are different from a killer's desires, doesn't know what a woman is. But in attempting to set right that confusion, *Tightrope* plunges deeper into another kind of confusion concerning male sexuality. Block's younger daughter, Penny—the only female in the film who escapes a sexual identity—asks a question, intended superficially as comic relief, which serves as a kind of pivot to the film: "What's a hard-on, Daddy?" The daughter speaks from a position not unlike that of the feminist, a position of detachment (innocent in the daughter's case; critical and theoretical in the feminist's). The film has no answer for the question she asks. Wes Block sleeps with women, and the murderer kills them, but what indeed is a hard-on? Is it the desire to kill, *or* the desire for sex, and is it possible to resituate the polarities of violence and sexuality in any but either-or terms? If the director of a rape crisis center is a sexual being, how is she sexual? The only time we actually see Beryl Thibodeaux in the context of the crisis center is when she demonstrates attack points on a dummy to a female self-defense class. After demonstrating kicks to various sensitive parts of the body, she tells her class that if the attacker continues to act "tacky," there is one final point of attack—a final swift kick to the groin. "Tackiness" is, of course, a term that would be more applicable to the etiquette of dating than to sexual assault—again, a symptom of the film's confusion between the two. And when the kick is delivered to the groin of the dummy, its eyes light up. Block, who has been observing the class, winces in a gesture that can be read either as admiration or as repulsion.

Tightrope is as unsure of what rape is, as it is of what a hard-on is. Now the assertion that a Clint Eastwood film shares an affinity with feminism might seem somewhat delirious, but this confusion in *Tightrope* is analogous to the contradictory ways in which rape has been articulated as a theoretical and ideological issue within feminism. One feminist argument is founded on the incompatibility of sex and rape, and thus defines rape as a crime of violence and not a crime of sex. Another argument claims rape to be the very paradigm of male sexuality, or of male heterosexuality. However different these positions, in both cases there is the desire to rescue sexuality—whether in the name of lesbianism as a moment outside of patriarchal relations, or in the name of a utopian heterosexuality between free and equal agents.

The feminist politics of rape crisis centers and feminist theories about rape do not leave much room for a discussion of "men in feminism." In any case, the issue of rape evokes "radical feminism," and radical feminism seems to have become something of a spectre haunting the discussion of men in feminism. Critics of radical feminism have focussed on a variety of issues, such as the identification of men and women as belonging to inherently hostile and antagonistic camps, or the resurrection of the duality of oppression and emancipation, or the sometimes mocking attitude towards heterosexuality as a component of any kind of viable feminist identity. If a decade or so ago, the charges against "radical feminism" were reproaches against separatism, in the contemporary context those charges tend to focus on the sin of essentialism as a naive belief in a female identity that escapes patriarchal contamination and erupts in certain privileged contexts.

Current debates about sexuality and pornography in particular have polarized feminists, and the terms of the polarity are often reduced to essentialist claims about the purity of female experience, versus anti-essentialist positions which, while diverse in their points of emphasis, stress the difficult and contradictory nature of identity, whether male or female. While I don't question the necessity to be on the lookout for rampant essentialism, I do wonder about the usefulness of a "debate" in which the same oppositions emerge, again and again. And in particular, I question the *narrative* logic and the theoretical agenda served by invocations, conscious or not, of "radical feminism" or "essentialism." A provocative "in," like the one connecting "men" and "feminism," has an implicit "other," the other of radical feminism, of separatism (whatever that may be construed to mean). The radical feminist thus caricatured is part of a community (lesbian, or feminist, or both) in which men are not only addressed, but irrelevant. She is thus unwilling to engage with real men or masculinity. That there may be or have been historical reasons for separatist activity, or that the term "radical feminism" may include more diversity than the often-repeated slogan "porn is the theory, rape the practice" would suggest; that radical feminism might be about something more than, *other* than, the exclusion of men—in short, that radical feminism may itself be part of a complex *narrative* rather than the bad object of essentialist theory, is thus obscured.

Male desire in *Tightrope* also demonstrates a fear of irrelevance and a subsequent repression that makes the portrait of a feminist slightly askew. The portrayal of the Bujold character is surprisingly "accurate," remarkably free of the "libber" stereotype one might expect in an Eastwood film. But there is a mistake, a gap, in this portrayal of the discourse of feminism. Except for her relationship with the detective's daughters, Beryl Thibodeaux has virtually no relationship with women, no connection to anything remotely resembling a community of women. Feminism in terms so irreducible or inapplicable to the problematic nature of male sexuality is unrepresentable. Feminism in *Tightrope* is the object of a certain kind of male desire—the desire for resolution, to be sure, but also the desire for a heterosexual relationship where the transgression of boundaries can be pondered without losing one's self.

That the creation of a feminist in *Tightrope* is an ideological as well as a narrative gesture hardly needs to be emphasized. *Tightrope* is located within that ubiquitous and nebulous entity, the "classical Hollywood cinema," many analyses of which have demonstrated that narrative resolution often not only incorporates but turns on such blind spots. However much the projects of theory and narrative might overlap, it is the task of theory to interrogate the patterns of opposition and resolution, not to replicate them. The desire, in *Tightrope*, for a feminism that comforts and affirms is not unlike the desire of a male theorist to be "in" feminism, or to dismantle feminism from the comfortable vantage point of a certain kind of theoretical discourse. This is not to say that there is something "wrong" with that desire. But there is a fit between theory and narrative, and the intersection of feminism and male desire needs to be thought, and rethought, by submitting theory to the test of narrative.

7.
A Man's Place

ELIZABETH WEED

My comments are made in response to this morning's papers and comments by Paul Smith, Andrew Ross, and Stephen Heath. In principle, I am happy to be a respondent. The question of the relationship of men to feminism is, after all, men's problem—insofar as it is a problem—and it is good to see such a session at the MLA after all these years. Yet, being a respondent does itself pose problems, in that the papers of Paul Smith and Andrew Ross have produced a discursive battlefield which, of course, produces my position of respondent as one already in the fray, a position I would not otherwise choose. One reason I would not choose it is that the fray which has been produced involves some disturbingly familiar issues which do not take us very far in our look at men and women and feminism. That said, I will start with some comments on Andrew Ross's paper.

Ross uses the so-called Yorkshire Ripper's crimes and trial to display the danger and pathology of "an entire social logic based on the necessity of predicating men and women as fixed social categories." The court's ruling on Sutcliffe's apparent confusion about whether he was out to kill all women or on a divine mission to kill just prostitutes is taken by Ross as a way of demonstrating the twin ills of essentializing and totalizing. He argues that in finding Sutcliffe "sane" (meaning that he was out to kill all women and not just prostitutes), that in finding Sutcliffe not "mad" but just "bad," the law chooses to resolve the conflict by reaffirming the very "logic of universals that holds sway in the realm of social action that produces the likes of Sutcliffe."

I find some internal problems with Ross's argument, but for now my interest is elsewhere. It is with a detail of the paper which comes to assume inordinate importance within the argument as a whole. Near the beginning of his discussion, Ross mentions one of the feminist groups involved in the heated public reaction to the Sutcliffe case—a feminist group holding the position summarized by Ross as a syllogism: "Some men rape and kill women. All men are potential rapists-killers. Therefore all women are potential victims." After the syllogism, Ross pauses between parentheses to say that under other circumstances he would be tempted to argue that the logic of these feminists is just as false, just as reactionary as the puritanical persecution of prostitutes. The parentheses close but matters don't end there. Like inadmissible evidence, displayed but stricken from the record, the potential guilt of these feminists is not forgotten. Every mention of "all women" calls forth implicitly or explicitly "all men," and when Ross indicts an "entire social logic" at the end, we need only think of the syllogism at the beginning to give full closure to the paper. In short, Ross takes this opportunity to make it clear to all of us, in the name of radical theory, that the participation of certain feminists in a universalizing logic can be dangerous to our health.

This all too familiar gesture of indirectly implicating the victim is based on another all too familiar manipulation of the opposition universal/particular. The totalizing or universalizing operation that Ross censures is not, of course, an abstract problem; it has a history. And that history tells a story we all know of an operation performed in the interest of privilege, power, and domination. To universalize, in the West, has indeed been to erase difference in the name of, for example, Mankind. When feminists, speaking from the position of women, repeat the universalizing operation, no matter how problematic it may be, it can never, because of the circumstances of enunciation, be the *same* operation. Ross employs the universal/particular argument in the service of his demonstration of the danger of confusing the natural and the constructed, but in doing so he undermines his own radical project and repeats what can only be called the liberal gesture of arguing from the particular. And the history of that gesture is also well known. In the last two hundred years or so we have seen well how a dominant class or group can secure its power precisely because it has access to both poles of the universal/particular opposition. When arguments from the universal cease to work for whatever historical reason, there is always recourse to the particular, to the rights of the individual as against totalizing forces. And as long as the circulation of power remains closed, the ends are the same. Witness the recent phenomenon of accusations of reverse discrimination.

The point is not to repeat the argument of the universal and the particular as if one were living in an open field of power, but rather to articulate the positioning of the subject within the existing social field. By way of pursuing that argument, I want to move to Paul Smith's paper. In a gesture curiously similar to Ross's, Smith quickly establishes a certain feminism as the culprit. In his case, the guilty feminists are not vulgar, or theoretically incorrect. He quickly excises that part of the feminist project, naming it women's studies and declaring that it is quite well integrated into the structures of the academy. Having thus inscribed the boundary separating good and bad feminisms, he accuses good feminism—feminist theory—of having erected its own boundaries, its own law which keeps him from breaking and entering. What follows is a series of moves designed to turn the tables on feminist theory, accompanied by what one can only assume to be a series of ironic displays of the phallic as against the feminine. The tables turned, we are presented with a savior, a third term, the male theorist whose presence in the margins of feminism will provide the material sexual difference that will keep feminist theory radical and subversive.

There are problems with Smith's argument. Taken, first, at its face value, it doesn't work. For just as women, in the name of women, cannot perform the same universalizing operation as men, so men cannot play the subversive role with regard to feminist theory that Smith, at least, sees feminists playing with regard to what he calls theory in general. And for the same reasons. Such reversals do not work because, as we well know, the reversal of the constructed opposition male/female only exposes the excess of the female. And the male—or at least the white Western male—as things stand now, cannot be excessive and cannot occupy the margins. For all the talk about excess is not just theoretical, because what we are also talking about is access to power—or at least our different relations to power.

Smith's argument is even more disturbing when read through its rhetorical display and presumed irony. To what end does Smith reinscribe the problematic opposition of inside/outside, portraying feminism as a discourse intent on legalizing itself, naming transgressors, banning all but the authorized? He says he does so in the service of a struggle against institutionalization. But how to fight institutionalization when the very terms of the argument foreclose the possibility of thinking a different feminism, a feminism that might be a discursive strategy and not simply a self-authorizing institution?

It is interesting, in this context, that Smith's language about "men in feminism," "entering feminism, actively penetrating it" functions as a citation of Jacques Derrida—of the published proceedings of a seminar held last year at the Pembroke Center in which Derrida commented that "as the research in women's studies gains institutional legitimacy, it also constitutes, constructs, and produces guardians of the Law. It induces men from the country who come before the Law to try to accede it, to see it, to touch it, to penetrate it" (p. 189). Derrida was talking about women's studies—making no distinction between women's studies and feminist theory, by the way—in the context of his reading of the passage in Kafka's *The Trial* entitled "Before the Law." What Smith's "citation" leaves out, of course, is everything else, including a comment by Derrida that the most rigorous struggle to resist the Law, to dismantle it, inevitably entails another construction of the Law. As Smith himself says, there is no discourse without the operation of the law. Indeed, signifying practices are the Law, including the signifying practice of subversion. That is the law of the Law.

Thus, the question becomes that of one's relation to the law, in this case to the relative institutionalization or legislation of women's studies and feminist theory. And, at this point, I have to say that I don't find Smith's distinction between women's studies and feminist theory either useful or accurate. That is not to say that there is nothing reductive or essentializing going on within feminism. It is just that women's studies are not dominated by essentialism and as long as that is the case, I see no reason not to appropriate the whole field— that is feminist theory within women's studies—for radical ends. Thus, I use the terms "women's studies" and "feminist theory" interchangeably—which still addresses Smith's points, since both are subject to the same process of legalization.

Looking, then, at feminist theory's relation to the law, Smith is right in a sense: women's studies/feminist theory have become somewhat institutionalized, more so than other studies of the Other. And, to a certain extent, they have reinscribed conservative structures and claimed institutional territories. The relative success of that project can be gauged by institutional reactions to it by those who see women's studies as illegally appropriating someone else's ground. The recent report by an NEH committee on the state of the humanities, a report aptly entitled "To Reclaim a Legacy," certainly has nothing friendly to say about what it calls special interest politics in the curriculum.

In fact, women's studies are not nearly as established as the NEH report and Paul Smith would have it. Nor do most feminists aspire to erect an edifice to the Truth and Beauty of Woman. If that were the case, we would certainly demand centuries and centuries of equal time. The challenge for us, of course, is to do two things simultaneously, trying to make even conservative gestures as subversive as possible, trying to keep subversive gestures as really radical as possible, constantly displacing the meaning of feminism. That endeavor is, of course, an impossible one—impossible like the relation of women to Woman. For if, as Stephen Heath says, in "Male Feminism" (pp. 1–32), the relation of *men* to feminism is an impossible one, so, in different ways, is the relation of *women* to feminism. These are impossible relations, as Heath says, because although as individual human subjects we live our heterogeneity, we also live our positionings in the social field and have to assume both sets of operations. It is thus that men are carriers of the patriarchal mode and it is thus that women have to negotiate both essentialism and lack.

Understanding feminist theory, mastering it, is not, as Smith asserts, I hope ironically, the ticket of entry into some supposed inside, or into the place of the woman. It is not, because of the well-known difference between women's place and men's place. As we indeed all know, the white male theorist who understands that the subject

is not identical to itself has the relatively straightforward task of resisting the imaginary lures of the historically constructed fiction of
full male presence. The task of all the others is less straightforward.
Certainly the situation for women is additionally complicated by our
need to struggle against the lure of Woman as privileged figure of
undecidability, particularly in the texts of male theorists. For the many
feminists both inside and outside the academy who work to transform
systems of domination, the immediate task entails constructing a female subject in order to obtain for women a better, and in many cases
a less oppressive and literally safer place in the social field, while *at
the same time* always displacing boundaries, always shifting positions
to work against the erection of the same old phallocratic structures
in the name of identity and the unifying subject.

As Heath says, the impossibility of men's (and I would add, wom-
en's) relationship to feminism does not imply that we can do nothing,
but rather that the contradictions cannot be resolved. Accepting that,
the challenge, it seems to me, is to develop political, theoretical strategies, all the while keeping in mind to what extent our radical project
is a *utopian* one. The utopian vision, so necessary as the always re-
ceding horizon of any political project is, in the case of sexual difference, the realizing of *real* difference, of real hetero-sexuality, and
not the imaginary, constructed, determining two sexes with which
we live.

I find it interesting that Heath refers to at least two different uto-
pias. One is the utopian a-topia of continually deferred places. The
other—radically other—is Heath's evocation of Luce Irigaray's notion
of "admiration." Because it is suggested in the context of an ethics
(Irigaray's *Ethique de la différence sexuelle*), "admiration" could provide
a possible interim utopia for a possible politics. Interesting to think
about. However, because ethics are dangerous, precisely because
they are inscribed in the binary, it seems safer to opt for theory.

If we accept, then, the utopian vision of "real" sexual difference
as our working utopian horizon, what will be our strategies along the
way? I would like to suggest, for the sake of argument, that the relationship of feminist theory to so-called "theory" is not, as Paul
Smith would have it, constructed by a warring field of interpretation,
but rather that feminist theory and other theory operate within a field
of intersecting critical practices. If that is the case, where then do
some of those intersections occur? I will suggest three points.

The first is at the problem of the subject and its relation to existing
systems of power. At a very fundamental level, feminists have the
advantage of a long acquaintance with the notion of the personal as
political. Indeed, it may be worth mentioning that historically feminists learned many of the lessons of undecidability and irresolvable
contradictions from the Civil Rights movement. That is, from blacks

who articulated what it means to live simultaneously as subject and object and who taught whites what it means to live as an individual subject and also to be positioned in such a way as to make one complicitous with white power. It is true that feminists have at times fallen into a simple personalization of the political and into a simple confessional mode. But neglecting to account for one's position can also lead to excesses. Andrew Ross's choice, for example, never to address directly the question of men and feminism, while at the same time including in his discussion a textually manipulated anger against certain feminists seems to me an odd displacement.

With many feminists, at least, the need to textualize the subject is neither displaced nor neglected. It can't be. For throughout the entire feminist project runs the problem of experience. And if we are to theorize the female subject and texualize that subject, that is a problem we can't avoid. And *that*, of course, is a theoretical scandal. We know how women always seem to occupy the place of theoretical scandal. Years ago, when everyone was busy doing away with the referent, remember who was figured as the referent? In a text like Robbe-Grillet's *Le Voyeur* it was, indeed, the girl Violet who occupied that absent place—the place of violation and murder. Today things are a bit rosier. At least Woman can be respectable as the privileged figure of undecidability. But there is always the other side—the unacceptable place of experience. For women there is no choice but to assume both positions. What we need to do, as Teresa de Lauretis has recently written,[1] is to theorize experience on our way to theorizing and textualizing the female subject.

A second point of intersection is with sexuality and its relation to sexual difference. We know that the problems of sexual difference are not contained by the discourse of sexuality. And yet the discourse of feminist theory is often taken to be coterminous with that of sexuality. As Heath says, signification is certainly bound up with sexuality, but our societies have produced sexuality as "*the* meaning, including the meaning of feminism." The result for feminist theory is that it is then entirely spoken through and by the various well-known operations of the family drama. By thus always reinscribing feminism in the familiar, by keeping it in the family, we contain and trivialize it. In institutional settings of this sort, for example, we can fall so easily into the same old patterns, the same old battlefields. We dance so well the same old steps choreographed for us. The limiting of feminism means as well the limiting of the problematic of sexual difference. For if the history of the discourse of sexuality is a complex one, the history of the operations of sexual difference is even more so, and in order to interrogate those operations in a way that is not ahistorical or completely culture-bound, we need to attend to the specificity of women's relation to those very operations. It is not unusual to read cultural criticism involving problems of sexual difference from which women have been completely evacuated. For some of us, that is a curious practice.

The third point at which feminist theory intersects with other theory is around the ever-vexed question of theory and political practice. As one of the most recent large-scale discourses of oppression, feminism has raised again in different ways all the theoretical and political problems posed by the reinscription of the ethical and the just. In writing this response, I was constantly annoyed by its sententiousness—an annoyance I immediately displaced onto Andrew Ross and Paul Smith for having raised issues that I consider rather tired and from which I couldn't take much pleasure. But the sententiousness also comes with the whole discourse of oppression. The problem with oppression (in addition to the over-use of the word) is that it has a compelling descriptive power; it often seems very right. And yet, its limitations are well known. So, what to do with the part of feminist politics that is an ethical imperative, that constructs Woman as the subject of an ethics, that takes us back into the discourse of oppressor and oppressed, domination and liberation—a discourse that has limited usefulness in a post-modernist situation of radically altered relations of subjects and objects and an even more complex circulation of power in the social field? At the same time, what to do with theory from other quarters (usually not feminist quarters) that confuses the utopian and the present, that takes the ability to *theorize* a utopian heterosexuality for a solution to the woman-problem of today? How to deal with the sleight of hand by which "real" sexual difference takes over and women disappear? How to keep utopia in its place?

The point, finally, is not to set up a polarity that can somehow be resolved, but rather to continue working with sometimes unresolvable, and always interlocking problems. That is something that I think both women and men can do from our different positions.

8.
Femmeninism

P. KAMUF

In answer to a question:

Yes, I'm giving a paper at the MLA—in a session titled "Men in Feminism." You see, there is "Men in Feminism I" where some men, some supposed men, are supposed to talk about men in feminism, and then there is "Men in Feminism II" where some women who are supposed to be women are supposed to talk about men in feminism too, that is, as well. Now, guess which one of the two I'm in?

Would this exchange—it is an answer to a question—be funny if spoken by a man? if spoken from this same place but slightly in the past, this morning? Yes, of course, why not? The answer's a quote, so perhaps I'm quoting Stephen Heath or Andrew Ross or Paul Smith. There's no way to tell in this context because the "I" of a phrase like "I'm giving a paper" does not state its gender, much less its proper name. What is more, in the quote, the dual structure of gender is reproduced and repeated by the dual structure of the roman numerals I and II of "Men in Feminism" (which I'm going to propose we try to pronounce according to the graphic rebus "femmeninism," although this runs the risk of introducing a new shibboleth, a word with which to discriminate insiders from outsiders merely by one's ability to pronounce it). Within this symmetry, how can we—you and me, you plural and you singular, me singular and me plural—how can we be sure who's speaking here? Fortunately (but also unfortunately), a certain organization of rules and exclusions, a whole institutionalized, incorporated legal apparatus of convention is in place to provide some measure of certainty. But what are we supposed to think about the certainty of the "I" as conventionally structured, for example by the procedural rules of the MLA convention? The question is that of the spatial limits of conventional metaphor which it is crucial to set out, to posit or suppose if one is to be able to state, with any reliability, where one stands with relation to "femmeninism," inside or outside, for or against, left or right, in rejection or projection. If the decisive question to be put here is "where do I, where does the 'I' stand," then at most we have a thread to follow through this crush of conventional spatial metaphors, obligingly given an incorporated reality every year by the MLA, and which this year we celebrate—but by what kind of coincidence?—in Washington, D. C. I'm

proposing to follow the thread from a conventional question such as
"Are you giving a paper at the MLA?" to watch how the "I" answers
when constrained by place and by time to decide where it stands. If
you like, I will say I am borrowing—or quoting—this way of reading
from *A Room of One's Own* where the narrator is both an admiring
and an admirable reader. "All this was admirable. But after reading
a chapter or two a shadow seemed to lie across the page. It was a
straight dark bar, a shadow shaped something like the letter 'I.' One
began dodging this way and that to catch a glimpse of the landscape
behind it . . . Back one was always hailed to the letter 'I.' One began
to be tired of 'I.' Not but what this 'I' was a most respectable 'I';
honest and logical; hard as a nut, and polished for centuries by good
teaching and good feeding. I respect and admire that 'I' from the
bottom of my heart." As you can see or hear, perhaps, such a reference has already considerably complicated the thread to be followed. Woolf's "'I'"/"I" is not a beam of theoretical light, but "a
straight dark bar, a shadow . . . "

Who, when, what, and where is the "I" that has to answer all
these questions, that also has to answer *for* all these questions?

At the moment of writing—today, December 13th—"I" already
must address this moment of reading my paper, performing it here
(there) now (then). At this moment, I have before me three texts to
which to refer, two of which, at least, assume with more or less insistence the "maleness" of their first persons, of their signatures and
their performances. So, as I write, "femmeninism" gets its spatial
contours from three very fine papers, contours which, I hasten to
add, do not correspond mimetically with men's bodies nor do they
in any simple way represent men's bodies. The same must be said
of that particular piece of the text called the signature. By convention,
of course, texts and signatures have and will be projected into this
relation of representation. By convention, as well, one writes of a
future present in which body is made to coincide with text, or rather
to punctuate it or interpret it as one says of a theatrical performance.
By convention, there is an "I" addressing an absent "you," but as if
this "you" were already or still present. All of this, already, just by
convention.

(As I write, back on the farm in Ohio, the only other animate bodies
in the room are two cats, male and female, one neutered and the
other spayed. However, it is true—although you're just going to have
to believe I'm not making this up—that earlier in the evening, I got
a phone call which, if forced to guess at its intention, I might call
obscene—a brief, anonymous, disembodied voice asking me a question. And now I'm wondering if—in two weeks—I can recount this
in such a conventional place without making you wonder what the
question was and how I answered. But who, "you"? there is still no

"you" yet, the address remains as anonymous as an obscene phone caller's.)

If "I" is like an obscene phone caller in its mode of address, does that mean I can say anything whatsoever here? "n'importe quoi" as one says in French to indicate the general interchangeability of a thing? I say no, but what does the "I" of our convention say? Is it not posed—for example by the conventions of our double session, but by at least eighty other sessions as well—to be interchangeable, substitutable according to the characteristics of sex? If one attributes the "logic" of this conventional "I" to the strict biological or genealogical or genetic code of two-sexes-reproducing-each-other, then this "I" will be read as human female no matter what it says about itself—it can say, in other words, n'importe quoi.

Well, I could try to follow the paths of the various "I"'s which are deployed by these three very moving and mobilizing papers. They certainly deserve more response, more responsible response than anyone can expect to give in fifteen minutes. A conventional time constraint here on all our "I"'s, theirs and mine, ours. How can "I" act responsibly, then, given such a limit on response? Does not the reduction to such strict temporal and spatial limits constrain one to speak almost at random of this or that feature traced in shadowy outline by "the straight, dark bar"? As in Hegel's night, where "A" looks just like "not A," in this night where all cats are black and crossing paths, doesn't one take a chance whenever one tries to read in the dark?

Another question here: is reading in the dark a mode of writing the imaginary? Paul Smith asks "What does a male writing his imaginary actually produce? I am, I must confess, stumped by that question; the only answers at which I could guess seeming unlikely to be 'correct'." I notice that the "I" here says "I must confess" and thereby enters—however ironically, however rhetorically—the confessional or autobiographical mode at the very place where what it confesses to is being "stumped" by the question of, exactly *how* one can enter an autobiographical mode "correctly" as a man. We may see here an "I" in a double bind, circumscribed by a demand which it is as impossible to read as it is necessary to understand. For this reason, one may expect that the "I" cannot *not* write what it calls the "imaginary" and which it defines as "a pornographic defense against the mother's body," but by its own prediction it will do so "incorrectly," out of place.

I realize that the "I" realizes or understands its predicament in terms that are not all that different from the ones I have just used. But it should not be presumed that this understanding—his or mine—constitutes or effects a resolution. As Paul Smith reminded us this morning, there is a risk of things seeming to settle too quickly,

giving one but an imaginary resolution of the problem of the "imaginary," settling too quickly the question that stumps the "I" every
time. He writes: "in the context of academic feminist theory these
men might perhaps do something akin to what women do within
theory more generally: that is, they can be there to help to subvert,
unsettle and undermine the (seemingly rather fast to settle) laws of
the discourse. . . . This they might do purely by virtue of existing in
it as a difference." Why am I retained, held back by the "purely" and
the "virtue" of the claim made in this last sentence? What have purity
and virtue got to do with "men in feminism"?

Unless we are talking already, but without knowing it, about the
immaculate birth of a thing to which we have had to give the monstrous, stuttering name of "femmeninism"?

By announcing such an untimely, uncertain (unwanted?) birth, am
I being "ahistorical and irresponsible"? Does not the forced reproduction of this unutterable stammer defer the referent which the correct title, "Men in Feminism," might, as Smith writes, help keep in
view? "From the point of their impossible . . . position in or near
feminism, [men] might be able to help keep in view the referent which
most of our current theory is all too eager to defer." I cannot disagree
with this idea, but I am prompted to wonder about the reappearance
of a representational clarity which passes by way of a visual metaphor
once again—to "keep in view the referent"—and which, at the very
place where it discerns "most of our current theory" deferring the
referent, nevertheless performs a *theoretical* construction of space
along the fold or turn from inside to outside: "when poststructuralist
feminist theory turns to construct its public sphere, or when it has
done with codifying itself in the contested but limited sphere of the
academic, that is the point where we can really talk about alliances
between men and women feminists, between people engaged in a
political struggle on many fronts." In this passage, the metaphoric
turn follows a clearly dialectical path, passing through the roadforks
or signposts marking off opposite one-way streets (men and women
feminists), turning (left or right?) onto main highways ("alliances,"
"people") which feed into the final term bringing together identity
and difference ("political struggle on many fronts"). In keeping with
my own pattern of spatial metaphors, I suggest we can take this final
term to be something like a cloverleaf over a four-lane interstate where
traffic is permitted to move in at least four different directions at once.

A cloverleaf, of course, is a symbol—a kind of metaphor—for good
luck, "the luck of the Irish," as one says. The question, however, is
always to know whether the cloverleaf has three leaves or four, since
it is only the four leaf clover that is supposed to bring good luck. So,
if the dialectic of "Men in Feminism" promises that its complete operation will be carried out under a good luck sign, that the cloverleaf

will cover all the bets and all the guesses one has to make reading the exit and entrance signs in the dark, then it must have some reliable way of counting these exists and entrances.

Whether the cloverleaf of the dialectical promise has three leaves or four cannot be said to be *seen* in the same sense as one sees—and can therefore simply count—the leaves on a real cloverleaf, or even the exit, entrance ramps on those all-the-more-real-because-more-dangerous traffic regulators called cloverleaf overpassses. Everyone knows how these things are supposed to work, but nevertheless many accidents happen when the concept is realized in concrete. Is there any rule, then, that can allow us to count the number of ins and outs of this promise? What is the rule—or the law—that stands outside that which one is trying to count? Smith makes this suggestion: "When [feminist theory] has had done with codifying itself in the contested but limited sphere of the academic. . . . we'll really be able to talk . . . " If, at that point, one can begin to talk *really*, it will be because some codified principle can be counted on to exclude uncertainty from our numbers. The question, however, of whether this codification has had done with itself or not takes up our other question of whether the concept has three or four leaves. If it has had done with itself, then it is outside of that which it serves to count. There are, then, three leaves to be counted, the fourth having excluded itself. If, however, it— "feminist theory in the contested but limited sphere of the academic"—has not had done with itself, then there are perhaps four leaves but no way to count them.

Has feminist theory had done with codifying itself, giving itself the law so that we have a new, truer convention for counting our numbers, counting off the ins and outs? Or are we still trying to read in the dark? Is there a law—or a rule—that directs blind reading?

By convention, the answer might be yes. For example, PMLA practices an editorial policy of "blind reading," a policy which was instituted largely because of successful pressure from women's caucuses on the legislative mechanism of this association. Does this rule always work? That is, does it have general applicability as a principle for discounting the signature in order to count more safely and surely, which is to say, by multiples of three? By convention, the answer seems to be no. There are other sets of rules governing the omission of signatures, for example the rules which governed the omission of Andrew Ross's name from the program of "Men in Feminism I." (By some coincidence—or chance—Ross's paper is also the only one of the three that does not assume the "maleness" of its signature.) Thus, counting mistakes can still occur because the rules for counting (or discounting) signatures are themselves, between themselves disjointed.

To project a codification of feminist theory in any sphere—even the limited, apparently trivial sphere of the MLA—is to imagine, it seems to me, a body of law with no internal contradictions, a rounded-off form that has everything sewn up, leaving no hidden pockets or recesses. Such a projection might be called a devagination, or, since a fourth term drops out, collapses or lapses, a prolapse—here, the prolapse of a feminine signature.

Has feminist theory given itself—and us—the law of how to count signatures, of how to count *with* signatures that are both inside and outside what counts? Do we now know how to stand on the signature without jumping from one leg to the other, do we have a leg to stand on that lets us count past three, at least up to four, or, like Mr. Ramsay, are we still stumped by the letter "R," this initial, unable to get to "q"? Has feminist theory figured out how to stand the signature up as a ruler against which to measure a new hierarchy of values or to lay it out on the ground like a tape measure that will point exactly to the limit beyond which out is out and in is in? Has feminism learned to absorb its "own" difference, the unreliability of its signature, so that it can sign for everything else?

I'll end, abruptly, by returning the reference to Irigaray's "admiration." As Stephen Heath notes, the term comes from *Les Passions de l'âme* where Descartes makes admiration the first of all the passions. Specifically, Irigaray reads this passage, as I translate it:

> When the first encounter with some object surprises us, and we judge it to be new or very different from what we have known up to then or from what we might have supposed it to be, we are then caused to admire it and be astonished by it; and since this can happen before we have any sure knowledge whether or not this object suits us or not [*si cet objet nous est* convenable *ou s'il ne l'est pas*; that is, whether it is appropriate to us, adequate, conform, expedient, pertinent, favorable, decent, etc., etc., from *venire*, to come, *con-* together], it therefore seems to me that admiration is the first of the passions, and that it can have no contrary; this because, if the object that presents itself has nothing in itself which surprises us, we are not moved in the least and can consider it without any passion.

Admiration has no identified contrary, it does not, in other words, already depend on a binary or dual repetition. It is thus both before the appropriate binary convention and gives the law to that convention but as the rule of a perpetual newness, perhaps the lawless rule of the monstrous.

With admiration, have we found a four-leaf clover or have we, rather, broken the mirror? If the latter, is there not a sense in which breaking the mirror has to be counted on to bring, not seven years

bad luck, but to bring into view something other that is not yet or
still a contrary, an opposite, a complement, an appropriate, that is,
a (necessarily) *convenable* object? It seems to me that both Heath and
Smith find themselves constrained (but by whom or by what?) to
locate "admiration" on a more or less imaginary map. Heath moves
or is forced to move to the side of utopia; Smith leaps or is forced to
leap back because he reads warnings of dystopia, a pornograaphic
production. Each move, each jump—forward or back? onto the left
leg or to the right?—constructs a contrary of admiration, divides it
between two scenes—best possible and worst possible scenarios. Is
there any surprise in this?

To take a leap of my own here, but one which lands again on the
path of road metaphors, such scenarios bring *Road Warrior*—the
movie—to mind. There the utopic/dystopic fold of represented space
over visual, narrative time depends on an impossible frame narration
from a child's point of view. The frame doesn't hold together, is impossible because, for the child to tell the story, it has, in effect, to
coincide (spatially, temporally) with "Mad Max," its spiritual father
and the hero of the film. This feral child, the foundling born of
"mother nature," as they say, tells the story as if he were his "own"
father. The narrative works only if one agrees to disregard its frame,
one which in this case is laughingly incoherent—it's child's play to
see the joining cracks. Elsewhere than in the movies it's more difficult,
I'll admit, to see the cracks that break up the father's dream of im-
mortality through a son because, having been repeated generation
after generation, it can now seem to be imputed to the child as his
own dream. But isn't it time we all began to break up whenever we
hear talk of or from an oedipal imaginary?

So, maybe there's something pretty funny going on here. I'm
tempted to understand it according to one of the first principles of
feminist consciousness—the notion of the double standard, the double measure or rule. When an imaginary line is being drawn, dividing
precisely what will be called the imaginary from the rest, who is going
to be ready to sign on the dotted line guaranteeing the reliability of
all other signatures? And if we're still asking whether the authorizing
signature will itself be masculine or feminine, even male or female,
can we ever expect to be surprised again by the advent of what counts
differently?

P. Kamuf

Members of the MLA panels were invited to add here any further comments they might wish to make and we received the two following essays. Stephen Heath and Judith Mayne chose to incorporate their afterwords into their original text.

9.
No Question of Silence

ANDREW ROSS

The concept of "correctness," last enshrined in the stern, prescriptive body of Left-Leninist thinking, ought to be long since dead and buried. That, at any rate, was the laudable claim (although I am too young to remember it myself) which helped to launch the women's movement and inspire a politics of the personal which would honor, among many other things, the practice of pleasure. How successfully that claim to bury correctness has been historically borne out among feminists is not my business, although I do know how exemplary and consequential it has been for the politics of everyday life which my generation of men and women inherited. It is all the more ironic and disquieting, then, to think that it may be the phenomenon of male feminism—the recently heralded reentry of men into the political orbit of women—that will finally prompt feminism to resurrect prescriptions about correctness in order to better rehearse and apprentice its newly enlisted male allies. Surely there would be more to lose than gain in this rejection of praxis.

Nevertheless, anyone who reads closely enough will find invocations of correctness and fears of incorrectness alike, whether resonant or *sotto voce*, in all of the papers presented by men and women at the MLA sessions on "Men in Feminism." If I single out the example of Alice Jardine's "pragmatic agenda" of prescriptions for men to follow and live up to (and it offers good, sound advice for all that), it is only because it is the easiest and clearest example to cite. Assuming, then, that correctness is *already* at issue, just as it once *was*, in a different way, for women expressing their disaffection with a sexist and hierarchical Left, what does it have to do with male feminists now? The question can have no meaning for us as *biological men* (we very rarely are defined simply as biological men and women). It is already implied, however, in our relation to feminism as what I shall call *men-in-practice* (our response, in actions, to the privileged contours of social maleness; in style, to the currently dominant or hegemonic images of masculinity; and in fantasy, to particular configurations of masculine sexuality—with the proviso that there is no *necessary* or determining relation between these three realms of practice), and as *theoretical men*, by which I mean the set of discursive positions which we occupy most as intellectuals, and with which I shall therefore be concerned here.

By *theoretical men*, then, I do not simply mean academic male theorists, but rather the wide variety of discursive positions through which men culturally engage with feminist issues—contexts in which men discursively construct themselves, or are discursively constructed by others, as "men in feminism": whether in the workplace, bar or, *pace* Godard, in the bedroom; whether responding to sexism or voicing it; whether reading, interpreting and making sense of our culture in ways that either challenge the oppression of women or reproduce it; and whether we, or anyone else for that matter, actually recognize what we say to be "feminist" or not. Of the many positions defined under *theoretical men*, there are those which will exclude men from feminism as men, on the grounds that the most they can hope to deserve is a show trial (for all of its troubled pathos, Stephen Heath's advice—that the best we can do is "try not to be anti-feminist"—is not too far away from this self-excluding role: *la parte maudite*, or "accursed portion," of male feminism to be exact). Alternatively, there are those for whom the *facticity* of feminism, for the most part, goes without saying; in other words, there are men who are young enough for feminism to have been a primary component of their intellectual formation (I offer my own as an example: the politics of feminism came first, democratic socialism later). In this respect, Alice Jardine's observation, that "Anglo-American male critics *do* seem to be very much *into* feminism these days. Younger . . . older . . . gay . . . straight men . . . " strikes me not at all as a multiple or overdetermined symptom of the same phenomenon. Each of these categories in themselves implies a fundamentally different history in relation to feminism, and a fundamentally different set of problems for male feminism. In fact, I take these categories to be more important in preserving the differences among male feminists than those which Jardine actually goes on to invoke in her own class breakdown of men in feminism: the Silent Majority, the Divide and Conquerors, and the Allies. It seems to me that these latter categories already carry with them a prescribed and hierarchical structure of correctness which promises to tell us very little about the multiplicity of the male response to feminism. It is more plausible to expect, say, an *older* male feminist to occupy all three of Jardine's categories at different times, or at the same time in different contexts (this is not intended as an ageist slur on older male feminists; I am referring to men whose personal intellectual history includes a substantial pre-feminist phase), than it is to expect him to occupy only one.

In addition, there are those *theoretical men* whose devotion to the gender cult is lavished upon libertine fantasies of mobility—going beyond gender, or, at least, the phallus. Their blend of poststructuralist indeterminacy with the confessional mode of experiential feminism advertises, at every turn of phrase, its privileged, Utopian claims, but it is just as likely to end up, as Paul Smith observes of Barthes's case, in a vanguardism that goes beyond sexual politics, nay, politics itself. Finally, there are those, quite appropriately academics, who received particular attention in the MLA panel debates; those who have learnt feminist theory well and are familiar with the rationality of its various strategies. How can they not be "correct"? For Jardine, it is because they do not have the "grain of the voice" ("intonation," "syntax") which would otherwise distinguish a woman's expression of the same concepts and discourses. For Elizabeth Weed, it is because they use feminist theory against feminism itself, constructing a good and bad feminism out of its unitary ranks (e.g., my critique of radical feminism, Smith's critique of women's studies, and, although Weed does not comment upon it, Heath's critique of psychoanalytic feminism in "Male Feminism"). On the one hand, then, for Jardine, male feminism is an imperfect simulacrum, a body-snatching pod whose new mind is not yet quite synchronized with its renovated body. On the other hand, for Weed, it is merely a new breed of colonizer who has learnt the native language, this time around, in order better to divide and conquer. Clearly, there are many different ways of being incorrect.

What hardly needs to be said again about theoretical men and women who are also academic theorists is that they do not inhabit an autonomous political realm, remote from practice. In fact, as practicing intellectuals, inside or outside the academy, all of the contributors to this volume will recognize that their use of theoretical argument is one of the political sites proper to their social function. That theoretical concepts, however, have concrete social and political effects for all members of the much larger category of theoretical men and women is less frequently pointed out and is nowhere more evident than in the case of the law. Indeed, the polemical motive behind my paper, "Demonstrating Sexual Difference," was precisely to show how an "abstract" logic of universals irradiated the case of the Yorkshire Ripper at all levels, from popular consciousness to legal nicety to the response of radical feminists. In arguing that this response merely reaffirmed the social logic that produces killers like the Ripper (a logic that constructs them both as *theoretical men* and *men-in-practice*), I was suggesting that this logic is too deeply constitutive in our society to be transformed by simply "correcting" our discourse of generalizing about "all men" and "all women." Nonetheless, Elizabeth Weed was correct to interpret this argument as, in part, a criticism of radical feminism; it came as no surprise, in fact, to find yet another man having problems with radical feminism. She is mistaken, however, in suggesting that my argument about universals rests upon an "abstract" sleight of hand. To be more precise, her counterclaim is that when feminists, speaking as women, repeat the "universalizing operation," in other words, when they speak of "all women," it can never be the same operation as that through which men historically spoke, in the West, of "all men" in the name of all Mankind (all men and all women). I agree with Weed that there are indeed more than just historical differences between the two acts of enunciation. Her criticism puzzles me, however, because I don't at any point in my argument invoke this historical universal in which "all men" connotes "Mankind." On the contrary, I am exclusively concerned with the use of "all men" as a discursive term within the history of the essentialist idea of a sexual politics: a term used to describe anatomical men as distinct from anatomical women. Accordingly, the difference between this anatomical "all men" and the historical universal "all men" (Mankind) is, in fact, a difference in kind and not descriptive degree. In effect, my complaint is with a sexual politics that reduces the complexities of sexual difference to an antagonistic relation between two mutually exclusive groups of people. Perhaps, as both Weed and Jardine respectively point out, this critique of essentialism is "rather tired" or "by now rather familiar" for feminist theorists, but this does not make it any less cogent for a larger world (of *theoretical men and women*) in which the initiation of men and women into sexual politics is still so hegemonically informed by this mutually exclusive division between anatomical groups. In such a world, the need to repeat this critique, even at the risk of its sounding "tired" to academic ears, seems to me to be a ceaseless political task, at least if we do not want to live in a lesser world.[1]

Where I do agree with Weed, however, is in her assertion that the relation of women to feminism is just as "impossible" (albeit in different ways) as that of men to feminism, because our lives as "social" men and women are heterogeneously composed of many different positions. Because of this array of subject positions, there is no guarantee that we are ever likely to be non-contradictory social agents. There is nothing unitary, for example, about belonging to the categories of *biological men, men-in-practice*, and *theoretical men* at one and the same time, as many men do. For the same individual can be different kinds of theoretical men and men-in-practice, some progressive for feminism, others not, at different times and in different discursive contexts. There is nothing pluralistic about this; it is simply a consequence of the way in which we are socially articulated as subjects and not as unitary "persons" (as a result, a politics of the personal is much more complex than, though it always risks being reduced to, a "politics of persons").

In the case of sexual politics before the law, we are faced with a different, but related, "impossibility." As I suggested in "Demonstrating Sexual Difference," the law recognizes subjects, with rights pertaining to their discursive positions as subjects, and not persons. For a sexual politics to have some purchase upon the law, it must recognize that fact, or else fall back upon the double-edged appeal of universal categories with (as I have been arguing) all their attendant dangers. A recent Dutch film, *A Question of Silence (De Stilte Rond Christine M.)* raises this question in interesting ways. The film turns upon the legal proceedings against three women, strangers to one another hitherto, who spontaneously kill the male owner of a women's boutique after he catches one of them shoplifting. In the course of the investigation and the trial itself, many of the structural elements of the Ripper trial are reproduced. The police and the court assume that the accused women cannot simply be "bad," given the extraordinarily gratuitous circumstances of their crime. However, a female psychiatrist, called upon to argue the case for diminished capacity, decides that they are neither "bad" nor "mad." On the contrary, she has come to believe that their actions and "symptoms"—in particular, the persistent silence of one of the defendants, Christine, in the face of the psychiatrist's interrogation—are, in fact, lucid and rational when judged against the logic of patriarchal oppression. In voicing this belief, she puts herself on trial, not only before the court, but also before her husband, a lawyer who believes that the law is not there to be interpreted, but to "preserve the status quo." This completes the logic of the film itself, in which all of the characters, male and female, are reduced to their respective responses to the "universal" of male domination. The court, of course, cannot subscribe to this logic, and the prosecuting counsel expresses the convictions of his training thus: "What difference does it make? I see no difference than if they had killed a woman, or if three men had killed a woman." The resulting, uproarious laughter of all the women in the court replaces the belligerent silence of Christine M., whereupon they are ejected from the courtroom, leaving the officers of the court, all men, to deliberate in peace. Outside the courtroom, the psychiatrist appears to desert her husband for the other women. There is no doubt that this conclusion is a representationally and affectively satisfying one, but it clearly leaves unexamined and unresolved the question of difference raised in the course of the trial. It reduces the question of difference—What differences does it make if it is a woman?—to a question of silence/laughter—how to make a nonsense of the male game of question and answer. So, too, it leaves lingering the proposition that a sociolegal liability predicated upon something like diminished capacity ought to be extended to all women in similar circumstances because of their universal subjection in a male dominated society. As I have said, the symbolic effects of this gesture are entertaining and affectively satisfying; indeed, the identificatory demands of the film's narrative elicit this kind of response from all viewers, women and men. The practical effects of such a politics are another matter, however. And it is in the gap between the two, between silence/laughter and difference, that we move in and out of the realm of universals, in and out of theory and practice, acknowledging the continuity and discontinuity between what we say, what we expect to do, and what we resist being done to us as a result. That is why our attention to what we mean when we use universal propositions seems so important.

To pursue further the practical effects of such propositions for the law, we might consider the special case of the battered-wife murder defense. In an article called "Killing Husbands," Lisbeth Hasse observes that California law, which already recognizes the only felony wife-beating statute in the U. S., could extend special dispensation to battered wives who murder the husbands who abuse them. Would this lead, Hasse muses, to an "open season" on married men? More specifically, she considers the disadvantages for women that are borne along with legal defenses based upon the universality of the social subjection of women. Feminist lawyers have indeed argued that the battered-wife murder is a rational response to the social logic of women's oppression; it is not only "a systematic product of a male supremacist society, but also a legitimate reaction thereto." Of the two exculpatory defenses available in criminal law, a feminist lawyer could argue a defense either from *excuse*—that the defendant was under the immediate duress of a violent attack—or, in the absence of duress, from *justification*—that the defendant's response "was a rational and correct one, that is, a justifiable one, because the condition of women is such that she is permitted no other reasonable response." Hasse suggests, however, that such a feminist approach, which bases this *justification* on the universality of women's experience is "beset with insurmountable analytic difficulties, difficulties that are practical as well as theoretical." Such a lawyer, for example, would have to expect a judge and jury to understand the defendant's actions from a *feminist* point of view, and thus recognize them exclusively and specifically as *political* acts.[2] Moreover, Hasse suggests that equal treatment could then extend this justification to men, who would be seen, no less than women, as "trapped in the customary roles that male dominated society fashions for them." How then could a husband be charged for committing acts of physical aggression that his society has taught and encouraged? Hasse goes on, more persuasively, to point out that any sexification by law which would create a battered-wife murder defense would only serve to further institutionalize sexual inequality. For such a provision would recognize not only an "essential" and "natural" relation between every woman and "the universal weakness of women," but also between any woman and the "essential" and "natural" phenomenon of male violence. In short, the universalist basis of this claim demands that *to be defined as a woman* is to be helplessly abused by violent men.

To move back now from the law to the question of male feminist correctness is not simply to take a metonymic leap; it is also to call into question my reasons for addressing the topic in this way. Perhaps it is indeed nothing more than a symptom of my litigious male mind that thoughts of "men in feminism" should invoke discussion of trials, defenses, prosecutions, diminished capacities, criminal liabilities, justifications, excuses, verdicts, and various murderous acts. It seems more likely, however, that the invitation to talk about *prescriptions* for male feminism should inevitably call forth reflections about *prescriptiveness* itself, and the various ways in which the prescriptiveness of sexual politics lives out an uneasy relation to the *proscriptions* of the law *as it exists*. Perhaps that explains what some saw as my initial reluctance to address directly the question of male feminism in the form of an MLA paper. Perhaps it also helps to explain the attachment of each of the MLA participants in their own way to some principle of correctness.

In the course of reconsidering my own initial reluctance, I was encouraged to write this present response by thinking about a popular Scottish saying which my mother was fond of citing: "There are those and there are such as those." It was, of course, intended as a scathing criticism of those with middle-class (in the British sense) pretensions. On the other hand, and like most popular sayings, its ideological effect was to "essentialize" or "naturalize" the class system as if it were fixed and unalterable, and ought to be vocally defended against those who sought to transcend their place within it. Like most prescriptions for political correctness, then, it bristles with contradictions which actually sanction and extend social inequalities even while they promise to eradicate mere pretensions to justice. As the debate about male feminism gets under way (even if only to get it out of the way), it may proceed, unavoidably, according to certain precepts of correctness; it already involves right-thinking dictates and wrong-thinking mandates, native speakers and alien impersonators, admirers, fetishists and voyeurs, bona fide originals and flawed simulacra, gift-bearing Greeks and cultural appropriators, impulse buyers and critical cross-dressers, not to mention the multifarious discourses of authentification that serve to distinguish each from the other. Much will no doubt be said about "those" and "such as those," and in each of the four realms of practice in which sexual politics is articulated: words, actions, fantasy, and experience. Insofar as that versatile distinction—those/such as those—devolves upon categories of difference and not mutually exclusive divisions, then it will present contradictions that men and women can live with and live by; contradictions that are not necessarily resistant to change. Insofar as it does not, then male feminism should stop here and now—a prospect which seems much less likely.

10.
A Double Life
(Femmeninism II)
PEGGY KAMUF

"Permets m'Amour penser quelque folie:" "Permit me, Love, to think a certain madness" or "Permit my Love to think . . . " Is "my Love" a term of address, or is it rather the active subject of "to think"? Is "Love" an other from whom permission is sought to think mad thoughts? Or is it "itself" the subject of this thinking? What if the alternative were undecidable and one could not discern the subject of thinking from its address to another? That undecidability might well be the "folie" which is asking to be thought here.

Here, which is to say first in this line from Louise Labé's famous sonnet XVIII ("Baise m'encor, rebaise moy et baise").[1] But here, as well, in a volume on men in feminism to which I propose this addendum to "Femmeninism." In particular, I want to add some notes on the "in" which articulates the phrase "Men in Feminism" and inarticulate (if you'll permit the word) "Femmeninism." I realize that such a proposal risks seeming to complicate things unnecessarily (but first we should ask: what exactly is the necessity of a volume titled *Men in Feminism*?); that is also why I have invoked at the outset Labé's request to be permitted to think mad thoughts.

Permit me, then, my love / Permit my love to think . . . In whichever sense one reads its syntax, "Permets m'Amour penser" brings one back to the fact that it is "Love" which gives thinking its support. Whether to read Love as the (so-called) active subject of *penser* or as the other on whom thought depends for its activity is not to be decided because perhaps it comes down to the same thing. The sameness without which thinking would not be permitted is called here "Amour." All of this is not without consequences for what can be thought about the situation of an "in" like the one in our title. Louise Labé's sonnet has much to say about that "in."

However you read it, this line solicits thinking from "Amour," by "Amour." What does it mean to say love (my love, me love, you love) *thinks*? This is not an allegorical figure, an allusion to the mythological Cupid which elsewhere (in the *Débat de Folie et d'Amour*) Labé pitted against Folly. Love, rather, names a place of thinking that cannot be identified *with* or *in* a person, falling as it does between the Poet and her addressee, a "je" and a "tu," joining them in a name which is neither the one nor the other because it is both one and the other. It is indeed this insituability of "Amour" which can lead to its allegorization, the putting in place of a figure for what has no single place or face. For Labé, however, even an allegorized Amour is no simple thing since, as the *Débat* argues, without (feminine) Folly, (masculine) Cupid's arrows would be just so many blind shots in the dark describing meaningless, pointless arcs. *Amour* cannot be itself—*Amour*—without Folly's intervention. But even this kind of disabused allegory is set aside when "Amour" is made to hover in a space without identity, figure or face as it does in the line from this sonnet.

What if (permit my love such a mad hypothesis) Love were a true name for "the thinking subject"? Not an allegorical name (because it has no face nor figure), nor a proper name (because it never designates just one), but a *true* name for that which occurs only *in* (the relation to) some other? A true name also insofar as it gives the lie to the Subject named *in* itself which is but an allegory or a fable within which to contain what is always dispersing itself outside itself and gathering itself together but *in* the other.[2]

This would be the "mad" topology of Love (of thought) that Louise Labé's sonnet contrives to describe. Through a certain doubling, the logic of the "in" is turned inside out so that it finds its true sense and place in the outside:

> Lors double vie à chacun en suivra.
> Chacun en soy et son ami vivra.

Commentators on these lines have persisted in invoking a neoplatonic theme of, as one put it, "two souls become one through the power of the feeling that unites them."[3] Labé's language, however, quite clearly resists precisely this assimilation of the two into the one which is a platitude compared with the "double vie" that both discerns one from the other and repeats the one *in* the other.

With the "double life," the poem proposes a "mad" way of counting by two. (Sonnet XVIII is all about numbers. Besides the one and the two, there is a four in l.4/"Je t'en rendray quatre plus chaus que braise"/and a ten in l.6/"En t'en donnant dix autres doucereus"/. Labé's numerology adds a gloss on certain numerical propositions in "Femmeninism." The "double life," what I will call the indiscrete two, would be factored in the four which, I suggested, counts differently than the dialectical three. The latter, on the other hand, is at work in the interpretive grid of "two-souls-become-one" too easily laid over the sonnet's assertion of a difference *in* similarity.) The final lines are inscribed within and by the permission the other grants to think outside reason's discerning limits. They are spoken thus from the "double vie," "en soy et son ami":

Permets m'Amour penser quelque folie:

Tousjours suis mal, vivant discrettement,
Et ne me puis donner contentement,
Si hors de moy ne fay quelque saillie.

The couplet rhyme "discrettement"/"contentement" displays a re- markable concentration of doubled meanings which, in accord with the explicit thematizing of "hors de moy," carry these lines outside any simple identification of the thinking, writing subject with a "moy." First, "vivant discrettement" has here the sense of living pru- dently, in observance of the social rules for discreet conduct—keeping to oneself, you might say. But the other, etymologically prior sense of "separately" (from *discernere*, to separate) cannot be discounted since it is, quite simply, the same word but without the charge of any moral judgment. One may, I think, read the complaint about "vivant discrettement" in the play between these two senses: the social code of (particularly feminine) discretion is a figurative displacement of the arithmetical model of discrete entities or numbers. This assimilation of the arithmetic concept to a system of value (a system in which the number one is discerned to be of greatest value) produces "tous- jours," says the Poet, a *mal-être*. Permit me to read "suis mal" in the strong sense of un-being, being which is not in the full mode, a lack- of-being because a discrete/discreet one.[4]

Secondly, the word "contentement" is made to bear a sense almost contrary to its standard meaning. "Contentment" derives its standard associations from the close alliance with "containment," that is, from the notion of limits or bounds that keep in (or keep out), or the notion of a filled space or vessel. The last two lines of our sonnet take up this notion in order to turn it inside out because it is said that con- tentment can be found only "hors de moy," outside myself. This is to say that "I" (the pronoun which is never pronounced in these three lines where it is a matter of an outside-me) gives me contentment, fills the un-being of the discrete self *on* the outside or even *in* the outside. The self's inside is outside itself, "in" the other. It is con- tented only when uncontained, indiscrete.

The sallying forth or extrusion of a sense of contentment that is not contained by or within a *moy* suggests a more complex design within the double life than first suspected. If one counts by positive and discrete numbers, then the double life is a simple addition: 1 plus 1 equals 2. But with the "I" which is always a negative un-being (because discrete, individual), a different calculation must be made. Rather than a product, the double life would be an originary excess:

excess because it is double, a repetition, more of the same (recall that
the poem begins in repetition: "Baise m'encor, rebaise moy et baise"),
and originary because the one depends—for its contentment, its containment, its constitution—on what exceeds it. Before counting one
by one, one *and then* two, there will have been the double which is
neither one nor two, neither one nor the other but the repetition of
one *in* the other and the other *in* one. The indiscrete double is not
an arithmetical figure and therefore it exceeds the calculation of even
the purest science.

Is the "double life" a figure with which to think "men in feminism"? Yes, if one may be permitted to insist on the "in" in such a
phrase as the mark of an interior spacing of difference within the
same. This lever for deconstructing the closures of sexual and other
oppositions has far from exhausted its usefulness, to say the least.
The impatience with deconstructive practices (writing practices
whether or not they produce texts in the limited sense of the word)
that lately marks or mars theoretical discussions would frequently
like to make one believe that deconstruction can and has been assim-
ilated, as if it were a body of information rather than a practice *on*
writing *in* writing. When Elizabeth Weed writes that "the immediate
task entails constructing the female subject . . . while *at the same time*
always displacing boundaries, always shifting positions to work
against the erection of the same old phallocratic structures in the name
of identity and the unifying subject,"[5] the urgent tone, the impatience
to get on with the task should not be allowed to disguise the fact that
this task is plotted as a *text* since it calls for a spacing of different and,
on the surface at least, incompatible gestures: "constructing"/"displacing" (indeed elsewhere in the same essay Weed speaks of the
"need to textualize the subject"). Neither of these gestures can take
place without the other; neither can take place at all outside a field
of forces, a text. Or again, is it indeed "thought-provoking," as Alice
Jardine writes quoting Gayatri Spivak, to read that "women today
may *have* to take 'the risk of essence,'"[6] or is it not rather a mark and
an encouragement of the impatience with the thinking subject as deconstructed by the necessity of textualizing itself? How is one supposed to understand essence as a *risk* to be run when it is by definition
the non-accidental and therefore hardly the apt term to represent
danger or risk? Only over against and in impatient reaction to the
deconstruction of the subject can "essence" be made to sound excit-
ingly dangerous and the phrase "the risk of essence" can seem to
offer such an appealing invitation to anyone who, similarly impatient,
nevertheless doesn't like to think that there may be something cring-
ing in that attitude. "Go for it," the phrase incites. "If you fall into
'essence,' you can always say it was an accident." Through this struc-

ture of denegation, deconstructive writing practices that pose everywhere a risk *to* essence have been themselves . . . essentialized! Ironically, therefore, such a provocation can be issued only because of an
assurance in advance that there is *no* risk of an essential (feminine or
masculine) subject ever evacuating the differences among forces from
the field of their play.

But this impatience also translates the sense that it is urgent for
women to write, even if it sometimes disguises from itself why this
might be so. Might it not be the same urgency one reads in Sonnet
XVIII where "vivant discrettement" is synonymous with *mal-être* and
where a double life already figures as an in-discrete text? It is thus
my love allows me to think.

Peggy Kamuf

11.
Dreaming Dissymmetry: Barthes, Foucault, and Sexual Difference

NAOMI SCHOR

> . . . the risk of essence may have to be taken
>
> Stephen Heath, "Difference"

On the very first page of the important preface to *Powers of Desire: The Politics of Sexuality*, a bulky 1983 anthology bringing together some of the most significant recent texts on feminism and the discourses of sexuality, the three editors pay hommage—or is it femmage—to Michel Foucault, historian of sexuality. Briefly summarizing Foucault's paradoxical reading of so-called sexual liberation as in fact a further turn of the screw of repression or oppression, the editors praise Foucault for his, "subtle rendering of the general argument that sex and capitalism have gone hand-in-hand too long for sex to be interpreted at face value as a radical force."[1] On the very next page, however, Foucault is summarily dismissed as just another purveyor of "the obsessive male sexual discourse that runs through the centuries from St. Augustine to Philip Roth."[2] The editors point out that if for men who have regulated the discourse of sexuality throughout the history of Western civilization, silence is an option, for women whose relationship to sex has traditionally been aphasic, "it is too soon . . . for silence."[3] Setting aside for the moment the question of Foucault's phallogocentrism, of the inscription of his discourse on sexuality in the order of male discursive practices, I want to make another point. The mention of Foucault at the very beginning of this lengthy preface is striking in two ways: it is the only mention both of a *French* and a *male* theoretician in this otherwise indigenous, not to say ethnocentric overview of the burgeoning field of feminist discourse on sexuality. One could imagine a homologous anthology which would represent the French point of view, and while I will not speculate here on its table of contents, I think it is safe to assume that though most likely equally ethnocentric, it would be less gynocentric, because as historians of French Feminisms have often pointed out, in France recent feminist thought has always functioned in dialogue with the reigning male *maîtres à penser*, notably Lacan and Derrida. One figure is almost never mentioned in this context and that is Roland Barthes. And yet, I will want to argue here that it is perhaps in Barthes, who was in his own words a sort of "echo chamber"[4] of contemporary French thought, that we can most easily grasp the dominant male discourse on sexuality in poststructuralist France, what I will call the *discourse of in-difference* or of *pure difference*, for they are in fact one and the same.

Barthes's major rhetorical strategy is seduction, and many feminists—there are some notable exceptions—[5] have succumbed without much resistance to his subtle persuasion. Nor is this seduction totally misguided, for there is much in Barthes that speaks to some of the central preoccupations of French neo-feminisms. Most seductive, most resonant has been the later Barthes's valorization of the body and its pleasures, his insistence that one must write the body, that writing must render the very grain of the voice, that most intimate and idiosyncratic corporeal imprint. Then there is also Barthes's valorization of jouissance, the most intense form of sexual pleasure which French women writers and theorists have in the wake of Lacan claimed for the feminine.[6] There is another more subtle reason why so many feminists have felt a special sympathy for Barthes: even at his most doctrinaire, Barthes's voice is never strident; it is a voice whose grain reveals vulnerability and not an obsession with force and penetration. Rejecting the violence of "arrogance," Barthes speaks from the margin, aligning himself with the excluded of the bourgeois social order, with all those who resist ordering. There are, however, a growing number of signs that in the ongoing process of dismantling the master discourses of the past twenty years feminists are beginning to resist the seductions of Barthes's texts and to examine the ways in which these seductive texts participate nonetheless in a masculine discourse on sexuality, which is not to say, of course, that women, indeed feminists do not also practice this discourse, for they do. In what follows I propose to answer the question of the feminist critique of and complicity with what I take to be one of the dominant discourses on sexuality by undertaking to read from a feminist perspective some texts first by Barthes and then by Michel Foucault, with particular emphasis on his more recent work, notably the second and third volumes of his *History of Sexuality*.

In a fragment of *Roland Barthes by Roland Barthes* entitled *"Pluriel, différence, conflit*—Plural, difference, conflict," speaking of himself in the third person, Barthes writes:

He often resorts to a kind of philosophy vaguely labeled
pluralism.

Who knows if this insistence on the plural is not a way of
denying sexual duality? The opposition of the sexes must not
be a law of Nature; therefore, the confrontations and paradigms
must be dissolved, both the meanings and the sexes must be
pluralized . . . (p. 69)

Denied sexual difference shades into sexual indifference and, following the same slippery path, into a paradoxical reinscription of the
very differences the strategy was designed to denaturalize. This se-
quence of events is traced out in a recent review article on Barthes's
A Lover's Discourse (Fragments d'un discours amoureux) by Stephen
Heath who writes: "The subject of *Fragments*, of its discourse on love,
is unisex, an indifference, only a 'lover' (the scenes permutate 'he'
and 'she', hetero and homosexual love, marking as little as possible
the differences of sexes)." Heath is quick to point out the dangers
inherent in this sort of erasure of the inflections of gender, what we
might call the *effet pervers* or perverse effect of Barthes's sexually un-
marked erotics: the return of a "certain myth of the 'feminine'," as
when Barthes writes: "the man who waits and suffers from it is mi-
raculously feminized," and, further, "the future will belong to the
subjects *in whom there is something feminine.*" Heath comments, "To
envisage a future that will belong 'to the subjects in whom there is
something feminine' might be heard on the one hand as the projection
of a new order, beyond the phallic (. . .), on the other as a derivation
from the existing order, a repetition of its image and essentialization
and alibi, its perspective of 'Woman'."[7] Jane Gallop, on the other
hand, speculates a propos of Barthes's *The Pleasure of the Text*, that
"the wish to escape sexual difference might be but another mode of
denying women."[8] To decide whether or not Barthes's discourse of
indifferentiation ends up reessentializing woman and/or denying her
specificity altogether I want to study in some detail a recurrent strategy Barthes deploys when confronted with the question of difference,
a synecdoche for femininity since in Western conceptual systems the
feminine is always defined as a *difference from* a masculine norm. It
is the recurrence of this strategy or move that interests me, for on
this matter there is no gap between Barthes's prestructuralist, high
structuralist and poststructuralist discourse. Redundancy, according
to Barthes, does not always ensure communication; on the contrary,
as he notes in the fragment of *Roland Barthes* entitled "Les idées mé-
connues—Misunderstood Ideas," the recurrence of an idea from one
book to the other virtually guarantees its incomprehension: "it is *pre-*

cisely where I dare encourage myself to the point of repeating myself that the reader 'drops' me" (p. 103).

I would like to begin with perhaps the most famous example of Barthes's displacement of sexual difference. It is located in *S/Z*, Barthes's brilliant and highly influential analysis of a bizarre tale by Balzac which tells of the ill-starred love of the sculptor Sarrasine for la Zambinella, a Roman castrato whom Sarrasine willfully persists in mistaking for a woman despite the many early warnings he receives. Barthes's choice of this formerly obscure tale by Balzac seems motivated in part by a desire to dramatize the dangers of essentialism— "Barthes," according to John Sturrock, "began . . . as an enemy of essentialism and he has remained one"[9]—and in late Western culture those dangers can best be dramatized by de-essentializing woman, woman as cultural construct, universal woman as oppposed to women as historical subjects, Woman with a capital W. And no text could better serve to dramatize the dangers of essentializing woman than *Sarrasine*, for it is precisely Sarrasine's blind reliance on the conventional signs of femininity that lead to his death; essentialism in the case of Sarrasine is fatal.[10] In order to de-essentialize "woman," Barthes enlists a familiar strategy: what Heath first termed displacement, Barthes's general strategy for shaking up the "habits of intelligibility" of the doxa.[11] Noting that the female characters of the novella are split by a difference internal to femininity, Barthes writes:

> sexual classification is not the right one. Another pertinence must be found. It is Mme Lanty who reveals the proper structure: in opposition to her (passive) daughter, Mme de Lanty is totally active: she dominates time (defying the inroads of age); she radiates (radiation is action at a distance, the highest form of power); bestowing praises, making comparisons, instituting the language in relation to which man can recognize himself, she is the primal Authority . . . In short, the precursor of Sappho who so terrifies Sarrasine, Mme de Lanty is the castrating woman, endowed with all the hallucinatory attributes of the Father: power, fascination, instituting authority, terror, power to castrate. Thus, the symbolic field is not that of the biological sexes; it is that of castration: of *castrating/castrated, active/passive.* It is in this field, and not in that of the biological sexes, that the characters in the story are pertinently distributed.[12]

At first glance there is much here that is of use to feminist theory. What Barthes does here in exemplary fashion is to de-naturalize difference, stressing what Kaja Silverman has called the "disequivalence between sexual and symbolic differentiation in Balzac's tale,"[13] uncoupling man and activity, woman and passivity. If the characters in

Sarrasine cannot be usefully classified according to their biological sexes it is because that classification relies on the double equation: masculine = active, feminine = passive which has at least since Aristotle fixed woman in the inferior position in the sexual hierarchy. Feminists have long fought to break down the assignation of fixed sexual roles to biological men and women and claimed for women but also for men the possibility of oscillating between activity and passivity, and to that extent Barthes's substitution of the active/passive for the male/female paradigm can be seen as beneficial. However, if one takes a closer look at what is going on in this passage we note the following: no change has really been effected in the representation of woman, since Mme de Lanty does not cease to be classified as a woman; rather she has been reclassified as that most fearsome of female monsters: the castrating woman, the phallic mother with all her terrifying attributes of super-power. What Barthes calls the women's camp has now become that of "active castration," a questionable reversal: first because it lends credence to a phantasmatic construct of maternal super-power, second because it is *merely* a reversal, which leaves standing what Barthes was to call some years later the "binary prison" (*R.B.*, p. 133) of sexual classification.[14]

In *S/Z*, Barthes seeks to debiologize difference by substituting the paradigm castrating/castrated for the paradigm male/female. This suggests that what is really at stake in *S/Z* is sexual difference, but a symbolic rather than an anatomical one. This presumption is quickly dispelled when one turns to an essay Barthes wrote on the same Balzac tale, entitled "Masculine, Feminine, Neutral." In this early version of what was to become *S/Z*, Barthes suggests that the centrality of sexual difference in *Sarrasine* is in fact illusory, a lure: "Its apparent center is sexuality."[15] Because for Balzac—and, of course, for Barthes—the castrato escapes the binary sexual taxonomy into the neutral, Barthes argues that in *Sarrasine* we are in fact outside the symbolic realm of sexuality altogether. "In reality, and linguistics attests to this fact, the neutral cannot be directly implicated in a sexual structure; in Indo-European languages, the opposition of the masculine and the feminine is less important than that of the animate and the inanimate; indeed it follows from it:

Animate (Masculine/Feminine)/Inanimate (Neutral)."

If this is so the question in *Sarrasine* is not the transgression of the bar of castration that separates the masculine from the feminine—since they are located on the same side of the bar which divides the animate from the inanimate—rather what Barthes calls a "transgression of objects" (ibid.). Thus the paradigm of sexual difference is cancelled by the opposition of life and death.

So far we could speak merely of displacement: the paradigm man/ woman is displaced by two other paradigms, in the first instance castrating/castrated, in the other, animate/inanimate. But as I turn to my third and final example of Barthes's strategy of indifferentiation, I want to introduce another term to characterize Barthes's move. Borrowing, however loosely, from Lucretius via Harold Bloom, I want to call Barthes's movement away from sexual difference, a _clinamen_ or swerve.[16] I prefer this term to the more common displacement, because displacement implies taking a concept or a word and transporting it over to another conceptual field, thereby creating a new and startling configuration. Whereas displacement denotes a _shift_, the clinamen as I am using it here denotes a _shift away from_; whereas in displacement the two paradigms coexist, in the Barthesian clinamen one paradigm is literally effaced by the other. But in order to demonstrate that what is at stake here is not a displacement (either single or double), rather a clinamen (however minimal), and further that the clinamen is a swerve away not merely from sexual difference but specifically away from femininity, let us look at my third and final example, which is drawn from _The Fashion System_.

The Fashion System was originally meant to be Barthes's doctoral thesis. It was begun in 1957, completed in 1963, and first published in France in 1967. Its long voyage into print spans roughly Barthes's years as a high structuralist. The book is intended to be, "the structural analysis of women's clothing as currently described by Fashion magazines."[17] Now although _The Fashion System_ is essentially an attempt to carry out Saussure's program for a general science of signs by studying the language of fashion, Barthes subsumes the signifiers of fashion to those of language and is concerned here exclusively with fashion in its textual inscription, that is in the captions that gloss the pictures in the glossy magazines. Because as Barthes notes in one of those parentheses where he tucks away some of his more memorable asides, Fashion is a discourse that "deals only with the Woman, for women" (p. 258), one might expect that Barthes would at some point in the book have to deal with woman or at the very least femininity. And that expectation seems to be borne out when we note that one of Barthes's subheadings is precisely "Femininity." Because _The Fashion System_ is possibly Barthes's least pleasurable text to read I skip ahead to the section on femininity. It begins on a fairly conventional note, but then comes the clinamen, the moment at which Barthes's paradigm shift becomes an erasure of the very femininity foregrounded in the section title. Fashion, according to Barthes, "understands the opposition between masculine and feminine quite well; reality itself requires that it do so" (p. 257). What distinguishes women's clothes from men's are often details and despite the clear distinction between men's and women's fashions some degree of cross-dressing is permissible, at least for women, for whereas:

> there is a social prohibition against the feminization of men, there is almost none against the masculinization of women: Fashion notably acknowledges the *boyish look. Feminine* and *masculine* each have their own rhetorical version: *feminine* can refer to the idea of an emphatic, quintessential woman (. . .); when noted, the *boyish* look itself has more a temporal than a sexual value: it is the complementary sign of an ideal age, which assumes increasing importance in Fashion literature: the *junior*; structurally, the *junior* is presented as the complex degree of the *feminine/masculine*: it tends toward androgyny; but what is more remarkable in this new term is that it effaces sex to the advantage of age; this is, it seems, a profound process of Fashion; it is age which is important, not sex . . . (pp. 257–58)

Perhaps the best word to describe Barthes's erasure of sex, now to the advantage of the neutral, now to the advantage of age, is Foucault's term "desexualization." Foucault's use of the word "desexualization" occurs, perhaps not coincidentally, in his response to an interviewer's question regarding the women's and homosexuals' liberation movements. Foucault says:

> The real strength of the women's liberation movements is not that of having laid claim to the specificity of their sexuality and the rights pertaining to it, but that they have actually departed from the discourse conducted within the apparatuses of sexuality. These movements do indeed emerge in the nineteenth century as demands for sexual specificity. What has the outcome been? Ultimately, a veritable movement of de-sexualization, a displacement effected in relation to the sexual centering of the problem, formulating the demand for forms of culture, discourse, language, and so on, which are no longer part of that rigid assignation and pinning-down to their sex which they had initially in some sense been politically obliged to accept in order to make themselves heard.[18]

In both Barthes and Foucault, the move toward desexualization takes the form of a fascination with limit-cases of difference: to Barthes's *Sarrasine* corresponds Foucault's *Herculine Barbin*. The volume whose English edition bears the mock-libertine title, *Herculine Barbin: Being the Recently Discovered Memoirs of a Nineteenth-Century French Hermaphrodite*, is made up of an introduction by Foucault, the memoirs of Herculine, excerpts from the medico-legal texts on the case, and finally a fictionalized version of the story by the German psychiatrist Oscar Panizza. Herculine Barbin was born in 1838 in Vendée. She was educated in Catholic women's schools, first a convent then a normal school where she obtained her teaching certificate. Herculine's first post as a schoolmistress was with a widow with three daughters. During the three years Herculine spent there, she and one of the daughters became lovers. Found out by a doctor who examined her, Herculine decided to request an official change of her civil status. In 1860, when Herculine was 22 years old, she was officially reclassified as being of the male sex, and changed her name to Abel. Alone, miserable, and destitute, Abel committed suicide in Paris in February 1868, leaving his memoirs and body to posterity. For Foucault what is of interest in this sad story is the new relationship between desire and the law that was being put into place at the very moment when Herculine's story was unfolding. Whereas in the past hermaphrodites were free to choose their sex, in the eighteenth and nineteenth centuries a new order of discourse decreed that all hermaphrodites were "pseudo-hermaphrodites," that is: beneath the ambiguity of their anatomy lay concealed a single "true" sex, whose discovery it was the task of the medical profession to carry out. Accordingly Foucault reads the memoirs of Herculine as utopianism masquerading as nostalgia. He contends that the memoirs reveal a longing for the "happy limbo of a non-identity."[19] Indeterminacy is bliss; if only Herculine/Abel had been able to continue indefinitely in her/his sexual in-between stage, she/he might have lived happily ever after.[20] In his fragment, "Active/passive," Barthes describes the utopia of indeterminacy this way: "once the alternative is rejected (once the paradigm is blurred) utopia begins: meaning and sex become the object of a free play, at the heart of which the (polysemant) forms and (sensual) practices, liberated from the binary prison, will achieve a state of infinite expansion. Thus may be born a Gongorian text and a happy sexuality" (R. B., 133).

The memoirs of Herculine Barbin first appeared in 1978 when Foucault was still committed to pursuing the *History of Sexuality* inaugurated in 1976 in its originally announced form. The five volumes Foucault projected writing suggested that the entire project would be ruled by the dream of escaping from what he termed the "austere" binarisms of the sexual order. However, in the course of working on his History, as he explains in the preface to the first volume of what we might call the new *History of Sexuality*, he found himself obliged to revise completely his original plan. He realized that in order to carry out his project it was necessary to study the genealogy of man as subject of and to desire:

in order to understand how the modern individual could experience himself as a subject of a "sexuality," it was essential

first to determine how, for centuries, Western man had been
brought to recognize himself as a subject of desire.[21]

To do this he would have to return to the classical foundations of
Western civilization, to the ethics of sex elaborated by the philosophers of Ancient Greece and Imperial Rome. The archaeological move
backward to the origins of Western sexual discourse on sexuality provides a much needed perspective on the discourse of sexuality. Sexuality, it will be remembered, is the term Foucault reserves for the
discourse on sex elaborated by the bourgeoisie during the nineteenth
century in order to codify the respective and complementary places
of men and women in society. Now precisely because sexuality is a
discourse with fairly precise spatio-temporal boundaries, the question
becomes what came before. In his latest books, Foucault sketches out
a more comprehensive periodization than that proposed in *The Will
to Power*, where Church doctrine had constituted his historical horizon. In the West, man's relationship to his own desire has according
to Foucault's Hegelian design passed through three phases: 1) the
aphrodisia, which is to say the classical discourse on sexual ethics; 2)
the "flesh," that is the Christian discourse on sexuality; and, finally,
the very recent 3) sexuality in its restricted Foucauldian sense. Foucault's last two books explore in depth only one of these stages, the
first, but look ahead to the others. Three diverse but related aspects
of Foucault's curiously restrained and limpid final works—so different in tone from the feisty polemics of *The Will to Power*—seem to me
of particular interest to feminist analyses of sexuality: first, the scrupulous attention Foucault pays to the gender of the enunciating subject; second, the subtle way in which he decenters the "woman question"; and third and finally, the pride of place he accords a model of
heterosexual relations based on reciprocity and mutual respect.

    From the outset Foucault makes clear that the *aphrodisia* was a dis-
course which circulated only among men: "It was an ethics for men:
an ethics thought, written, and taught by men, and addressed to
men—to free men, obviously" (p. 22). Given this remarkable statement it becomes difficult to maintain as do the authors of *Powers of
Desire* that Foucault participates in the obsessive male discourse on
sexuality. Or rather, if he does so, he does so in his last works with
an intense awareness of the phallocentrism of that discourse; though
Foucault can never write from the place of enunciation of a woman—
nor does he attempt to—he makes it very clear that he is not complicitous with the "hommosexual" (Lacan and Irigaray) communication circuit he so insistently lays bare. Because of the eminence of
Foucault's position on the intellectual scene, his categorical assertion
of woman's exclusion from the aphrodisia, as both sender and receiver, encoder and decoder, matters; that Greco-Roman civilization

excluded woman, as well as other marginal members of society (slaves, young boys) from access to the symbolic codes will surely come as no surprise to students of classical antiquity, but that it is Michel Foucault who is insisting on this exclusion will surprise feminists. What Foucault does here is to recognize as he never had before in his work the centrality of gender—a question which simply does not arise in *The Will to Power*. Woman as object of discourse and subject of history is, of course, spectacularly in evidence in *The Will to Power*, where Foucault argues that one of the key strategies deployed by the power-knowledge system to ground its tentacular investment of the human body is what he calls the "hysterization" of the female body: a three-step operation involving first a reduction of woman to her sex, second a pathologization of that sex, third a subordination of the female body to the reproductive imperative. But the question of gender cannot be said to inform Foucault's project. In *The Will to Power* we are introduced to a History of Sexuality wherein the notion that the history of sexuality might be different if written by women is never entertained; a single universal history is presumed to cover both sexes, as though the History and, more important, the Historian of sexuality himself had no sex.

Throughout Foucault's presentation of the aphrodisia he continues to insist on their phallocentrism though, significantly, the word is conspicuously absent from the text. Thus he observes that temperance, that discipline of self-mastery which ensures the exercise of one's freedom, is a masculine virtue par excellence. This does not mean that women are not enjoined to practice this virtue, but: "where women were concerned, this virtue was always referred in some way to virility" (p. 83). In other words temperance, like Freudian libido, is always masculine. Similarly, Foucault emphasizes the ways in which what he calls the "ejaculatory schema" of the sexual act is in the teachings of a Hippocrates simply transferred from male sexuality onto the female: in this old dream of symmetry—which survives well into the pornographic texts of a Sade or a Cleland—the two are assumed to be isomorphic. "This 'ejaculatory schema', through which sexual activity as a whole—and in both sexes—was always perceived, shows unmistakably the near-exclusive domination of the virile model." However, even within the isomorphism of masculine and feminine sexual activity, a hierarchy is at work: "The female act was not exactly the complement of the male act; it was more in the nature of a duplicate, but in the form of a weakened version" (p. 129). Female sexuality in this schema has no specificity other than its distance from the male norm.

In Freud the valorization of the same does not preclude—indeed it requires—the centrality of the Other; phallocentrism revolves around the riddle of femininity. What Foucault reveals is that in

Greco-Roman moral discourse—mythology tells another story—phallocentrism is not also a gynocentrism; what is problematic and intellectually challenging for classical thinkers is the pederastic relationship to boys, that is the erotic relationship between two free men separated only by an age difference; what is problematic in the conceptual framework of the aphrodisia is not female passivity, which is viewed as so natural as to be non-problematic, but masculine passivity, the feminization of man. The line of demarcation passes here not so much between men and women, or even between homosexuals and heterosexuals, but between active and passive men, with the result that the opposition between men and women and the concomitant obsessive focus on the enigma of femininity is decentered, even as the myth of a happy pederasty is exploded:

> Later, in European culture, girls or married women, with their behavior, their beauty, and their feelings, were to become themes of special concern; a new art of courting them, a literature that was basically romantic in form, an exacting morality that was attentive to the integrity of their bodies and the solidity of their matrimonial commitment—all this would draw curiosity and desires around them. No matter what inferior position may have been reserved for them in the family or in society, there would be an accentuation, a valorization, of the "problem" of women. Their nature, their conduct, the feelings they inspired or experienced, the permitted or forbidden relationship that one might have with them were to become themes of reflection, knowledge, analysis, and prescription. It seems clear, on the other hand, that in classical Greece the problematization was more active in regard to boys, maintaining an intense moral concern around their fragile beauty, their corporal honor, their ethical judgment and the training it required. (pp. 213–14).

But then again, the aphrodisia is not a monolithic discourse; in the course of its passage from Greece to Rome a subtle and gradual shift takes place and eventually the fascination with boys is displaced by a preoccupation with woman. In the section of *Le souci de soi* entitled "Woman," woman assumes a new centrality in the context of a reconceptualization of marriage. "The intensification of the concern with the self goes hand in hand with the valorization of the other."[22] And with this dawning recognition of alterity what I will call conjugal man is born. The model of conjugal relations posited by the Stoics is radically opposed to the model that prevailed in Athens; if under both regimes woman has no existence outside of the marital couple, under this new ethos, the couple becomes a privileged social unit, bound together by mutual respect and obligations. Fidelity is no longer woman's natural destiny, men too are held to the same standard. Reciprocity replaces domination. And heterosexual married love displaces pederastic love as the valorized model of eroticism and privileged locus of problematization. This does not mean, of course, that homosexual love ceases to be practiced or permitted in Imperial Rome, merely that the love for boys no longer is problematized. Foucault's tone throughout these two books is as already noted remarkably dispassionate; he exposes the interlocking discourses on pederasty and conjugality without ever suggesting the superiority of the one to the other, without ever taking a clear position in regard to them: the texts are, as it were, allowed to speak for themselves, presentation preempts representation. And yet despite the impersonality of the voice, or perhaps because of it, a system of values is established, and a model of human sexual relations which is both heterosexual and conjugal is promoted, precisely because it recognizes the alterity of woman.

There are from a feminist perspective at least two problems with Foucault's eerily timely reconstruction of the Stoic ethics of sexuality—an ethics of sexual austerity fueled by a preoccupation with what we might call anachronistically physical fitness: the woman who becomes in Foucault's words, "the other par excellence" is "the wifewoman [*la femme-épouse*]" (p. 192) and, furthermore, alterity is, of course, not specificity. And therein lies the clearest and most persistent dissymmetry between men and women in feminism today: whereas many theoreticians, some of them women, have eagerly seized upon and used the tools of deconstruction to dismantle metaphysical woman, no feminist theoretician *who is not also a woman* has ever fully espoused the claims to a feminine specificity, an irreducible difference. Even the most enlightened among the male feminists condone claims to female specificity *only* as a temporary tactical necessity for pressing political claims; in the promised utopia of sexual indifferentiation and multiple singularities, they assure us, there will no longer be any place or need for sexual difference; it will simply wither away. At the risk of being a wallflower at the carnival of plural sexualities, I would ask: what is it to say that the discourse of sexual indifference/pure difference is not the last or (less triumphantly) the latest ruse of phallocentrism? If one lends an ear to what some of the most sophisticated feminist theoreticians are writing these days, the resistance to the hegemony of the discourse of indifference is powerful and growing. That difference does have a future is forcefully argued by Myra Jehlen who, taking note of the emergence of a politics of difference in recent American feminist writings, comments:

In the evolution of feminist analysis . . . this about-face hardly signifies that women have, typically, changed their minds. On the contrary, it reflects a deeper analysis. In the first place the claim of difference criticizes the content of the male universal norm. But beyond this, it represents a new understanding that if the other is to live, it will have to live as other, lest the achievement of integration be crowned with the fatal irony of disappearance through absorption.[23]

A chiasmus best figures the cross-purposes of those who currently maintain, respectively, masculine and feminine positions on difference: whereas those who adopt the masculine position press for an end to sexual difference and only grudgingly acknowledge claims for feminine specificity, those who adopt the feminine position concede the strategic efficacy of undoing sexual oppositions and positionalities, all the while pursuing the construction of difference. The most active site of the feminine resistance to the discourse of indifference is a certain insistence on doubling, which may well be the feminine mode of subverting the unitary subject: mimeticism (Irigaray and Kolodny), the double and even double double identification of the female film spectator (Mulvey, Doane, De Lauretis), women's writing as palimpsest (Gilbert and Gubar), female fetishism (Kofman, Berg, Schor), the foregrounding of the "other woman" (Gallop), the elaboration of a "doubled strategy" of deconstruction and construction (Martin) are some of the varied forms this insistence on doubling has taken and is taking.[24] Whether as producers or consumers of cultural artifacts and theories, the claim in all these texts is that women occupy in modern Western culture a *specific liminal cultural position* which is through a tangled skein of mediations somehow connected to their anatomical difference, to their femaleness. Women are bilingual, bifocal, bitextual. Now perhaps, as Simone de Beauvoir writes in *The Second Sex*, "these differences are superficial, perhaps they are destined to disappear. What is certain is that right now they do most obviously exist."[25] Or as Hélène Cixous writes in *La jeune née*, after having imagined a utopia of multiple differences not unlike those of her male contemporaries, Barthes and Foucault: "But we are still floundering about—with certain exceptions—in the Old order."[26] Doubling holds open *for now* a space that has only begun to be explored: the pitch black continent of what patriarchal culture has consistently connoted as feminine and hence depreciated. Before tearing down the cultural ghetto where the feminine has been confined and demeaned, we need to map its boundaries and excavate its foundations in order to salvage the usable relics and refuse of patriarchy, for to do so is perhaps the only chance we have to construct a post-deconstructionist society which will not simply reduplicate our own.

12.
French Theory and the Seduction of Feminism

JANE GALLOP

A good number of us have, in recent years, been swept away by something both charming and dangerous which, for lack of an honest name, I will call French Theory. One of the peculiar things about this particular intersection of Seduction and Theory is that, according to local mores, seduction can function as a positive term. I, for one, wrote a book a few years ago called *The Daughter's Seduction*. Among the ambiguities of that title is the question of whether seduction constitutes a defeat or a triumph for the daughter. The possibility of valorizing seduction occurs either through some sort of equation between seduction and femininity, or at least through casting seduction as a threat to the uprightness of phallogocentrism.

At this point in time, I would like to consider a book entitled *De la séduction* (Of Seduction), published in 1979 and written by Jean Baudrillard. Baudrillard is, by discipline, a sociologist and, by stance, a very provocative thinker. He is certainly not as well known in Anglo-American circles as a number of other contemporary French theorists. The book I am discussing has never, to my knowledge, been translated into English, although a few of his other books have, notably in the *Semiotexte* series. His work is quite interesting, if totally outrageous to a liberal humanist sensibility. I introduce him here, however, not to give you yet another French theorist whose works you must tackle, but because he is the French theorist who has written a book called *Of Seduction*, because I want to talk about seduction as we find it in French theory.

The form of the title—*De la séduction*, which I translate as "Of Seduction"—is reminiscent of one of the best-known monuments of contemporary French theory—Jacques Derrida's *De la grammatologie*, which Gayatri Spivak translated as "Of Grammatology." Derrida's book makes the point that, although writing appears to be a secondary form, mediating speech, there is actually a kind of writing or difference primary within speech. The secondary form that would appear to adulterate the original is exposed by Derrida as actually more fundamental than, as constitutive of, the so-called "original." *De la sé-duction* makes a similar sort of point. Although we think of seduction as a secondary adulteration of truth, production, or sexuality, Baudrillard contends that seduction is a primary, constitutive form.

"We were led to believe that everything was production. . . . Seduction is only an immoral, frivolous, superficial . . . process, of the order of signs and appearances. . . . And what if everything, contrary to appearances . . . if everything marched to seduction?" (p. 115). Not only does Baudrillard, like Derrida, promote a secondary something to the rank of primary, but there seems to be a kinship between the two causes championed. According to Baudrillard, "seduction is superficial, of the order of signs and appearances." Writing is precisely of the order of signs and appearances, the surface which mediates pure spirit or thought or logos. And just as there is a certain paradoxical logic to thinking of writing as anterior to speech, to Derrida's use of the term writing to designate something originary, so "seduction" must always connote a leading away (*se-ducere*) from something else which would be logically anterior. Both French theorists choose to promote terms that must necessarily connote something secondary and adulterated.

In the quotation I just read you from Baudrillard, he is caught up in just such contradictory logic. On the one hand he says that "seduction is of the order of appearances," on the other hand he asks "and what if everything, contrary to appearances, marched to seduction?" In promoting seduction, throughout the book, he frequently valorizes the realm of appearances. Yet here he asserts that there might be a hidden order "contrary to appearances," and that seduction might be that hidden order. In fact, right after he writes "contrary to appearances," he adds a parenthetical correction, cognizant of the contradiction. The actual sentence with its parenthetical insertion reads: "And what if everything, contrary to appearances—in fact according to the secret rule of appearances—if everything marched to seduction?"

What does it mean for something to be both "contrary to appearances" and at the same time "according to appearances"? What would be a "secret rule of appearances" if not something precisely hidden, some aspect of appearance which does not appear? Similar contradictions are constantly at work in *De la séduction*. For example, seduction is supposed to, everywhere and at all times, undermine truth, and yet Baudrillard is announcing the truth (he even uses the word) that everything is seduction. And then, of course, there is the enormous problem that—although he announces the superiority of seduction over truth and distinctions and categories—the book operates by assertions, by setting up categories and distinctions. In other words, the writing itself is far from seductive.

Now these sorts of contradictions are by now familiar to those of us who have strayed down the path of French theory, where the rule is the breakdown of metalanguage, the impossibility of theorizing about something without the theory itself being nastily entangled in the very problematic on which it would like to pronounce. Every theory, however masterful it would be, has always already been seduced, including and especially the theory of seduction.

Those of us who have, at least to some degree, accepted the necessity for entanglement, contradiction, and loss of mastery have learned to take such contradictions not as failings but as the mark that someone is trying to think his way out of the very logic with which he thinks, with which we all, more or less, seem forced to think, trying to think our way out in the hope that we will not always be quite so forced.

Nonetheless, Baudrillard's contradictions seem less subtle than those of other practitioners of such theory, since he remains within a classical theoretical rhetoric of assertion, category, logic. If Baudrillard's case is interesting to me, it is, first of all, because of the blatant enormity of the contradictions which are better hidden by the stylistic charms of a Derrida or a Lacan. And second of all (this second reason being for me the primary one—my hidden agenda, in fact), because the contradictions seem linked to a rather rabid attack Baudrillard makes on feminism. Many of us have seriously wondered about the effect of French theory on feminism's health. Baudrillard is, to my knowledge, the male French theorist who most explicitly and most frontally adopts an adversarial relation to feminism.

I would like to quote you a passage from the first chapter of *De la séduction* where the theoretical contradiction occurs within Baudrillard's pronouncement of the proper course for women: "Now, woman is only appearance. And it's the feminine as appearance that defeats the profundity of the masculine. Women instead of rising up against this 'insulting' formula would do well to let themselves be seduced by this truth, because here is the secret of their power which they are in the process of losing by setting up the profundity of the feminine against that of the masculine" (p. 22).

When he writes "insulting formula," he puts the word "insulting" (*injurieuse*) in quotation marks. He does not consider it an insult to say that woman is only appearance. Baudrillard is writing against the history of writing against appearances. He is for appearances, and against profundity, so that when he says that "woman is only appearance" it should be taken as a compliment.

Nonetheless, when I read this passage, as a woman, I feel insulted. Baudrillard would have it that my feeling of offense is a great error which stems from my inscription within the sort of masculinistic essentialist thinking which condemns appearances as misleading mediations of essences, realities, and truths.

Yet, in considering the passage carefully, I decide that it is not what he says about "woman" that offends me so much as what he says about "women": "Women would do well," he advises, "to let themselves be seduced by this truth." It is the phrase "would do well" (*feraient bien de*) that irks me. Although he puts "insulting" in quotation marks, he uses the word "truth" (*vérité*) straight. He knows the truth—the profound or hidden truth, I might add—about women, and women "would do well to let themselves be seduced" by the truth he utters. He speaks not from the masculine or masculinist position (which he identifies as against appearances and for profundities) but from a position that knows the truth of the feminine and the masculine and can thus, from this privileged position beyond sexual difference, advise women how best to combat masculine power. It is his assumption of this position of superiority, of speaking the truth—more than any content of "truth" that he may utter— which offends me. Women, he warns, are in danger of losing their power, but if they would only let themselves be seduced by what he says . . . A line if ever I heard one.

The problem may not lie with the women—that women are not "letting themselves" be seduced—the problem may lie with Baudrillard's "technique." Perhaps truth never seduces, or at least not self-certain truth or certainly at all. Baudrillard asserts, in this book which is, after all, very insightful about how seduction works, that "It is by our fragility that we seduce, never by powers or by strong signs" (p. 115).

As opposed to truth, which is necessarily irreversible (the opposite of the truth cannot be true), seduction, as Baudrillard understands it, is the very principle of reversibility. Hence the very best "technique" for seduction turns out to be that which can never be simply a technique at all. As Baudrillard puts it: "To be seduced is yet again the best way to seduce. . . . No one, if he is not seduced, will seduce others" (p. 112). Truth cannot seduce; only seduction seduces. Baudrillard cannot seduce feminism with his truth, because he protects his truth from being seduced by feminism.

Throughout the book he persists in seeing feminism as stupid, wrong, mistaken. Only at one point does he even come close to imagining a reversal of that judgment. This in a book where he reverses almost every judgment, where he is championing seduction as a generalized principle of reversibility. At one point he writes: "Even the most anti-seductive figures can turn back into figures of seduction," and he immediately adds the following parenthesis: "(it has been said of feminist discourse that it rediscovers, beyond its total nonseduction, a sort of homosexual seduction)" (pp. 67–68).

He is announcing the reversibility of seduction itself (the opposite of seduction can seduce). This is, I contend, the central moment of the book, the moment when seduction itself must be seduced so that reversibility rather than a new truth will reign. And at the very moment when seduction as truth would be seduced, feminism appears. If antiseduction can seduce, than surely even feminism could be seductive. Yet there is one, and to my knowledge only one, reversal he cannot allow himself. The reversal of the negative judgment of feminism is not a complete 180 degrees. "It has been said . . . ": Baudrillard cannot assert feminism's seduction but only reports something to which he does not add his assent. And what he reports is only "a sort of seduction." And besides, it is homosexual; it is not for him. Baudrillard cannot imagine—except through the defenses of a triple mediation—finding feminism seductive. Feminism can only be an adversary, forcing him away from seduction's reversibility into the strategy of irreversible truth, the very position he has designated as weaker, stupider, inferior.

At this point, I would just like to conclude with a statement Shoshana Felman makes about the relation between psychoanalysis and literature, but I will take the liberty of substituting "French theory" in the place of "psychoanalysis" and the word "feminism" in place of the word "literature": "It is usually felt that [French theory] has much or all to teach us about [feminism], whereas [feminism] has little or nothing to teach us about [French theory]." My wish is that a reversal of what is "usually felt," of the *doxa*, can make possible a real seduction in and of theory, so that my title—"French Theory and the Seduction of Feminism"—has a chance to experience the exhilaration of going both ways.

13.
Critical Cross-Dressing; Male Feminists and the Woman of the Year

ELAINE SHOWALTER

It's better to be a woman in our day. With us is all the joy of advance,
the glory of conquering . . . Thank heaven we are women!
  —from George Gissing, The Odd Women *(1983)*

A number of prominent English and American male theorists have recently begun to recognize the intellectual claims of feminist criticism, and to connect it with their own critical positions. Wayne Booth led the way by linking feminism and interpretation at the conference on "The Politics of Interpretation" at Chicago, when he declared his conversion to a feminist criticism that had finally persuaded him that "our various canons have been established by men, reading books

This essay by Elaine Showalter was originally published in Raritan *(Fall, 1983). We thank both Elaine Showalter and the editors of* Raritan *for their permission to reprint it.*

The essay was first presented as a review essay of the following books: Jonathan Culler, On Deconstruction: Theory and Criticism After Structuralism *(Ithaca: Cornell Univ. Press), 1982, Terry Eagleton,* The Rape of Clarissa *(Minneapolis: Univ. of Minnesota Press), 1982; Terry Eagleton,* Literary Theory: An Introduction *(Minneapolis: Univ. of Minnesota Press), 1983; Nina Auerbach,* Woman and the Demon *(Cambridge: Harvard Univ. Press), 1982; Terry Castle,* Clarissa's Ciphers *(Ithaca: Cornell Univ. Press), 1982; Susan Dworkin,* Making Tootsie *(New York: Newmarket Press), 1982.*

The inclusion of Showalter's essay in this collection is obviously justified—beyond the piece's own not inconsiderable merits—by the fact that it was perhaps the first to try to take stock of a certain brand of "male feminism." We thought that it could be productive to reprint it in the context of a dialogue or an exchange with at least one of the men whom it queries. Thus we invited a response from Terry Eagleton. We received a short essay from him which follows immediately after Showalter's essay, and which is itself followed by a further comment from Elaine Showalter.

mostly written by men for men, with women as eavesdroppers,"
and that "now is the time for men to join women in working at the
vast project of reeducating our imaginations." Robert Scholes allied
feminism and semiotics in a racy chapter on the literary supression
of the clitoris in his *Semiotics and Interpretation.* Jonathan Culler
used feminist theories of reading to bring deconstruction down to
earth, political earth, that is, in his *On Deconstruction.* And Terry
Eagleton, in his sustained advocacy of Marxist and feminist criticism
in several recent books and TV appearances, seems to be even more
interested in leading women than in joining them in their educational
project.

To women who have been writing feminist criticism this phenomenon must be both gratifying and unsettling. To begin with, we can
hardly fail to welcome male feminist criticism when we have so long
lamented the blindness, deafness, and indifference of the male critical
establishment towards our work. "As every feminist critic knows,"
Sandra Gilbert has protested, "many—indeed, most—of our male
colleagues don't come to our talks, don't read our essays and books,
don't in fact concede that we exist as thinkers, teachers and writers
who are part of a significant intellectual movement." The exclusion
of feminist criticism from the institutions of critical discourse, the
omission of feminist criticism from histories of modern criticism (such
as those by Gerald Graff, Grant Webster, and Frank Lentricchia),
shows how, in Jane Marcus's words, "male bonding" is a more co-
hesive force among American critics than the theoretical enmities that
divide them intellectually.

The move to feminist criticism on the part of other male theorists,
in fact, seems motivated in many cases by the recognition that it offers
the mixture of theoretical sophistication with the sort of effective political engagement they have been calling for in their own critical
spheres. In *Walter Benjamin: or Towards a Revolutionary Criticism* (1981),
for example, Terry Eagleton imagines the ideal shape of revolutionary
criticism. It would:

dismantle the ruling concepts of "literature," reinserting "literary" texts into the whole field of cultural practices. It would
strive to relate such "cultural" practices to other forms of social
activity, and to transform the cultural apparatuses themselves.
It would articulate its "cultural" analyses with a consistent political intervention. It would deconstruct the received hierarchies
of "literature" and transvaluate received judgements and assumptions; engage with the language and "unconscious" of literary texts, to reveal their role in the ideological construction of
the subject; and mobilize such texts, if necessary by hermeneutic
"violence," in a struggle to transform those subjects within a

wider political context. If one wanted a paradigm for such criticism, already established within the present, there is a name for it: feminist criticism.

After this announcement, one might have predicted that it would not be long before Eagleton would try to incorporate the revolutionary paradigm of feminist criticism within his own problematic stance as an English Marxist aesthetician, a political position whose historical impotence he has often remarked.

Jonathan Culler has also taken note of the success of feminist criticism in opening the literary canon, changing the curriculum, and challenging entrenched theoretical positions. In an interview with Fredric Jameson in *Diacritics* (Fall 1982), he asked whether other modes of criticism that seek political impact might have lessons to learn from feminist criticism, which he calls "the most politically effective movement in literary criticism." Jameson (whose political unconscious, like his political conscious, has been unabashedly phallocentric) conceded that feminism had been a force whose power he attributed to its "collective dimension, its status as the culture . . . of a genuine social group," and asked rather plaintively in return "with what organic social group the straight white male intellectual has any particular affinities?"

The organic social group with which this lonely soul found a bond used to be called the Old Boys' Network; and if, at last, it no longer provides a secure status and a collective identity, then the women's movement has been more successful than it often thinks it has. Indeed, feminist criticism is currently so appealing to male theorists that some feminists are beginning to regard the development with some suspicion. In the 1890's, Gissing's "odd women" congratulated themselves on their fortunate position in history, and pitied men who had no movement to serve. As one of his fin-de-siècle feminists remarks, "A woman with brains and will may hope to distinguish herself in the greatest movement of our time—that of emancipating her sex. But what can a man do, unless he has genius?" Gissing's heroes acquired a vicarious sense of history through their contact with these ambitious feminists. Gayatri Spivak, however, is sharply skeptical of the motives of "straight white male intellectuals" who have turned to feminism: "Why is it that male critics in search of a cause find in feminist criticism their best hope?" she asks in *Critical Inquiry*.

> Perhaps because, unlike the race and class situations, where academic people are not likely to get much of a hearing, the women's struggle is one they can support "from the inside." Feminism in its academic inceptions is accessible and subject to correction by authoritative men; whereas . . . for the bourgeois

intellectual to look to join other politico-economic struggles is to toe the line between hubris and bathos.

Feminist critics disagree, moreover, about the potentialities of male feminist reading. Annette Kolodny sees feminist reading competence as a skill that men can learn through patience, practice and effort. Reading, she maintains, is a "learned activity . . . inevitably sex-coded and gender-inflected." Although most men are poor readers of women's writing because they are ignorant of women's values and inexperienced in interpreting female codes, they "will be better readers . . . of women's books when they have read more of them." But others would find this functional view of feminist reading as an acquired expertise superficial and politically suspect. Ten years ago Carolyn Heilbrun and Catharine Stimpson warned that feminist techniques could be copied and lifted out of their personal and political contexts: "Like French or Esperanto, they will comprise a language that a person may practice or learn, learn or practice, without having it affect his or her actions outside of the study or classroom." Kolodny's argument is limited to the reading of women's texts, but other feminist critics would also question the reduction of feminist reading to a cognitive skill easily transferable to male texts or critical theories. Gayatri Spivak is one who insists on the "political or historical and indeed ideological differential that irreducibly separates the male from the female critic of phallocentrism."

In general, I think Spivak is right to question the contexts in which male feminist criticism is produced, to point out the different stake that men and women have in a critique of phallocentrism, and to remind us that the habits of academic training make women critics peculiarly susceptible and vulnerable to the judgments of male authority figures. Feminist criticism has worried too much already, in my opinion, about communicating with the white fathers, even at the price of translating its findings into the warp of their obscure critical languages. If some of them are now learning *our* language, all the better; but there is more than a hint in some recent critical writing that it's time for men to step in and show the girls how to do it, a swaggering tone that reminds me of a recent quip in the *Yale Alumni Magazine* about a member of the class of 1955, Renée Richards: "When better women are made, Yale men will make them."

Nevertheless, we must not prejudge male feminist criticism, refuse to give it a hearing, or go after it with a hatchet *pour encourager les autres*. It strikes me, in fact, that this first wave comes from friends rather than rivals, that it is genuinely exciting, serious and provocative, and that it has large and important cultural implications. Booth, Scholes, Culler, and Eagleton have taken some chances of their own in supporting a feminist politics. Culler, for example, has been attacked by Robert Alter in the *New Republic*, ostensibly for making feminism his latest "true revolution" and for trying to "harness Deconstruction to a political program," but more likely for having betrayed the patriarchy by finding feminist criticism intellectually challenging. It's no accident that these initial recognitions should have come from strong and secure writers of criticism who have little to gain by aligning themselves with a constituency or a cause.

Still, there are questions raised by the phenomenon of male feminist writing which are both pragmatic and theoretical. Why does this criticism make its appearance now? What does male feminist criticism tell us about the current impasse in literary theory? Most important, what are its uses and its dangers for women, and for feminist criticism in general? Is male feminism a form of critical cross-dressing, a fashion risk of the 1980s that is both radical chic and power play? Or is it the result of a genuine shift in critical, cultural and sexual paradigms, a break out of the labyrinth of critical theory? In pursuing these questions, I want to begin with a parallel phenomenon in popular culture: the rise of the male heroine. What is the sudden cultural appeal of serious female impersonation?

Acting as a Woman: Dustin Hoffman and Making *Tootsie*

> *"One of the things about being a man in this society is giving away as little as possible,"* Mr. Hoffman notes. *"Part of manhood is not to be taken advantage of. Poker is a masculine sport, where the whole thing is bluff and knowing where someone's vulnerability is so you can attack and try to take something away from them"*

> —*"Tootsie Taught Dustin Hoffman About the Sexes,"* New York Times, *December 1982.*

The 1980s' fascination with cross-dressing, manifested in such recent and popular plays and films as *La Cage Aux Folles*, *Torch Song Trilogy*, *The World According to Garp*, *Victor/Victoria*, *Cloud 9* and especially *Tootsie*, is symptomatic of a fin-de-siècle ambiance in which sex-roles are under attack, and gender anxieties take a variety of cultural forms. The parallels with the nineteenth century are striking. In the 1880s and the 1980s, New Women, homosexuals, and sexual radicals symbolized the apocalypse to Victorian patriarchs, and warnings of epidemic syphilitic infection convinced frightened conservatives that racial degeneration or extinction was at hand. Yet the androgyne became a compelling figure in theater and art; themes of cross-dressing began to appear in popular fiction and feminist fantasies; and some advance novelists of the period (including Gissing, Hardy, and Wells) imagined a better social order beyond what Gissing called "sexual anarchy." In the 1980s, as Reaganism tries to demolish every legislative and social advance of the women's movement, and as epidemics of herpes and AIDS convince the Moral Majority that God is punishing the perverted, the promiscuous, and the depraved, we are seeing ludicrous, panicked reactions to the erosion of gender distinctions. In 'La Différence," for example, a last ditch Op-Ed polemic in the *New York Times* against the admission of women to the Century Club in Manhattan, Lewis Lapham insists that only Nature's "dynamic symmetries" of masculine and feminine keep us from chaos: "The clarity of gender makes possible the human dialectic. Let the lines of balanced tension go slack and the structure dissolves into the ooze of androgyny and narcissism." This could be straight from the 1890s, an echo of its urbane diatribes against feminist "erotics, neurotics and Tommy-rotics."

Yet the immense popularity of *Tootsie*, and the reverently received Hollywood hype about gender meanings that accompanied it, indicates the contemporary mass appeal of the androgynous ooze, and also of the narcissism of sexual introspection. American audiences took very seriously the questions that *Tootsie*'s several makers raised in interviews about the film: "What does it mean to be a man? What does it mean to be a woman? What would a given individual be like if he or she were to change gender?"

Dustin Hoffman's motivations received especially close media attention and praise, often from feminist film critics. According to Susan Dworkin, in her book *Making Tootsie*, Hoffman and his producer Sydney Pollack located the film in the "sexually political atmosphere" of the 1980s, and described its origins in "the ferment of feminist awakening." Even before Pollack signed on as director-producer, Hoffman had been earnestly researching feminist theory; in July 1981 I saw him several times in London sitting attentively in the audience at avant-garde feminist plays (two were on George Eliot and Virginia Woolf), presented in the dark attics or dank basements of small lunchtime theaters. Hoffman's motivations, according to Dworkin, were more personal than political. In playing Dorothy Michaels, he was "not looking for the truth about women. He was looking for the woman in himself."

American film critics seem to have accepted this; Molly Haskell, for instance, calls Dorothy "the first genuinely mainstream feminist heroine of our era." I should make clear, however, that to my mind, *Tootsie* is not a feminist film. In England, where the drag act is one of the last preserves of a virulent misogyny, the minstrel show of sexist culture, film critics were skeptical of *Tootsie*, seeing the buxom Dorothy as a familiar caricature, and the film's pretensions to raised consciousness as insulting to women. Insofar as *Tootsie* is a commentary on the women's movement, teaching women how to stand up for their rights, it borrows what little politics it has from *Nine to Five*, even using the same actor, Dabney Coleman, to play the male chauvinist boss. It says more, I think, about Dustin Hoffman's sense of the actor's career—its passivity, its vulnerability, and physical exposure—as feminine. The woman in Hoffman is the rejected actor; as Dworkin notes, "the insecurity of the actor, who knows what it's like to wait by the phone for twenty years, parallels the insecurity of the woman who is less than pretty, who has waited by a few silent phones herself."

At the same time, to act as a woman means access to a kind of biological stardom or supremacy. "There's a lot about being a woman that I've always felt robbed about," Hoffman told a reporter. "I can't carry children; I can't bear children. I can't breastfeed. When it comes to all that, I've always felt like a stagehand." In *Kramer vs. Kramer*, Hoffman took centerstage as the parent, getting Meryl Streep offscreen fast to demonstrate that he could be a better mother than a woman could. In one of the original takes for the courtroom scene in this film, Hoffman improvised his own dialogue about the child: "I'm his *mother*! He didn't come out of my vagina, but I'm his mother!" (Molly Haskell has called the films in which women are cast out or killed in order to make room for Daddy in his new role as male mother, "male weepies.") For Hoffman, maternity seems to be the essential attribute of feminine completion; the most positive (real) woman in *Tootsie*, Jessica Lange's Julie, has a baby, and Hoffman has joked in interviews that in a sequel to Tootsie he too will give birth.

The actor's need to be a star is also at variance with some of Hoffman's views of the character of Dorothy Michaels. For him, she is not only childless, but a homely sexual loser. "This character makes me cry," he told Gene Siskel of the *Chicago Tribune*. "She doesn't have a man. She never got married. She never had kids. And it hurts me 'cause she's not pretty." The pain of identifying with this feminine marginality and frustration, according to the press releases about the film, humanized both Michael Dorsey and Dustin Hoffman, and taught them both how to be better men. The crudeness of Hoffman's criteria of feminine success is amply revealed in his remarks; but oddly enough, the film never *shows* Dorothy Michaels as a lonely and unattractive woman who is rejected by men. The two men in her age group both pursue her hotly; she has more sexual invitations than she can accept. Whereas in nineteenth-century feminist literature cross-dressing is the redressing of an emotional debt owed to women, and dressing like a woman is the hero's penitential and instructive immersion in humility, impotence, and subordination, Michael Dorsey is a male failure who becomes a female success. Playing Dorothy is an ego trip.

This success comes primarily, the film suggests, from the masculine power disguised and veiled by the feminine costume. Physical gestures of masculinity provide *Tootsie's* comic motif of female impersonation. Dorothy Michaels drops her voice to call a taxi, lifts heavy suitcases, and shoves a hefty competitor out of the way. Dorothy's "feminist" speeches too are less a response to the oppression of women than an instinctive situational male reaction to being treated like a woman. The implication is that women must be taught by men how to win their rights.

In this respect, *Tootsie's* cross-dressing is a way of promoting the notion of masculine power while masking it. In psychoanalytic theory, the male transvestite is not a powerless man; according to psychiatrist Robert Stoller, in *Sex and Gender*, he is a "phallic woman" who can tell himself that "he is, or with practice will become, a better woman than a biological female if he chooses to do so." When it is safe or necessary, the transverstite "gets great pleasure in revealing that he is a male-woman . . . The pleasure in tricking the unsuspecting into thinking he is a woman, and then revealing his maleness (e.g., by suddenly dropping his voice) is not so much erotic as it is proof that there is such a thing as a woman with a penis." Dorothy's effectiveness is the literal equivalent of speaking softly and carrying a big stick.

Acting as a woman, therefore, is not necessarily a tribute to the feminine. If, however, the female impersonation of *Tootsie* often seems to be part of a masculine sport of knowing where people are vulnerable so you can then try to take something away from them, the film winningly and finally mocks and deflates this characteristic in itself. As Hoffman/Dorsey, drunk with success, fantasizes playing Medea, Blanche DuBois, and Eleanor Roosevelt, his agent reminds him that he has nothing to say to women. *Tootsie* does, in fact, have a message for women, although not the one the filmmakers intended. It says that feminist ideas are much less threatening when they come from a man.

Reading as a Woman: Jonathan Culler and the Deconstruction of Feminist Criticism

It's a quantum leap from the flamboyant self-promotion of *Tootsie* to Jonathan Culler's account of the theoretical issues of women's reading in *On Deconstruction*. If the seriousness of a book is in inverse relation to the figuration of the cover, the white jacket of *On Deconstruction*, adorned only with the title, and three small lines, is the peak of minimalist prestige. Scrupulous, lucid, and tough-minded, *On Deconstruction* not only clarifies debates within feminist criticism, but moves the arguments a step ahead. Culler takes feminism seriously as a political ideology and a critical practice, describing it as "one of the most powerful forms of renovation in contemporary criticism." He takes to task "self-styled historians of criticism and critical theory" who have left feminist criticsm out of history; and he is one of the few critics under discussion here who gives detailed and knowledgeable references to feminist texts, instead of vague well-meaning gestures in the direction of *Signs*.

The alliance of feminism and deconstruction is not new; male theorists such as Derrida and Lacan have for some time used woman as the wild card, the joker in the pack who upsets the logocentric and phallocentric stack of appellations, and a number of brilliant young feminist critics, including Jane Gallop, Nancy Miller, Peggy Kamuf, Gayatri Spivak, and Margaret Homans, have made common cause with deconstructionist theory. But Culler's analysis cuts two ways. First he uses deconstructive techniques to demonstrate some difficulties in the feminist appeal to the woman reader's experience, an experience and an identity which is always constructed rather than given. Second, he uses feminist criticism to give deconstruction a body, to link its philosophical abstractions to specific literary and political choices. Feminist critics confront, on immediately practical terms, many of the issues deconstruction defines. Where Derrida insists that hierarchical oppositions (such as man/woman) must be deconstructed through reversal rather than denial, feminist critics must put this principle into action, must choose whether to ally themselves with the reformist position of sexual equality, which denies difference, or with the radical position which asserts the difference, the power and the superiority of the feminine. Their position on the specificity of women's writing, their critical style and voice, will be determined by this choice. Culler recognizes that both positions are valid, although as a Derridean he prefers the rhetorical reversal. Most feminist critics, in fact, play both ends against the middle, advocating social, academic, institutional equality, but textual difference. These positions are not oppositional, but responsive to women's different roles as citizens or as writers.

Feminist criticism also poses in dramatic and concrete terms the poststructuralist concern with the reader's experience as constitutive of the text. While reader-response criticism in general proposes a reading self or an informed reader who produces textual meaning, it prefers not to discuss the nature of the reader in specifically human terms. But as Culler observes, feminist criticism "has a considerable stake in the question of the relation of the reading self and the experience of the reader to other moments of the self and other aspects of experience." The question of the *woman* reader brings this relation forward, and "issues often swept under the carpet by male stories of reading are brought into the open in the debates and divisions of feminist criticism."

In tracing out feminist approaches to "reading as a woman," Culler sees three modes or stages. In the first, the critic appeals to female experience as a source of authority on female characters, on values, and on phallocentric assumptions. Yet, he points out, the "nature" of woman is a social construct, so "to ask of woman to read as a woman is in fact a double or divided request. It appeals to the condition of being a woman as if it were a given and simultaneously urges that this condition be created or achieved." In its second phase, feminist criticism confronts the reasons why women often read as men do, given their indoctrination by male literary and critical values. While identification with male experience may, as Dorothy Dinnerstein has argued in *The Mermaid and the Minotaur*, be the widespread result of nurturing arrangements which lead both sexes to reject and resent the female mother on whom they are initially dependent, it is reinforced and intensified in the case of academic women by their professional training and their prolonged immersion in patriarchal institutions. Reading as a woman thus becomes a willed project of unlearning, a resistance to what Judith Fetterley has called "immasculation." In this mode, the hypothesis of a woman reader, rather than a call upon female experience, serves to expose the misreadings, distortions and omissions of phallic criticism.

Culler sees the third mode of feminist criticism as the investigation of the "ways our notions of the rational are tied to or are in complicity with the interests of the male." This investigation includes the French feminist attack upon phallogocentrism and the interrogation of current critical assumptions. Its task is to "develop critical modes in which the concepts that are products of male authority are inscribed within a larger textual system." More theoretical than the other two, this third phase is still nevertheless linked to female experience, Culler argues, through its stress on maternal thematics and marginality. He concludes that "reading as a woman" is always a paradoxical act, in that the identity as "Woman" must always be deferred: "For a woman to read as a woman is not to repeat an identity or an experience that is given but to play a role she constructs with reference to her identity as a woman, which is also a construct, so that the series can continue: a woman reading as a woman reading as a woman."

But can a *man* read as a woman? Culler does not ask what might

happen when a man attempts to produce a feminist reading, a situation in which the construction of the reader's gender identity is
foregrounded. He does not present himself as a feminist critic, but
rather as an analyst of feminist critical work. For the most part, Culler
places himself outside of, although sympathetic to, feminist reading.
Yet in two instances, he does offer his own feminist readings of texts,
and these raise interesting questions as to whether a male feminist
is in fact a man reading as a woman reading as a woman.

Near the beginning of the section on feminist criticism, Culler comments on Geoffrey Hartman's observation in *The Fate of Reading* that
"much reading is indeed like girl-watching, a simple expense of
spirit," explaining that "the experience of reading seems to be that
of a man (a heart-man?) for whom girl-watching is the model of an
expense of spirit in a waste of shame. When we posit a woman reader,
the result is an analogous appeal to experience; not to the experience
of girl-watching, but to the experience of being watched, seen as a
'girl', restricted marginalized." Here Culler invokes the woman
reader as a preamble to his inversion of Hartman's text.

By the end of his excursus on "Reading as a Woman," Culler has
abandoned the hypothesis of a woman reader and produces his own
rhetorically unmediated reading of Freud's *Moses and Monotheism*.
Freud, he points out, links the development of speech, the Mosaic
prohibition of material images of God and the turn from a matriarchal
to a patriarchal social order, and treats the result as an advance to a
more symbolic and thus higher stage of intellectuality. In doing this,
says Culler, Freud is really promoting the elevation of the paternal
principle which values the invisibility and the symbolic nature of its
own relation with the child. Culler proceeds from this argument to
speculate on the relation between the "promotion of the paternal"
and the likely concerns of literary criticism in a patriarchal culture:
(1) the conception of the author's role as paternal and the assimilation
of any valued maternal function to paternity; (2) the investment in
paternal authors; (3) the obsession with the legitimacy of meaning
and with the prevention of illegitimate interpretations.

I would argue that what Culler has done here is to read consciously
from his own gender experience, with an ironic sense of its own
ideological bounds. That is to say that he has not read as a *woman*,
but as a man and a feminist. Indeed, Culler's deconstructionist priorities lead him to overstate the essentialist dilemma of defining the
woman reader, when in most cases what is intended and implied is
a *feminist* reader. Reading as a feminist, I hasten to add, is not unproblematic; but it has the important aspect of offering male readers
a way to produce feminist criticism that avoids female impersonation.
The way into feminist criticism, for the male theorist, must involve

a confrontation with what might be implied by reading as a man and with a questioning or a surrender of paternal privileges.

Writing as a Woman: Terry Eagleton and the Rape of Feminist Theory

But when male theorists borrow the language of feminist criticism without a willingness to explore the masculinist bias of their own reading system, we get a phallic "feminist" criticism that competes with women instead of breaking out of patriarchal bounds. Terry Eagleton's *The Rape of Clarissa: Writing, Sexuality, and Class Struggle in Samuel Richardson* (1982) brings together three "revolutionary" reading strategies: feminist criticism, historical materialism, and poststructuralist textualism. Although Eagleton refuses to give priority to any of these methods (indeed the copyright page of the American edition states that "The University of Minnesota Press is an equal opportunity educator and employer," as if to guarantee the constitutional equality of ideas as well), the aggressive title and the erotic cover of *The Rape of Clarissa* (Fragonard's *Le Verrou*) certainly foreground the sexual issues. Eagleton also acknowledges the centrality of the feminist revolution in his text when he declares that "if Richardson may once again become readable, it will be in large measure because of the women's movement."

Eagleton presents the book as a bold incursion into several alien territories, and it is meant to have the dash and daring of a highwayman's attack. First, it is a foray into psychoanalysis, a "terrain," he notes, "which the English have always found a little unnerving." Second, it is an invasion of the eighteenth century, "long the preserve of literary conservatism, rarely penetrated by Marxist criticism." And finally, it is a raid of feminist criticism, in order to claim overdue recognition for *Clarissa* as "the major feminist text of the language." Richardson, according to Eagleton, was the most "gifted and popular ideologue" of the eighteenth-century exaltation of the "feminine," and *Clarissa* is "the true history of women's oppression at the hands of eighteenth-century patriarchy." Like his "eighteenth century," Eagleton's "feminist criticism" is another well-barricaded preserve to be penetrated by the daring Marxist Macheath. Obviously more is at stake than the recuperation of Richardson.

Clues to precisely what *is* at stake may be deciphered in the textual strategies Eagleton employs, the "hermeneutic violence" he deploys in the name of revolutionary criticism. He is very good at exposing the sexism of those critics who have been of Lovelace's party: Dorothy

Van Ghent, V.S. Pritchett, and especially William Beatty Warner, who reads the rape as Lovelace's clever way of deconstructing Clarissa. But Eagleton's own reading sees Clarissa, in her apparently infinite accessibility to interpretation, as the Lacanian "transcendental signifier"—the phallus itself. It is her phallic power that the anxiety-ridden Lovelace really craves: "Lovelace must possess Clarissa so that he may reunite himself with the lost phallus, and unmask her as reassuringly 'castrated'."

What then, we ask, is Lovelace so anxious about? In part, Eagleton suggests, he is anxious about writing, about the appropriation of a womanly, or at any rate, an unmanly act. "What is worrying about Lovelace," according to Eagleton, "is that for a man he spends too much time writing." If the letter, in the eighteenth-century context, is associated with the feminine entrance into literature, and, more generally, with the expression of those concerns for the individual and for the emotional that Eagleton also describes as part of the bourgeois "feminization of discourse," then the scribbling Lovelace may be less than virile. And on a different level, the written word in fiction seems to share the metaphoric properties of the feminine. As Eagleton asserts, "The problem of writing is in this sense the problem of the woman: how is she to be at once decorous and spontaneous, translucently candid yet subdued to social pressure? Writing, like woman, marks a frontier between public and private, at once agonized outpouring and prudent strategem."

The allegory here of "Writing as a woman" seems forced, especially when we recognize that what is being described is neither female anxiety of authorship, such as Sandra Gilbert and Susan Gubar analyze in *The Madwoman in the Attic*, nor the dilemma of Clarissa herself as correspondent and narrator. Instead it is the male gender anxiety of the character, the novelist, and ultimately the Marxist critic, who fears that his writing (rather than revolutionary action) is effeminate. By possessing feminist criticism, so to speak, Eagleton effectively recuperates for himself its "phallic" signifying power. In his synthesis of feminism, Marxism and poststructuralism, Eagleton also intermingles (or ignores) critics, so that there is no sense of a background of feminist readings of Clarissa against which his reading defines itself. This may be the inadvertent result of haste, or an aspect of English critical style, but it also suggests a disconcerting insensitivity to the politics of acknowledgment.

What happens if we contrast Terry Eagleton's reading of *Clarissa* to another feminist reading by a woman? Like Eagleton, Terry Castle, in *Clarissa's Ciphers*, locates her reading in an intersection of feminism, deconstruction, and politics. Like him too she deplores the Lovelacean bias of Warner and Van Ghent, and sees Lovelace as infantile and banal. But unlike Eagleton, Castle sees Clarissa as the *victim* of "hermeneutic violence" practiced against women. Interrupted, "shut up," censored, silenced, violated, Clarissa's powers of expression, her access to language and to literary modes of production are severely constrained, while her oppressors' rights to language go unquestioned. Despite her eloquence, Clarissa's rhetoric is powerless because it is not grounded in the political authority and force that backs up the patriarchal discourse of Lovelace and the Harlowes. In the "black transaction" of the rape, *Clarissa* as novel inevitably tends to polarize its male and female readers, encouraging us to "examine the ways in which the gender of the reader (along with the resulting differences in socialization and *power*) may condition the meanings he or she finds in the text." In particular, Castle argues, the female/ feminist reader responds to the silences in *Clarissa* and these correspond to the silences in the cultural history of women. The rape is the ultimate silencing, and a form of "hermeneutic intimidation" for Clarissa's efforts to define her own nature.

Terry Eagleton describes *Sir Charles Grandison* as Richardson's effort to appreciate the "tide of feminization" for patriarchy, to produce a new kind of hero who would combine Clarissa's feminine virtues— tenderness, feeling, goodness, chastity—with masculine power and effectiveness. The effort failed, however, because without the reality of female powerlessness and dependency behind it, goodness seemed priggish, chastity pointless, and tenderness merely effeminate. Thus Grandison's unreality indicates "a genuine ideological dilemma." If Eagleton had gone one step further, to consider his own ideological dilemma, *The Rape of Clarissa* would have been a more important book for feminist critics. Energetic, entertaining, and inventive though it be, Eagleton's phallic feminism seems like another raid on the resources of the feminine in order to modernize male dominance. We are led back to the politics of *Tootsie*—the appropriation of the tide of feminist feeling in the interests of patriarchy, the production of a new kind of (critical) hero. Whereas Terry Castle, breaking hermeneutic silence by reading and writing as a woman, testifies to the increased power of women to define their own nature, and builds her case on the work of such feminist critics of *Clarissa* as Nancy Miller, Janet Todd, Rachel Brownstein, Judith Wilt, and Margaret Doody, the effect of Eagleton's text is to silence or marginalize feminist criticism by speaking for it, and to use feminist language to reinforce the continued dominance of a male literary canon.

As Eagleton points out with reference to Sir Charles Grandison, the "genuinely progressive drive to generalize the discourse of femininity to men, exposes, in the very thinness of the text, an insurmountable sexual difference." In critical terms, as Larry Lipking disarmingly concedes in his essay "Aristotle's Sisters," sexual difference begins with "a fact that few male theorists have ever had to confront:

the possibility of never having been empowered to speak." As women understand it, the problem of writing as a woman is initially one of overcoming fear. Eagleton notices that the people around Clarissa would prefer her *not* to write, that Mrs. Harlowe, for example, would prefer her daughter to read—that is, "to conform herself to another's text rather than to produce her own meanings." Like other kinds of criticism, feminist criticism is both reading and writing, both the interpretation of a text and the independent production of meaning. It is through the autonomous act of writing, and the confrontation with the anxiety that it generates, that feminist critics have developed theories of women's writing, theories proved on our own pulses. What I chiefly miss in *The Rape of Clarissa* is any sign from Eagleton that there is something equivocal and personal in his own polemic, some anxiety of authorship that is related to his own cultural position.

It has to be added, nevertheless, that in his latest book, *Literary Theory: An Introduction*, where he is no longer scolding feminist criticism for its separatist tendencies and lack of theoretical rigor (as he does in his book on Benjamin), or speaking for it (as he does in *The Rape of Clarissa*) for his own interpretative ends, Eagleton is persuasive, pungent and self-aware. At his best—and *Literary Theory* is his best—Eagleton is a persuasive analyst of literary culture, and his clearheaded account of the mutual goals—yet mutual independence—of socialist and feminist criticism makes this book immensely valuable. If in *The Rape of Clarissa* Eagleton's use of feminist crticism is self-interested, here he accords it a full measure of autonomy and respect. One senses in this book that feminist ideas have penetrated Eagleton's reading system everywhere, and that, along with Marxist aesthetics, they inform his entire account of the development of contemporary critical discourse.

Looking for the Woman: Demons, Diacritics, and the Woman of the Year

Mercedes Kellogg, at table with Raquel Welch, who wore a bow tie, wing collar and tuxedo: "What does it mean when the 'Woman of the Year' dresses like a man?"

John Duka, New York Times, *December 1982*

To a considerable degree, recent debates within feminist criticism about the importance of gender in the production of the feminist text have made space for male theorists like Eagleton, Culler, Booth, and Scholes to enter the field. Nina Auerbach's *Woman and the Demon: The Life of a Victorian Myth* challenges the feminist critical commonplace that literary sterotypes of women (such as the angel in the house, the victim, the queen, the witch, the old maid, and the fallen woman) are male mystifications, reducing and dehumanizing women. Properly understood, she argues, these figures are paradigms, or better, myths of ascendant womanhood. George MacDonald's malevolent Lilith, Rossetti's monumental "stunners," Dickens's expiring angels, all testify to female grandeur and to the woman-worship of an age losing its religious faith. In textual terms, then, male writers and artists inscribed "subversive paradigms of a divine and demonic female power at the cultural center of Victorian patriarchy and chivalry." Auerbach's analysis turns conventional interpretation on its head: although she does not exactly claim that Dickens, Rossetti, and Thackeray are feminist writers, she explains that their work is part of a Victorian "feminism" so "pervasive—in the broad power of this many-faceted myth of a mobile presiding woman—that the word has lost its meaning." Certainly, for Auerbach's purposes, there is no point in distinguishing between male and female purveyors of the myth.

Within French/deconstructionist feminist criticism, these issues take a different and even more enabling form for male critics. First of all, after the decentering of the human subject, and the alleged disappearance or death of the author, "the question of whether a 'man' or a 'woman' wrote a text," as Alice Jardine explains, "becomes non-sensical." Second, for French theorists, *"l'écriture féminine,"* or women's writing, stands for a style, not a signature. Writing is feminine when it is open-ended, playful, avant-garde, audacious, non-linear; *l'écriture féminine* can as well be signed by a man as by a woman.

In recent years, in fact, it has been necessary for American feminist critics to argue in behalf of our special commitment to women's writing as a historical and social category. The material conditions and contexts of women's writing have to be repeatedly stressed, because the patriarchal literary canon has a centripetal force and a social power that pulls discussion towards its center; women's writing gets left out unless feminist criticism insists that historically speaking, the question of whether a man or a woman wrote a text is of primary importance. Reviewing the first wave of male feminist criticism, one notes that it nearly all "happens" to be about texts signed by men: Rabelais, Richardson, Hemingway, Lawrence. As Culler predicts, patriarchal criticism tends to disclose whatever it values in the maternal by assimilating it to the paternal function. Unless male feminist critics become more aware of the ways they too have been constituted as readers and writers by gender systems, their books may continue to be written for men and in behalf of male literary traditions.

Without closing the door on male feminists, I think that Franco-American theory has gone much too far in discounting the importance of signature and gender in authorship. The male author occupies a different literary place; the author of an *écriture féministe* needs to consider his or her own cultural circumstance. The movement away from the historical specificity of gender is hinted in the cover of the *Diacritics* special issue of summer 1982, titled "Cherchez La Femme: Feminist Critique/Feminine Text." On a white background is a figure in a black tuxedo and high heels, resting one knee on a bentwood chair à la Marlene Dietrich. The figure has no head or hands. On the back cover, a dress, hat, gloves, and shoes arrange themselves in a graceful bodiless tableau in space. No "vulgar" feminist, the chic Diacritical covergirl hints at the ephemera of gender identities, of gender signatures.

There is an interview with Derrida in this issue of *Diacritics*, but all the other contributors are women, as are the editors. Yet I am haunted by the ambiguity of that cover. Sometimes I have a dream of the feminist literary conference of the future. The demonic woman rises to speak, but she mutates before our eyes into a mermaid, a vampire, a column of fire. The diacritical woman rises to speak, but she has no head. Holding out the empty sleeves of her fashionable jacket, she beckons to the third panelist. He rises swiftly and commands the podium. He is forceful; he is articulate; he is talking about Heidegger or Derrida or Lévi-Strauss or Brecht. He is wearing a dress.

14.
Response
TERRY EAGLETON

In seeking to address these issues not in the first place abstractly or theoretically (thus risking one form of appropriation), but in terms of my own experience, I shall inevitably appropriate the issues into that experience by way of an—unavoidably falsifying—allegory, one which if it succeeds in its task of cautiously elucidating a certain partial parallelism will do so only at the expense of suppressing a certain difference, a move which may well render the entire piece redundant, which may be no bad thing.

In the early 1960s I went from a working-class North-of-England background to Cambridge, at a time when the university was even more male- and upper class-dominated than it is today. I found myself one of a dismally miniscule group of proletarian students, besieged by gun-toting aristocrats like some exotic endangered species. My roommate, a Cockney, was hauled in by his Tutor and asked why he dressed like a garage mechanic. All the young men around us (there were hardly any young women) seemed chinless, well over six foot, and brayed rather than spoke. They all seemed to be called Jeremy or Alisdair, stamped their feet in cinemas and elbowed the Cambridge townspeople off the narrow pavements. We plebeians clung defensively together, cracking bitter jokes about the arrogance of the English ruling class and flamboyantly drinking the most socially disreputable beer we could find.

The group we *really* couldn't stand, however, were the English public school socialists. With Conservatives you knew where you were; what really spooked us was to discover a minority of chinless braying Jeremies who actually spoke our own political language, quoted *Capital* in languid tones and ran the university Labour club. None of them had ever clapped eyes on a row of back-to-back houses, but they were genuine in their socialist views and interested in learning about our own very different social experience. We spent a lot of time huddled in pubs venting our spleen upon them. Who the bloody hell did they think they were, claiming our cause for themselves? They didn't have any *experience* of being working class: they were just full of a lot of highfalutin phrases they had picked up in books alongside their public school Virgil, oedipally on the run from their city director fathers. We mocked their Brideshead accents in private and were severe with them in public, scrutinizing their socialist credentials for the least flicker of ideological impurity. We made them feel bungling, inept, wet behind the ears, second-class socialists. We spent most of our time working out our justifiable aggression on them, not on the real enemy. They needed us, so as to be able to boast back home of working-class friends; but we needed them too, to be gloriously reinforced in our unsullied proletarian essence.

Most of my Cambridge working-class friends are now Tories, social democrats, or political cynics. Because their politics were so closely bound to an intense, bitter personal experience, they couldn't survive the changes brought about by later middle-class affluence. Most of the public-school Marxists, by contrast, are still on the Left, some of them doing substantial radical work. Their politics were also of course bound by inversion to personal experience: they weren't just being altruistic. But the connections were more complex and oblique, and in certain ways, though not in others, there had never been much in it personally for them to become socialists. On the whole their commitment came through in later life, surviving our adolescent jeers.

Looking back on this gloomy experience, I now think I can see what was most wrong about our sectarianism. It wasn't only its tedious self-righteousness—its unreflective fear of the troublingly uncategorizable other/ally. It was the bland assumption that we could ever really afford to be that choosy. It was the unexamined belief that in a world groaning in agony, where radicals of any sort are hardly thick on the ground, we had time, leisure, and allies enough to sit comfortably loose to the bungling, well-intentioned Alisdairs. We watched them setting their faltering feet on the lowest rungs of the ladder, making all the inevitable mistakes of tone and style; and having climbed that ladder securely ourselves, we turned round and kicked it casually away.

The history of the Labour Party in Britain is littered with smooth-talking ambitious men who climbed to power on the backs of working men and women, took over their language, claimed empathy with their sufferings, and then proceeded to sell them out. The recurrent mistake of working people was to be generous-hearted enough to trust these opportunists—allow them to speak in their name, be grateful for allies from elsewhere, believe that support from any quarter was better than none. Working people were advised to drop their sectarian prejudices, sink their differences in some fetish of unity and recognise that left-talking middle-class politicians were really on their side. With impressive good will, the working class listened to this advice and allowed itself to be hijacked by a bunch of patronizing well-wishers who mouthed socialist sentiments while running country houses and buying an expensive private education for their children. When the heat was on, these men (along with a few women) turned the judiciary, and occasionally the troops, on the working men and women who had trusted them as allies.

I still think that we were wrong to have been so self-righteous. Yet of course we were not.

15.
Elaine Showalter
Replies

I'll trade a story with Terry Eagleton. In a recent study of male-female interaction in conversation, Pamela Fishman discovered that men dominated, both by ignoring topics introduced by the women, and by developing topics that they had initiated themselves. As Fishman comments: "We have seen that, at least among intimates in their homes, women raise many more topics than men. They do so because their topics often fail. They fail because the men don't work interactionally to develop them, whereas the women usually do work at developing topics raised by men. Thus the definition of what are appropriate or inapproriate topics for a conversation is the man's choice. . . . Men control topics as much, if not more, by veto as by a positive effort."[1]

Could this possibly have any bearings on the question of men and feminist discourse? Terry Eagleton's "response" invites two possible interpretations:

1) He has not read "Critical Cross-Dressing" and has produced an all-purpose response to what he imagines feminist critics feel about male feminism.

2) He has read "Critical Cross-Dressing" and has decided not to respond to any of the topics it introduces, but rather to change the grounds of discussion by initiating a narrative of his own.

In either case, I don't see the point of continuing a one-sided dialog, and I will leave the story of Terry and Jeremy for others to consider.

16.

Man on Feminism: A Criticism of His Own

NANCY K. MILLER

Tell them to read our books
Tell them what we do.
Tell them we don't do what they think we do.
Tell them why they think we do what we don't
really do.

—*Anon., in Sandra M. Gilbert,*
"What do Feminist Critics Want?"

Deconstruction is a style of accusation.

—*Denis Donoghue, "Deconstructing Deconstruction"*

Midway through his brief survey of "feminist criticism and scholarship," of which, he assures the reader—but what reader?—he has been reading "a good deal," Denis Donoghue wonders: "Am I really guilty of the allegedly phallocentric enforcement of meaning in discourse? When did I commit the crime?" Framed in such aggressively disingenuous terms, it is as hard for a feminist critic—Irigarayan or not—to indict the man as to let him off the hook of incredulity. Of course no "particular man" is uniquely responsible for the global power effects of the dominant discourse, but yes Denis, since you ask, you are "really guilty"; in every line of this article of yours, beginning with the cheap shot of its title; you're doing it now in the flamboyant bad faith of your rhetoric. Throughout the essay, Donoghue's language is inhabited by a metaphorics of the Law: crime

---

For the reader's convenience the article by Denis Donoghue to which Nancy Miller refers is reprinted below. Donoghue's article purports to be a review of the following books: Sandra Gilbert & Susan Gubar eds., The Norton Anthology of Literature by Women: The Tradition in English *(New York: Norton, 1985); Nina Auerbach,* Romantic Imprisonment: Women and Other Glorified Outcasts *(New York: Columbia Univ. Press, 1986); Carroll Smith-Rosenberg,* Disorderly Conduct: Visions of Gender in Victorian America *(New York: Knopf, 1985); Elaine Showalter ed.,* The New Feminist Criticism: Essays on Women, Literature, and Theory *(New York: Pantheon, 1985).*

and punishment, guilt and innocence, enforcement and entitlement, rights and wrongs. In fact, it is the constant recourse to this language, the preferred codes of phallogocentrism itself, and the mode of enunciation borrowing its gestures from the grandiloquent flourishes of the courtroom that make Donoghue guilty as charged. But who is on trial here, and why? What guilt, whose crimes are being rehearsed?

What is Donoghue after in a piece subtitled "feminism's agenda in literary studies"? He explains that he wanted to see what's been happening in feminist criticism since the publication of *Sexual Politics* in 1970. Unfazed by the vast amount of reading such a task generates—that comes with the territory: "Who can keep up with anything these days?"—the man admits to being perplexed by a more elusive quantity: "The difficulty, rather, is to determine what the present context of feeling is." Why is it necessary for the man to take the measure of women's feelings? Donoghue's move to cast feminist criticism as a matter of *feeling*, rather than intellectual debate will prove to be both crucial to the shape of the essay and symptomatic of its animating pathology. (He thus takes *Sexual Politics* as *origin*—as opposed to say, Mary Ellmann's *Thinking About Women* or Ellen Moers's *Literary Women*—because of the "sentiments and passions" it provoked.) The decision to understand the context of feminist thinking as a climate of emotion—angry ones, as it will shortly emerge—sets the stage for the trivialization and domestication of feminist scholarship Donoghue orchestrates in the rest of the piece and in which the challenge to epistemology that underwrites feminist literary studies takes on the simplicities of melodrama, when it's not cat fights.

The field report begins in the profession's mainstream with findings from the MLA's Annual Report for 1984 of the American Literature Section; Annette Kolodny's remarks about the impact of recent scholarship on canon-formation, to the effect that "in the wake of all the new information . . . all prior literary histories are rendered partial, inadequate, and obsolete." Donoghue doesn't comment immediately or directly on Kolodny's discourse—one is to draw one's own conclusions about the present context from such statements— but waits to accumulate evidence, which he finds in the very same document: Marianne De Koven's claim that according to an "official [Hugh Kenner's?] version," modernism is "a revolted flight, by means of the 'fabulously artificed', Dedalian wings of male technology, from the primary horror of female (pro)creativity." Donoghue wonders whether the "sentiments" expressed here are a valid indication of the context, or a fluke, a quirky excess: "some bizarre hyperbole," a "willed turbulence worked up for the occasion." Are the women really angry (as in really guilty) or are they just getting carried away by the sound of their own voice: is this a "real fury in the words" (a fake rage like a faked orgasm)?

We thus come rather quickly to Donoghue's central thematics, a recurrent set of descriptive concerns we could perhaps think of as a poetics of anger: female rage on the one hand; the state of literary studies on the other. But as if the implications of that conjuncture (Athena and Derrida) were too abstract—too academic, perhaps—for his (sensible, implied, *New Republic*) reader, Donoghue takes care to ground his case with what he calls a "tangible episode" from the pages of *The New York Times Book Review*. To bring home his point, he picks Gail Godwin's review of the Sandra M. Gilbert and Susan Gubar *Norton Anthology of Literature by Women*.[1] Donaghue is attracted to the publication of the review as an "especially significant" episode ostensibly because this gives him a chance to show what is at stake in feminist literary history. What turns out to be more tangible here, however, is not so much the terms of the review and the content of the replies it generated (summarized in a single sentence), but what he will describe as an "interesting moment of telegrams and anger" (I read the promotion of letters into telegrams a "bizarre hyperbole" on Donoghue's part). Thus, in a classically p.e.m. (phallocentric enforcement of meaning) move, Donoghue plays the women off each other. In this performance, which will culminate at the end of the essay in an invocation of the Furies (and their domesticated incarnation at the end of the trilogy as Eumenides) of the *Oresteia*, Donoghue's preference (to mix tragedies for a moment) is for Cordelia, the good daughter, not Clytemnestra, the woman in revolt. Godwin's account of the *Norton*, he writes, "was quietly severe." In her mournful concern (empathy almost) for the fate of women writers wrongly (and wrongfully) collected together in the anthology, Godwin "silently appealed" to other grounds for inclusion, those, for example, "generally accepted in literary criticism." Despite the reasonableness of these criteria of excellence, feminist critics were angered by her judgment (sent telegrams?), and "accused her" (more trials).

Donoghue spends several paragraphs defending Godwin's position on the anthology by displaying his *own* belief in those undefined but generally-agreed-upon-by-teachers-of-literature "criteria of critical discrimination" as opposed to the editors' "political and sociological" thematic obsessions. He thus uses the woman to put the man's problem on the table. The context of feeling once again proves to be the monster in the man on feminism's mirror: the Norton editors have turned their back on literature in order to assemble "documentary evidence to support a case against men—or against the world."

There is no transition from the account of the Norton as a brief against men to the rehashing of a very particular piece of what is typically known as "French feminist" theory identified, amazingly, as a larger of *the* "two agendas" of feminist criticism. The first agenda, in this topology, is the theoretical one; the second and smaller one—

a "matter of politics and sociology"—has to do with the practical
realities of institutional life (women's studies courses, for example).
(The anger of the women and the question of literary merit have only
been bracketed, however.)

Like me, many feminists will be startled to learn that they look for
their larger sense of purpose to Jacques Derrida's "several polemics
culminating in *Eperons*." The fact that Derrida's work is named in
French has its internal figural importance: it authorizes the vulgar-
izer's account of the material; and it proves that if the reader finds
this continental stuff rough going, it is not a problem of translation.
Before explicating Derrida's seminal role in the big picture of feminist
criticism, however, Donoghue attaches two women's names to the
Derridean hegemony, albeit in subordinated clauses: Luce Irigaray,
author of *Speculum* and *This Sex Which Isn't One* (again, titles are given
in French); and Gayatri Chakravorty Spivak as the author of "Derridean essays." But adding women's names to the master's in no way
mitigates the outrageousness, nor redeems the impoverished wit of
consigning to the ambiguous fluency of Derrida's zones the attempts
feminists have made—since Woolf—to theorize woman's place in
language and the question of female subjectivity. On the contrary.
Indeed, if Donoghue is truly at a loss to know when exactly he might
have committed the crime of p.e.m. he need look no further. It is not
without a little irony that the crime whould locate itself around the
questions of origins and authorization. Since Donoghue gets more
excited by the targets of his own polemic than the difficulty of analyzing the feminist enterprise, he doesn't bother to take the time to
unpack the complex relations between Irigaray's "agenda" and Derrida's; not to mention the place these critics occupy in France, and
have within feminist criticism; or the place (marginal) of "continental"
theory within the U. S. feminist scene. Thus, for example, to stay
with the books ostensibly under discussion—*The Norton, Romantic
Imprisonment, Disorderly Conduct, The New Feminist Criticism* (these are
grouped within an inserted box as though this were a review essay)—
for none of the critics in these books and collections is Derrida's position on writing and subjectivity an informing or authorizing one;
nor, for that matter, is Irigaray's.[2]

There are two points to be made here. The first, as I have just said,
concerns the lurid representation of feminist critical theory as mas-
sively Derridean. Donoghue fails to address and doesn't seem to get
what relation might obtain between Derrida and U. S. feminism and
how it might have come about (this is in fact a complicated and interesting subject); nor does he make or get the connection (and more
important still, the disjunction) between the feminist project of the
Norton, and the feminist project of, say, Spivak's pointed critique of
Spurs (in "The Double Displacement"). The second is really a more

speculative question: to what extent is Donoghue's attack on feminism as bad literary criticism, and feminism as the theory of phallogocentrism not about feminism at all, but instead an attack on "Deconstruction" and a political criticism in the name of common sense; a retro view of literature and its readers speciously supported in his parting shot by a humanist appropriation of Bakhtin's notion of dialogism? For instance, when Donoghue concludes his dismissal of Irigaray's claims ("complaint" in his lexicon) he caps the evaluation by calling it revisionist, and by that logic places her work under the umbrella of Deconstruction, which for Donoghue is "an old quarrel by now."[3]

This looks to me very much like a struggle between men in which the woman's function is the classical position of mediator: her body—the body of her criticism will do—keeps the men together and apart on a continuum of rivalry and identification. The fight between the girls leaves the Daddies to their old struggles over ownership of the discourse. This is part of why we so often feel in presence of the Law. Thus, unlike the men "who profess to be ashamed of possessing" the attributes of "phallogocentric power," Donoghue carries on with the arrogance of the old regime.

Confident that nothing is new in the big picture, Donoghue takes on the second, smaller, "tangible" story (with "tangible" we return to the more accessible zones of comprehension, like *The New York Times*). Here no quotations or masters are required. Donoghue lays it on the line: "Women want a bigger slice of the cake, but not a transfigured cake." About women and cakes. Here we arrive at the fatal flaw in Donoghue's understanding—it is, indeed, we must see, his understanding that is at stake—of the link between politics and epistemology that makes feminism neither deconstruction, nor yuppism (the ladder of success). From a feminist perspective the question of the cake is posed differently. Thus, for example, in the case of women's literature and the canon: the point, as the homily goes in feminist circles: the point, very precisely, is *not* to "add a woman and stir." This recipe, we know, does not result in a "transfigured cake," but the same old dessert, served last, in the same old order. (What woman would want *those* calories?) Of course women want "a bigger slice," a redistribution in the economy that would result in something resembling equity, for instance.

Contrary to what Donoghue may have "gathered," these demands have neither been "universally accepted," nor granted. Yes, there are feminist series at several major university presses, journals, conferences, and women's studies programs. But again, contrary to what Donoghue imagines (fears?) these accomplishments, which are real enough and hard won, thus far only *add to* the existent institutional arrangements. Put another way, feminist criticism is not about more of the same. It is about the imagination of difference that does not break down into two agendas, but opens onto a complicated map of contiguities. At stake is not, then, for feminists a "change of disposition," a matter, as Donoghue puts it, of observing the proprieties that would, for example, pay lip service to the notion of a female subjectivity by referring (occasionally) to the readers as "she," but a radical revision and restructuring of the study of literature; something indeed resembling a transfiguration on the order of what Donoghue calls a "change of heart." At stake in the field of feminist criticism is an analysis (which is not a matter of feelings, or sentiments, hearts or furies) that challenges not only the exclusion of women writers from the canon, but the criteria that underwrite and regulate the formation of the canon itself. This is also to say the very notion of literature and its place in the anthologies and institutions that house it; the pronouns of subjectivity and the organization of knowledge; power and the transmission of cultural values.

As far as the canon goes, Donoghue is not on the face of it opposed to the recovery of neglected works and writers. Indeed, to have drawn attention to such writers and writings is, as the man puts it, "the most obvious merit of feminist criticism" (also the only one he lights on). But even here problems arise for him. The critics who deal with these works either fail to raise the question of their "literary merit"; or fail to raise it with sufficient critical savoir-faire. Thus, Donoghue finds feminist criticism in the main reductive, even "insultingly reductive"; and "so far as critical theory arises, regressive." Given Donoghue's well-published antitheory position, his touchstones here of old masters known by their power initials (like the old-school tie)— L. C. Knights, D. W. Harding—and his characterization of Nina Auerbach's readings as "lurid," it is a little hard to know exactly what standard is being evoked here. But if there is nothing new, and what tries to be new is naive and reductive, these complaints are side issues to the main course, which is that of "literary merit."

A bit like the ladies in the Groucho Marx joke who complain that the food is bad and that they get such small portions of it, Donoghue's gripe is that on the whole feminists don't face "the issue of merit and value," but when they do, the argument, he writes, "is desperate." This is of course the flip side of Donoghue's struggle with the master of Deconstruction. In this moment of the essay what we see writ large are Donoghue's beliefs about literature, critical theory, and institutional arrangements. More pointedly, since the word does not seem to be on his agenda, he displays his unexamined relation to *ideology*, both as an operative category of analysis and as a self-conscious agenda item for feminist theory. The man can only sigh in exasperation: "We are to believe that literary criteria are incorrigibly manmade values, and are compromised by the power they enforce." The problem of enforcement returns; this is definitely a law and order man. Trading incredulities, I will confess to being at somewhat of a loss to understand in what sense this "argument" is "desperate." Why yes, Denis, we really believe that literary criteria are man-made. What else might they be? Divine? (Is there a paradigm I'm missing here? man-made as opposed to genuine leather? or does he mean man-made vs. woman-made?)[4] Or is this just a matter of the (unexamined) notions of literature teachers who "have a general sense of critical discrimination, like a passport; they don't carry it around, but they could produce it if they had to."

Curiously, in his quest for a good argument about the important issues he finds an ally in the person of Lillian Robinson, whose essay earns some of Donoghue's rare praise: "one of the best . . . in *The New Feminist Criticism.*" I hasten to add that I too admire the Robinson essay; I'm just puzzled by his use of it.[5] Donoghue cites at length Robinson's argument that it is not enough to insist upon the representation of women writers within curricula that claim to represent the canon; it is also essential to question the construction of the canon itself: is it a "compendium of excellence" or is it "the record of cultural history"? True. The whole debate rides on the answer institutions historically have made to that question. Now as I read the Robinson essay, replacing the passage Donoghue excerpts in the context of its own argument, and the body of her work as a cultural critic, there is, I think, no way to understand Robinson's point as the *acceptance* as a valid alternative of "the (unexamined) name of excellence." Donoghue tries to tune out the implications of the parenthesis in his characterization of it as "the only swipe in that passage" (she writes like a gentleman?) But the thrust of the ( ) is not so easily bracketed, for it comes to underscore an analysis by the more "desperate" feminist critics of the *values* (including merit) that inform the male mainstream tradition; and the ways in which the very question of women's writing as an interrogation of the institution of literature "alters our view of the tradition" (Robinson). To return to Donoghue's metaphors, the ineffable but legitimately *literary* criteria he thinks he finds evoked in Robinson's piece, like the produceable passport, are instead about the *man-made* values and concerns, tradition, and institution he has so much trouble with elsewhere. What I'm saying here is that Donoghue can only assimilate Robinson to his position by taking this piece of her argument out of its contexts of feeling, away from its central political alignments. Robinson's ( ) is the trope in punctuation of Donoghue's romance with ideology.

So where does that leave us in the field of literary studies?[6] Donoghue can't see "anything happening" with Irigaray; Auerbach is not persuasive and repeats (nonfeminist) commonplaces; feminist critics of women's literature have "matronized their writers" (confirmed for

Donoghue by Brigid Brophy in the *TLS*; nice to have women do it for you). But Donoghue is not done yet. He has not yet reached the turn in his essay that requires the rhetoric of a parting shot and a peroration about what might yet be. Too clever to call for a return to the old new critical traditions, he plays instead the much fetishized card of "critical theory" that his feminist critics resolutely fail, it seems, to play. Donoghue piously invokes the name of Bakhtin. Against the "plurality of consciousnesses, with equal rights and each with its own world" that Bakhtin finds in Dostoyevsky, Donoghue sees feminist critics as denying "women writers dialogic imagination." Feminist criticism, Donoghue declares, "consigns women to their fate, and recognizes them only when they transcribe their fatality." With the dialogic in place as the ultimate in Continental passports, Donoghue feels free to condemn all feminist critics with total conviction. The judgment begins with "it is evident" and includes not merely the much lamented selection of the *Norton* anthology. One might also wish to return the judgment: it is his own involvement in the world of monologic values that blinds him to the plurality of consciousnesses at work in the worlds of feminist criticism.

Donoghue's final remarks about the "smaller agenda" are equally, if differently, sweeping in their dismissiveness. These demands, we learn, are "well in hand." But this is not to suggest that Donoghue has anything but scorn for their claims. Or rather, the anger that is thematized in his opening moves as a characterization of feminist discourse returns here both as description and as the unsaid motor of his own sovereign position; his identification with what for academics must pass for the royal "we": "Our institutions know how to deal with its demands, reducing the number of telegrams and appeasing the anger." (Earlier he had wondered aloud; and he gets in a last swipe in closing: "What is to be done to placate Irigaray?")

Donoghue, we recall, began his trip into the land of feminist criticism by saying it was "an attempt to see what has been happening." It seems to me that what we get is less the travel diary of an explorer than the notes of an angry man, much like the "Professor von X." that Woolf sketches in *A Room of One's Own*, working away in the Library on the "truth about W.": "His expression suggested that he was labouring under some emotion that made him jab his pen on the paper as if he were killing some noxious insect as he wrote, but even when he had killed it that did not satisfy him; he must go on killing it; and even so, some cause for anger and irritation remained" (31). When Professor Donoghue sets out to discover whether there's "a real fury in the words, or a willed turbulence worked up for the occasion," it seems to me that he has misplaced the question, a bit like Oedipus: the anger he tracks turns out to be his own. How could he be guilty of enforcing meaning in discourse phallocentrically? In the establishment of the two agendas; making one the larger, the other the smaller; locating the grounds of the larger within the precincts of Jacques Derrida; dismissing the demands of both: what else could this be an example of? Let us return, in closing, to the status of Donoghue's agendas. As I said earlier, feminist criticism does not have two separate agendas. In U. S. academic circles—since it is crucial to locate these issues in their contexts—theory and practice function dialogically (*pace* Bakhtin). The question of "the feminine" (Derrida's question, which may or may not have anything to do with women: Donoghue should reread Spivak); of woman's positioning in language—Irigaray's; of womens' experience; of women's writing; the canon; curricula; institutions; journals; conferences; hiring; firing; these all exist and interact *on a continuum.* Nor is feminist criticism the monologic space Donoghue makes it out to be: not all of feminist criticism is represented in *The New Feminist Criticism; The Norton* accounts for *a* tradition.

One is tempted to provide Professor Donoghue with a bibliography; a list of works that could broaden his horizon; complicate the picture.[7] But that would no doubt supply the angry professor with more material to jab at with his pen. In the epigraph to this piece I excerpted some lines from an essay of Sandra Gilbert's subtitled, "A Postcard from the Volcano," originally presented as a talk to the Association of Departments on English in 1980. In it feminist colleagues make suggestions about what to tell *them,* the male colleagues like Donoghue out there unheeding in the pages of their criticism and the exclusionary clubs of establishment scholarship. Six years later one has to wonder about the urgency of "them" reading "us," if the result is the sustained (Oedipal?) blindness to feminist insight and the "willed turbulence worked up for the occasion": telegrams and anger.

Earlier, in his muddle about Irigaray, Donoghue puzzles over the "status . . . in feminist rhetoric" of the argument (presumably Irigaray's) that "woman should keep to their own company, pursuing the possibilities of sisterhood and planning eventually to make a separatist difference."[8] What I think becomes vividly clear in Donoghue's open letter to his colleagues, those readers and teachers of literature who participate in the gentleman's agreement to know what makes for a good poem, but not tell, is that the notion of a "separatist difference" (the tip of homophobic anxiety always lurking in these rehearsals of identity) is in fact a man's preference for the company he has learned to keep. What Donoghue says over and over again is his desire for nothing to change, for the indifference of Literature. This is a dangerous nostalgia, and to use the man's own words, the argument is "desperate."

A Criticism of One's Own
Denis Donoghue

I have been reading a good deal of feminist criticism and scholarship. Not all of it—I am sure to have missed many books and essays I should have read. But I have made an attempt to see what has been happening in feminist criticism since 1970, when Kate Millett's *Sexual Politics*, the book usually taken as having started the feminist field by provoking sentiments and passions in its favor, was published. The main problem I have encountered is not the multiplicity of books and essays in the field. That is merely a quantitative matter, endemic in every area of scholarship: Who can keep up with anything these days? The difficulty, rather, is to determine what the present context of feeling is.

The annual report for 1984 of the American Literature Section of the Modern Language Association, for instance—but is it an "instance," and of what?—includes Annette Kolodny's claim that "in the wake of all the new information about the literary production of women, Blacks, Native Americans, ethnic minorities, and gays and lesbians; and with new ways of analyzing popular fiction, non-canonical genres and working-class writings, all prior literary histories are rendered partial, inadequate, and obsolete." In the same report, compiled by Donald Yannella, Professor Marianne De Koven evidently holds "that women have the same claim as men to having 'invented' modernism in America," and cites as evidence three fictions by women: Charlotte Perkins Gilman's "The Yellow Wallpaper" (1891), Kate Chopin's *The Awakening* (1899), and Gertrude Stein's *Three Lives* (1903–6). She also claims that there is "an official version of modernism," as in Hugh Kenner's *A Homemade World*, which defines it (these are De Koven's words, not Kenner's) as "a revolted flight, by means of the 'fabulously artificed,' Dedalian wings of male technology, from the primary horror of female (pro)creativity." I'm not sure whether these sentiments, which seem wild to me, accurately indicate the context of feminist criticism or some bizarre hyperbole; a real fury in the words, or willed turbulence worked up for the occasion.

But there are some tangible episodes, one of which is especially significant. On April 28, 1985, the novelist Gail Godwin reviewed the new *Norton Anthology of Literature by Women* for the *New York Times Book Review*. Her account of the book was quietly severe. She disapproved of the editors' "stated desire to document and connect female literary experience rather than present a showcase of the most distinguished writing by women in English from Julian of Norwich in the fourteenth century to the present day." *The Norton Anthology*, she maintained, forced "the individual female talent to lie on the Procrustean fainting-couch of a 'dis-eased' tradition."

Godwin's review angered several well-known feminist critics, including Elaine Showalter, Alicia Ostriker, Carolyn Heilbrun, Nina Auerbach, Myra Jehlen, Nancy K. Miller, and Catharine R. Stimpson. They accused her of "denying the existence of a female literary tradition" (Ostriker). In her reply, Godwin went a step further than her review: she "mourned the authors who were slighted in the *Anthology* by having their most trivial or least representative works selected because these works helped the editors establish a sisterhood of themes and images they felt ran through most women's writing."

It was an interesting moment of telegrams and anger, but the critical issue was not well defined. Godwin made it clear that she wanted to see in a *Norton Anthology of Literature by Women* an ample selection of the best writing by women writers, to demonstrate once if not for all that women have written well and continue to write well. The criteria she silently appealed to were those generally accepted in literary criticism; criteria by which it is agreed, for instance, that Yeats's "Among School Children" is a much better poem than his "The Lake Isle of Innisfree." But she failed to make clear that the criteria adopted by the Norton editors in this anthology are not critical at all. They are political and sociological. The literary merit of the items chosen is not a major consideration for the editors. They are concerned to document the range of experience—and the resultant constraints and anxieties—peculiar to women. George Eliot's minor poem "Brother and Sister" was chosen because "it explores the same sibling relationship she had placed at the center of her semi-autobiographical *The Mill on the Floss*." It is evident that "explores" in that sentence suppresses every critical or qualitative consideration; it sets aside the questions of crucial concern to literary criticism in favor of documentary value and thematic relevance.

If literary criticism were to have its way, *The Norton Anthology of Literature by Women* would be a textbook in sociology rather than in literature. But literary criticism has so often failed to define its way, so often failed to know what its way is, that one more failure won't amount to a scandal. It is common practice for courses in literature to roam into considerations of history, nationality, theology and indeed sociology. Courses on "the English Novel" are rarely confined to a strict account of forms and genres. But teachers keep their consciences reasonably clear by choosing the best novels; or at least the novels that seem to be the best, according to the criteria of critical discrimination. True, these criteria are rarely defined, and teachers often rely upon a conventional or habitual notion of their deliverances. I suppose most teachers have a general sense of critical discrimination, like a passport; they don't carry it around, but they could produce it if they had to.

But the distinctive mark of the *Norton Anthology* is that it does not even pretend to select its material according to the criteria of literary criticism. Just as historians and sociologists choose their documents without reference to literary merit, the Norton editors have assembled documentary evidence to support a case against men—or against the world. The fact that some of the items chosen are also works of literary merit is a coincidence, however congenial. The *Anthology* would make a good textbook in a course in sociology called "Women and Their Fate." It is flagrantly misleading as a selection of literature by women.

It is my understanding that feminist criticism has two agendas. The first is the larger one: it can be found in Jacques Derrida's several polemics culminating in his *Éperons: Les Styles de Nietzsche*; in Luce Irigaray's *Speculum de l'autre femme* (1974) and *Ce Sexe qui n'en est pas un* (1977); and nearer home, in the Derridean essays by Gayatri Chakravorty Spivak and other critics. The agenda says that there is no discourse but masculine discourse, that women are trapped in a syntax that is phallocratic and phallogocentric. As a result, women are condemned either to adopt the masculine discourse that leaves them essentially unexpressed, or to engage in a masquerade by which they mime the masculine syntax and take upon themselves, speciously of course, the signs of presence and power. It is the fate of women, therefore, to gratify their masters. The paradigm of this fate is the faked orgasm.

I allude to this agenda so far as I can understand it. Many feminists would claim that by physiological definition I can't understand it. So I quote a passage from *Ce Sexe qui n'en est pas un* to let Irigaray speak in her own words, though it is crucial to the agenda that no woman has her own words. I give the passage in English, but the French to me is just as opaque:

> I am a woman. I am being sexualized as feminine. I am sexu-
> alized female. The motivation of my work lies in the impossi-
> bility of articulating such a statement; in the fact that its utterance
> is in some ways senseless, inappropriate, indecent. Either be-
> cause *woman* is never the attribute of the verb *to be* nor *sexualized*
> *female* a quality of *being*, or because *am a woman* is not predicated
> of *I*, or because *I am sexualized* excludes the feminine gender. In
> other words, the articulation of the reality of my sex is impossible
> in discourse, and for a structural eidetic reason. My sex is re-
> moved, at least as the property of a subject, from the predicative
> mechanism that assures discursive coherence. I can thus speak
> intelligently as a sexualized male (whether I recognize this or
> not) or as asexualized. Otherwise, I shall succumb to the illog-
> icality that is proverbially attributed to women. All the state-
> ments I make are thus either borrowed from a model that leaves
> my sex aside . . . or else my utterances are unintelligible ac-
> cording to the code in force.

Now, virtually every modern writer has claimed that the words available to him or to her are somehow wrong. It could be argued that Irigaray has said what she wants to say not only in words but "in other words." Or that men don't feel themselves released from what T. S. Eliot called the "intol-erable wrestle with words." But even if we grant—who are the "we" who grant?—that Irigaray's complaint is valid, it is not clear what the same "we" can do to satisfy it, or even to mitigate it. The agenda amounts to an im-putation of Original Sin, except that the official Original Sin was ascribed to the whole human race and this one is confined to men.

The charge is so omnivorous, moreover, that no particular man need feel intimidated by it. It reminds me of Hannah Arendt's account of "the banality of evil," an accusation so grand that it left every individual free to go about his or her business. Am I really guilty of the allegedly phallogocentric en-forcement of meaning in discourse? When did I commit the crime? Besides, if a new discourse were to be devised, vaginacentric rather than phallogo-centric, a "fault" would remain, wouldn't it? And presumably the whole revisionist process would have to be undertaken again, this time in favor of men. (To be fair to Derrida, he wouldn't want a mere change of center, the Mother displacing the Father; he wants to dislodge every center by an endless play of signifiers.)

So what is to be done to placate Irigaray? The gestures that several critics have made seem to me further examples of patronage. If Jonathan Culler, Terry Eagleton, and Fredric Jameson refer to the reader as "she" rather than the conventional "he," what purpose is served? I have no answer. I have read several essays that argue that women should keep to their own com-pany, pursuing the possibilities of sisterhood and planning eventually to make a separatist difference. But I don't know the status of this suggestion in feminist rhetoric as a whole.

It may be the case that the first agenda is strictly women's work, and that the best a man can do is keep out of their way. Irigaray is determined to ensure that speech about women is not to be taken as "a recuperation of the feminine within a logic that maintains it in repression, censorship, non-recognition." I'm not sure what she means, unless she thinks that recuperation would only be yet another instance of repressive tolerance (Marcuse's phrase), the strategy by which a man's world expands to make room for women and merrily proceeds upon its powerful way. To prevent this from happening, Irigaray proposes, as she says, to jam the theoretical machinery. Instead of trying to construct a logic of the feminine that would still take the "ontotheologic" of masculine discourse as its model, she would aim to disrupt every discourse.

I assume she sees her work as the Luddite phase of feminism. But she also sees herself, more conventionally, as revising Freud's phallocratic psychoanalysis, a job already in the hands of Karen Horney, Melanie Klein, Marie Bonaparte, and other critics. In America, the most "reasonable" place for such revisionists is in Deconstruction, which undertakes to reveal discourse as the sovereign predicate of the Father. Presumably this project satisfies not only women who resent phallogocentric power, but men who profess to be ashamed of possessing it. The fact that the project seems to me largely specious, and indeed "in bad faith," is an old quarrel by now.

The second agenda of feminist criticism is smaller, and far more tangible. Women want a bigger slice of the cake, but not a transfigured cake. In practice, this entails readier access to publishers, fellowships, and grants; affirmative action in their favor in the professions; more space and time at the M.L.A. conventions; steadier promotion in the universities; more magazines devoted to feminist issues; women's studies in the curriculum of universities and colleges. The demands on this agenda are now, I gather, universally accepted. They have been implicit in feminist sentiment since Mary Wollstonecraft's *A Vindication of the Rights of Women* (1792) and Margaret Fuller's *Women in the Nineteenth Century* (1855), their motto Fuller's: "Let them be sea-captains, if you will." Or rather: "if they will."

Immense progress has been made on the second agenda. There are dozens of magazines given over entirely to women. Columbia University Press has announced the publication of a new series of books on "gender and culture." The editors are Carolyn Heilbrun and Nancy K. Miller, and the first batch includes Nina Auerbach's *Romantic Imprisonment* and Naomi Schor's *Breaking the Chain: Women, Theory and French Realist Fiction*. Discourse may still be as Irigaray describes it, but it has not reduced women to silence or to forms of expression that are self-evidently frustrating.

The most obvious merit of feminist criticism is that it has drawn attention to writers and writings that have been neglected. The Norton Anthology prints, complete, Chopin's *The Awakening*, Toni Morrison's *The Bluest Eye*, and (hardly a neglected work) *Jane Eyre*. Other feminist essays make strong cases for Rebecca Harding Davis's *Life in the Iron Mills* and Alice James's *Diary*. (It wouldn't worry me, by the way, if I were asked to pay just as much attention to Alice's diary as to her brother Henry's *Notes of a Son and Brother*.)

But the question of literary merit, as distinct from sociological interest, is rarely raised by feminist critics. When it is, the argument is desperate. We are to believe that literary criteria are incorrigibly man-made values, and are

compromised by the power they enforce. Lillian S. Robinson at least faces
the issue of merit and value in one of the best essays in *The New Feminist
Criticism:*

> Is the canon and hence the syllabus based on it to be regarded
> as the compendium of excellence or as the record of cultural
> history? For there comes a point when the proponent of making
> the canon recognize the achievement of both sexes has to put
> up or shut up; either a given woman writer is good enough to
> replace some male writer on the prescribed reading list, or she
> is not. If she is not, then either she should replace him anyway,
> in the name of telling the truth about the culture, or she should
> not, in the (unexamined) name of excellence . . . It is ironic that
> in American literature, where attacks on the male tradition have
> been most bitter and the reclamation of women writers so spec-
> tacular, the appeal has still been only to pluralism, generosity
> and guilt. It is populism with the politics of populism.

The only swipe in that passage is the reference to "the (unexamined) name
of excellence." The alternative to pluralism is the examined name of excellence; anything less is disgraceful. As for her last sentence, the appeal she
refers to is populism without the name of populism—that is, sociology. But
Robinson is right. If a feminist critic wants to dislodge a male writer and
install a woman writer in his place in the curriculum, she should make a case
for her on literary grounds that she would herself choose and expound; or
insist on installing her anyway, as Robinson says, "in the name of telling the
truth about the culture." But she should not fudge the issue.

It is also a distinct merit that feminist critics and scholars are compelling
attention to forgotten or ignored moments in the past. Carroll Smith-Rosenberg's *Disorderly Conduct* is exemplary in this regard. Its theme is "the nature
and the origins of the separate world of nineteenth-century women." Smith-
Rosenberg's methods are taken mainly from anthropology (Mary Douglas,
Victor Turner) and semiology (Roland Barthes). Her documentary materials
are gathered for the light they cast upon mothers and daughters, friendship
between women, marriage, menstruation, menopause, the New Woman, androgyny, the New York Moral Reform Society, prostitution, women of the
Second Great Awakening, the American Medical Association and its attitude
toward abortion. I can't imagine that an American historian would have studied these moments and issues with such concentration if a context of feminist
criticism were not already available to take account of them.

But the context sometimes produces lurid results. Nina Auerbach could
have written her essays on nineteenth-century fiction and poetry even if an
official feminism had never existed. But she would not have pressed or
pushed her perceptions if extreme feminist motives had not claimed her al-
legiance. I don't find anything distinctively feminist in her account of the
separation of the sexes in *Dombey and Son,* but this passage from her essay
on the Brownings has the feminist ring to it:

> Having survived a poet who made epic claims for herself, Robert
> Browning perpetuated her voice by turning it into his own; he

"married" Elizabeth Barrett one more time when he appropriated her after her death, weaving her declarations into the cor-
rosive fabric of his dramatic monologues. According to Irvine
and Homan, she had found from the first something sinister in
his ability to read her: "She had been frightened of him at first.
She felt he had a power over her, that he could read her thoughts
as he might read a newspaper." This initial ability to read Elizabeth ripened into an ability to write her and finally, with love
and reverence, to silence her.

I don't find this persuasive. The paradigm seems to have preceded the
need of it; it has an air of applied romance. The springs of Browning's poetry
are to be sought in his relation to Shelley in particular, and to several other
voices offering him a poetic strategy. Elizabeth's voice was one of those, but
a minor one. The feminist drama of a man's possession, co-option and final,
loving suppression of a woman seems to have provoked Auerbach into finding it exemplified, however implausibly, in Robert and Elizabeth.
    Auerbach also seems to me to claim as distinctively feminist perceptions
notions that in fact have long been commonplace. Her essays on Jane Austen,
for instance, don't amount to a radical revision of the standard sense of Austen's novels that has been current since D. W. Harding published, many years
ago, an essay called "Regulated Hatred," in which he argued that Austen's
artistic problem was to find a form and a style that would enable her to settle
her account with a society she in great part hated.
    "The task of feminist critics," according to Elaine Showalter, "is to find a
new language, a new way of reading that can integrate our intelligence and
our experience, our reason and our suffering, our skepticism and our vision."
The task "should not be confined to women," though she confines it to
women in *The New Feminist Criticism*. Studying "woman as reader," she calls
for a feminist critique, "a historically grounded inquiry that probes the ideological assumptions of literary phenomena." For "woman as writer," Showalter proposes a "gynocriticism" that concerns itself with "the psychodyn-
amics of female creativity; linguistics and the problem of a female language;
the trajectory of the individual or collective female literary career; literary
history; and of course, studies of particular writers and works."
    That sounds like a full day's work. In practice, however, feminist critics
have much reduced the range of their literary interests. Many of their essays
are, so far as critical theory arises, regressive. I have read feminist essays that
study the characterization of Emilia in *Othello* as if L. C. Knights had not
shown the penury of such questions fifty years ago (in his famous essay "How
Many Children Had Lady Macbeth?"). Was Jane Austen opposed to marriage? Did she dislike children? What did she think of motherhood? Did
Shakespeare restrict women to a narrow range of emotions? Did Yeats pa-
tronize Maud Gonne and other women? These are wretched questions, even
if they are excused as marking a primitive stage in the development of a more
interesting feminist criticism.
    Indeed, feminist criticism seems at its present stage to me to be a libel
upon women. The questions it asks are insultingly reductive. The situation
is very odd: feminist critics are selling their literature short while promoting
it at every turn. Promotion belongs to the history of advertising, but not less
to the history (with its drifts and turns) of political sentiment. Where women
should beware women—that is, where women writers should refuse the em-

brace of feminist critics—is in their implication that a woman writer can only transcribe the experience she has been given, and cannot imagine experience other than her own. Feminist critics have matronized their writers; they have set them a list of themes, motifs, and situations amounting to one physiologically ordained predicament, and told them that it is their destiny to annotate it. A woman writer is supposed to be merely an amanuensis of her fate. For her, there is one story and one story only.

So I was pleased when Brigid Brophy protested, in the *Times Literary Supplement* on July 26, 1985, that many feminist critics forget that there are writers "whose imagination is fired by what they have not experienced. Shakespeares who create *Romeo and Juliet* out of not visiting Verona and *Antony and Cleopatra* out of never setting eyes on the Nile." If feminist critics libel women, they also, in the same reductive spirit, deny the imagination.

Specifically, they deny women the imaginative power that Bakhtin calls "dialogic." His distinction between monologic and dialogic imagination is one of the most valued references in contemporary criticism. The writer with monologic vision insists that every thought gravitates to him as a sign of his power, a power he exerts unremittingly throughout his composition, controlling every ostensibly different point of view. The dialogic vision projects "a plurality of independent and unmerged voices and consciousnesses, a genuine polyphony of fully valid voices." What occurs (Bakhtin takes Dostoyevsky as his example) "is not a multitude of characters and fates in a single objective world, illuminated by a single authorial consciousness; rather a plurality of consciousnesses, with equal rights and each with its own world, combine but are not merged in the unity of the event." It is evident that feminist criticism denies women writers dialogic imagination; it consigns women to their fate, and recognizes them only when they transcribe their fatality.

What now? The smaller agenda is well in hand. Since it presents itself as a matter of politics and sociology, our institutions know how to deal with its demands, reducing the number of telegrams and appeasing the anger. Women's studies are a new area of growth in university departments, and welcome mainly for that reason. At the end of the *Oresteia*, the avenging Furies have been transformed into the benign Eumenides, a change of disposition that authorities can indeed bring about by observing the propriety of discourse. Nothing as fundamental as a change of heart is required. As for Luce Irigaray and the large agenda: I can't seen anything happening there. A change of heart wouldn't be enough to effect the transfiguration she demands.

17.
Men, Feminism: The Materiality of Discourse

CARY NELSON

If I am to begin at all, I must begin by trying to say why I find the topic of this book, men in feminism, to be such a wretched and intractable one. As I start to write, I feel that the topic asks me to articulate and identify with a gendered vantage point, to make masculinity the primary ground of my voice. Since I generally agree with feminism's critiques of the cultural construction of masculinity—its alienation from emotional and physical life, its obsession with falsely objectified forms of knowledge, its idealization of models of culture based on hierarchy and dominance—the vantage point seems at best unsavory. Moreover, the topic appears to fix—by way of a unitary gender—relationships that are plurally and unstably constituted and immensely contextual. To be a man in feminism can mean simply a man reading a feminist book, an activity that holds no special self-consciousness for me. Or it can mean a man writing about/within/ without feminism, an activity that entails all the anxieties of writing in general, some contextual and singular, but, again, none radically problematic for me. Feminism is part of my social and intellectual life, has been so for many years, and so, to the extent that writing is ever "natural," it is natural that I write about feminism. But writing about "men in feminism" seems a regressive move. At the same time, there are many material contexts in which my own personal history has no bearing on my role or how I will be received. At a National Women's Studies Association meeting, as the only man in some of the smaller sessions, there are moments when I feel awkward, unwelcome, or invisible; superfluous would perhaps be the more accurate reading of my actual status, a status, however, that does not in fact prevent me from enjoying the meeting. On the other hand, at a feminist session at the Modern Language Association I am simply a member of a mixed audience. At a Feminist Scholarship Interest Group meeting at the 1985 International Communications Association I was again the only man; there, unexpectedly, I was, I felt, too generously welcomed. Finally, there are feminist events that men, especially sympathetic men, should have the sense not to attend. We must not, it seems to me, lose sight of these material, social, and institutional moments; we must not imagine that the topic of "men in feminism" is one altogether resolvable in the scene of writing alone.

Thus, although I find it very useful for Andrew Ross, in "No Question of Silence," to remind us that men intersect with feminism not only discursively but also "in the workplace, bar, or, *pace* Godard, in the bedroom," I find his strict separation between *"theoretical men"* and *"men-in-practice,"* despite the charm of these italicized categories, to be a serious practical *and* theoretical error. Interestingly, in "Demonstrating Sexual Difference" he works very hard to overcome that division, rather dramatically pointing out the very real social consequences of a static and oppositional construction of sexual difference, but in "No Question of Silence" he feels placed on the defensive and the division is affirmed again; that he relegates discussion of "men-in-practice" to a few sentences merely confirms the traditional hierarchism of this split. As I write about men and feminism now, I cannot help but think of a series of socially constituted engagements with feminism:

1. Early in 1986, my department, considering offering a senior position to a feminist, was presented with a summary of reviews of her books. We were informed (by a person *advocating* her appointment) that reviews from feminist journals had been omitted "since they would all automatically be positive." Thus we were urged to appoint a feminist at the same time as feminism itself was marked as non-scholarly, uncritical, and illegitimate. It would have been counterproductive to take issue with this unacceptable double message during the meeting (though I did afterwards), since the important thing was to support the appointment. But the claim about feminist reviewing was simply inaccurate. In the early days of the contemporary feminist movement, there was a political and intellectual need for reviewers to emphasize advocacy, but feminist reviewing has been as critical as any other kind since about 1975, the year, as it happens, that *Signs* was founded.

2. At an academic meeting in 1983, two men were offering formal responses to a paper just presented by a woman, her paper having nothing to do with feminism. The first man opened his remarks by apologizing for looking like he was "participating in a gang bang." Several people expressed their outrage at his vulgar sexism. He was shocked and affronted, feeling that he had been displaying his sensitivity to feminist issues. In fact, his response to feminism seemed to have had mainly the effect of bringing his own violent sense of sexual difference to the surface.

3. Anyone who has attended a meeting of the Modern Language Association in the past decade or taken note of what books are being published will be aware that feminism is perhaps the single most vital area of the intellectual life of literary academics. But there is a great distance between those active in publishing and the large majority of humanities and social science college teachers, among whom resistance to and ignorance about feminism remains widespread. Concrete examples of this kind of disjunction between the world of scholarship or intellectual debate and the daily life in a university department abound: 1986—a department is considering opening a search for an assistant professor specializing in feminism. "Does a traditional discipline really need a feminist?" asks a senior scholar, "Shouldn't such a person be appointed in Women's Studies?" 1985—a feminist faculty member is up for tenure. The department decides not to write to other feminists for letters of evaluation. Feminists, the only people fully knowledgeable about feminism, are considered not to be objective. 1985—a graduate student struggles to get approval to teach a course in lesbian writing, a subject some faculty members simply assume is wholly inappropriate for a college course. Whenever we move from our reading and writing to negotiating these kinds of problems, our illusions about "the state of theory" are brutally readjusted.

4. At several conferences in the mid-1980s I was struck by the difficulties both men and women have in presenting themselves as feminist speakers. A man delivers a paper on feminism in a soft, hushed voice, his shoulders curved inward; he makes every effort to diminish his physical presence and make his style unassertive. In the question period, however, he is challenged several times and his voice and bodily posture become distinctly more aggressive. At another conference, a woman is presenting a paper on feminism. She invites the audience to dismantle her patriarchal authority as a speaker by interrupting her with questions and requests to expand on other related issues. The audience soon obliges, but she becomes annoyed at being interrupted and asks that they delay these requests until the question period. The institutionalized power of a structure that honors the *subject supposed to know* is sometimes stronger than our efforts to overthrow it.

I offer these four paragraphs as characteristic examples of the current complex, contradictory social inscription of feminist theory. They are not simply narratives about traditional sexism, since they represent instances of feminism's special reception in daily life.[1] The stories in these paragraphs suggest, respectively: the disjunctions between what can now become the relative straightforwardness of an intellectual commitment to feminism and the compromising politics of university life; the libidinally driven articulation of gender differences in purportedly academic settings; the often deluded sense of the state of theory produced by the narrow framing of the social terrain in which we do our intellectual work; the uncanny ways in which traditionally male academic practices can return to haunt us even as we try to disavow them. These are the kinds of contradictions lived every day by feminist critics. No theorizing of "men in feminism" can be adequate if it does not think these contexts and integrate them into its argument.

Nor is any theorizing of feminism adequate without some positioning of the person who is doing the theorizing. So, feminism has been part of my life, though not all of it, since the early 1970s; its importance to me and my commitment to it have both changed and grown steadily since then, though some of its lessons, indeed, have taken me many years to learn. In the late 1970s I began to write about feminist topics, teach feminist texts, and attend feminist conferences. More importantly, the woman I live with has been involved with feminist organizing and feminist scholarship for many years. I cannot therefore easily place myself *in* feminism in any unitary way. My connections with it are by now too many and too various. But finally, as I read my personal connections in the light of those traversing both universities and the society at large, I have to readjust my perspective. Despite the effects of attacks from the political Right, despite the incomprehension of many of my colleagues, feminism's strength as a movement demonstrates that it can go its own diverse and transformative way without, for now, troubling itself about its relations with men. I cannot think of an obvious topic lower on the list of feminist discursive priorities. That, it seems, is how it should be.

As a discourse, moreover, feminism has no special need for male practitioners. As a series of discourses, feminism is structured, to be sure, by its differences with patriarchy, so it is able to use (in *that* sense) the rejected but paradoxically enabling otherness of a history of oppression. Like other theories grounded in its practitioners's knowledge of a history of discrimination, feminism can gain a powerful (if necessarily partial) distance from the culture it critiques. That is not, however, the same as saying that feminists need (or are enamored of) the history of women's oppression; that is an argument grounded in the pathology of male power and pride. It is clear, however, that in many specific moments of social life generally, though by no means all moments, feminists at present can benefit from the advocacy and self-reflection and alliance of men. This is not the same, however, as saying that feminists *need* men's political cooperation, a claim that men may find reassuring but that may not be in women's best interest. It deflects energy from what feminists can accomplish on their own and diminishes feminism's independent political force. Moreover, it may not always be the case that there are immediate benefits to be gained from alliances with men, and in the long term progress will be made with or without men, but the good will of men may be necessary (for now) if various specific ends are to be achieved in various male-dominated institutions.

Yet I do not think men realistically have anything unique at present to contribute to feminist writing. Thus I must take issue with Paul Smith's suggestion that men can help destabilize feminist theory and make it more self-reflective. "They can be there," he writes, "to help to subvert, unsettle and undermine the (seemingly rather fast to set-tle) laws of the discourse." This does not reflect my own experience of the disputations and differences within feminism, which seem to be more diverse and mutually critical than the differences within any other body of theory in the contemporary critical scene. Is there a special difference in perspective that men can add? A difference other than that readily available in the sexist practices that pervade the culture? Is there a sympathy, a skepticism, an intimacy, or a distance unique to men as a class that we have to offer to feminist writing now? I do not think there is. This is not to say that individual men cannot make useful contributions to feminist writing. They have in fact already done so. But feminism does not need either discursive interventions or generous admiration from the vantage point of a culturally constructed masculinity. Such interventions are almost certainly guaranteed to be destructive.

At a certain utopian remove, if we are ever able to write our bodies in the way Alice Jardine recommends in "Men in Feminism: Odor di Uomo or Compagnons de Route?," then men may have a vital collective contribution to make to the discourse on gender. Jardine reminds us of Irigaray's statement that "the bodily in man is what metaphysics has never touched" and of Cixous's observation that "Men still have everything to say about their sexuality." But of course we all write our bodies all the time, at least in the sense that what we want and fear is inscribed in our language whether we will it to be or not. Even the rhythms of language, its pauses and stresses, its periodicity, are somatically negotiated and inscribed with physical effects. Discourse is socially and libidinally constituted; gender and the life of the body are continually at issue, are continually put forward, in everything we write. Writing is at once a mediated form of bodily expression and an externalized encapsulation and rejection of bodily life. Moreover, certainly novelists and poets have written the body with as much tropical richness as we are likely to be able now to imagine—Monique Wittig, Samuel Beckett, and so forth. From Walt Whitman to Adrienne Rich the body has been written in its historical facticity and in its autobiographically expressive ecstasy and despair. So Jardine must be asking for a special self-expressive and self-critical somatic awareness in critical writing, a new willingness to deal overtly with these issues in critical discourse, especially—in the light of feminism—with the social construction of one's sense of one's own body. Neither men nor women, it seems to me, have yet achieved that willingness; if they do, the social construction of gender will itself begin to change. Moreover, it is true that feminism itself provides the basis for a more radical critique of the socially lived body. To write that body in critical prose would, of course, be to overturn our whole notion of academic writing. In some sense, then, Jardine's recommendation is utopian. We can perhaps now write *in relation* to that utopian aim, but we are unlikely actually to achieve it for some time. It is useful as a provocation and a basis for reflection and self-critique, but it is unrealistic as a condition for feminist writing by men.

This is not to say, therefore, that men cannot now write feminist criticism, whether from deep commitment or intellectual curiosity or even simple opportunism. Unless writing is taken to be transparently and consistently self-expressive, there is nothing to guarantee it must be gender marked in any way that is necessarily obvious or even recoverable. Neither the discourses of writing nor the discourses of social life necessarily offer us the essential being of the human agents involved. Women, for example, can certainly pass falsely as feminists; indeed, they do all the time. Mary Daly is quite right when she points out that institutions select women for positions of power on the basis of their implicit willingness to kill other women, especially feminist women.[2] Based on the models of achievement men have promoted, male institutions sometimes label as "feminist" women who merely defend their own self-interest ruthlessly; such women often have no commitment to feminist issues generally. Indeed, such women may even disingenuously publish work that is taken to be feminist. Men can do the same. Feminist writing, after all, in part provides a series of verbal strategies that can be learned and convincingly imitated. Both men and women, of course, can also do feminist work out of deep conviction. But it is foolish and dangerous to *assume* that writing necessarily entails, documents, certifies, expresses, deep inner commitment. Writing is words on a page; a political movement is better off assuming no more than that zero level of discursive meaning. I suppose one test of the relations between writing, politics, and gender would be to determine whether men could write feminist criticism and publish it under a woman's name; can we really argue that that would be impossible? As a program for deception, this would be an outrageous suggestion, but my aim is merely to be persuasive on the issue of whether writing necessarily and dependably communicates a gendered essence. I believe it does not.

On the other hand, publishing under female pseudonyms might be a good experience for men. Women have often published under men's names and thus have had to endure that sort of marginality and self-extinction often enough; there are feminist lessons men cannot learn without perhaps being in women's place. For example, on a few occasions on visiting another school I have found myself in the role of the "wife" of the invited speaker; it's not a role I can say I much enjoyed, but I nonetheless recommend it as instructive. Lacking the direct experience, this is the kind of status many men will not credit as a problem. But *some* men of course often are in a position of subordination that has instructive points of similarity with woman's structural place in patriarchal society—moreover, they are not necessarily in such positions of subordination temporarily and not always in ways over which they have any control. First, because not all men are white, European, and empowered. The West has numerous hierarchically disenfranchised *others* by way of which it asserts and maintains its confidence and prestige. Variations on categories of race, class, religion, and ethnicity regularly place men in some respects in the situation of women; indeed, these are experiences that some men draw on in seeking ways of empathizing with and being "in" feminism.

Alice Jardine argues that it is "the inscription of struggle—even of pain" that most distinctively marks feminist texts and that is, presumably, most notably absent from texts that are not truly feminist. The inscription of struggle *with* feminism, a common feature of writing by men and women, would not seem a very dependable instance of this. What I find as a credible referent for Jardine's claim is something different: the shock of recognition that feminism often provokes—the sudden recognition that one's prior experience has been reread, reinterpreted, rendered intelligible by feminist knowledge. For feminism at its core is nothing less than a recasting of one's world view, a collectivizing of experience that may until then have seemed only individually painful. But it is not only one's own past and destiny that is at issue and is susceptible to that shock of recognition. For feminism throws into relief the pain of all the women one knows and cares about; that experience is not restricted to women. Where I would differ with Jardine, however, is in noting that there is also much joy in entering into this generalized knowledge, for it constructs a community—reaching back through history—of comparable pain and comparable achievement. That inscription of community seems equally central to the enterprise of feminist writing.

Women have every historical reason to doubt whether men—writing to, about, or within feminism—are part of this community, are also writing as feminists. If men come to write about feminism (or in relation to feminism)—as some now are by choice and some are implicitly by unacknowledged influence, offering interpretations of texts and social practices they would never have arrived at without feminism's dispersion throughout the culture—they will presumably do so in their own interests.[3] It cannot be an entirely unselfconscious and easy relationship; if it were, it wouldn't be called feminism, a term whose historical meaning involves resistance to patriarchal culture, extensive social critique, and an increased awareness of the nature of one's own social interactions. Men writing about or as feminists will be scrutinized and, at least for now, will be partly unwelcome. They may also lose some of the respect of their male colleagues, quite possibly an overrated commodity in any case. They will also frequently be misunderstood and misrepresented, a condition that applies to the reception of most activities on the planet, so hardly surprising in this context, and, in any case, particularly inappropriate ground for sympathy for feminist men. Is the relation of men to feminism also an *impossible* one, as Stephen Heath argues in "Male Feminism"? Yes, if by that one means it will always be one of unstable and socially constituted difference, not one of inner or outer identity.

Certainly elements of men's affirmative relations with, commitments to, feminism can become so ingrained as to be instinctive and unselfconscious. But there will remain other areas of behavior to be worked through, rethought, unlearned, negotiated, and challenged. Moreover, the tiresome and not overly interesting burden of chaperoning other men through the early stages of feminism—a responsibility feminist men might undertake, since the mixture of resistence, discovery, and self-congratulation that men undergo is not always productive for (and can be quite distracting to) feminist women—requires us to make conscious and rearticulate feminist commitments that had come to seem automatic. For all these reasons—and because feminism remains primarily and deeply women's project—a multiplicity of differences and commitments, not some simple, straightforward identity, will continue to characterize men's relations to feminism.

But then all relationships are impossible in that sense. This is not to erase the specific cultural impossibilities that traverse feminism but rather to recognize that people can never wholly identify with an individual discourse. Although the relationship between women and feminism is clearly more possible than that for men, it is, as Elizabeth Weed points out in "A Man's Place," also, in various ways, an impossible one—not only, as she suggests, because of the inevitable conflicts and misalignments between our inner heterogeneity and our multiple social positioning, but also because there is no unitary feminism with which women can identify. In committing themselves to feminism, women must negotiate an impossible identity with difference. If individual experience is devalued as a source of knowledge by some feminists, will others necessarily identify with that view of feminism? If cultural feminists find that any use of male theorists invalidates a feminist position, will all feminist theorists feel that feminism is their own? If some academic feminists urge their colleagues not to publish in feminist journals until after they get tenure, will all feminists find that an appropriate politics? Will Black, Asian, or Hispanic women, reading this book, find that it speaks to their specific experiences of the various difficulties men in those communities have with feminism?

Despite these differences, feminism remains women's project. If men take on feminist knowledge, they will do so not merely in intellectual admiration but because it is in their own interest. They may find it irresistible to be where the most vital intellectual activity is in their profession. They may find feminism the only practical, culturally possible route to their own personal growth. They may come to feel that not to be in feminism is virtually not to be in the world. They may come to realize, as I believe is the case, that feminism represents, among other things, the only historically effective discourse now available by which academic disciplines can come to reflect on and critique their enterprises. But it is absurd for men to assume that women will take a feminist commitment as something men are doing entirely *for women*. Thus men's status in feminism must, at least in the present society, remain mariginalized, no matter how great their commitment.

Given this secondary status, there is a need for something like an ethics that enables us to acknowledge and negotiate the specific impossibilities in men's relations with feminism. If I write within feminism it is because I choose to; I do it because I want to, because not to do so would now be to induce a radical self-alienation. Feminists, however, have every right to protect their own sense of community (and, for that matter, their own peace of mind) by being distinctly, even excessively, suspicious of anything I write. I, on the other hand, am not bound to accept any critique just because it issues from a woman who is a feminist. For one thing, not all the feminist critiques one receives will be in agreement with one another. Nonetheless, I will listen as carefully as I can to such critiques—because it is my political responsibility to do so if I wish to resist the influence of a patriarchal society, because I owe it as a matter of human decency, and because it is altogether in my own interest to try to learn from those feminists who are willing to try and teach me—but I also have a right to the insights and errors of my own work in its current state of development. It is merely that I should not anticipate being routinely congratulated for them, an anticipation that is typically built into men's ego structures. Finally, since feminism is about change, men need to anticipate that they *will* change as a result of their contact with feminism; feminist positions they reject today may seem necessary and inevitable tomorrow. As a result of learning this, I now repeatedly rethink feminist positions I rejected in the past. It is an error reinforced by the culture's construction of sexual difference for men to imagine their opinions will hold for eternity.

But as I reread the last paragraph, with its rather neutral language, its struggle to negotiate equal rights across sexual difference within the social inscription of feminism, I realize its tone is the product of a much messier struggle. The contractual conclusions are misleading without some sense of the process that led up to them. For there have been several times when I have found no real negotiation possible, when I have been told that I was mistaken and I just could not agree. Once, when I was told that an essay could not *be* feminism because it cited men approvingly, we talked, argued, and in the end agreed to disagree. On another occasion it did not go so well. I had suggested in a paper that feminists should remain "envoys of otherness" within Western culture, meaning that they should continue to articulate a radical and politically destabilizing difference from the existing order.[4] One reader felt this argument was incredibly cruel to women, since women were already *other* and had suffered for it for centuries. I responded that I had in mind such things as the plural, textually rich otherness that feminists like Luce Irigaray and Hélène Cixous had evoked, not the vacant otherness of male fantasy, but this did not help, and the woman I was talking with left in great distress. To be sure, there were other issues at stake, including a growing separatism on her part, but the conversation still troubles me—not because she disagreed with me but because her pain was very real. Causing pain is usually not one of the risks of academic writing. Realizing that unresolvable pain *can* be a result of men's interrelations with feminism throws discourse into a material domain that academics are generally wholly unprepared for—a domain in which we are humanly present in our work and responsible for its social and personal consequences.

Of course men will also quite often simply get feminism wrong, making errors that are understandably more annoying and potentially more damaging than those by women. The most frequent error—for academics—will be the one Stephen Heath anticipates: the conclusion that feminism is just another critical approach, another interpretive method, not a politics and a way of life. People will obviously *use* feminism, just as they use Marxism and psychoanalysis—the other modern bodies of theory that challenge the nature of the social formation and undermine the independence and self-determination of the interpreter—in a detached and unreflective way. I see no point in objecting to this; since it will happen anyway, there's no stopping it, and it's better than indifference because supposedly neutral academic feminist discourses often have politically subversive effects

their authors do not intend. Moreover, and more importantly, feminist readings that pretend to a detachment having no social consequences—a sociologist's reading of cultural attitudes toward gender, a close reading of the representation of women in a literary text—can then be rearticulated by others to political projects. Nonetheless, I do object strongly to the judgment (always moralizing and always ideological) that all feminism (as an interpretive practice) is and should be is a disinterested form of intellectual inquiry. The most recent attempt to mount that kind of depoliticizing operation is K. K. Ruthven's, appropriately criticized by Toril Moi and others.[5]

In any case, feminist critiques of feminist practice have been a part of feminism from the outset. They are not merely a matter, as Andrew Ross seems to argue in "No Question of Silence," of policing violations of law, of obliterating difference; they are part of a struggle to shape the social formation of the future. This struggle can be a cruel and brutal one because the stakes are high—the nature of the lives that women especially can live today and will be able to live tomorrow. But it remains true that women in feminism have been harder on one another than they have been on men, just as at other times they offer one another greater support and encouragement.

Perhaps the most intractable difficulty among feminists has been over the issue of women and power. Women are often given authority in feminist organizations both because temporal demands require some limits on feminist process (decentralized authority, greater effort to hear and acknowledge what people are saying, etc.) and because the outside world insists on some hierarchizing of responsibility. That outside world, including government funding agencies and upper-level university administrations, is of course often male, and thus feminist organizational structures are partly compromised by the necessities of establishing relations with authorities that only understand hierarchy. Partly as a result, women in power are often endlessly critiqued by their sisters. At the same time, women in power can become especially resistant to feminist critiques. Feminists are aware of this problem; Judith Fetterly addressed it quite eloquently at MLA in 1981, describing why she felt an administrative role in her largely male department would, in fact, be less personally destructive than an administrative role in NWSA, and urging greater generosity and self-reflection in women's power relations amongst one another; but solutions have not yet been forthcoming. If feminism were only an interpretive practice, the intensity of these and other continuing disputations—directed toward both women and men—would be merely petty and destructive. But because feminism is also a vision of human possibility it is necessarily also an ethics and a challenge to daily life. Thus intellectual differences have continual implications

for practice in all domains. It is not simply a question of reaffirming
a tolerance for diversity (though it is also that).

There is no easy way of negotiating these problems. We might as
well accept the fact that men and women are (and for some time will
continue to be) defensive about their interrelations with feminism, a
defensiveness obvious in all the essays in this book—including, however much I wish it were not true, this essay. Given the history of
the oppression of women, there is simply no way for feminists to
extend a benign and accepting generosity to every man who makes
his first clumsy steps in the direction of feminist commitment; nor is
there any way for a sophisticated discourse whose signature is male
to be unproblematic. There is quite simply no way for any man to
behave correctly in respect to the whole range of influential feminisms. The effort to be entirely correct—consider the tears of Robin
Morgan's husband in *Not a Love Story* and John Stoltenberg's pathetic
"Refusing to be a Man"—is arguably as regrettable as any other
tactic.[6] In fact, Stoltenberg's essay suggests that, for this historical
moment, complete correctness is only readable as castration. At the
same time, taking on the burden of correctness—not only in its ma-
crological sense but also in its tangible, day-to-day specificity—is part
of what feminism is about for men. Men who resent the difficulties
of gaining acceptance for their feminist commitments might keep in
mind one reality: as an intellectual project, feminism does not need
men. Its vital differences will certainly keep it productive throughout
our lifetimes. And its commitment to community will give its female
practitioners all the intellectual and interpersonal support they need.

This fragile sense of community—continually at risk, regularly
threatened—is all that keeps the multiply fractured feminist project
together—that, I suppose, and feminism's false hypostatization by
the culture of patriarchy. Which is why I find Paul Smith's image of
a potentially monolithic feminism inexplicable. Feminists have always
disagreed with one another; feminism has radically differed from itself since its inception, differed from itself in fact in *all* of its discursive
and political incarnations at different historical moments. It does not
need men to insure disagreement and diversity and to prevent a hard
legalization of its codes.

There are in fact a number of binary divisions within feminism,
but they do not divide feminism neatly in half; issues like abortion,
pornography, separatism, race, heterosexuality, lesbianism, activism,
academicism, and the place of theory create overlapping and sometimes contradictory constituencies, alliances, and disputations. Consider, for example, two nationally known figures in the feminist
movement who would seem at least on the surface to have virtually
nothing in common—Catharine MacKinnon and Ellen Willis, the first
among the most uncompromising crusaders for antipornography leg-

islation, the second with a long history of advocating both feminist issues and free speech.[7] There could hardly be two people who consider each other's public positions to be more destructive. Yet they have certain beliefs in common: 1) that women have been historically discriminated against and disenfranchised; 2) that men have traditionally appropriated many human activities and distorted them in the process; 3) that feminism has deeply utopian aims. MacKinnon and Willis each give these points of similarity very different inflection indeed, but the fact that such networks of similarity and difference exist gives feminism some coherence as a body of theory.

But these shifting alignments also continually undermine the hierarchizing and exclusionary mechanisms Ross and Smith identify. The one division Smith does recognize I find particularly problematic for him to privilege—a division between feminist theory and women's studies. This division seems an extension of the traditional, sexist binarism of maleness and femaleness, with intellect and philosophical discourse on one side and a debased materiality and experience on the other. His argument also implies a dangerous theoretical distaste for feminist activism and a misplaced and disingenuous condescension toward the often wholly marginalized institutionalization of women's studies. On the other hand, one might fairly divide feminism between cultural feminists (who believe in a redemptive, alternative women's culture) and feminists who remain in dialogue with many of the other discourses of the West, including those by men. But there is *theory* and *women's studies* (and consciousness-raising) on both sides of this division, so Smith's view of a split within feminism won't hold up. Moreover, one of feminism's achievements is to call into question our confidence about which cultural sites, practices, and discourses are dependable and important sources of theory production, indeed about what kinds of discourse will count as theoretical. For feminism, the production of theory is certainly not confined to the academy.

The impossibility of demarcating the theoretical is suggested, in fact, by offering a few answers to what might first seem an uncomplicated question—What is women's studies? Among other things, it is a place for cross-disciplinary contacts among students and faculty; an organizing point for feminist political constituencies; a possible site for university/community interactions; a home for feminist courses not offered by individual departments; a place where feminists with different agendas have a history of coming into conflict with one another; an institutional structure divided between bureaucratizing and revolutionary impulses; an appropriate vantage point from which to critique the division of knowledge into academic disciplines; a place oddly at once within the university and outside it; an institutional incorporation and encapsulation of difference; and a promoter of consciousness-raising and new intellectual commitments for women on campus. Given all of this, what does it mean for a male theorist to imagine he is located *elsewhere* than women's studies? That imaginary elsewhere apparently serves an inner split between theory and experience, between mental constructs and bodily life. It is a way of saying that the *important* problems of consciousness can be resolved in the absence of any engagement with social life.

Yet Smith is right that theory (both of feminist and nonfeminist persuasions) has at some moments and for some practitioners been deliberately distanced from women's studies. One reason for this has been the women's studies commitment to articulating individual experience and using it as a valid source of knowledge. For theorists to reject that women's studies tradition without reading it in the context of the continuing debates over the value of experience within other bodies of theory seems to me to be particularly sexist and irresponsible. The positivist and scientistic attack on experience—an attack that many find outdated but one that survives nonetheless— would seem to have been plausibly countered by phenomenology's way of theorizing experience outside traditional versions of the subject/object dichotomy. Of equal importance for feminism (and for anyone who would dismiss feminism's accounts of experience) should be the Marxist-humanist reading of experience as historically determined by class position and thus a tremendously rich source of broadly applicable knowledge about how people live their lives. Feminism in fact does not typically treat experience as the unique property of individuals but rather as a route to understanding the historical position of women. Even the poststructuralist critique of narrated experience can be countered if we do not see it as the history of a unified subject but rather as the discursive register of particular subject positions. That experiences are *constructed* does not, finally, invalidate them as forms of knowledge, a recognition that psychoanalysis has made available for some time.

Yet none of this does away with the fact that feminism deals with kinds of gender specific experience typically ignored within many of these other theoretical positions. There is a real need, in fact, to continue theorizing both experiential and material domains that may appear to be outside traditional theoretical concerns. One division in feminism, for example, that needs appropriate theorizing is that between those feminists who will versus those who will not typically give professional assistance to other women. A purely intellectual feminist commitment can be more than self-interested careerism; it can be very deep, and it can help change the world. But it is also worth theorizing the interrelationships amongst one's commitments. It is also crucial to recognize whether or not feminist men make this kind of practical/theoretical commitment, whether they risk their professional status and use their professional contacts and prestige on behalf of women. "Theoretical men" need to realize that those commitments may be more important than the truth content of their insights into feminist discourse.

But are there, then, other contributions men can make to feminist writing? As I suggested above, men can write feminist criticism and thus can do valuable feminist analyses of texts and social practices. Furthermore, though feminist discourse does not need the intrusion of men as a class—and here, perhaps, the metaphors of penetration that Jacques Derrida and Paul Smith seem to use with a less marked and deconstructed self-consciousness than they might are quite apt; i.e., if men as a class are to contribute to feminism it will be as an unwarranted aggression, unless men as a class are transformed—individual men can make unique theoretical contributions to feminism. Men may even make contributions to feminism without intending to. I don't imagine, for example, that Roland Barthes was thinking of feminism when he began to rethink the semiotics of sexual difference in *S/Z*, but the book has nonetheless proven useful for some feminists. If one wishes to map the whole territory of feminism, then some lines of affinity, influence, and rearticulation will have to run to Barthes. To deny this is to exclude from feminism the work and experience and intellectual histories of some women (those who have found Barthes useful) against their will. Some will find such exclusion necessary, which is understandable enough, but they should surely know what it is they do.

With Barthes, the issue is whether women's rearticulation of his work *to* feminism rewrites his name and his discourse within a wider feminist project. To a certain extent, whole strains of the discourse of the West are necessarily rewritten both this way and more obliquely within feminism. In a visionary passage toward the end of *This Sex Which Is Not One*, Irigaray asks what the world might be like if women took themselves out of the existing systems of exchange, if they ceased to be commodities. She imagines in its place an "economy of abundance": "Exchanges without identifiable terms . . . Nature's resources would be expended without depletion, exchanged without labor, freely given, exempt from masculine transactions."[8] In a famous passage in Act II of Shakespeare's *The Tempest*, Gonzalo wonders what sort of world he might create if he had "plantation of this isle." He would, he promises, reverse the existing notions of nationhood; there would be "no sovereignty . . . All things in common nature should produce . . . nature should bring forth, / Of it own kind, all foison, all abundance, / To feed my innocent people." When this passage was discussed in a faculty seminar in 1985, several men concluded that the echoing and rewriting of utopian discourses in Irigaray proved that her work was not original. Actually, as semiotics made clear some time ago, it is this similarity with past discourses, this often unconscious quotation of our multilayered cultural inheritance, that makes it possible for readers to process and begin to comprehend new texts. At the same time, the rewriting of utopian discourses in terms of a radical vision of sexual difference is part of what makes Irigaray's work decisively *new*. In any case, Gonzalo, it would seem, is now implicitly rewritten *in* feminism, as are, arguably, many of the utopian discourses of the West, as are, for some feminists, Barthes and Derrida.

With Derrida, however, there are also a series of more direct problems, since his work has for some time been immensely useful for some feminists and since he has himself now been repeatedly questioned about his positions on sexual difference and his relations to feminist politics. Derrida's least problematic contribution to feminist discourses has been his critique of "phallogocentrism"—"the foundations or anchorings of Western rationality . . . the complicity of Western metaphysics with a notion of male firstness."[9] Widely influential both here and in Europe, with echoes in attacks on phallocentrism not only in feminism linked with poststructuralism but also in cultural feminism, some of Derrida's work here is about as close to being "in" feminism as any male theorist has come. Yet Derrida himself has felt it necessary to put some distance between himself and a complete feminist commitment: "I am not against feminism, but I am not simply for feminism."[10] His difficulties with feminism as a totalizing cultural project are several: feminism is sometimes linked to teleological notions of progress that imply an impossible capacity to speak for history and truth; it risks maintaining the dichotomous cultural division between the sexes, which he feels masks a more diverse field of sexual differences; finally, feminism's very conviction sometimes becomes its own version of "phallocentric mastery." All these criticisms and hesitations, of course, feminists themselves would sometimes register. What is needed is a commitment nonetheless to real social change, a recognition that monological and militantly certain discourses are often strategically necessary if people's lives are to be bettered. On some local fronts, we need to believe that there are wrongs to be righted and real forms of progress to be achieved. Derrida does actually acknowledge this, but he tends to put his reservations first. Thus his sympathy for feminist political action seems secondary to his own intellectual project, a pattern duplicated in some female academics, but a pattern that is arguably more damning for men to emulate. Moreover, his failure for many years to take a stronger stand for political action makes it easier for some of his followers in America to use their theoretical distaste for monological discourses as an excuse for avoiding a commitment to combatting discrimination. This is not simply a result of misreading Derrida, though it is a misreading; it is also an *effect* of Derrida's rhetorical strategies, which make such a misreading easier to maintain.

All these problems become more intractable still when we take up a much more controversial element of Derrida's work—his use of the terms "hymen" and "double, chiasmic invagination." In addition to his rather neutral terms for a semiotics of unstable difference, displacement, and supplementation, Derrida has for some time also made use of this much more provocative vocabulary to suggest the social construction of meaning in terms of a phantasmatic version of sexual difference. Almost too predictably, many male American deconstructive critics have simply ignored this more challenging element of his enterprise. Derrida himself has plausibly argued that his use of this vocabulary is too unconventional for it to evoke any simple, anatomical representation, but these terms, like Irigaray's experimental prose about female sexuality, are nonetheless traversed by problematic representational effects. If his use of "hymen" suggests that new meaning is always in part a sexualized broaching of established and codified differences, his image of "invagination" suggests that every encapsulation and formalization of an exterior reality involves a libidinal dynamic that is coded by the cultural history of the social construction of masculinity and femininity. If these are among our most powerful versions of an analysis of the relations between semiosis and sexuality, they are also overtly contaminated by the same system they would critique. Derrida of course would insist on that very paradox, though that does not make it any easier for feminism to deal with the fact that a man is basing a powerful critique of semiosis on what is in part a sexual joke.

Related problems surface in another influential element of Derrida's enterprise—his use of the trope of woman, in *Spurs* and elsewhere, to locate and generalize about the continuing other of Western metaphysics. Femaleness becomes a metaphor for the pervasive undecidability that Western rationality represses and distances from itself. To speak for that undecidability is thus, in a sense, to speak for or within that femaleness and, in the process, to give it a depth and rhetorical diversity it has not had in mainstream philosophy. It is also, inevitably, to make a certain libidinal investment in the image of woman in one's own work, an investment that writers need to acknowledge and address. Not to discuss this issue is to engage, inevitably, in struggles over who will keep possession of the metaphysical body of woman, a struggle that places male feminists in exactly the gendered role they had hoped to reject.

Stephen Heath's case is equally problematic, since his recent work is explicitly informed by, sympathetic to, and, in fact, dependent for its very existence, on feminism. He has clearly written work which is pertinent to and very much available to feminism. Heath, however, disclaims a vantage point within feminism: "I do not at all think, even less claim, that these are feminist writings, it is just that they depend on learning from feminism." As Judith Mayne argues, for men "any notion of writing a feminist book or being a feminist, is a myth, a male imaginary with the reality of appropriation and domination right behind." But these are not in fact Judith Mayne's words. They are part of the same passage in Heath's "Male Feminism." I apologize for this momentary deception, though its aim was heuristic. The point is that we will read these words differently depending on whether we take them as coming from a man or a woman. If we take them as coming from Heath, then, despite his elaborate efforts at self-effacement, we will hear him as prescribing the terms of his own marginalization, as mastering his own irresolution, as producing his own masochistic subordination, as possessing certainty about where it is he is speaking from, as occupying the site of a phallic truth, however veiled. One could argue, moreover, that Heath's apparent struggle with feminism is an altogether internal or metaphysical one. Feminism to Heath is to some extent a problem in how his own voice is to be constituted, how his self-image is to be reshaped. Through most of "Male Feminism" there is little evidence of an engagement with the material and social conditions of sexual difference. At the same time, it may be that my reading of Heath (and of other men in feminism) is the result of a distancing that enables me to situate myself within a discourse about feminism—treating men within feminism as the other within my prose.

In this context, it may be useful to look more closely at the opening of Paul Smith's "Men in Feminism: Men and Feminist Theory." In an effort to make explicit "the provocation, the offense, the trouble that men are for feminism," he uses language that many feminists will find offensive. Moreover, he uses that language to characterize not the reactiveness of antifeminist men but the efforts of men, like himself, who have read widely and intelligently in feminism and are now attempting to speak within its discourses:

Men, some men now—and perhaps by way of repeating an age-old habit—are entering feminism, actively penetrating it (whatever 'it' might be, either before or after this intervention) for a variety of motives and in a variety of modes, fashions. That penetration is often looked upon with suspicion: it can be understood as yet another interruption, a more or less illegal act of breaking and entering, entering and breaking, for which these men must finally be held to account. Perhaps the question that needs to be asked then, by these men, with them, for them, is to what extent their irruption (penetration and interruption) is justified? is it of any political use to feminism? to what extent is it wanted?

In talking with Smith, I suggested that this paragraph presented a whole scenario of violently imposed sexuality and interrupted ejaculation. "Penetration" is used three times, once followed by "interruption." Men's efforts to be in feminism, Smith suggests, are read as robbery or rape—an "illegal act of breaking and entering." Smith in turn suggested that all this was deliberate, that he had aimed for a kind of "desperate irony." Clearly, he would have had a better chance of being understood if he had reflected openly on this language while using it, talking perhaps about how men cannot for now altogether escape the air of sexual appropriation and possessiveness that surrounds their intellectual passions. He might have talked more directly about his own frustration and anger at being misunderstood and misrepresented as an aggressor. At a certain point, I think, his impossible masquerade—performing as the male theorist burglarizing feminist language—becomes something else, as when the cliché "breaking and entering" becomes the rather more aggressive "entering and breaking." I sense real rage here, at the same time as I realize this whole range of feelings may be of little use to feminists. They may reasonably say this is Smith's problem, not theirs. It is also not clear whether Smith realizes how much this opening colors the rest of his essay. Thus, when he asks to what extent men's penetration into feminism is "wanted," we are as likely to hear the defense at a rape trial as we are to recall Freud's famous question. Finally, one needs to ask what this language offers to feminists. Is this really the moment to ask them to apologize for their wariness about men's intentions?

Part of Smith's aim in taking on the masquerade of male intellectual aggressor, even in exagggerating this masquerade, was presumably to register his distress at having all his investments in and comments on feminism read so reactively and reductively by other feminists. To exaggerate the role is thus to draw attention to it and potentially make it an impossible one. In highlighting the tendency to see all male feminist discourse exclusively in terms of sexual difference he hoped, perhaps, to persuade women to read men's feminist writing more diversely. He may, in short, have simply wanted a more humane and tolerant reading of his commitments. I fully sympathize with him here, but, again, I do not think this is yet the time for men to make that request of feminism. I have made that request myself often enough in the past, but I do not make it any more.

In the end it is less a question of determining the essential nature of men's contributions to feminism than of deciding what the effects of those contributions will be. For I think my misquotation of Judith

Mayne above shows that passages from essays by men could be transported into feminist essays—invisibly and without difficulty. There are certainly many sensitive passages in Smith's essay that could seamlessly be transported into women's essays as well. How these passages will be read is thus partly a question about the connotative effects produced by a gendered signature, connotative effects which are an inescapable consequence of our history. Put simply, the words will mean something else if a woman says them. That may not always be the case; the connotative effects, the reception and social meaning, of a gendered voice may change, but we are not now part of that future in which gender may be more diversely inscribed in our lives.

Yet there are things we can do to bring that future closer. Men can contribute to feminism in their social practices and in their writing; that they are not *in* feminism in the same way is in no way a decisive prohibition. But if we are to take advantage of the contributions of both women and men we may have to unlearn a certain phallocentric way of reading prose. I refer here at once to the arguments over essentialism and to the continuing disputes over the proximity to truth exhibited by various feminist practices. We tend to read any discourse as if it were trying to take over the world, as if it aspired to absolute truth claims. Men in particular may be vulnerable to making the error of seeking the one true feminism, of deciding that the job of theory is to decide which discourse wins first prize. And indeed discourses do partly aim for that sort of power, and some can achieve it for a time. But it seems an instance of unnecessary masculine paranoia to read everything in those terms. It is instructive to ask not only what essentialist claims a writing practice makes but also what its actual social effects are, what field of alliances and differences it establishes. An analysis of that more interactive and combinative kind of power will show some discourses to be more harmless and others to be more dangerous than we now suppose. It will also be a more realistic assessment of their social inscription. In the process, we can ask what role essentialist claims play in our lives, not whether or not they are true. And at the same time we will begin to see how men and women—in feminism or in its margins—may enable us to have a chance at remaking the world.

18.
in any event . . .
MEAGHAN MORRIS

PRIMAL SCENE: . . . Scene of sexual intercourse between the parents which the child observes, or infers on the basis of certain indications, and phantasizes. It is generally interpreted by the child as an act of violence on the part of the father.
J. Laplanche and J-B. Pontalis, The Language of Psycho-Analysis

I can still remember with glee the first occasion on which I saw a man ejected from feminism.

The setting of the scene shall be vague—some cold hall, a large and noisy crowd. I suppose I am very young, and very lost in feminism—short, buffeted, out of it, overwhelmed through a skin too thin to fend off these loudly ebullient women jostling me to and fro. My clothes are clumsy: too softly suburban, and the weight of them makes my voice catch with a self-conscious insincerity that I wish I didn't feel. Sinking, I hang grimly to the edge of some little group and try to join in with jokes, slogans, and stories that fall flat as soon as I form them in the unctuous tones of insecurity. Then deliverance, fresh air: the crowd settled, a woman took the stage, began to speak, and stopped. A couple of men had sneaked through, and now stood quite close to the front. In the long prickling silence, panic tightened my chest and strangled my cowardly pulse. Now there'd be a brawl. But the speaker laughed—*would they go quietly, or would they like a little help?* . . . And as all movement elsewhere ceased, she walked alone off the stage towards them. To a slow rise of clapping and hooting, they backed off and out of the hall.

I couldn't believe it. *We* couldn't believe it. Two great bruising Australians, bounced, banished, pulverized, *flattened!*—and not a black eye in sight. As the crowd dissolved in a laughter that picked me up and swept away one and many lifetimes spent in a physical fear of men, some small, selfish center swelled in me with a rush of petty relief. It was all right now, I'd made it. When the story was told, I'd have been there. I was in.

The zone of influence of the division produced by philosophy is . . . a very limited one. This idea of woman as sphinx and chaos is no doubt only current today in certain fractions of the dominant class. In the popular strata of society, the woman is seen rather as a force for order,

"rational"—indeed, a killjoy, it being assumed that the pole of imagination and carefree fancy is the province of masculinity.
Michèle Le Doeuff, L'imaginaire philosophique[1]

Of course, my glee in remembering that incident simply serves a present purpose. I don't know what really happened, who those men were, what they wanted, or why they left. I represent them, I *see* them, as threatening barroom hulks—volatile, dangerous, unpredictable. It's more likely that they were miffed or inquisitive leftists, couldn't fight their way out of a wet paper bag, and didn't know or didn't care how their presence might be felt. Many men do interrupt women's meetings out of a puzzled sense of their own individuality, rather than a will to reassert their prerogatives—not perceiving that the two can be one and the same.

In any event . . . the form of revelation which I've given this memory wants none of that to matter, any more than the frightening ambiguity of a collective moral force as it drives out its enemy within. My purpose now is to understand how it comes about that, in the name of something to do with "feminism" and "feminist theory," I could be sitting round fifteen years later making up a response to this:

Men, some men, now—and perhaps by way of repeating an age-old habit—are entering feminism, actively penetrating it (whatever "it" might be, either before or after this intervention), for a variety of motives and in a variety of modes, fashions. That penetration is often looked upon with suspicion: it can be understood as yet another interruption, a more or less illegal act of breaking and entering, entering and breaking, for which these men must finally be held to account (p. 33)

In the dossier of MLA seminar papers that gave rise to the project of this book, I read several references to possible irony in Paul Smith's presentation. As a non-participant in that event, what I read in this passage isn't irony, but innuendo: good-"humoured," perhaps well-meant, but emerging smoothly nonetheless from a political rhetoric that constructs with ease a coherence between sex, or a sort of sex (*"actively penetrating"*), rape (penetration as *"a more or less illegal act"*—the *"less"* there serving to intensify rather than moderate the suggestion, given the judicial favour accorded to rapists in many a legal scene), crime against property (*"illegal act of breaking and entering"*) and then hymen rupture and property damage understood simultaneously (*"entering and breaking"*).

The extraordinary thing about this passage is not merely the insensitivity with which its wit reaffirms those links (for the amusement of what reader?) between sex, rape, and theft. What strikes me first, with something like the force of a slap, is the way the wordplay here works not to multiply possibilities and to institute differences, but to bind and to unify: the complexity of feminist politics, and of any politics of "entrism," for women as well as men, is collapsed into a single, emblematic, heterosexual primal scene (that *"age-old habit"*). Punning is a treacherous method. If it may assist in the "careful teasing out of warring forces of signification within the text" that Barbara Johnson looks for in a deconstructive reading,[2] it can also (and I think in Smith's text does) mark the moment when, *for* a text, the significance of painful social conflicts is teasingly smoothed away.

For the most remarkable gesture in the passage I've been holding, I know, to account, is the way that it presents itself as *not* so serious after all. Responsibility for the logic linking raped bodies to broken locks is not really accepted (even as a loan . . .) by Smith, but rather imputed hypothetically to a possible feminist *"suspicion."* That is to say, we are asked to think this rhetoric not as an instance of how Smith thinks feminism, but as an instance of how Smith asks us to imagine that feminism might think Smith. If we are feminists with female bodies, attempting to think, and live, this feminism and these bodies without resort to the *topoi* of possession, I suspect that there may indeed by some trouble in taking Smith's text as a serious invitation to rethink men's relations to either.

It's heavy-footed to state the obvious, and make things over-explicit. A wise woman knows when to stop.

Indeed, I'm stumbling heavily here into a trap prepared for feminist critics, opened in the passage I've quoted, which snaps shut at the end of Smith's paper—playing policewoman-judge of discourse, defending her fortress Feminism against irruptions of unruly masculinity. I'm aware, as I read, that Smith is stressing the reversibility of loose talk about transgression in romantic literary theory. And it *is*, of course, reversible, once freed from consideration of complex social contexts. The very condition of the romantic game is that noone, whatever their position in political and social power, wants to be seen to be playing the cop. Therefore, the roles are always already reversed: reading Smith on men as a "dark unlegislatible area for feminist theory" I am reminded irresistibly not of femininity-burble about the excluded other, but of an issue of *The New York Times Magazine* (February 9, 1986) on deconstruction, in which full-color photographs of various portly old gentlemen in fabulous surroundings are held to represent the *"wild men"* of contemporary criticism.

Reversing the reversals is easy to do if we can take, with Smith, this restricted literary field as our terrain for further debate. But for a feminist, about to write, that's difficult—and so is avoiding Smith's trap. Any writer may fear the opprobrium incurred by an ugly over-insistence in a culture that values—however horrid the topic—a "lightness" and "delicacy" of touch. A woman writer, however, is confronted by a doubled, or intensified, *terror* of appearing "legal-istic," defensive or accusatory—all highly pejorative terms. The rea-sons for this have to do with a history of misogynist representation that Smith seems able to ignore, but which can be far more paralyzing in practice to women than demands for girlish display. It's a history of the distribution of myths of woman as constitutionally *heavy*—the stolid, earthbound beast, the killjoy, the moral overseer, the puritan-ical cleaner of speech, the guardian of social custom (if not symbolic law). If literary critics love to see themselves as criminals, what woman does not dread (whatever her occupation) being seen as some man's gaoler?[3]

So there is indeed a thudding inevitability about my argument here, and its bristling tone of combativeness. One can sympathize, easily, with the problems men at all alert to feminism face now in writing anything about women; misogyny's history is so rich in rhet-oric that any step can become a *faux pas*. But feminist theory is one of the ways in which feminism tries to challenge that history and refuse its inheritance. To enter into feminist debate is to accept to face both those tasks. In the note from *L'imaginaire philosophique* with which I began this, my strident section, Michèle Le Doeuff goes on to suggest that we need a "fine sociology" of the *variety* of "masculine/feminine" images; not only as they structure relations between men and women in particular milieux, but as they create difficulties *between* women from different social groups, or any one woman in shifting social contexts. Such a sociology might help also to make it harder for anyone of any sex "in" feminism to think through difficult political problems (pornography and rape come to mind) by allocating rejected positions to the bad, the "heavy" feminist.[4] It takes no particular refinement here to see in the latter, and in her up-market legalistic sister as invoked for the academy by Smith, that most terrifying of media bogeys, that dreaded figure who looms so large in our language that women toil untold hours over their prose to write her off—the humorless feminist.

Yet she's really a helpful soul. For humorless feminism, unlike philosophy's "dark, unlegislatible" femininity, insists on metalan-guage: not metalanguage understood as a policing of discourse, or as a primacy accorded to one discourse (say, philosophy, or "theory" in literary terms) over others, but, more simply, as a critical shift *in relation to* a given discourse, in a particular place and time. Such shifts enable, if they cannot alone achieve, the re-statement, re-working, re-mapping of the terms of our social existence. Without the Hu-

morless Feminist's Move—clumsy, indispensable, insufficient—the
spriteliest feminist politics can find itself rapidly blocked.

So I shall lumber one step further with my commentary on Smith's
text. In his scene of penetration, men are seen to be entering feminism
"for a variety of motives and in a variety of modes, fashions." I shall leave
aside the motives. I'm interested in the way that, given the broader
context of the article's restricted emphasis on feminist "theory" as a
distinct activity, and on theory as academic, the terms *"modes, fashions"* hint already at a certain externality of (here male, later feminist)
theoretical action to the assaulted body of *"it"* (here feminism, later
a broader "political struggle"). Modes and fashions pertain, after all,
to *dress*, easily shed for dramatic action, and also to the *ephemeral*—
perhaps the French "modes," the theoretical "fashions," already
over-familiar from Anglo-American cultural journalism and paper-
back polemics. The notion that in the final analysis theory remains
in some sense *ornamental* in relation to political action is in my view
more crippling to feminism than any stylish thrusts from men. Feminist theory, with or without participation from men, in the academy
as elsewhere, is feminism extending, understanding, transforming
itself and its fields of operation. And yet Smith fears, while inviting
feminists to talk about men and feminist theory, that our response
to his tableau of men-in-feminism as violence might only be that it's
just about wasting time—*"yet another interruption."*

The problem may not be women's speech, but men's hearing.

Helen Grace, ' "For all her shouting, she was as if mute' . . ."[5]

Is responding to such a provocation a waste of time? I did waste
some time worrying about this. After all, why *write,* "why waste
time?"

Yet I chose to single out the text that might lead me to that worry.
Why not take a point of departure from one of the women's papers?
Why repeat, with a simplistic tone, so much that's already been said?
Why not ignore the MLA papers, American academia, and begin with
some experience that might be closer to home?

I'm bothered too by the unrelenting negativity of my chosen response, with its structure of double rebuff—an infantile parable, a
wrangling scene of reading, with a whole political narrative ("feminism") suggested *in elision* between.

I have a fondness, however, for BEFORE/AFTER advertisements
addressed to women in magazines, selling skin care or weight loss
programs. Their rhetoric depends not primarily on the act of elision
(an absent tale of acquiring and using the product), but on presenting
simultaneously two almost—nearly, not quite—incompatible ver-

sions of the same body. Gazing at these images, we are fascinated by the possibilities of contradiction, almost incoherence—being fat and thin, spotty and radiant, *at once*. Perhaps this is one of the difficulties for men imagining the effects of feminism for them. Model tales of transformation addressed to them by Western culture take the form of the grand conversion (Paul on the road to Tarsus . . .) and a stress on the single event. The few available contemporary images of common, everyday change correspondingly acquire a demeaning quality (one thinks of hairpiece ads for the bald, or the eight-stone weakling having sand kicked in his face before discovering muscle development). It's the ridicule, the indignity of lived change in all its incoherence that men must deal with in feminism—and in feminist theoretical practice.

And so my bother with my own negativity so far is that while the negativity is deeply felt, it quite elides my daily attitudes and past experience of frequently working (in writing, publishing, journalism) *with* men, *as* a feminist. But they weren't men "in" feminism, nor would they have "placed" themselves so, whatever their relation to feminist politics, feminist discourse; and if and when their maleness became an issue, it was occasionally, *eventfully*, and not as a fixed condition defining a constant state of affairs.

There's something deeply embarrassing, and inhibiting, about the title *Men in Feminism*. (This is certainly why I've addressed Paul Smith's paper, for without articulating my urge to turn away I find no other way to make sense). As others have remarked, the embarrassment congeals upon that odd word "*in*," blocked between two nouns to produce an apparently spatial—indeed, territorial—problem for feminism, but in terms that make that problem only thinkable as an action problem for men. So what can a woman say?

She can shrug, if she does say something; make some vague gesture of syntax (to take a term from Alice Jardine); affirming, if only to refuse the ins and outs of (r)ejection, a certain lack of connection, a reluctance, in fact, to connect: *in any case, in any event* . . . it really isn't an issue. Feminists might be justly uneasy about saying even so much. Whatever our personal motives and desires, the artificial creation of issues, hot topics, events and non-events is one of the most disturbing, difficult-to-manage processes defining the media, and the academic institutions, with which any political practice may engage as a means to continue its work.

I believe in the necessity of that engagement (including acts of discretion and silence). Media-innocence is an arcane state that seals off many a fading radical voice left sobbing in the library over the good old days of the bourgeois public sphere. Without engagement, we risk a profound misapprehension of the culture in which we presume to act, an inability to listen to those whom we hope we might address, and a convenient naivete about the impossible contradictions defining any "place" of intellectual political activity. Within such engagement, however, we always risk myopia and deafness: seeing only as the media see in the moment of cynicism, hearing only the academy's voice as we speak a discontent with that academy's narrow range.

The real embarrassment of *Men in Feminism* seems to me to have something to do with this double difficulty. It's a difficulty I can't dismiss by invoking, with Stephen Heath, the difference of my everyday feminism from an "academy-enclosed feminist theory," nor by separating, with Paul Smith, an academic "kitchen" from some other "public sphere." The academy, like the kitchen, as feminist theory must never tire of repeating in case it might be heard, is not enclosed or enclosing; not separable in its workings from other social relations; not "private." Writing, speaking, media-practice, theorizing, in a classroom or on a newspaper page . . . *is* my everyday feminism.

Therefore, the problem that emerges is this.

It's true that feminism is not, as Heath cautions, just another male "*topic.*" Neither, for that matter, is "men" a female topic, for feminism: works like Phyllis Chesler's *About Men*, for example, or Maxine Hong Kingston's *China Men*, are not about making space to take "stands." *Men in Feminism*, on the contrary, is just that—the name of a topic. It's a composition topic, and it does define a space—a commodified space, a space for publication, this book. And it's a space that can only emerge, in this form, from precisely those processes of "institionalization of feminism" that Paul Smith suggests (in suggesting the topic) that male "entry" might help to forestall!

I sympathize with Smith's anxieties about institutional processes (and of course, most feminists do). To some extent I share them, though I don't accept the terms of his formulation and the solution they permit. If embarrassing contradictions of the kind afflicting this project cannot easily be resolved, they can, however, be stated in the hope of countering the paralysis they can cause when complex political dilemmas (in this case, to speak or not to speak—and *how*) are collapsed into moods of moral anxiety about cooptation, and ingrown academic, or activist, communities. Institutionalization is not another name for doom, that fate always worse than death. It's an opportunity, and in many instances a necessary condition, for serious politics—including the failures, the repetitions, the reversals and the betrayals that any living politics entails.

So it's not a waste of time, not another interruption, to take an opportunity to insist that a topic like "men in feminism" is only intelligible as an *effect* of institutionalization as it works in particular contexts (and here I don't mean just this book). Therefore, it cannot usefully be abstracted from analysis of, and action in, contexts considerably more narrow again—that is, more precise, more local—than any generalizing myth of limitation (like "academia" or "American academia") can hope to define. Presented as a free-floating proposition, men in feminism probably isn't "an" issue for women: not that it doesn't matter, but because the intricate politics of lived social relations, and the incoherent passions always at work in any event (including territorial anxieties, and the desire to exclude the other as a means of becoming for one's self) are, after all, among the basic issues that feminism has always explored.

Specified as a local conflict about a job teaching feminist theory, of course, men in feminism is a problem at issue immediately. (My own "stand" on that is quite simple. Men have no business in feminism, when they've nothing but business therein.)

I'm reluctant to end, nonetheless, on such a narrowly businesslike note. The suggestion that we might make a problem of hearing, rather than women's speech, seems to me to be a useful one in general, and for one particular reason here.

I am sincerely astonished to read Paul Smith's claim that "feminist theory. . . . however 'feminist' it may be, and howsoever 'feminist' is construed, does not exist outside the academy . . . " (p. 34), and I suspect that he hasn't been listening very hard. Having carried out my own work in feminist theory (reading, talking, thinking as well as writing) without an academic base, and in nonacademic contexts with women and men in that same situation, my gasp of astonishment here may be inflected by purely regional customs—though I'm reluctant to believe that even in the United States, feminist theorists don't live, act, and write unemployed, or in nonacademic occupations.

The real trouble, however, is the construal of "theory" and "existence"—what discourses one accepts to hear as "theory," and where and how, what conditions are recognized as defining theory's "existence." Even if one makes the initial blocking-out gesture of restricting feminist theory to an "array of post-structuralist discourses" (which I most certainly would not, since my own interest in those discourses derives precisely from practical experience in feminism, and not the other way around), even if one consents so to limit one's attention, it's easy enough to hear that feminist theory being developed, debated, challenged, transformed and enjoyed in many different sites—if one leaves the academy to listen.

For surely, the "existence" of any theoretical work is defined in the activities of the people who read it and use it (in all the intimate ways that count as a "use" of reading), rather than by the institutional placing of some of those who produce it in a first instance as one of their activities. The existence, the making of theory is also defined by ripples of talk, hearsay, casual appropriations of a good idea by women who may never, or rarely, read theory, read at all.

I've no wish to be disingenuous here. I'm sure that the professional conditions of production of much American feminist theory entail particularities that I (reading it avidly at a distance) might quail to imagine. Nor do I wish to exaggerate the circulation of such theory, fancying the farreaching consequences following every theoretical tremor. But if it is, as Gayatri Spivak pointed out some years ago for the context of Marxism, quite misleading as well as discouraging for radical intellectuals to represent themselves as "lonely personalities proselytizing in the wilderness,"[6] it's misleading as well as abusive to represent academic feminists, and men, as overly close siblings squabbling in the kitchen. If the movement of ideas in industrialized capitalist societies did respect limits in the way implied by the rhetoric of confinement (besides academy and kitchen walls, "ghettoes" and stormy "teacups" are commonly occurring figures), then the tasks of ideological struggle might be at once simpler, and less important, for us all.

It's precisely because of movement, then, that the limit on, as Paul Smith puts it, "men *in* feminist theory" cannot possibly be the limit *of* feminist theory "itself." As one of the practices of the women's movement, the only limit that feminist theory need accept is that which appears in moments of fading energy, blockage, or wearying repetition, the ragged edge of theory's usefulness to particular women at any given time. This sort of limit is not a normative border, but an operational experience—and it's perhaps in terms of the latter, rather than the former, that the limitations of men's contributions to feminism, in feminist theory, might better be understood.

In any event, if we must resort at all to "age-old habits" and think our actions through territory and war, then men supportive of feminism are not entirely disarmed by giving away the romance of possession and entry. If the habit of active penetration does create the conditions for a scene of wearisome repetition, then there's something to be said for men in feminism to begin again by exploring the uncertainties that follow any act of strategic withdrawal.

19.
In, With

RICHARD OHMANN

Before sitting down to write this piece, I *may* have spent an hour or so in feminism today. I wrote a letter to my colleague Christina Crosby, suggesting items for discussion in a meeting we are planning with the president and vice-president of our college, Wesleyan University, on the future of our Women's Studies Program; then I phoned my colleague Jill Morawski, to go over some of the same points, and get further ideas from her. Christina was coordinator of the Program this past year; Jill and I were co-coordinators the previous year, and in 1981–2. The Program is only six years old, under-funded, and scrambling. We mean to press the advantage gained from a favorable review of it, just completed by the college's Educational Policy Committee. We will argue about secretarial help, about released time for the coordinator (Jill, next year), about getting commitments to the Program from some crucial departments that are now void of feminist scholars, and so on. The president and vice-president will say yes to some requests, maybe to others, not now to still others. We have had such meetings before, and there will probably be another in a year or so. We make a few gains, take a few disappointments. The Program slowly picks up strength. I take some satisfaction in the process, and in my role within it.

When the meeting takes place, Jill will be on the other side of the continent, so only Christina and I and the two administrators will be talking. Christina is an assistant professor in my own department; for her this is also a meeting with three men who will be deciding, two years hence, whether she gets tenure or not. She is our junior by twenty years (as is Jill). My relation to the administrators—Nat and Colin, thank you—is rather different: one of them was my subordinate, the other my counterpart, when I was in the administration sixteen years ago, and when Wesleyan was an all-male college. You could say that the three of us are part of the old boy network. To the likely readership of this volume, I don't think I need underscore the strange yet familiar power dynamic of the upcoming meeting, or the implicit contradictions of my local work in women's studies.

I say "work in women's studies." Does that work mean that I am a "man in feminism"? I frankly don't know, and the phrase makes me a bit uneasy. It reminds me of that old icebreaker at MLA conventions: "What century are *you* in?" To speak of men (or women) as in feminism surely does not (yet?) imply that sort of academic reduction of the person to a specialism, but it does smack of guild credentials—of an intellectual membership earned through writing centripetally toward an established group that has the authority to admit or exclude. Even though I know Jardine and Smith did not intend that emphasis, I wonder if it is not latent in the phrase, and strong enough to load the issues of this book with some unnecessary confusions. Can a man really *be* a feminist? be *in* feminism? What must I do to get certified? Who decides on membership? These strike me as dead-end questions that bypass the strategic issues for women's liberation, and for human liberation.

In this essay, then, I want to nudge the discussion toward questions of action and of politics, acknowledging the sorts of anomaly—or perhaps absurdity—framed by the example with which I began, but arguing that these are not very different in principle from others that we have learned to cope with. "We," in this article, are white, academic, progressive men in the United States, over thirty-five years of age. I believe that the account I give of how feminism came into my life has much in common with the stories that other such men might tell.

We were actively opposing the war in Vietnam and racism at home when the new feminist movement suddenly exploded around and amidst us. We had begun with individual protest: writing letters, signing petitions, then going to teach-ins, rallies, marches. The protests gathered a collective force. We joined or started organizations. We began to call ourselves "the movement," gliding optimistically past all the rifts and conflicts that divided us, taking in the attacks and critiques from black activists, trying to sort out nationalist woofing from warranted exposure of our blindness and arrogance, mainly accepting as historically necessary the separatist tendencies of black militancy, believing somewhat naively that all oppressions were one at some deep level, and that the enemy of my enemy is my friend.

I allude to those tensions as a reminder that we had a rather sharp experience of exclusion before the women's movement took shape, which started to happen about the end of 1968 in organizations with which I worked. By contrast, I did *not* experience that new articulation as excluding us, in spite of the separatist tendencies that grew within it, and in spite of the often-justified anger directed at us. (Marge Piercy's "Grand Coolie Damn" was a paradigmatic text, for that anger.) Most women in the MLA Radical Caucus, in RESIST, in New University Conference, later in *Radical Teacher*, did not leave; the characteristic expression of their politics was the caucus, which sought both to provide a male-free arena of discourse *and* to carry ideas and grievances spoken there back into the larger organization. The process worked through constant personal encounters, too—Florence Howe calling Louis Kampf and me on our supposedly innocuous jokes;

Elaine Hedges persuading me that the switch to "he or she" did make a difference; Susan McAllester opening my eyes to the maleness of a journal we worked on. (I'm not relaxed enough with the identity of personal and political to bring the tensions and troubles of my marriage into this discussion, but it too was an important part of the process I describe.) Women's caucuses and individual feminist women brought the import of privilege and liberation into the center of our political work and our lives. They were saying, "our demands are implicit in yours," and "change your conduct"; not "go away." Meetings and organizations became more democratic, talk less abstract. We began trying to *hear* women. We learned a few things. The quality of politics improved.

Politics spilled over into our jobs, in the early and middle seventies. We were trying to integrate our lives around new centers. It seemed urgent, and natural, for teachers of literature to bring *The Bell Jar* and *Sula* into the syllabus, to welcome *Their Eyes Were Watching God* and *Daughter of Earth* and *The Awakening*, as feminists rediscovered them, to raise issues of stereotyping and objectification articulated by early feminist criticism, to assign Kate Millett and Sheila Rowbotham, to bring gender into focus as we had tried to do with race, and were doing with class. There were more women colleagues now; we learned from them at home campuses, and from the intense and revelatory feminist sessions at professional meetings. In our classes (women were there, now, at the previously all-male colleges) we contended with piggery and tried to help authorize the interests and perceptions of the women students. I don't mean to suggest that the infusion of feminist texts, insights, and pedagogies into our teaching took place without failures and embarrassments, or that we shrugged off our former selves as easily as we had stopped wearing coats and ties a few years earlier. But along with the discomfort and dislocations, there was always the sense of fighting old deformities in ourselves, of participating in a just movement, and (not least) of teaching better courses.

For many of us who researched and wrote as part of our jobs, feminism was an enabling force in our scholarship, too. Feminist criticism, from Showalter and Gilbert and Gubar on, has of course transformed the field of literary studies. For me, as I moved toward cultural studies and took on an attempt to understand the origins of mass culture, other kinds of feminist scholarship have been even more crucial: work on the reconstruction of family, home, and domesticity a hundred years ago by Dolores Hayden, Gwendolyn Wright, Susan Strasser, Ann Douglas, Barbara Ehrenreich, Dierdre English, and many others. I regard those women as both my teachers and my collaborators, though as I appropriate their work, it remains to be seen whether they regard what I write in the same way. But the point is not whether I can somehow qualify myself through cultural scholarship (much less theory) as an *echt* feminist; what sort of ventriloquism would that require? The point is that for fifteen years I and many male comrades have worked politically with feminists, and come to believe that no radical politics unconnected to feminism is worth pursuing; and that I and many male academic radicals have learned from feminists to transform our teaching, our writing, the ways we think and feel about the world.

As for being *in* feminism, what more can it mean for us, other than joining in feminist struggles when we have a chance to do something useful on that terrain? I became part of the Women's Studies Program at Wesleyan in a peculiar way, yet one that illustrates the point. The Program was new; it had come into existence mainly through the efforts of students, though a number of faculty members had given the proposal support. At the end of its first year it looked as if no faculty members might be able and willing to act as coordinators the following year. There were still few tenured women (not all of them feminists); some disliked the idea of working with a collective composed mainly of students; some untenured feminist women were sensibly worried that putting volunteer time into administration of women's studies would make their futures even more insecure. I knew many of the students in the collective, through political work and from my courses. After they ran unsuccessfully through the plausible women candidates, they asked if I would be a co-coordinator for a year. They knew as well as I did what was wrong with that idea, but there had to be two faculty coordinators. I agreed to be one, expecting that I would mainly sign expense vouchers and front for the Program with the administration, while Jill really worked with the collective.

But it turned out that I could contribute more than that, and liked doing so. I knew how budgets worked, how faculty committees worked, how a program without a faculty T.O. could influence departmental hiring; I knew what senior faculty members and administrators were likely to be hostile and helpful. I did belong to the old boy network, and knew what would or would not carry weight with the vice-president. On the other side, from my experience in movement organizations I knew how democratic process could work or collapse, and I had learned (partly from women in the movement) how to be part of a collective, and not a big shot. Also, I had a fair idea of what was going on in women's studies. I found myself taking more satisfaction from this work than from other academic tasks; I put more energy into it, and have stayed close to the Program since then.

Well: it takes no genius to see what's fishy about all this. When I negotiate for Women's Studies with department chairs or with the administration, I draw upon—precisely—male privilege, funded over

many years. Furthermore, my presence in a meeting like the one
coming up inevitably familiarizes women's studies, and perhaps feminism, to the men who run our college. Perhaps more surprising
things, and in some ways more radical ones, would get said if the
delegation included only women. Perhaps the challenge that wom-
en's studies poses to old structures and habits of education would be
clearer. Perhaps Christina and the others would conceive more re-
sourceful strategies and goals by themselves, without someone like
me putting on the voice of local wisdom. (This is how things are done
here; this is what we can reasonably hope to win; etc.) Surely my
presence in the collective limits what might be thought or said there,
not just because I am a man (there have usually been one or two other
men in the collective), but because in that setting I represent practical
rationality, the old institution, the old boys.

As if those were not enough contradictions, I am also present in
this feminist context not because I am, historically, a feminist, but
because radical, socialist, and marxist commitments brought me here.
Do those commitments run cross-grain to directions that the program
might take up were I absent? Certainly I am hostile to some tendencies
represented among students in the group: Dalyism, Dworkinism,
Friedanism, one might name them. How much should I speak my
mind on these positions, given that they are at least organic growths
from an experience I have not shared?

Enough said, without even gesturing toward a deeper emotional
level (how do I feel, for instance, about being an influential and generally well-liked man in a room full of younger women?), to indicate
that there is nothing simple about a progressive man's involvement
in feminist projects. So what else is new? It wasn't simple to relate
ourselves to black liberation in 1968, but should we have scrapped
the effort? Our class privilege (as I write, I am on sabbatical, not on
unemployment) makes our efforts at solidarity with workers unceas-
ingly problematic. A typical article (in this case a pretty good one) by
a committed leftist winds up its analysis of intervention, take-backs,
and economic decline with a section titled "Strategic Problems for the
Left," and launches that section with a sentence beginning, "The area
where the left, at this point, has the greatest chance to organize mass
action. . . . " (Robert Brenner, "Austerity and Interventionism: Political Effects of Economic Decline," *Against the Current*, vol. I, no. 3,
new series, May-June, 1986, p. 35.) The image that comes to mind is
of an intellectual like me, at a meeting of some coalition group, explaining to the trade unionists there that protectionism or the rigid
defense of seniority is not in their long-term interest. OK, it's embarrassing; yet we do know that unless the struggle joins the interests
of workers and peasants around the world, of people of color and
women in the U. S., *and* of the traditional working class, it will be

ineffectual and wrong. So we keep trying to find the right alliance, and a rhetoric to use within it that is neither presumptuous nor self-hating. We are not Palestinians, we are not Nicaraguans, we are not Navahos, most of us are not gay, but. . . . If we were to stick humbly to a politics derived strictly from our own experience and interests, we could be satisfied with membership in the AAUP—or even (why not?) with endorsing the politics and policies of Mr. Secretary William Bennett.

My point, as it applies to the concerns of this volume, is just that progressive male intellectuals and professionals have arrived at feminism by an inexorable development, and by a moral logic that flows from our strongest allegiances. We understand that a movement without a commitment to (e.g.) abortion rights, without full internal equality of women and men, and without a realization of politics in personal life, is a movement crippled both practically and morally. Of course we didn't discover this for ourselves, most of us. And the memory of how belatedly we learned it, and from whom, should guarantee a measure of lifelong humility. If we are "in" feminism at all, we were dragged into it kicking and screaming, and now that we're there we should think of ourselves as on extended probation, still learning. What we do there with our experience, our competence, and our gender and class confidence, is a matter to be negotiated through caution, flexibility, improvisation, listening, and often doubtless through a strategic fade into the wallpaper. But I don't see drawing back from the knowledge that feminism is our fight, too.

So is racial equality, so is gay liberation, so is antiimperialism. I see the difficulties of our participation in these struggles as parallel to those of our joining in women's liberation, and in consequence I see alliance politics as our challenge and our aim. But I want to acknowledge that in two important ways our relation to feminism differs. First, institutional racism and homophobia have their historical roots in the soil of capitalism. Imperialism of the present sort grew directly from capitalism's motion and needs at a particular time. Ending the reign of capital would of course not automatically or easily end these oppressions, but at least it would eliminate their historical rationality. Patriarchy is much older, maybe as old as the species. To be sure, capitalist relations have penetrated deeply and subtly into relations of male dominance; as capitalism requires great inequality, and as bourgeois democracy must proclaim itself to be in principle egalitarian, *any* socially entrenched hierarchy with an accompanying belief that one group is intrinsically less deserving than another is grist for capitalism's mill. But male supremacy responds to other needs than those of the bourgeoisie. For that reason, those of us who are socialists have to maintain a special relation to feminism, recognizing that it is not quite so inevitably a part of the one struggle as are the other liberations.

Second, for most of us patriarchy was a far more intimate part of our socialization than were the other oppressions, and it far more completely suffuses our daily lives. On many days I can feel antiracist for all my waking hours, and never be tested. My commitment idles in neutral, to be engaged in political meetings, curricular discussions, or the like. Not so my commitment to gender equality, which meets challenges, and small or large defeats, on even the most apolitical day. My very affections, which are the strongest personal incentive to live a feminist life, simultaneously threaten to call old, antifeminist habits and routines into play. I can't be "in" feminism the way Jill and Christina are, and the effort to be *with* it is more problematic.

I'll try to remember that in the president's office. But what the hell, the Women's Studies Program does need a halftime secretary, and that will be at the top of my agenda.

20.

Women in the Beehive: A Seminar with

JACQUES DERRIDA

INTRODUCTION: In reference to the lecture on Kafka's text, one can say that if the Law is the condition of the institution, if the in-

---

"Women in the Beehive: A Seminar with Jacques Derrida" was first published in subjects/objects (Spring 1984), a journal produced by students associated with the Semiotics Program and the Sarah Doyle Women's Center at Brown University. We thank Jacques Derrida and the editorial board of subjects/objects for permission to use this material, and particularly those members of the board—James Adner, Kate Doyle, and Glenn Hendler—who originally edited the text from transcripts of the seminar. James Adner translated those parts of the transcripts which were originally in French. We also want to express our gratitude to Elizabeth Weed and the Brown University Pembroke Center for their cooperation and help.

The text printed here has not been reedited by us except for the removal of a couple of contextual remarks, and the changing of the punctuation in a very few places.

At its original appearance the transcript was prefaced by the following remarks:

The text printed here is situated somewhere between speech and writing. It is a modified transcript of a seminar given by the Pembroke Center for teaching and research on women with guest speaker Jacques Derrida. *The speaker referred to as "Response" is not the writer Jacques Derrida,* but is rather our account of his responses. The category "Question" denotes edited versions of queries posed by members of the seminar and visitors. . . . Due to the improvised nature of the seminar's dialogue and the vulnerable philosophical position M. Derrida is placed in [no] quotation marks appear in this edited text. We thank M. Derrida for allowing us to publish this transcript—this text, authorized but authorless.

We include this interview in our collection partly because it gives a good sense of how Derrida negotiates the difficult questions which feminists inevitably will have about the treatment of "the feminine" in his work. It is perhaps worth remarking that in the original (i.e. unedited) transcripts Derrida often makes comments in the first person about his own relation to such questions. Those comments would have considerably affected the tone of the seminar, but we are not "authorized" to publish them.

stitution is the Law, then the guardians of the institution are also the guardians of the Law. And as the research in women's studies gains institutional legitimacy, it also constitutes, constructs, and produces guardians of the Law. It induces men from the country who come before the Law to try to accede it, to see it, to touch it, to penetrate it. Thus departments of women's studies in America are now becoming a relatively solid institution. It is certainly important to acknowledge the problems, limitations, and resistances to the institution met even in the United States.

Yet one can say without error that the United States is a pioneer in this aspect, that there are more women's studies programs in the United States than anywhere else in the world. And from this point of view, to criticize women's studies—from whatever aspect—is an error, a mark of ignorance, of obscurantism, since anywhere else in the world women's studies does not have the institutional power that it already has in the United States. One can only wonder: what are the risks and the stakes of the institution of women's studies? Do the women who manage these programs, do they not become, in turn, the guardians of the Law, and do they not risk constructing an institution similar to the institution against which they are fighting? In other words, the first question could be, what is the difference, if there is one, between a university institution of research and teaching called "women's studies" and any other institution of learning and teaching around it in the university or in society as a whole? It is certain that the range of work in women's studies is enormous, and that there are already considerable problems to pose, of bodies of work, of objects to define, and that women's studies has a great future. Nevertheless, if this future is of the same type as that of all other departments, of all other university institutions, is this not a sign of failure of the principles of women's studies?

In the universities of Western Europe and the U. S. we see an institutional model reproduced which on the whole was constructed at the beginning of the nineteenth century in Germany, in Berlin— and the U. S. is probably more faithful to this model than are most of the European countries. All the objects, all the fields which presently structure the university today were already established by the nineteenth century, whether studies of literature, philosophy, physics, mathematics, geography or social studies—nothing new, *except* women's studies. There was no place forseen in the structure of the classical model of Berlin for feminist studies. Thus with women's studies, is it a question of simply filling a lack in a structure already in place, filling a gap? Fascinating things would be done, new things discovered, knowledge advanced, and this is necessary—but one would not alter the model of the university, and in consequence, one would insidiously reproduce in the modern university, whether one knew it or not, the old model, which is fundamentally phallocentric or "phallogocentric."

As much as women's studies has not put back into question the very principles of the structure of the former model of the university, it risks to be just another cell in the university beehive. If one tries to analyze, to gain an overview of the state of women's studies in the world and notably in the U. S., where the movement is the strongest, one has an ambiguous feeling. One has the feeling that on the one hand a certain positivity of research is very successful, one discovers all sorts of things, one exhumes new corpuses, one studies women's literature, one uplifts from under the repression, from out of the realm of the forbidden all sorts of feminine signatures, feminist discourses which were obscured, one brings out not only literary but anthropological, political, and social dimensions. All that is very positive, certainly. On the other hand, the effort to put back into question the structural principles which I mentioned before, which construct the university law, the academic law, that is to say, in the end, the social law in general—because the university is not a separate bloc, it represents society, society represents itself through the university—one has the impression that the questioning of this principle is unequally developed in comparison to those studies which we could call "positive." This question concerns the fundamentals of the institution. In that sense, the risk of failure of women's studies is the risk of its very own success. The more it proves its positivity, its necessity, and brings proofs to the masculine directors of the university—masculine, whether women or not—the more it legitimizes itself by this power; the more then, it risks to cover up, to forget, or to repress the fundamental question which we must pose.

Thus, the risk is not only the unequal development between positive and progressive research, both political and scientific, which are necessary to pursue, but there is a more dangerous and adventurous question. It is that whoever asks questions by definition not coded on these principles of progress risks to appear—in the eyes of women who are activists for women's studies—reactionary, dangerous, only limiting the progress of their positive research. This would include, for example, whoever suggests that we do not need Women's Studies departments at all, and that it's not necessary to construct institutions of this sort, that it is necessary that the concern finds other routes outside the universities where departments are established on the old model. Those—whether men or women—who risk that question, also risk in one form or another being rejected by that which calls itself Women's Studies.

This is a question of the Law: are those involved in women's studies—teachers, students, researchers—the guardians of the Law or not? You will remember that in the parable of the Law of Kafka, between the guardian of the Law and the man from the country there is no essential difference: they are in oppositional but symmetric positions. We are all, as members of a university, guardians of the Law—people who assure a tradition, who maintain a heritage, who are critics and evaluators, and at the same time who are men from the country, naive in front of the text, in front of the Law. Does that situation repeat itself for women's studies or not? Is there in the abstract or even topical idea of women's studies something which potentially has the force, if it is possible, to deconstruct the fundamental institutional structure of the university, of the Law of the university?

There seem to be two hypotheses, two responses. On one hand, there is the positive deconstruction, which consists of saying that one cannot be content with only positive research, but that one must push to the end of the radical question concerning the university Law, and do more than simply insitute a department of Women's Studies. That is the optimistic deconstruction, the deconstruction which would not submit to the Law. And then there is another deconstruction, perhaps not resigned or fatalist, but more conscious of the law of the Law and of the fact that even the radical questioning, even the radical deconstruction of the institution of the university by women's studies would not be able to reproduce the Law in the face of the Law. It is not a question of transgressing the Law. In any case, if one takes again Kafka's text, if one were to radically deconstruct the old model of the university in the name of women's studies, it would not be to open a territory without Law—the theme of liberation if you like. But it would be for a new relation to the Law. It is necessary to establish the departments of Women's Studies which would resemble their brothers and sisters of literature, philosophy, anthropology, etc., but after one had done that, one would already have found the Law again. But at least one would have radically changed the situation. One would have rediscovered the Law, but at least one would not be bored any longer. That would be the pessimistic deconstruction.

It is a question of two affirmations, one which appears in classically coded language—optimistic, liberating, revolutionary—and the other which appears on the contrary more modest, more conscious of the fact that at least one radically changed things. One will have brought a better situation, again in front of the Law, which would give one time to grow old, to die like the man from the country. This is the first question—it is a question about strategy. Of course, it has been a necessary phase, strategically speaking, to build women's studies. But what should be the next step? Only this first move, this first effort? Or something totally new? And is it only a question of strategy—is not strategy itself the real risk?

QUESTION: I was just wondering to what extent one can carry your discussion of the Law last night over to this question by thinking about the practitioners of women's studies as women subjects, who can, unlike men, identify with the Law—neither with the man from the country or the keeper of the Law, but with the Law itself: the hymen, the forbidden place, and use that as some kind of strategy by subverting from within. Not through building women's studies, but through feminizing disciplines, which, in very simple terms, is tried sometimes in this country. It's called "integration" of women's studies into the curriculum. But this integration is often a simple way of subverting the curriculum. *Feminizing* the curriculum on the other hand, is trivializing it, is dismantling it, is displacing it; it is making it as trivial as women, and I wonder if it isn't our real strategy: that we work from the base of an operation such as this in order to trivialize philosophy, to trivialize history, to trivialize economics.

RESPONSE: The best choice would be to have the two gestures at the same time: to have a Women's Studies department with a solid, autonomous structure, without giving up the idea of penetrating all other fields, to remain within a department, would be a failure. On the other hand, if you give up the idea of a feminine studies program, then you will weaken the feminine cause. So, the only response to this question would be—joint appointments! Now . . . coming back to the first step in your question—as to the Law—you will remember, the Law in Kafka's story was neither male nor female. The doorkeeper and the man were subjects—subject to the Law, and "subjects." So a problem arises: if you keep the philosphical axiomatics, implying that *women* are subjects, considering women as subjects, then you keep the whole framework on which the traditional university is built. If someone tries to deconstruct the notion of subjectivity within women's studies, saying "well, woman is not a subject, we no longer consider woman as a subject"—this would have two consequences: one radically revolutionary or deconstructive, and the other dangerously reactive.

This is the risk. The effect of the Law is to build the structure of the subject, and as soon as you say, "well, the woman is a subject and this subject deserves equal rights," and so on—then you are caught in the logic of phallogocentrism and you have rebuilt the empire of the Law. So it seems that women's studies can't go very far if it does not deconstruct the philosophical framework of this situation, starting with the notion of subject, of ego, of consciousness, soul and body, and so on. The problem with this strategy is that it's difficult to make so many gestures at the same time. Doing research in classical fields—and we need such research in anthropology, in literature—under the titles of subjectivity and soul and body, and civil rights, and at the same time undermining the very structure you're trying to transform.

QUESTION: I wonder if there isn't some use in the de-naturali-

zation of man as a universal; in making men—not "Man," but *men*—
the specific objects of study.

RESPONSE: Yes, that's a necessary gesture. What we could call
the neuterization of sexual marks, has as you know, the effect of
giving power to man. When you say, "well you are in a neuter field,
no difference," we all know that in this case the subject will be man.
So, this is a classical ruse of man to neutralize the sexual mark. In
philosophy we have such signs all the time; when we say that the
ego, the "I think," is neither man nor woman, we can in fact verify
that it's already a man, and not a woman. It's always the case. So,
to the extent which universality implies neutralization, you can be
sure that it's only a hidden way of confirming the man in his power.
That's why we have to be very cautious about neutrality and neutralization, and universality as neutralization.

QUESTION: I wanted to pursue the question of subject/object. In
a piece of Gayatri Spivak's,[1] a review of *La Carte Postale*,[2] she, in
talking about the privileged place of woman in your work, says, "of
all the names that Derrida has given to originary undecidability,
woman possesses this special quality—she can occupy both positions
in the subject/object oscillation, be cathected as both something that
différance, writing, the *pararegon*, the supplement, and the like. Other
names of undecidability *cannot*, without special pleading. Derrida's
arrival at the name of woman seems to be a slow assumption of the
consequences of the critique of humanism as phallogocentrism . . .
" and so forth. I want to ask you about the difference between woman
and Woman, and the deconstruction of subjectivity and subject/object
around woman. How does one do it?

RESPONSE: That's a difficult question. Of course, saying that
woman is on the side, so to speak, of undecidability and so on, has
only the meaning of a strategical phase. In a given situation, which
is ours, which is the European phallogocentric structure, the side of
the woman is the side from which you start to dismantle the structure.
So you can put undecidability and all of the other concepts which go
with it on the side of femininity, writing and so on. But as soon as
you have reached the first stage of deconstruction, then the opposition between women and men stops being pertinent. Then you
cannot say that woman is another name, or a good trope for writing,
undecidability and so on. We need to find some way to progress
strategically. Starting with deconstruction of phallogocentrism, and
using the feminine force, so to speak, in this move and then—and
this would be the second stage or second level—to give up the opposition between men and women. At this second stage "woman"
is clearly not the best trope to refer to all those things: undecidability
and so on. The same could be said for undecidability itself! Undecidability is not a point of arrival. It's also a letter, a misconceived letter,

because undecidability—the theme, the motif of undecidability— has to do with a given situation in which you have an opposition or a dialectical logic.

So, the motif of undecidability is linked to a given situation in which opposition is strong. But once you have deconstructed this opposition, you do not need undecidability any more. And there are many many kinds of undecidability. There is one kind of undecidability which is a kind of calculus, a kind of logic, a kind of programming or unprogramming a program, but with a symmetrical relationship to the program. And then there is another undecidability which is totally heterogeneous to the former one, which is totally foreign to the realm of calculus, to the realm of opposition, to the realm of programming and so on. By analogy, we could say the same about "woman." There is one meaning to the word "woman" which is caught in the opposition, in the couple, and to this extent you can use the force of woman to reverse, to undermine this first stage of opposition. Once you have succeeded, the word "woman" does not have the same meaning. Perhaps we could not even speak of "woman" anymore. Of course, these two stages are not chronologically altered. Sometimes you can make the two gestures at the same time, and sometimes you cannot go from one to the other.

QUESTION: But if we use a new triad that still had an opposition of man and woman but had a homonymous yet different tropic use of "woman" as the third term, wouldn't we have the same sorts of reservations that we have with the reigning triad of man and woman with the homonym "man" as the third term? That homonym there seems to imply a synecdochal relationship in that a man can represent the higher category of "Man." Perhaps the tropic use of "woman" is so unfamiliar that we would not slide into homonymy as safely and as routinely as we do with the current use of "man." Perhaps because it's not a metaphoric use, because every one of us in the room has felt the difficulty of undertaking the responsibility to be the Capital W, "Woman." What is the difference between the two systems?

RESPONSE: First of all, the two systems carry similar danger. "Triad" has not been named, you know: triadic structure, which is a dialectical solution. There is no dialectical solution to the problem. Then: in our situation, in this cultural and historical situation, the terms "Man" and "Woman" are not at all the same. This is not an eternal and universal situation. This could change. But in the Western countries, in phallogocentric cultures and so on, the situation implies that there is a difference. In our language, when one says "Man" with a capital M and "Woman" with a capital W . . . it's not at all the same, not at all, because "man" with a capital M means "mankind." Woman with a capital W means . . . "Truth" or things like that, but doesn't mean mankind or womankind.

QUESTION: You have this question about woman's studies, that it might simply add something to the existing structure of this academic institution and not question it. I think it's a problem that's very, very important, and I don't know if we're answering it. I have no illusions about the road to freedom and liberation, but a Women's Studies program does institute some different relationship to the Law, and if women were absent before in the traditional academic institutions, maybe now women are more present. So it's a very relative progress, but I suppose it *is* a progress. But then with this background, how do you feel as a . . . I don't know if I dare call you a deconstructionist philosopher. What is the relationship of your research and pursuit, and the way that deconstruction is absorbed—I can't say absorbed, it's *swallowed*—with tremendous eagerness by American universities, even more than in France?

RESPONSE: It's more complicated, even in the United States. Of course the reception is larger in the United States than it is in France, but it's not . . . "swallowing." In fact, there are many signs of a very strong and growing resistance in the United States. And it seems to be exactly the same resistance—and there's nothing fortuitous in that—exactly the same resistance which is opposed to women's studies. Exactly the same people, and the same arguments and the same schemes. For instance, and this is only an anecdote—but a significant one—it has been written somewhere that deconstruction in the United States was successful among feminists and homosexuals. And there is always something sexual at stake in the resistance to deconstruction. Of course it's never simple. It's never easy to formalize, but we can be sure that the force for resisting deconstruction is the same. It's probably the reason why feminists or feminist scholars are to some extent interested in deconstruction, because the struggle is the same. Now, why is it the same? Because deconstruction has developed itself as a deconstruction of a system which is called phallogocentrism, which is a whole structure, which is a system so to speak. And it's not only a matter of concepts, of philosophical battle, but it's also a problem of how to write, how to behave in front of texts, in the institution, and of the relationship to literature and philosophy and so on. That's why it seems to me that there is a strong link between deconstruction—deconstruction*s* and feminine studies, women's studies; but these strategic difficulties are also the same; with the same aporias, the same traps.

QUESTION: In your interview with Christie McDonald,[3] there's an implication that there are two kinds of feminism. The first is a sort of emancipatory movement that is within the tradition of progress, and in some ways very boring, but very secure also. Very necessary but also not imaginative. It works more or less within the framework. In that interview the optimistic deconstruction says that we must not be content only to enact or conduct positive research, and I think that

that kind of feminism is a little bit like the women's studies that does positive research and which also exists, and which is important. And then that same optimistic deconstructionist says that we must do something more than build a supplementary. And that looks a little bit like the maverick feminist who dances. It's a way of doing things which can think almost beyond, or re-think the existing structure. I can see that, but I think that that is not really an opposition, necessarily, to the other kind of position which, as you said, is the one that is conscious of the law of the Law, in the sense that you think that you can do something different but you may not think, therefore, that you can go beyond the existence of the Law. It's one thing to say I destructure the subject, and it's another thing, I think, to say I destructure structure or I destructure Law.

RESPONSE: We cannot be sure there is a way of destructuring Law. You see, deconstruction cannot be transgression of the Law. Deconstruction *is* the Law. It's an affirmation, and affirmation is on the side of the Law. This is rather difficult. Usually we represent deconstruction as a negative or de-structuring movement, which it is not. It is an affirmative movement, first; and then, *as* an affirmation, it is not an affirmation against the Law or going beyond the Law. What's difficult to think is that the Law *is* an affirmation, has the structure of an affirmation. It's not something which limits the desire or forbids the transgression. As soon as you affirm a desire, you perform something which is the Law. The Law says, "yes." That's difficult to understand. The Law is not simply negative.

That's why writing in a deconstructive mode is another way of writing Law. And this is paradoxical. That's one thing that was demonstrated last night, that when Kafka writes "Before the Law," of course he describes a powerful structure, and then he deconstructs all the systems of the Law and shows you how impossible it is to see the Law, to enter the Law, to trangress the limit past the door. But what he is doing, in the meantime, is writing a text which in turn becomes the Law itself. "Before the Law" *is* the Law. We are in front of it as in front of the Law. He reproduces the situation, and the Franz Kafka signature, or the signature of the text, makes the Law—in a deconstructing movement. So deconstruction affirms a new mode of Law. It becomes the Law. But the Law is guaranteed by a more powerful Law, and the process has no end. This is why deconstruction is not a movement of transgression, of liberation; of course, it has some effects of—in a given situation—effects of emancipation, of transgression, of liberation, but, in the end, it is not.

QUESTION: When we were reading "Choreographies," there was one passage we stopped over and spent a lot of time trying to deconstruct. It is precisely one where you talk about the gift; this is in your response to Christie McDonald. You say, "I am moving much too rapidly but how can I do otherwise here? From this point, which is not a point, one wonders whether this extremely difficult, perhaps impossible idea of the gift can still maintain an essential relationship to sexual difference. One wonders whether sexual difference, femininity for example, however irreducible it might be, does not remain derived from and subordinated to either the question of destination, or the thought of the gift." Do you think that you could unpack that for us?

RESPONSE: Let's begin with the idea of destination. In general, when one speaks of "man" or of "woman" one supposes, for example, that a man speaks to a woman, that a woman speaks to a man, that they are identifiable subjects, and that between them there exists an exchange. The messages, the gifts, caresses, desires, objects, etc., have a giver and a receiver, a destination between two subjects. In as much as a gift has an assignable destination, it is an exchange—therefore, it is *not* a gift. There is a difference here between a gift and an exchange. If there is, from the man to the woman, or from the woman to the man, a destination of whatever kind, of an object, of a discourse, of a letter, of a desire, of *jouissance*, if this thing is identifiable as passing from subject to subject—from a man to a woman, or from a woman to a woman, or a man to a man, etc., etc.—if there is a possible determination of subject—at that moment, there is no longer a gift. Consequently, there is no gift except in that all determinations—particularly sexual determination as classically defined—are absolutely unconscious and random. And this randomness is the chance of the gift—the gift must be given by chance.

If the gift is calculated, if you know what you are going to give to whom, if you know what you want to give, for what reason, to whom, in view of what, etc., there is no longer any gift. And in order for this chance to arise, it is necessary that there be no relation with consciousness, experience, or the representation of sexual determination. When we speak here of sexual difference, we must distinguish between opposition and difference. Opposition is two, opposition is man/woman. Difference on the other hand, can be an indefinite number of sexes and once there is sexual difference in its classical sense—an opposition of two—the arrangement is such that the gift is impossible. All that you can call "gift"—love, *jouissance*—is absolutely forbidden, is forbidden by the dual opposition.

In consequence, to "unpack" the ellipse, we cannot be sure that there is ever a gift. If someone says to you that there is a gift, you can be sure that that person is mistaken. But if there is the gift, it can only be on the condition—not of non-sexuality—but of sexual non-determination, in the sense of opposition. That is, not in sexual indifference, but in a sexuality completely out of the frame, totally aleatory to what we are familiar with in the term "sexuality." There can be a heterosexual or a homosexual relation; homosexuality does not exclude itself from this situation.

This does not mean that there is the gift only beyond sexuality but that the gift is beyond sexual duality. To refer to the recently published text called *Geschlecht*, a reading of Heidegger's notion of *Dasein: Dasein* is neither man, nor spirit, nor subject, consciousness nor ego, but sexually neuter; that is, it has no sex. Heidegger did not consider this non-sexuality to be a negative attribute with regard to the opposition man/woman; in other words, it is not a term denoting a-sexuality. *Dasein* is not indifferent to the marks of difference. Heidegger's discourse is not simple, nor simply beyond classical thought on this subject; certainly this motif on neutralization in his discourse could also reconstruct phallocentrism. There is a certain neutralization which can reconstruct the phallocentric privilege. But there is another neutralization which can simply neutralize the sexual opposition, and not sexual difference, liberating the field of sexuality for a very *different* sexuality, a more multiple one. At that point there would be no more sexes . . . there would be one sex for each time. One sex for each gift. A sexual difference for each gift. That can be produced within the situation of a man and a woman, a man and a man, a woman and a woman, three men and a woman, etc. By definition, one cannot calculate the gift. We are in the order of the incalculable, of undecidability which is a strategic undecidability where one says "it is undecidable because it is not this term of the opposition or the other." This is sexual difference. It is absolutely heterogeneous.

QUESTION: I have a question about the relationship between sexuality and identity. It seemed to me that, from the analysis of the problem of the gift, in order for the system to work, when you have sexual inderterminacy in this binary way, then you have no possibility that the individual, or that the parties be identifiable, recognizable, determinable. Sexual indeterminacy implies the indeterminacy of the people, of the subjects. However, one could say that you're sexually indeterminate, but you're not indeterminate racially, for example. Or there's the possibility of identification, and of destination, therefore, which is not bound to sexuality. Is that right?

RESPONSE: In the moment, in the core instance of gifts, it doesn't mean that we have to give up any sexual determinations, but the experience of gifts itself—if it takes place—implies such a sexual indeterminacy. The gift, effacing all determination, sexual or otherwise, produces the destination. Supposing that a gift has been given; that supposes that before it took place, the giver is not determined, and the receiver is not determined. But the gift determines; it is the determination, it produces the identity of the giver and the receiver. The gift is not simply floating in a definitive determination. It gives itself the right to determine. That is why the gift is always a strike of force, an irruption. As an example, in *La Carte Postale* there is a text which is called "Télépathie." In this text it says that such enunciations are not always addressed to anyone, but will only be determined in their destination after their answer. The one who responds, receives it, becomes the receiver. The performativity of the text produces its receiver, but in no way does it pre-exist it. It is the receiver who is the determining factor of the gift. It is not really a "message" structure, for a message presupposes that "X" sends "Y" for "Z," and in the situation of the gift there is no message. It is only the other, at the moment when it receives it, who decides the destination, and who says "it is me who answers" or, "it is mine."

Consider the Declaration of Independence. Jefferson wrote the first draft, the other representatives corrected his text—they were not at all satisfied with it—and the Declaration was signed. But the question is "Who signed the Declaration of Independence?" If one analyses the text, one can first of all say that not Jefferson, for he was the editor, and not the representative, for they spoke in the name of the "good people," but the American people signed the Declaration of Independence. And if one reads the text, one can see that the good people of the United States signed the text in the name of God. It is God who guarantees their good faith, and it is ultimately God who signs the Declaration of Independence. That means that the American people did not exist as the American people before having signed the Declaration of Independence. And it is in signing that they conferred upon themselves the right to call themselves the American people and the right to sign. It did not exist before the signature. Thus, the scriptor does not exist before the signature. The signature itself, which imposes the law, is in itself a performative act which in a certain way produces its own subject, which gives the person the right to do what he is doing. Here is an enunciation—the Declaration of Independence—which arises with a burst of force before there is even a receiver. Thus there is a gesture which, at the limit, produces the receiver, and at the same time produces the sender. When there is such a gesture, an enunciation, it speaks of indetermination but produces determination. It is by the gift that the Law is produced. It is this signature which engenders the sender, the receiver, the signer. It is a performative act—not to put great trust in this concept, but to use it only for convenience—of the gift which produces the giver and the receiver, who at that time become determined, determine themselves as such. It happens all the time, when one says "yes" in marriage for instance.

QUESTION: What is the relation between the performative function of the gift and the conception derived from Heidegger of a kind of limit-notion that might never even exist but points beyond and might also liberate into a kind of non-role-specific diversity of sexualities? It's pretty clear that *Dasein* is quite curiously neutral; I think everyone has noticed that. What is the connection between these two dimensions of the gift?

RESPONSE: The relationship between the theme of indeterminacy on the one hand and the performative on the other could be clear under the condition that one does not simply accept the opposition of performative to constative. You always arrive at a point where this opposition doesn't function any more, but if you take the concept of performative as a conventional assumption then you have to do with a way of speaking or writing—of promising—which is presupposed by any other form of language. The promise, for instance, is a fundamental assumption of any speech act. As soon as one speaks, one is promising. And this promise doesn't simply fall under the concept of performative. If you agree that a signature or everything that amounts to a signature in a statement or in a writing or even in a gesture is performative inasmuch as it doesn't rely on a ready determination, then you cannot rely on the sexual opposition.

In the classical theorization of speech acts, a performative must rely upon conventions. So that's why one cannot be confident of the category of performatives in this case, because there can be no performative if there is no law, if there is no convention which guarantees the efficiency, the pertinence of any performative. There is a performative which creates its own conventions, or if not creates, at least upsets or transforms the system of conventions. For instance, the Declaration of Independence relies on many conventions, but also creates a new framework for new conventions. To this extent it's a performative, and it is a kind of subversion of the existing situation, of the relationship with Great Britain. In that sense, every event of gift is subversive, because it doesn't rely on any given program.

Perhaps it's not even subversive because subversion is a way of relying on given conditions. A gift is something else; it's not subversive, it's not conservative. Subversion is also a program. It has to do with the programmed destruction of a certain amount of conditions. It is totally heterogeneous to subversion as well as to conservation. That is, if it takes place, which is never guaranteed.

QUESTION: As you posed the optimistic and the guarded reading of Women's Studies Programs, I wondered by what standard one would read it as either the optimist or the pessimist. I'm a historian, and so I kept thinking that one could write a history of these programs either way, and yet could one try to articulate the measure or the standard by which one could say the subversion had been accomplished, or the transformation achieved, as opposed to the institution incorporating this potentially subversive force?

RESPONSE: There is no measure, not in the form of a theoretical statement, of a theoretical statement signed by a historian. If you want to write the history of women's studies in this country, you won't be able to stop the movement. Your own history can be an active interpretation and can be part of a conservative interpretation of women's studies or another part. So, there is no historical metalanguage on women's studies. But within the space of women's studies, both gestures are always possible. In the same room, in the same seminar, each one of you may sometimes make a conservative gesture and sometimes a subversive one. The history that you could write of women's studies belongs also to the movement; it is not a metalanguage, and will act either as a conservative moment or a subversive moment. Because there is no theoretically neuter interpretation of the history of women's studies. The history will have a performative part in it.

QUESTION: This then brings us to the question of political strategy. And maybe then one asks: in what terms does one understand which of the gestures—or both of the gestures—that you describe as possibilities is better. It seems to me that when you were asking the question you stood outside and posed it as the "optimistic deconstructionist." One can maintain a radical critique and open up new territory and on the other hand one that is more aware of the law of the Law.

RESPONSE: This may not answer the question, but one way of dealing with these problems, not necessarily within women's studies, but on the whole, is to try to do both things at the same time, to occupy two places, both places. That is why deconstruction is often accused of being conservative and . . . not conservative. And both are true! We have to negotiate. To maintain, for instance, Women's Studies as a classical program, a now classical program, and at the same time to ask radical questions which may endanger the program itself. And what is the measure? You must check everyday what is the measure. One thing may be the good measure at Brown, but perhaps it would be the worst thing at Yale for instance. There is no general device. In some situations you have to behave in a very conservative way, in tough conservative ways, to maintain, and at the same time, or the day after to do exactly the contrary.

QUESTION: The gift: in every one of its appearances, we get a new configuration of subjects, objects, of identities. That is, with each occurrence of the gift, I suppose, one could occur as male or female in a certain configuration of subjects. In every production of this gift situation we assume that all of us could appear as something different. Even historically different, I suppose. I wonder if you take that as a positive limit, if it's a limit-case. I'm not sure it has any value, moral value, whatsoever.

RESPONSE: It has no *a priori* value. There is no value before it has taken place. Once it has taken place, one will see what is the worth. If you are the receiver of a gift which makes you "woman," you will see. You will say if it has a positive or a negative value. It will be your evaluation of the gift. One can't say ahead of time, "well, this will endanger you."

QUESTION: Then, relating it to the positivity or negativity of the situation of women's studies. If there's merely a reversal, in which men become objects of study and women become the mastering subject, you merely recapitulate the same structure you had previously. But every repetition of the gift would be a repetition not of the same, but exactly a repetition of the different. If that's possible. It seems to me that for women's studies, then, that can be taken as a positive strategy. If there's a battle of the sexes, then women can't win it, they can just end it. It seems to me that this gift implies an interesting notion, where the notion of sexuality disappears in the triumph of feminism.

RESPONSE: No one ever said that sexuality would disappear. Without a doubt, if the success of women's studies would be to constitute men as an object of study, and women as mastering subjects, nothing will have happened. It is necessary not to reproduce the same structure. And you can't say that the gift must always produce something. The gift is not a production. But there are gifts which are gifts which only call upon repetition and not reproduction. To receive a gift, in the Nietzschean sense, is to say "I want it to begin again," that it happens again, not that it reproduces. And that suggest something on the order of repetition. The "yes" of the gift must be repeatable from the start. Thus it is necessary not to mix the value of production and reproduction, newness, repetition of the other.

QUESTION: This question is related to something you said earlier. You said that in Western culture, the word "man" means "mankind" and the word "woman" means "truth." But in your own writings woman seems to be theorized as a whole list of things mentioned earlier, in the quotation from Gayatri Spivak. And to use one phrase from "The Law of Genre,"[4] a "random drift" which affects the masculine genre and threatens to make it other. I guess I'm asking you to explain how woman as man's "random drift" is different from woman as man's "truth."

RESPONSE: This is an abyssal question, for there is a certain determination of truth which permits one to answer that woman as truth is that which stops the drift, that which interrupts and assures truth. But there is a way of thinking about truth which is more adventurous, risky. And at that point, truth, which is without end, abyssal, is the very movement of the drift. There is a way of thinking about truth which is not reassuring, which is not in general what we think of truth. That would bring us into a discourse about the truth of truth, and Heidegger who says that truth is non-truth; the field is open. As is the case with women's studies and any discipline, at a certain moment one can no longer improvise or hurry. You have to go slowly, look at things in detail. At a certain point it is necessary to stop; one cannot improvise on a question of truth. It would not be surprising, considering all the fields of research in women's studies, that one day, in a program of Women's Studies, there will be the question of truth, and that someone will spend three or four years researching "truth."

21.
Reading Like a Man

ROBERT SCHOLES

. . . if we consider for example what is called a writing man—for example me, to the extent that I'm supposed to be a man . . .

J. Derrida

What is reading? How should we read? These are questions that begin before Kindergarten and extend beyond all schooling. In recent years literary theoreticians have contributed to our understanding of reading by raising two other questions: who is the reader? and whose text does the reader read? On this occasion we shall be most concerned with the first of these two latter questions, that which asks about the nature of the reader, but it will be useful to approach that one by way of the other: whose text is read? Our best guide here—as in other cases—may prove to be a blind bard:

> Menard (perhaps without wanting to) has enriched, by means of a new technique, the halting and rudimentary art of reading: this new technique is that of the deliberate anachronism and the erroneous attribution. This technique, whose applications are infinite, prompts us to go through the *Odyssey* as if it were posterior to the *Aeneid* and the book *Le jardin du Centaure* of Madame Henri Bachelier as if it were by Madame Henri Bachelier. This technique fills the most placid works with adventure.
>
> (J. L. Borges, *Labyrinths*, p. 44)

We shall never know with what degree of seriousness Borges allowed the narrator of "Pierre Menard" to advance these suggestions for the improvement of reading. Personally, even without "the deliberate anachronism and the erroneous attribution," I have found reading sufficiently adventurous, but the Borgesian text is rich in suggestion nonetheless. In what the eccentric narrator doubtless intends as a mere insult to his enemy, Madame Henri Bachelier, he suggests reading a book of hers as if it were indeed written by her. We, reading these words as if they were indeed written by Borges (and I have long maintained that Borges wrote in English and hired journalistic hacks with improbable names to translate his glittering prose into rather pedestrian Spanish, which now, with the original texts lost, has become the basis of the English versions we have)—

reading, as I say, these words as if they were written by Borges, we may find in them a deeper wisdom about the art of reading.

We do read as if. As the whole of "Pierre Menard, Author of the *Quixote*" is calculated to demonstrate, in reading a text we control its fecund excesses of potential meaning by postulating a historical personage whose intentions, however confused or schizoid, provide the grounds for that recuperative activity we call "reading." If the text of *Don Quixote* is attributed to Pierre Menard, or as the Borgesian narrator suggests in his concluding sentence, the text of the *Imitatio Christi* to James Joyce, we should inevitably read it differently. And we all make this sort of attribution when we read. That admirable reader Jacques Derrida, for instance, is absolutely dependent in his readings upon the intentional presences he calls Husserl, Saussure, Láevi-Strauss, Rousseau, and so on. He reads the text of Rousseau as if it were written by Jean-Jacques Rousseau. And so do we all read in this way, though we may not find the same Rousseaus in the same texts.

We do not, in fact, need the erroneous attribution and the deliberate anachronism to make reading adventurous. Our reading is inevitably erroneous and always more or less anachronistic, but this is neither a sin to be atoned for nor a deficiency to be remedied; it is simply an aspect of the textual condition. We are all constituted as readers by powerful cultural forces. Whatever freedom we have in reading will come through consciousness of what these forces are and how they work. This is why in recent years the most interesting theories of interpretation have all—in one way or another—addressed the question of the reading subject.

On the present occasion I wish to take up this question—who is it that is reading?—in the light—and shadow—thrown by two theories of reading, each of which is also a practice of reading. The two theories are deconstruction and feminism, and I turn to them because they represent two powerful approaches to the problem of reading and because recent attempts to align them seem to me both misguided and illuminating. What I find most misguided—and most illuminating—are attempts by deconstructive critics to locate feminism within deconstruction. I am opposed to this because I believe that at the deepest levels of presupposition and the furthest range of implications feminism is right and deconstruction is wrong.

I shall have a good deal to say (here and elsewhere) about what I think is wrong with deconstruction. What is right with feminism will also be a theme of this discussion, which I will introduce here by simply mentioning the way that feminists have forced upon a largely unwilling critical establishment new and persuasive readings of classic texts and important changes in the literary canon. In terms of literary theory, feminism has made a powerful contribution by fram-

ing the question of reading inside the question of gender. More than
any other critical approach feminism has forced us to see the folly of
thinking about reading in terms of a transcendental subject: the ideal
reader reading a text that is the same for all. This does not happen.
Readers are constituted differently and different readers perceive different features of the same texts. Both texts and readers are already
written when they meet, but both may emerge from the encounter
altered in some crucial respect. Feminist critics have made this semiotic process concrete and intelligible for us all, for gender—if not
destiny—is one of those rough spots by which destiny, in the form
of culture, grasps us and shapes our ends. Because women in this
culture have been an underprivileged class, they have learned lessons
in class consciousness that many men have not. Because it cuts across
social class, gender brings the lessons of class consciousness into
places normally so insulated by privilege as to be unconscious of the
structure that supports and insulates them.

The issue of class has been important for feminist criticism as it
has not been for deconstruction—and this is a major point upon
which my treatment of these two critical modes will depend. For this
reason it is important to clarify the notion of *class* that I will be using
in this discussion. I do not mean to restrict the term to socioeconomic
class, though that remains as a central type or model for the concept
of *class* I am deploying here. Readers who read as members of a class
can be distingushed from those who are members of what Stanley
Fish has called an *interpretive community* (a concept with weaknesses
I have discussed elsewhere) in that membership in a class implies
both necessity and interest. A member of the class *Jew* in Hitler's
Germany or of the class *Black* in South Africa at present, is a member
of those classes by necessity and has an interest in the situation of
the class as a whole. And so, in those same societies, would a member
of the class *Aryan* or *White* have such an interest. A class, in this sense,
is a cultural creation, part of a system of categories imposed upon all
those who attain subjectivity in a given culture. One may belong to
a party or faction through choice—or what is perceived as choice—
but one is assigned to a class by a system that allows no abstentions.
One may choose to be a feminist or not but one is assigned one's
gender and may change it only by extraordinary effort. The relationship between being female and being a feminist is neither simple nor
to be taken for granted, but there is no comparable relationship between being a deconstructionist and belonging to a class—which is
of course not to say that deconstruction is free of interest or beyond
ideology. Deconstructive critics constitute a party or faction within
academic institutions and discourses. One joins this party only by
actively professing the deconstructive faith and producing discourse
that partakes of the deconstructive paradigm. The model here is quite

clearly that of the sciences, even though the burden of deconstructive discourse is often antiscientific. Within academic institutions deconstructive critics, like those of other persuasions, seek power, status, and such other rewards as the institution may provide.

Within academic life feminism has come to be constituted in a similar fashion, but with some absolutely crucial differences that turn precisely on this matter of class. Feminists claim a purpose and an authority that is based on their membership in a class extending beyond the bounds of academic institutions and their discourses. A male critic, for instance, may work within the feminist paradigm but never be a full-fledged member of the class of feminists. On the same problems, the same texts, he will never work with the authority of a woman. Feminism is especially interesting and especially valuable because of the way that class and paradigm come together under its banner.

The female reader proposed by feminism is not an individual reading for herself but a class-conscious member of the class *woman* reading on behalf of all the members of that class including herself. The power of feminist readings of texts depends to a great extent on the size and solidarity of this group and the clarity of the paradigm of reading that they share. Feminism has made its way against considerable open and tacit resistance from male critics, because the individual members of the class *woman*, reading consciously as women, have produced highly similar readings of a variety of texts, and found similar structures of patriarchy operating throughout the established canon and in the works of male interpreters of the canon. A shared critical paradigm driven by feminist class-consciousness has enabled these achievements.

The notion of *class* operative in feminism has a powerful social dimension, then, but there is also a linguistic/logical dimension to this notion, which is an indispensable part of the social functioning of the concept. In language most nouns denote categories or classes of objects, as the word *cat* denotes not this or that particular animal but a class of animals to which certain individuals can be assigned, and the word *woman* denotes a class of humans to which certain individuals can be assigned. In the history of Western thought attitudes toward these universals have shifted in a way that W. K. Wimsatt summarized usefully in an essay written four decades ago:

One main difference between all modern positivistic, nominalistic, and semantic systems and the scholastic and classical systems is that the older ones stress the similarity of the individuals denoted by the common term and hence the real universality of meaning, while the modern systems stress the differences in the individuals, the constant flux even of each individual in time and space and its kinetic structure, and hence infer only an approximate or nominal universality of meaning and a convenience rather than a truth in the use of general terms. (*The Verbal Icon*, p. 70)

Deconstruction, then, would be one of those modern systems that, as Wimsatt said, "stress the differences in the individuals." What Wimsatt could not have predicted forty years ago was that a modern system would come along and reject "approximate or nominal universality" as if it were a fatal flaw in Western thought never noticed until now—indeed as if the Wittgensteinian concept of "family resemblance" had not been developed in response to a widespread awareness of the imperfection of universal categories. But deconstruction did come along and found itself upon the impurity of class concepts. Which means—in the present context—that we should be aware that feminism and deconstruction—and you can see it in the very names—are founded upon antithetical principles: feminism upon a class concept and deconstruction upon the deconstructing of all such concepts. This is why attempts to reconcile them should provoke the horrified fascination of an acrobat attempting an impossible feat—even if in academic life there is usually a net under the performer.

In this case our performer will be Jonathan Culler or, more accurately, the Jonathan Culler I perceive in the section of his book *On Deconstruction* called "Reading as a Woman," and some other related passages from the book. I shall not attempt a full reading of Culler's text but rather will meditate upon some of his more acrobatic textual moves. The difficulty—and even danger—of Culler's attempt will become clearer as we see it against the background of Derrida's own position on the same question, which is much less risky because it remains within the bounds of deconstructive orthodoxy.

According to Culler, all of feminism is divided into three parts— as Caesar observed of Gaul after he had conquered it. In the world of discourse to divide is to conquer. Analysis is a form of mastery. We shall return to this matter of power in a moment, but first let us follow the analysis, in which the three parts of feminism are sometimes called "sorts," sometimes "cases," sometimes "modes," sometimes "moments," and sometimes "levels." Now *sorts, cases,* and *modes* are sufficiently undifferentiated to function as a mere variation of signifiers, employed to avoid excessive repetition, but the words *moment* and *level,* combined with the enumerative terms *first, second,* and *third* introduce two new dimensions into the analysis: temporality and hierarchy, three moments or stages in a developmental process in which each moment equals a new and higher level. With *feminism* as the nominative term or character that passes through these three phases of development, we have a familiar narrative structure. This is the story of Feminism's Progress, which is similar to the progress of every pilgrim. For Culler, feminism's first moment finds the heroine at a level of naive belief in the feminine as a quality given by experience. In the second moment she has progressed to an awareness that the feminine must be generated by a struggle against the false consciousness imposed upon all readers by a patriarchal culture. The third moment is the present, and in it we find our heroine approaching the Holy City, which she may or may not be found worthy to enter. This pilgrimmage has been a passage from a too earthy obsession with experience—with living as a woman—toward a nirvana in which all experience is transcended. In the perfection of the third stage—if our heroine can attain it—she will find "a larger textual system" (p. 61), and with this new instrument she will obtain power over the categories of thought produced by male authority: namely, "notions of realism, of rationality, of mastery, of explanation" (p. 62). This power will be embodied in the heroine's ability to inscribe these notions in the achieved "larger textual system."

The larger textual system that contains and thus has power over *realism, rationality, mastery,* and *explanation* is, of course, deconstruction. There are, however, two serious problems in this positioning of deconstruction as the final level of perfection to be achieved by feminism. First, as will be clear when we examine the concluding words of the essay, and as Derrida himself has said quite bluntly, one of the things deconstruction deconstructs is feminism itself. And second, the reward for achieving the third level is couched in terms of a "larger system"—a phrase that clearly implicates *rationality, mastery,* and *explanation* in those two words, *larger* and *system.*

Culler's inability to avoid concepts of *order* and *power* must lead the critical reader to contemplate two possibilities: 1) Deconstruction is as interested in order and power as any other mode of discourse, and therefore just as thoroughly patriarchal. If this is the case, deconstruction is probably not the proper goal for feminism. 2) The second possibility is that order and power are such pervasive features of existence that there is simply no case for assigning them exclusively to one side of a binary system based on gender, nor is there any way that deconstruction itself can avoid them.

There is a third possibility, of course, that perhaps Culler has just got it wrong, that he has misrepresented deconstructive thought, and that his use of a term like "larger system" is neither a conscious revelation nor an unconscious one but a simple error. This may be the case, but I do not believe it. I think that he has, if anything, overrepresented deconstruction, explaining its implications too clearly, thus bringing to light difficulties that less gifted or less ingenuous expositors repress. For example, as he considers feminism and deconstruction together, he identifies certain problems that defy solution, and he expresses reservations about Derrida's attempt to bring the two together in *Eperons*, which he calls "a relevant but unsatisfying document in this case" (p. 61, n. 10). In this instance, it is precisely Culler's attempt to treat both feminism and deconstruction adequately that has led him to these "reservations" and perhaps to others, which sometimes take the form of narrative or assertive compensations for misgivings about the whole enterprise. One of the things that makes the conjunction of feminism and deconstruction interesting is that both positions have difficulty in determining their relationship to order and power. Culler's enactment of these difficulties seems to me exemplary.

The difficulties become especially apparent as the story of feminism's progress, and the text in which it is narrated, come to a conclusion. In this conclusion, as I read it, Culler suggests that one may seem to renounce that vile, male thing, authority, and yet have it after all by entering the pure, genderless discourse of deconstruction. Where this transcendence would leave those goals of feminism that are social and economic is one of the points that causes Culler and Derrida himself considerable difficulty.

Culler takes it up again in his section on "Institutions and Inversions," directing our attention to Derrida's observation in *Positions*, that the "phase of reversal" (Culler's translation, p. 165) or "phase of overturning" (Bass's translation, *Positions*, p. 41) hierarchical oppositions is necessary and must be gone through. Derrida is not talking specifically about the hierarchical opposition of *male* and *female* at this moment but Culler quite properly inserts this citation as reflecting Derrida's views on the matter of gender relations. Culler also deftly cuts off the quotation at the point where Derrida takes back the word *phase* with its narrative or temporal thrust—and then reinstates temporality, and the word *phase* itself, in the next paragraph:

> When I say that this phase is necessary, the word *phase* is perhaps not the most rigorous one. It is not a question of a chronological phase, a given moment, or a page that one day simply will be turned, in order to go on to other things. The necessity of this phase is structural; it is the necessity of interminable analysis: the hierarchy of dual oppositions always reestablishes itself . . .
>
> That being said—and on the other hand—to remain in this phase is still to operate on the terrain of and from within the deconstructed system. (*Positions*, p. 42)

The concepts of temporality and progress are used, then apologised for and apparently abandoned, and finally reinstated powerfully with the words _remain, still,_ and _phase_ itself. Buried in the midst of this verbal cloud is the question of whether the hierarchy that re-establishes itself is the same as the one previously established (in our case male over female) or some different one, such as female over male. In other words, the question that needs asking here is whether the phase of reversal ever accomplishes anything in social terms. Does deconstructive practice assume that it can change the world? Or does it hold such goals to be naive and vulgar?

I would say that this is not a rhetorical question, except that I fear an answer like, "Both. And neither." Still, it is not a question to be passed over. One of the large issues at stake in the conjunction of feminism and deconstruction is precisely the question of what the experience of being a woman has to do with one's ability to read as a woman. The relationship between experience and reading is ab-solutely crucial. Culler deals with it by deconstructing the notion of experience.

> In the third mode, the appeal to experience is veiled but still there, as a reference to maternal rather than paternal relations or to woman's situation and experience of marginality, which may give rise to an altered mode of reading. The appeal to the experience of the reader provides leverage for displacing or un-doing the system of concepts or procedures of male criticism, but "experience" always has this divided, duplicitous character: it has always already occurred and yet is still to be produced— an indispensable point of reference, yet never simply there. (p. 63)

"Experience" here, neatly veiled with quotation marks has a curiously vague and diffuse quality. When we achieve the third level we may refer airily to "maternal relations" or the marginality of "woman" in general, but not to anything so vulgar as the bodily experience of menstrual flow. "Experience," in this discourse, is something to be alluded to rather than something one lives through or, as we say, experiences.

I agree that a person may have experiences but, lacking the proper discursive codes, not be conscious of them or of their import. I only want to insist that there is a difference between having an experience and not having it, and a very large and significant difference between having the same experience over and over again and never having that experience at all. Deconstruction, I am afraid, must deny that very difference, for the following reasons. The fundamental gesture in the edifice of deconstructive thought is the denial of any significant difference between speech and writing, on the grounds that the ap-parent distinction between the copresence of speaker and listener in speech and their mutual absence in writing is not a real distinction, there being no such thing as pure presence. The same line of thought, if accepted, must lead us to the conclusion that there is no significant difference between reading about an experience and having an experience, because experience never simply occurs. As Culler puts it, experience "has always already occurred yet is still to be produced."

Very revealingly, Derrida's way of dealing with the question of feminine experience is to turn it into a question of essence, which he can then subject to the deconstructive formula, demonstrating that there is no such thing as a purely, essentially feminine creature:

> Now, when you say that "it's getting to be a watch word that in your writings the feminine can only be read as a metaphor," "then I would say "no" . . . It's not a metaphor. It's not a metaphor first off because in order for the feminine to be a metaphor one would have to be assured of knowing what the *essence propre* of woman is . . . And what I try to say particularly in *Spurs* (*Eperons*) is that woman has no essence of her very own, and that that's the phallocentric gesture. It's the gesture of considering that there is "*la femme*" and that she has her very own essence. (*Critical Exchange* #17, Winter, 1985, p. 31)

By collapsing the problem of feminine experience into the question of feminine essence, Derrida achieves mastery over feminism. He insists that feminism is in fact a form of phallogocentrism:

> . . . for me deconstruction is certainly not feminist. At least as I have tried to practice it, I believe it naturally supposes a radical deconstruction of phallogocentrism, and certainly an absolutely other and new interest in women's questions. But if there is one thing that it must not come to, it's feminism. So I would say that deconstruction is a deconstruction of feminism, from the start, insofar as feminism is a form—no doubt necessary at a certain moment—but a form of phallogocentrism among many others. (p. 30)

It is precisely the attempt of women to use their own experience as authority for reading or writing in a certain way that Derrida rejects or accepts as an evil necessary for a certain "moment." It is as though phallogocentric feminism will do the dirty work so that androgynous deconstruction can then enjoy the fruits of this labor—except that what deconstruction really enjoys is deconstructing feminism even while it is struggling to achieve its political and economic goals— goals that depend to some extent upon the ability of women to be conscious of themselves as a class—however impure—bound by a certain shared experience. The question of feminine experience is taken up several times in Culler's text, and always on those occasions we find difficulties at the surface of the text that are symptomatic of deeper conceptual problems. One such point is the final paragraph of "Reading as a Woman," in which Culler rewrites Peggy Kamuf's description of *writing* as a woman in the form of a statement about *reading* as a woman, drawing the following conclusion:

> For a woman to read as a woman is not to repeat an identity or an experience that is given but to play a role she constructs with reference to her identity as a woman, which is also a construct, so the series can continue: a woman reading as a woman reading as a woman. The non-coincidence reveals an interval, a division within woman or within any reading subject and the "experience" of that subject. (p. 64)

From the heights of deconstruction we are given a glimpse into the bottomless abyss of textuality, a vertiginous perspective in which constructs are erected upon constructs, without foundation and without end. Such a world seems to offer a dazzling textual freedom, but in practice deconstructive discourse rarely displays the liberated grace that one might expect to find in it, but seems constrained by fears of falling into locutions of presence and thus becoming prey for the monster, Phallogocentrism. In the present instance Culler's own discourse falters even as he describes the textual abyss, becoming ungrammatical, unclear, and phallogocentric all at once.

The phallogocentrism appears in the first clause, which makes a powerful truth claim: "For a woman to read as a woman is not to . . . but to . . . " In this expression one can find *realism, rationality, mastery,* and *explanation:* all those things that Culler has previously assigned to "male authority" and phallogocentric discourse. Culler is *explaining* to us here what *really* happens when a woman reads as a woman: not *that*, but *this*. He *reasons* effectively in this way because the "larger system" of deconstruction has given him *mastery* over such matters as reading and writing. This combination of textual order and power is in fact entirely typical of academic and many other forms of discourse. It would not be worth noting if Culler had not assigned it to the phallogocentric monster in the first place. Even so, it is probably the least interesting problem in the passage we are considering.

The logical problems appear next and are sufficient, perhaps, to refute the accusation of *rationality* that I levelled at Culler in the preceding paragraph. They appear largely in the following section of the first sentence in the passage we are examining:

> . . . not to repeat an identity or an experience that is given but
> to play a role she constructs with reference to her identity as a
> woman, which is also a construct . . . (p. 64)

In the first part of this passage I understand Culler to be saying that
reading is not guaranteed by the status of the reader. He is in effect
denying the truth of a syllogism like this one:

> All women read correctly.
> Mary is a woman.
> Therefore Mary reads correctly.

Leaving aside a number of problems with this syllogism that Culler
might wish to point out, the thrust of his argument is to deny that
Mary can simply be assigned to membership in the class *women*, to
insist that Mary may try to assume that role, but will never play it
fully and perfectly enough to belong to the class—and neither will
anyone else, which is why this sort of syllogistic reasoning (call it
logocentric) will not do.

This argument against the use of syllogistic reasoning in human
affairs seems to me very powerful. It is also very rational, so rational
that it would make all language and thought as we know them impossible, but that is the problem of deconstruction in general and not
a particular problem in this case. The logical problems in this case
begin when Culler turns right around and says that Mary can indeed
be a member of the class *woman*, that she can read "with reference
to her identity as a woman." So she has an identity after all, but it
is a *construct* not a *given*, and she can read with *reference* to it but
cannot *repeat* it. Now the logical problems that make the surface of
the passage difficult to understand are becoming clear. The word
identity here refers both to Mary's membership in the class *woman* and
to something repeatable that makes the Mary who reads the same as
the Mary who has experienced what it means to be a member of that
class.

Culler is assuming the identity of the woman who experiences and
the woman who reads. It is the same Mary in both instances. But
there is a gap, an interval, a division *within* this individual reader. In
order to locate his division *within* something he has to assume the
continuity of the something. If it were Mary who experienced and
Jane who read there would be no gap, no division, just two different
people doing different things. He must assume an identity in order
to locate the difference he wants—but this is exactly the sort of convenient assumption that deconstructive thought denies. When Culler
allows Mary an identity that is a *construct* but not a *given*, we must
ask what the difference is between these two terms, since he surely

doesn't mean that Mary constructs this identity herself as she does the *role she* plays as reader. If there are two roles or two constructs here, what allows us to see them as belonging to a single person— if not some notion of an identity that is *not* a role or a construct connecting the two?

There are similar, and perhaps even more important problems in the role played by the word *experience* in this passage. Brought on stage early, she is left off at the end when *identity* returns. Let us see what happens if she replaces her sister in the last act:

> . . . not to repeat an identity or an experience that is given but to play a role she constructs with reference to her *experience* as a woman, which is also a construct . . .

Experience is not so docile as her sister Identity. Whatever experience is, it is not just a *construct* but something that *constructs*. That is, Mary's experiences are things that have happened to her and are still happening to her, even as she writes. She does not step outside of them to refer to them in any simple or clear-cut way. To the extent that she is able to *refer* to them, to distance them by giving them verbal expression, we may say she is *outside* them, but she can never get completely outside them, and it is the recognition of this that constitutes her conscious membership in the class *woman*. Mary is what she is because she has had one set of experiences rather than another, some of which were typical of the experiences of most members of the class *woman* at a particular point in history. The introduction and later suppression of the term *experience* is a symptom of the text's inability to deal with this concept within the framework of deconstructive thought.

This particular difficulty surfaces again as a grammatical problem when the question of experience comes up in the last sentence of the passage we are considering:

> The non-coincidence reveals an interval, a division within woman or within any reading subject and the "experience" of that subject.

It is a strange and indeed a strained sentence, in which *différance* in three distinct avatars—*noncoincidence, interval,* and *division*—takes on the properties of a thing that lies inside some larger unified entity, as if the difference *between* Mary and Jane became a difference *within* Mary-Jane. This reification of *différance* is one of the most damaging weaknesses in deconstructive thought. Derrida, for instance, regularly speaks of traces as if they were things that could be located inside of signs, infinite numbers of them inside every sign, like angels on a pinhead.

In the present case the problem of *différance* appears as a grammatical difficulty in the use of the word *within*, when Culler speaks of a division "within any reading subject and the 'experience' of that subject." From the grammatical point of view, it looks as if the word *between* should have been used here: *between* the experience and the subject of that experience falls the inevitable shadow of *différance*. The word *within*, in this case, seems to propose something more mystical than my Jonathan Culler has led me to expect from him; the same difference in two places, or a difference within the subject and another within the experience, the experience and the subject perhaps being connected only by the identity of their differences—and so on. Perhaps it makes no difference whether this is mysticism or error, an ascent or a fall. It is a troubled spot on the textual surface and it comes when the word *experience*, now ironized by quotation marks, is about to return to the text after its conspicuous absence in the previous sentence. We can only take this troubling of the text as symptomatic. I interpret it as a sign of Culler's reluctance to either accept or dismiss the relevance of the reader's experience to her practice as a reader.

Derrida is troubled by the same problems, which he addresses in a light and impromptu manner at the end of the conference from which I quoted him earlier. Here are three short passages from his final remarks:

> In other words if we consider for example what is called a writing man—for example me, to the extent that I'm supposed to be a man—then writing on woman should be less writing on woman than writing from or on the basis of (*depuis*) what comes to me from a feminine place.

Following Culler, we can rewrite this as a comment on reading:

> If we consider for example what is called a reading man—for example me, to the extent that I'm supposed to be a man—then reading as a woman should be less reading as a woman than reading from or on the basis of what comes to me from a feminine place.

Yes, possibly, but where is this "feminine place" and on what basis does a man have access to it? In deconstructive terms it is the trace of femininity that inevitably is inscribed in something defined as *not* feminine. But to reason in this way is to give the trace a positive status as a place or locus of the feminine. The "feminine place" here is perhaps not strictly deconstructive but Jungian. Still, one must wonder exactly what does come from this feminine place and how it might be recognized or authenticated as feminine. Derrida's awareness of the problem is suggested by his immediate restatement of it in terms of—of all things—voice.

> . . . I too have learned from the _écoute_ of women, from listening to the degree I can to a certain feminine voice.

Of special interest here is the qualification—"to the degree I can." What is it, we must ask, that sets limits to Derrida's ability to hear "a certain feminine voice"? Why does he need to suggest that he hears this voice less well than he hears other (presumably masculine) voices? What can it be other than his own membership in the class of males, with all that implies in the way of experience? At some level the concept of _experience_, which was earlier dismissed and replaced by the more docile and vulnerable concept of _essence_, is returning to trouble this text also.

Quite properly Derrida wants to complicate the question of gender, to deconstruct it,

> Because it's not such a simple thing when we say that whoever bears a masculine proper name, is anatomically male, etc., is a man. This feminine voice can pass through trajectories that are extremely multiple . . . In other words, on the other side, and even in the most feminist women, the masculine voice is not silent. (p. 32)

After these words the text indicates "LAUGHTER." This laughter I read as symptomatic. Feminism and feminists have, however gently and gracefully, been put in their place—again. Whenever women speak up, it is the phallogocentric male voice speaking through them. And when they read actively and aggressively as members of the class, woman, are they then reading through male eyes as well? Or are they finally reading as women conscious of their own experience as members of a class who share that experience?

To put the problem another way, is there any difference between reading _as_ a woman and reading _like_ a woman? Can Mary actually read _as_ a woman because she _is_ a woman, or can she only read _like_ a woman because no individual can ever be a woman? To put the question still another way, can John read _as_ a woman or only _like_ a woman? If neither John nor Mary can really read _as_ a woman, and either one can read _like_ a woman, then what's the difference between John and Mary? My own feeling is that until no one notices or cares about the difference we had better not pretend it isn't there. Above all, I think no man should seek in any way to diminish the authority which the experience of women gives them in speaking about that experience, and I believe that women should be very wary of critical systems that deny or diminish that authority.

Experience, of course, sets limits even as it confers authority. If some irreducible minimum of space or time separates us from our own experience, it is also true that this separation is never complete. We are subjects constructed by our experience and truly carry traces of that experience in our minds and on our bodies. Those of us who are male cannot deny this either. With the best will in the world we shall never read as women and perhaps not even like women. For me, born when I was born and living where I have lived, the very best I can do is to be conscious of the ground upon which I stand: to read not as but like a man.

22.
Outlaws: Gay Men in Feminism

CRAIG OWENS

> Criminals come in handy.
>
> —*Michel Foucault, "Prison Talk"*

If the treatment of male homosexuality as delinquency and disease is a product of the same legal and medical apparatus that "castrates" women (by regarding them as always already castrated)—and I will be arguing throughout this essay that it *is*—then the gay male intellectual has a fundamentally different stake in feminism than his heterosexual "counterpart." How can he articulate that difference without setting himself up as the "exemplary" male feminist? To do so would not only be to appeal to a marginal—and marginalizing—(homo)sexual identity, rather than to investigate the construction of that identity; it would also be to posit a Genet-ic link between feminist and gay politics, rather than confronting the obstacles which stand in the way of such an alliance. Writing about Derrida writing about Genet, Gayatri Spivak observes that, in rewriting Freud by suggesting that the male homosexual may not be caught up in castration anxiety, Derrida is also suggesting "that the 'feminization' of philosophizing for the male deconstructor might find its most adequate legend in male homosexuality defined as criminality, and that it cannot speak for the woman." For Spivak, this admission indicates the limits of deconstruction as a feminist practice; as she points out, in the end Derrida opts, not for homosexuality, but for fetishism: *Glas*, she writes, "is the classic case of fetishism, a uniquely shaped object (his bicolumnar book) that will allow the subject both to be and not to be a man—to have the phallus and yet accede to dissemination."[1] The gay male critic must also point out that, in Derrida's de-Oedipalized homosexuality, Genet remains outside the Law. Is this not, then, a *re*construction of the "legend" of the homosexual outlaw?

Nevertheless, Derrida's effort to rewrite the Freudian scripture on male homosexuality is welcome, for the myth of homosexual gynophobia remains perhaps the most powerful obstacle to a political alliance of feminists and gay men. The "function" of this myth, I believe, is to obscure the profound link between misogyny and homophobia in our culture—a link that is nowhere more apparent than in Freud's texts, in which the scapegoating of women often appears in conjunction with a scapegoating of homosexual men. It is tempting, on this basis alone, to presume a common interest uniting women and gay men; however, as Eve Kosofsky Sedgwick cautions in her extraordinary recent study of male bonding in nineteenth-century British fiction, *Between Men*, in which she argues convincingly that male homophobia is a distinctly *feminist* concern, "Profound and intuitable as the bonds between feminism and antihomophobia often are in our society, the two are not the same. As the alliance between them is not automatic or transhistorical, it will be most fruitful if it is analytic and unpresuming."[2] It is in the same analytic and unpresuming spirit—and in the hope of forging just such an alliance—that I offer the following response to the recent tendency, on the part of certain feminist writers, to characterize (our) society as a "homosexual monopoly" (this phrase is Luce Irigaray's). I must say at the outset that, while I believe this formulation itself to be patently homophobic, I do not consider any of the women whose work I will discuss to be homophobes. To do so would simply be to scapegoat feminism for the oppression of homosexual men. But I do believe that, in employing powerful theoretical models devised by a number of demonstrably homophobic male thinkers—primarily Freud and Lévi-Strauss—some feminists have inherited the ideological biases embedded in those models. Before proceeding, however, I will pause to comment on the deployment of a clearly identifiable homophobic tactic in the male-feminist debate: I refer to the recent pastime of Tootsie rolling.

The woman shall not wear that which pertaineth unto a man, neither shall a man put on a woman's garment; for all that do so are abomination unto the Lord thy God.

—Deuteronomy 22:5

"Homophobia directed by men against men is misogynistic," Sedgwick writes. "By 'misogynistic' I mean not only that it is oppressive of the so-called feminine in men, but that it is oppressive of women."[3] What about homophobia directed by women against men?

In response to an editorial request for an endorsement to appear on the jacket of *The Anti-Aesthetic*, in which my essay "The Discourse of Others: Feminists and Postmodernism" first appeared, Linda Nochlin began by praising the book's "provocative and revitalizing critique of contemporary culture" (these words appear on the cover), but proceeded to criticize the paucity of texts by women in the collection, except those by Rosalind Krauss and "Craig playing a kind of 'Tootsie' role" (these words do not).[4] The association of transvestism and homosexuality is, of course, fully historical and contingent; however, in an ideological climate in which that association is presumed to be self-evident, to caricature a gay male feminist critic as a transvestite is tantamount to exposing his homosexuality. Perhaps Nochlin's characterization of the (gay) male feminist as a feminized man is to be read simply as an inversion of the Nietzschean characterization of the feminist as a masculine woman; even so, I would suggest—at the risk of confirming Freud's view of homosexuality as a paranoid structure—that it is as fully homophobic as Nietzsche's is misogynistic, for it deploys what has come to be recognized as a distinctly homophobic mechanism of social control.

Had Nochlin's letter remained an isolated incident, I might still be able to read it as I first did—as a comment on the fact that, in that essay, my homosexuality remains undisclosed. However, it turned out to be only a preview for the coming attraction, for Elaine Showalter's "Critical Cross-Dressing: Male Feminists and the Woman of the Year"—who turns out to be Dustin Hoffman in Sydney Pollock's film *Tootsie*—appeared in *Raritan* a few months later. (Because that essay appears in this volume, I will forego a summary.) In caricaturing Culler, Eagleton, and company as transvestites (a term which, in the homosexual subculture, is accurately perceived to be part of the clinical discourse on homosexuality, and therefore as hostile), Showalter is not, of course, questioning their masculinity. Quite the reverse: she is setting them up as straight men. But why is it presupposed that the male feminist is a heterosexual man? And why did Showalter not include a gay male feminist among the group?

Just as the blackmailing of homosexual men depends upon the public perception that they are straight, so too Showalter's—and Nochlin's—tactic relies for its effectiveness on the presumed heterosexuality of the critics whose work she discusses; this is what makes it a homophobic tactic. As Sedgwick demonstrates, homophobia is not primarily an instrument for oppressing a sexual minority; it is, rather, a powerful tool for regulating the entire spectrum of male relations. Homophobia is aimed not only at gay men, but also "at men who [are] not part of the distinctly homosexual subculture. Not only must homosexual men be unable to ascertain whether they are to be the objects of 'random' homophobic violence, but no man must be able to ascertain that he is not (that his bonds are not) homosexual." The imputing of a homosexual motive to every male relationship is thus "an immensely potent tool . . . for the manipulation of every form of power that [is] refracted through the gender system—that is, in European society, of virtually every form of power."[5]

Showalter skirts the issue of homosexuality in her text when she discusses "parallels" between the 1980s and the 1880s and '90s—the period in which the "modern" form of homosexual persecution began in earnest (the Wilde trial). However, every item on the list of "popular entertainments" she produces as evidence for a "1980s fascination with cross-dressing"—*La Cage aux Folles, Torch Song Trilogy, The World According to Garp, Victor/Victoria, Cloud 9*—makes the connection between transvestism and homosexuality explicit. (*Garp* is the exception, but then it deals not with a transvestite, as Showalter implies, but with a transsexual.) This list testifies, then, less to a fascination with cross-dressing and more to an intensification of mass-media stereotyping of gay men as feminine. Showalter avoids this aspect of the sexual politics of the Reagan era by zeroing in on the one character, Michael Dorsey/Dorothy Michaels in *Tootsie*, whose transvestism is motivated *not* by sexuality, but by careerism. Nevertheless, she invokes "psychoanalytic theory" in order to present Dorothy/Michael as if (s)he were the classic transvestite. And once again we encounter the figure of Derrida clutching his bicolumnar book, only this time he is Dressed to Kill:

> In psychoanalytic theory [Showalter writes], the male transvestite is not a powerless man; according to psychiatrist Robert Stoller, in *Sex and Gender*, he is a "phallic woman," who can tell himself that "he is, or with practice will become, a better woman than a biological female if he chooses to do so." When it is safe or necessary, the transvestite "gets great pleasure in revealing that he is a male-woman. . . . The pleasure in tricking the unsuspecting into thinking he is a woman, and then revealing his maleness (e.g., by suddenly dropping his voice) is not so much erotic as it is proof that there is such a thing as a woman with a penis."[6]

This is only the first passage I will cite in which "psychoanalytic theory" is deployed in order to polarize women and gay men by placing them in competition (for what? for straight men?). Besides, whose "theory" is being invoked here? Why does Showalter not inform her reader that Stoller regards homosexuality as a "gender disorder," or that he considers "feminine" boys who show signs of incipient homosexuality to be "in need of treatment"?[7] In aligning herself with the notoriously homophobic North American psychiatric establishment (Stoller is professor of psychiatry at the UCLA School of Medicine), Showalter uncritically perpetuates its biases. Thus, it is not surprising that her otherwise perceptive analysis of *Tootsie*'s antifeminism should include no mention of the film's homophobia— the source of much of its humor—or that the Julie Andrews character in Blake Edwards's *Victor/Victoria*, a female impersonating a female impersonator, should not be subjected to similar treatment.

But then Victoria poses as a (gay) man in order to get ahead in a man's (read: "homosexual-dominated") world: Edwards's film exploits the popular homophobic prejudice that show business (or fashion, or the art world) is controlled, not by Capital, but by a homosexual "mafia." Recently, a number of feminist writers have informed us that philosophy, fascism, even capitalism itself, are basically homoerotic formations. Philosophy: "Derrida comments repeatedly on the undisclosed homoeroticism of the official discourse of these phallogocentric philosophers [Hegel, Nietzsche, Freud, Marx]—a discourse supported by the relegation of public homosexuals like Jean Genet to criminality."[8] Fascism: "The Nazi community is made by homosexual brothers who exclude the woman and valorize the mother."[9] Capitalism: "Commodities . . . are the material alibi for the desire for relations among men."[10] In what follows, I will be concerned less with what these formulations have to say about philosophy, fascism or Capital, and more with what they *do* to openly homosexual men. How do these theories distinguish between latent and patent homosexuality? How do they account for the persecution of homosexuals, especially in the fascist state and under Capital? Have these writers confused homosexuality with homophobia?

Proscriptions against sodomy have very "ancient roots." Decisions of individuals relating to homosexual conduct have been subject to state intervention throughout the history of Western Civilization. Condemnation of those practices is firmly rooted in Judeo-Christian moral and ethical standards. . . . To hold that the act of homosexual sodomy is somehow protected as a fundamental right would be to cast aside millennia of moral teaching.

—*Chief Justice Warren Burger*, Bowers v. Hardwick, *6/30/86*

In the essays "Women on the Market" and "Commodities among Themselves," both reprinted in *This Sex Which Is Not One*, Luce Irigaray proposes that the other sex, the one which *is* one, is a fundamentally homosexual one. Irigaray extrapolates a "homosexual monopoly" from Lévi-Strauss's discussion of kinship structures as arrangements which facilitate the exchange of women among (groups of) men—exchanges in which women participate only as objects. "What the anthropologist calls the passage from nature to culture," she writes, "amounts to the institution of the reign of hom(m)o-sexuality. Not in an 'immediate' practice, but in its 'social' mediation." In characterizing what we customarily regard as male homosexuality as an "'immediate' practice," Irigaray implies that it is unmediated, that it does not pass through the circuits of desire and of representation that constitute (hetero)sexuality. That this is indeed her view

of male homosexuality is demonstrated by her (first) theory of homosexual oppression: homosexuals are "ostracized," she maintains,
because *"the 'incest' involved in homosexuality has to remain in the realm
of pretense."* Inverted commas notwithstanding, it is clear that Irigaray
is not speaking figuratively, for she continues: "Consider the exemplary case of *father-son* relationships, which guarantee the transmission of patriarchal power and its laws, its discourse, its social
structures. . . . [These relationships cannot] openly display the pederastic love in which they are grounded."[11] To reduce the social mechanisms which insure the transmission of property and the continuity
of the dynasty to homosexual desire, and then further to reduce that
desire to pederasty, is to align one's discourse with, rather than to
explain, the official legal and medical discourse on male homosexuality. (In France, only consensual private homosexual acts *with mi-
nors* are subject to prosecution.)[12]

Irigaray recognizes that not all homosexual relationships are pederastic, and so she offers a second explanation of homosexual oppression: "The 'other' homosexual relations, masculine ones, are just as
subversive, so they too are forbidden. *Because they openly interpret the
law according to which society operates."* (In this view, one supposes,
the homosexual subculture would be the utopia of patriarchy.) Thus,
homosexuality is forbidden because, on the one hand, it violates the
law (the incest taboo) that institutes the exchange of women and, on
the other, because it is in perfect compliance with the law. Here,
Irigaray believes she has uncovered a social contradiction: "Exchanges
and relationships, always among men, would thus be both required
and forbidden by law."[13] But I believe that what she has exposed is
actually her own imprecise understanding of the terms of Lévi-
Strauss's argument.

Closer feminist readers of Lévi-Strauss—Juliet Mitchell and Gayle
Rubin, both of whom have responded to the exchange argument without positing a homosexual monopoly—emphasize the fact that, for
Lévi-Strauss at least, the incest taboo is a prohibition against neither
intergenerational nor homosexual liaisons. In her influential 1975
essay "The Traffic in Women: Notes on the 'Political Economy' of
Sex," Rubin argues that the incest taboo in fact presupposes "a prior,
less articulate taboo on homosexuality. A prohibition against some
heterosexual unions assumes a taboo against non-heterosexual unions." Rubin characterizes this taboo, which institutes "compulsory
heterosexuality," as a "taboo against the sameness of men and
women":

> Men and women are, of course, different. But they are not as
> different as day and night, earth and sky, yin and yang, life and
> death. In fact, from the standpoint of nature, men and women

are closer to each other than either is to anything else—for instance, mountains, kangaroos, or coconut palms. . . . Far from
being an expression of natural differences, exclusive gender
identity is the suppression of natural similarities. It requires
repression: in men, of whatever is the local version of "feminine" traits; in women, of the local definition of "masculine"
traits.[14]

Although one wonders whether Rubin would maintain this "repressive hypothesis" after her association with Foucault, nevertheless
positing an ancient taboo against homosexuality allows her to connect
the suppression of homosexuality with the oppression of women:
"The suppression of the homosexual component of human sexuality," she writes, "and by corollary, the oppression of homosexuals,
is . . . a product of the same system whose rules and relations oppress
women." Rubin goes on to cite several instances of "institutionalized
homosexuality" in non-Western cultures, but argues that in every
case "the rules of gender division and obligatory heterosexuality are
present even in their transformations."[15] That is, one is sometimes
permitted to occupy either a masculine or a feminine position re-
gardless of one's sex, *but never both*—which suggests that Rubin's is
a taboo not against homosexuality, but against *bisexuality*.
    Locating the prohibition of homosexuality prior to the institution
of society (the incest taboo) can only lend support to the contemporary
tendency to regard the continuing criminalization of male homosexuality as a survival of ancient—even outmoded—prohibitions. In
most cases—such as *Bowers v. Hardwick*, in which the U.S. Supreme
Court upheld the constitutionality of the Georgia statute criminalizing
consensual sodomy when performed by homosexual men, while ad-
mitting that the law would be unconstitutional if applied to heterosexual acts—"ancient" sanctions are invoked in order to justify laws
criminalizing homosexual men, even when it is recognized that these
laws may be obsolete. (Justice Powell, concurring with the decision
of the Court: "The history of nonenforcement suggests the moribund
character of laws criminalizing this type of private, consensual conduct. . . . But . . . I cannot say that conduct condemned for hundreds
of years has now become a fundamental right.")[16] However, there is
also a "progressive" version of this argument, which deplores the
oppression of homosexuals while in the same breath celebrating liberal democracy: in this view, the persecution of homosexuals is "a
salutary reminder of the barbarities into which blind prejudice against
an unpopular minority can plunge an otherwise progressive
society."[17]
    Nothing could be further from the truth. The criminalization of
male homosexuality is a relatively recent phenomenon (the Georgia

statute recently upheld by the Supreme Court was ratified in 1968).[18] "Ancient" prohibitions—which applied to all subjects alike—must be distinguished from the "modern" form of homosexual oppression— denial of civil rights, housing, Party membership (Pasolini), military or teaching careers . . . —which began only in the nineteenth century. The stigmatization of homosexuality "as a suspect classification"[19] presupposes the metamorphosis of *the* sodomite into *a* homosexual; as Foucault writes in the first volume of *The History of Sexuality*:

> As defined by the ancient civil or canonical codes, sodomy was a category of forbidden acts; their perpetrator was nothing more than the juridical subject of them. The nineteenth-century homosexual became a personage, a past, a case history, and a childhood. . . . Nothing that went into his total composition was unaffected by his sexuality. It was everywhere present in him: at the root of all his actions because it was their insidious and indefinitely active principle; written immodestly on his face and body because it was a secret that always gave itself away. It was consubstantial with him, less as a habitual sin than as a singular nature. . . . The sodomite had been a temporary aberration; the homosexual was now a species.[20]

What the nineteenth century witnessed, then, was the appearance of the homosexual delinquent—an individual constitutionally predisposed to commit proscribed or illicit sexual acts, and therefore in need of supervision, correction, incarceration. And while sanctions against sodomy are the justification for the criminalization of the homosexual, nevertheless, the two must not be collapsed. To locate the repression of homosexuality in times immemorial is to ignore history, for the "homosexual" has existed for only a century.

What, you would like to marry your sister! What is the matter with you anyway? Don't you want a brother-in-law? Don't you realize that if you marry another man's sister and another man marries your sister, you will have at least two brothers-in-law, while if you marry your own sister you will have none? With whom will you hunt, with whom will you garden, whom will you go to visit?

—Margaret Mead's Arapesh "informants"

Juliet Mitchell's treatment of Lévi-Strauss's exchange argument in the chapter "Patriarchy, Kinship and Women as Exchange Objects" in *Psychoanalysis and Feminism* prompts speculation on the ways in which certain non-Western cultures have integrated, rather than repressed, "homosexual" impulses. For Mitchell, the differentiation of the sexes is not prior to the incest taboo (as Rubin argues), but accomplished through it. That taboo is not (*pace* Freud) a prohibition against intergenerational unions, but a taboo against the marriage of brother and sister; sexual differentiation, Mitchell observes, is instituted between these two through the prohibition of their incestuous coupling:

> The brother (maternal uncle) must give his sister away in marriage and not desire her incestuously; both he and his sister whom he gives away are as close as one can get to being each other. The distinction between them is minimal and the prohibition of their union (the incest taboo) establishes the smallest of differences which is necessary to inaugurate society.[21]

The most suggestive aspect of Mitchell's reading of Lévi-Strauss is her emphasis on the avunculate (a term that Rubin elides): "In order to establish the socio-cultural break with the biological given of two parents and their child," she writes, "a fourth term must intervene. This is where the mother's brother comes in, and he comes in with the very inauguration of society, he is essential to it."[22] For the maternal uncle is the agent of exchange; what he gives away is a sister and—reciprocity in future generations aside—what he receives in return . . . a brother-in-law—*two* brothers-in-law, according to the Arapesh theory of exponential return.[23]

Although the role of the maternal uncle varies from society to society, it appears to be especially important in groups which practice institutional or ritual forms of "homosexuality."[24] In New Guinea, for example, where initiation into manhood often requires the ingestion of sperm from adult males, the most important relationship is that between a boy and his mentor—ideally, *his mother's brother*.[25] And while one suspects Lévi-Strauss of suppressing evidence of homosexuality—his ad hominem homophobic outburst about Fire Island in *Tristes Tropiques* should be consulted[26]—his discussion in the same book of open homosexual relationships between Nambikwara youths confirms my speculation about the avunculate:

> Homosexual relationships are only allowed between adolescents who are "cross-cousins," that is, who would normally marry each other's sisters, so that the brother is acting as a temporary substitute for the girl. When the natives are asked about relationships of this kind, they invariably reply: "They are cousins (or brothers-in-law) making love." On reaching adulthood, the brothers-in-law continue to express their feelings quite openly. It is not uncommon to see two or three men, who are both

husbands and fathers, walking together in the evening with their arms affectionately around each other.[27]

As disarming as this passage may be, it also discloses the anthropologist's sexual politics, for he is able to regard a male lover only as a "temporary substitute" for a woman. Homosexual relationships are simply a "solution" to the shortage of marriageable women created in Nambikwara society because the chief has something that resembles a harem. But then, for Lévi-Strauss the number of available women *always* seems insufficient: "Even if there were as many women as men," he claims, "these women would not all be equally desirable . . . the most desirable women must form a minority." (To which Irigaray retorts: "Are all men equally desirable?")[28] Thus, the "same" ideology that manifests itself in the misogynistic complaint that there are never enough women leads the anthropologist to the homophobic conclusion that homosexuality is only a last resort.

Nevertheless, Lévi-Strauss's exchange argument prompts speculation—which will be confirmed or refuted by further investigation of societies which institutionalize same-sex relationships—that the incest taboo may actually work to integrate homosexual impulses into the sexual economy, and that the "repression" of homosexuality may be less universal than Rubin supposes. Before we can grasp the implications of this possibility for feminism, we will have to follow up on anthropological leads which suggest that societies which institutionalize "homosexuality" are more egalitarian, less hierarchical, than societies which do not, and that male dominance over women is emphasized more strongly in the latter.[29] In this way, the "repression" of homosexuality may well be linked to the ascendancy of men over women. Perhaps the alternative to the legend of the homosexual outlaw will turn out to be the role of the homosexual in-law.[30]

> It is not infrequently disappointment over a woman that drives a man to drink—which means, as a rule, that he resorts to the public house and to the company of men, who afford him the emotional satisfaction which he failed to get from his wife at home. If now these men become the objects of a strong libidinal cathexis in his unconscious . . .
>
> —Sigmund Freud, "Psychoanalytic Notes upon an Autobiographical Account of a Case of Paranoia (Dementia Paranoides)"

In "Function and Field of Speech and Language in Psychoanalysis," Lacan links Lévi-Strauss's kinship structures with the unconscious: "Isn't it striking that Lévi-Strauss, in suggesting the implication of the structure of language with that part of the social laws which regulate marriage ties and kinship, is already conquering the very terrain in which Freud situates the unconscious?"[31] It is not surprising, then, that a number of feminist writers employing Freudian theory should have arrived at conclusions similar to Irigaray's. For example, in "The Purloined Punchline: Joke as Textual Paradigm," in which she formulates a Lacanian theory of narration, Jerry Aline Flieger suggests that the narrative contract itself may be fundamentally homoerotic. Flieger traces Freud's version of the incest taboo (Oedipus) back to his analysis, in *Jokes and Their Relation to the Unconscious*, of the obscene joke—which Freud characterizes as a contract of mastery between two men at a woman's expense. When Flieger schematizes Freud's scenario, its homoerotic subplot rises to the surface: "PART I: BOY MEETS GIRL. . . . PART II: BOY LOSES GIRL. . . . PART III: JOKE CONQUERS ALL. . . . EPILOGUE: BOY GETS BOY?" (Flieger also provides a Lacanian update: "In Lacan's version of Freud's transparent master narrative, the closing line seems to read [comically] neither BOY GETS GIRL nor BOY GETS BOY but BOY *IS* GIRL.")[32]

It should be remembered, however, that the obscene joke originates in a failed attempt at *heterosexual* seduction; in the Freudian scenario, homosexual gratification remains supplementary, compensatory. (Flieger: "The locker room joys of male bonding have replaced the original aim of seduction.")[33] For Freud, however, homosexuality is a solution not to the shortage, but rather to the inaccessibility of desirable women: it is the woman's "resistance" that causes the erstwhile heterosexual seducer to turn instead to another man. (One is reminded of the famous passage on the inaccessibility of narcissistic women, who "have the greatest fascination for men [for Freud?] . . . since as a rule they are the most beautiful.")[34] Is it going too far to suggest that in the *Jokes* book, as well as in the passage from the Schreber case cited above, Freud uses male homosexuality as a threat against women in order to encourage them to be more responsive to men?

In any case, in both passages Freud appears to hold women responsible for male homosexuality. This is a familiar psychoanalytic tactic: Why is it always the mother who is blamed for a son's homosexuality?[35] Moreover, as I noted above, in Freud the scapegoating of women for male homosexuality frequently entails a scapegoating of homosexual men as well; here is one example, from *Das Medusenhaupt*: "Since the Greeks were in the main strongly homosexual, it was inevitable that we should find among them a representation of woman as a being who frightens and repels because she is castrated."[36] Since all men are supposedly frightened and repelled by the sight of female genitalia, why are the "homosexual" Greeks singled out here? Is gynephobia being defined as the "homosexual" component of masculine sexuality? Is the repression of a man's "horror of women" the repression of his homosexuality? But then how can the bisexuality of the drives precede the Oedipus complex?

This is not the place for an extended consideration of these questions, or of Freud's treatment of male homosexuality in general, which I reserve for another occasion. However, I do want to comment briefly on his argument, repeated over and over again, that the "social instincts"—camaraderie, esprit de corps, "the love of mankind in general"—are a manifestation of sublimated homosexual desire.[37] With this argument Freud himself comes close to positing a homosexual monopoly; but he also reveals what is at stake in the positing of such a monopoly.

In an interview published shortly before his death, Foucault speculated that the emergence of homosexuality as a distinct category is historically linked to the disappearance of male friendship:

> Homosexuality became a problem—that is, sex between men became a problem—in the 18th century. We see the rise of it as a problem with the police, with the justice system, and so on. I think the reason it appears as a problem, as a social issue, at this time is that friendship has disappeared. . . . The disappearance of friendship as a social institution, and the declaration of homosexuality as a social/political/medical problem, *are the same process.*[38]

Although Sedgwick rather summarily dismisses Foucault, claiming that he "suspends the category of 'explanation',"[39] her discussion of emergent homophobia in nineteenth-century England both confirms his speculation and allows us to sharpen it as an analytic tool. For homosexuality did not emerge as a problem because friendship had already disappeared; rather, as Foucault himself observed, intense male friendships were perceived as inimical to the smooth functioning of modern institutions—the army, bureaucracy, administration, universities, schools—which therefore attempted "to diminish, or minimize, the affectional relations."[40] And the primary weapon in this "progressive" campaign against male friendship was homophobia— the imputing of a homosexual motive to every male relationship; hence, the widespread tendency to regard such institutions of the military, the prison, and the boy's school as sites of rampant homosexual activity, rather than as machines for the reproduction, not of homosexuals, but of homophobes. As Sedgwick writes;

> The fact that what goes on at football games, in fraternities, at the Bohemian Grove, and at climactic moments in war novels can look, with only a slight shift of optic, quite startlingly "homosexual," is not most importantly an expression of the psychic

origin of these institutions in a repressed or sublimated homosexual genitality. Instead, it is the coming to visibility of the normally implicit terms of a coercive double bind. (It might be compared to the double bind surrounding rape that imprisons American women: to dress and behave "attractively," i.e., as prescribed, is always to be "asking for it.") For a man to be a man's man is separated only by an invisible, carefully blurred, always-already-crossed line from being "interested in men."[41]

Thus, Sedgwick deftly overturns received Freudian wisdom that repressed or sublimated homosexual desire lies at the origins of both the "social instincts" and of homophobia as well. Freud's theory of homophobia as repressed homosexuality has been celebrated by some gay writers for locating the "problem," not with homosexuality per se, but with homophobia.[42] However, this theory also makes it difficult—at times impossible—to distinguish homophobia from homosexuality; and I believe that the positing of a homosexual monopoly is predicated on precisely this confusion of terms. For it *would* make sense to speak of the undisclosed *homophobia* of the official discourse of philosophy, or to characterize the Nazi community as a *homophobic* brotherhood, and to investigate (as Sedgwick has) the way in which such homophobia affects women. Freud is not, of course, to be held responsible for the confusion of homosexuality and homophobia; his own confusion testifies to the historical limitations of his treatment of male homosexuality. But neither is Freudian theory to be invoked in support of theories of a homosexual monopoly, for it is a manifestation of the same homophobic mechanisms it purports to describe.

Homophobia, Sedgwick writes, "is by now endemic and perhaps ineradicable in our culture. The question of who is to be free to define, manipulate, and profit from the resultant double bind is no less a site of struggle today than in the eighteenth century, however."[43] That the single most important contribution to the redefining of the terms of this struggle should have been made by a *feminist* writer is highly encouraging. By demonstrating that male homophobia is directed at both gay and straight men, and by demonstrating that it affects women as well (by requiring that what Sedgwick refers to as male "homosocial" desire be mediated by women), Sedgwick has effectively transformed the fear of homosexuality from an isolated political issue into a central concern of any Left political coalition today. Nowhere is the importance of this issue for society at large more apparent than in the government's and the media's scapegoating of homosexual men for the AIDS pandemic—a homophobic tactic which is as threatening as the disease itself to the welfare of the entire population. Sedgwick's discussion of male homosocial desire departs from René

Girard's discussion of rivalrous erotic triangles in *Desire, Deceit, and the Novel*; in conclusion, I would like to cite a passage from Girard's *The Scapegoat*—a passage which has chilling repercussions today, as proposals for the quarantine, internment, tattooing, even the extermination of homosexual men resound in our ears:

> Medieval communities were so afraid of the plague that the word alone was enough to frighten them. They avoided mentioning it as long as possible and even avoided taking the necessary precautions at the risk of aggravating the effects of the epidemic. So helpless were they that telling the truth did not mean facing the situation but rather giving in to its destructive consequences and relinquishing all semblance of normal life. The entire population shared in this type of blindness. Their desparate desire to deny the evidence contributed to their search for "scapegoats."[44]

23.
Envy: or With Your Brains and My Looks

Rosi Braidotti

The male is a biological accident; the Y (male) gene is an incomplete X (female) gene, that is it has an incomplete set of chromosomes . . . . Being an incomplete female, the male spends his life attempting to complete himself, to become female . . . . The male, because of his obsession to compensate for not being female, combined with his inability to relate and to feel compassion, has made of the world a shitpile.

The SCUM Manifesto, Valerie Solanis, 1968

Mine is the century of Death. Mine is the century of male-birthed children, precocious with radiation.

About Men, Phyllis Chesler, 1978

I hesitate. There is something both appealing and suspect in the notion of "men in feminism"; like many of the other contributors, my gaze lingers on the preposition "IN" wondering about the spatial dimension it throws open. Is it the battleground for the eternal war of the sexes? Is it the space where bodily sexed subjectivities come to a head-on collision? I can only envisage this topic as a knot of interconnected tensions, an area of intense turmoil, a set of contradictions.

Somewhere along the line I am viscerally opposed to the whole idea: men aren't and shouldn't be IN feminism; the feminist space is not theirs and not for them to see. Thus, the discursive game we are trying to play is either profoundly precarious or perversely provocative—or both at once. A sort of impatience awakens in me at the thought of a whole class/caste of men who are fascinated, puzzled and intimidated by the sight of a pen-handling female intelligentsia of the feminist kind. I do not know what is at stake in this for them and thus, to let my irony shine through IN-BETWEEN the lines, I shall de/re-form a sign and write instead of phallic subtexts: "men in Pheminism." Why insist on a letter, for instance?

Contextual Constraints

Of all Foucault ever taught me, the notion of the "materiality of ideas" has had the deepest impact. One cannot make an abstraction of the network of truth and power formations that govern the practice of one's enunciation; ideas are sharp-edged discursive events which cannot be analysed simply in terms of their propositional content.

There is something incongruous for me to be sitting here in Paris, on a warm September day—police cars rushing past, sirens screaming; terrorists' bombs all over town; anti-Arab racism flaring up again—thinking about "men in Pheminism." I cannot say this is a major problem in my mind, or in the context within which I am trying to live. The sociopolitical impact of French feminism[1] has not been strong enough for feminist theory, women's studies, or women scholars to make anything like the impact they have had in the United States and in other Anglo-Saxon countries. There is something very American, in a positive sense, about this issue. The interest that American men display in Pheminism reflects a specific historical and cultural context: one in which feminist scholarship has made it to the cutting edge of the academic scene.

As a European feminist I feel both resistant to and disenchanted with the reduction of feminism to "feminist theory" and the confining of both within academic discourse. Paul Smith's provocative line about penetrating into feminism is amusing in a wild sense but is very problematic in the ways pointed out by others in this volume. This attitude points out a danger that the pioneers of women's studies courses had emphasized from the start: that our male "allies" may not be able to learn how to respect the complexity of the issues raised by feminism. Following a century-old mental habit which Adrienne Rich[2] analyzes so lucidly, they cannot resist the temptation of short-circuiting this complexity, in an attempt to straighten out feminist theory and practice, streamlining the feminist project in a mold which they can recognize. Blinded by what they have learned to recognize as "theory," they bulldoze their way through feminism as if it were not qualitatively different from any other academic discipline. They are walking all over us.

What they are lacking intellectually—the peculiar blindness to sexual difference for which the term "sexism" is an inadequate assessment—is a reflection of their position in history. They have not inherited a world of oppression and exclusion based on their sexed, corporeal being; they do not have the lived experienced of being historically denied the status of subject as a consequence of their sex. Thus, most of them fail to grasp the specificity of feminism in terms of its articulation of theory and practice, of thought and life.

Maybe they have no alternative. It must be very uncomfortable to be a male, white, middle-class intellectual at a time in history when so many minorities and oppressed groups are speaking up for themselves; a time when the hegemony of the white knowing subject is crumbling. Lacking the historical experience of oppression on the basis of sex, they paradoxically lack a minus. Lacking the lack, they cannot participate in the great ferment of ideas that is shaking up Western culture: it must be very painful indeed to have no option other than being the empirical referent of the historical oppressor of women, and being asked to account for his atrocities.

The problem is that the exclusion of women and the denigration of the feminine are not just a small omission that can be fixed with a little good will. They rather point to the underlying theme in the textual and historical continuity of masculine self-legitimation and ideal self-projection.[3] It's on the woman's body—on her absence, her silence, her disqualification—that phallocentric discourse rests. This sort of "metaphysical cannibalism," which Ti-Grace Atkinson analyzed in terms of uterus-envy, positions the woman as the silent groundwork of male subjectivity—the condition of possibility for *his* story. Psychoanalytic theory, of the Freudian or the Lacanian brand, circles around the question of origins—the mother's body—by elucidating the psychic mechanisms that make the paternal presence, the father's body, necessary as a figure of authority *over her*.

Following Luce Irigaray I see psychoanalysis as a patriarchal discourse which apologizes for metaphysical cannibalism: the silencing of the powerfulness of the feminine. Refusing to dissociate the *discourse* about the feminine, the maternal, from the *historical realities* of the condition and status of women in Western culture, Irigaray equates the metaphorization of women (the feminine, the maternal) with their victimization or historical oppression. One does not become a member of the dark continent; one is born into it. The question is how to transform this century-old silence into a presence of women as subjects in every aspect of existence. I am sure "they" know this, don't "they"?

"They" are those white, middle-class male intellectuals who have "got it right" in that they have sensed where the subversive edge of feminist theory is. "They" are a very special generation of post-beat, pre-yuppie 28-to-45-year-old men who have "been through" the upheavals of the 1960s and have inherited the values and the neuroses of that period. "They" are the "new men" in the "post-feminist" context of the politically reactionary 1980s. "They" are the best male friends we've got, and "they" are not really what we had hoped for. "They" circle round women's studies departments in crisis-stricken Arts Faculties, knowing that here's one of the few areas of the Academy which is still expanding financially and in terms of students' enrollment at both undergraduate and graduate level. "They" play the academic career game with great finesse, knowing the rule about feminist separatism and yet ignoring it. "They" know that feminist theory is the last bastion of radical thought amidst the ruins of the postmodern gloom. "They" are conscious of the fact that the debate about modernity and beyond is coextensive with the woman's question.

The age of so-called modernity which Alice Jardine has read critically in *Gynesis* has seen the emergence and the merging of two parallel phenomena: on the one hand the revival of women's movements and women-centered analyses; on the other hand, a crisis of the idea of rationality as a human ethical idea as well as the epistemological guideline in Western philosophical discourse. Ever since Nietzsche, passing through every major European philosopher, the question of woman has accompanied the decline of the classical view of human subjectivity. The problematic of the "feminine" thus outlined is nothing more than a very elaborate metaphor, a symptom, of the profound illness of Western culture and of its phallologocentric logic.[4] It is a male disease, expressing the critical state of the postmodern condition which J.-F. Lyotard describes; my argument is that this "feminine" bears no direct or even necessary relation to real-life women. In some ways, it even perpetuates the century-old mental habit which consists in assigning to the "feminine" disorders or insufficiencies pertaining to the male of the species.

Right across the spectrum of contemporary Continental and especially French philosophy the "feminine" functions as a powerful vehicle to convey the critical attempts to redefine human subjectivity. From Lacan's assertion that woman cannot speak[5] because her silence, her absence from, or ex-centricity vis-à-vis phallocentric discourse allows for the edifice of male discursivity; to Derrida's injunction that in so far as it cannot be said the "feminine" functions as the most pervasive signifier[6]; from Foucault's bland assertion that the absence of women from the philosophical scene is constitutive of the discursive rules of the philosophical game[7] to Deleuze's notion of the "becoming-woman" as marking a qualitative transformation in human consciousness[8]—the feminization of thought seems to be prescribed as a fundamental step in the general programme of anti-humanism which marks our era.

The combination of conceptual elements is quite paradoxical: deconstructing, dismissing, or displacing the notion of the rational subject at the very historical moment when women are beginning to have access to the use of discourse, power, and pleasure; while at the same time advocating the "feminine" or the "becoming-woman" of theoretical discourse—woman as the figure of modernity—seems to me highly problematic. What is missing from this scheme is the elaboration of a political project.

Well may the high-priests of postmodernism preach the deconstruction and fragmentation of the subject, the flux of all identities based on phallocentric premises; well may they keep reading into feminism the image of the crisis of their own acquired perceptions of human consciousness. The truth of the matter is: one cannot deconstruct a subjectivity one has never been fully granted; one cannot diffuse a sexuality which has historically been defined as dark and mysterious. In order to announce the death of the subject one must first have gained the right to speak as one; in order to demystify metadiscourse one must first gain access to a place of enunciation. The fragmentation of the self being woman's basic historical condition, as Luce Irigaray points out, we are left with the option of theorizing a general "becoming-woman" for both sexes, or else of flatly stating that women have been postmodern since the beginning of time.[9]

Knowing that the debate about modernity and postmodernism looms dangerously close to the subtle discursive grounds of feminism, I would just like to stress that the idea of the "death of the subject" has been over-estimated ever since the early days of structuralism in France. Just because, thanks to the formidable advances of science and technology, the so-called human and social sciences have had to come to terms with their own limitations as systems of interpretation and analysis of reality, it does not follow that there is no system, no interpretation or understanding and no reality. Just because modern philosophy has discovered an area of twilight within human subjectivity and discourse; and just because this is blurring the century-old distinction between self and other, it does not inevitably follow that there is no more certainty about the self. Just because ever since the end of the nineteenth century the ontological security of the knowing subject has been shaken up, it does not mean that all the old notions— such as subjectivity, consciousness and truth—are no longer operational. What the "Krisis" of modernity means is that philosophy must struggle to redefine the terms within which it would be possible for us to think adequately about our historical condition. What is needed is a reasoned critique of reason, paradoxical as it may sound.

I think that feminism and philosophical modernity can only be related in dialectical terms, that is to say in terms of power and strategy. While I remain extremely critical of the theoreticians of the "becoming-woman" or the feminization of the (postmodern) subject, I wonder what it is that makes them want to embark on this sudden programme of de-phallicisation? What is being exorcised by male thinkers in the act of their becoming "feminized"? What do these new hysterics want? I see nothing more in this maneuver than a contemporary version of the old metaphysical cannibalism: it expresses the male desire to carry on the hegemonic tradition which they inherited; it reveals their attachment to their traditional place of enunciation, despite all. Envy.

Envious of a history of oppression which the political will of the women's movement has turned into a major critical stance for women to use to their best advantage. As a close male friend put it, sadly: "Your position is, after all, *ideal.*" In whose imaginary? I wonder. Are we not confronted here by a variation on the theme of male mid-life crisis? Aren't "they" simply caught in a professional and personal context of intense disorder? Aren't "they" merely projecting on the feminists some of the traditional images of WOMAN as a threatening, all-powerful, devouring entity? Is the feminist woman, in so far as she claims to be neither mother nor whore and both of them at once, a new ideal *imago*? Are we stuck, once again, in hetero-sexist perversity thinly disguised as an authoritative intellectual inquiry on "feminist theory"?

In an age of advanced capitalism where the social manifestations of sexual difference are dislocated by a new androgyny,[10] while the reproductive technology revolution has given men the means of realizing their ancient dream of giving birth to children by and for themselves,[11] it seems to me that male uterus-envy is reaching a peak of paroxysm. Except for the few melancholy runaways who just sit and stare into a Beckett-like empty space in which the monuments and documents of the Phallus have already crumbled. What will be the place and role of real-life women in this fragmented universe? I fear that a postmodern world which will have made sexual difference redundant, proposing an image of the subject as deprived of fixed sexual identity, reproducing outside sexual intercourse, may even be able to afford the luxury of being Pheminist. Alone at last!

Three Guineas, Four Pennies and Other Bargains

Three books are lying at my side, on the bench which I am trying to keep all to myself on the sunny side of the Place des Vosges. Three titles to remind me of where I come from as a feminist: *La Presenza dell'uomo nel femminismo*, by radical Italian feminist Carla Lonzi; Virginia Woolf's *Three Guineas*; and Phyllis Chesler's *About Men*. I cannot think of a French feminist text about men in Pheminism.

Books—slices of female corporeal lived experience, to make sure that in raising the topic of "men" I will have exorcized what's left of my adolescent fantasies. Back in the days when the idea of "men" seemed to contain the answer to the question of my identity as not just *a*, but rather as *the* woman. My entire conditioning, enforced by a whole sociopolitical system, pushes me to rejoicing at having yet another opportunity to think talk dream about "men." And so I hesitate. There is something both appealing and suspect in the ease with which the topic pops up, offering itself to my attention. I am against compulsory heterosexuality, even of the sublimated kind;[12] I am not prepared to, or even interested in, sharing confidences about men in the pages of a book about Pheminism. It feels quite uncomfortable to coexist with men under this (book) cover; it is a form of cohabitation as strained as the Chirac-Mitterand couple, and just as loaded with potential for destruction. A solemn *de facto* discontent.

Where am I speaking from? So many links are missing. At least Virginia Woolf chose an in-transit position: she stood on a bridge and watched the crazed world of patriarchy—the learned men, the men of power, the war-lords—marching off to the fulfillment of their in-built death-wish. She wrote her magnificent *Three Guineas* on the eve of the Second World War and I think very strongly of her today, in post-Chernobyl Western Europe. Once again, as many times before, I feel great fear and an unspeakable sadness about our genocidal world.

Virginia Woolf watched it from afar, as if suspended in mid-air, ex-static—implicated and yet exterior, radically other but a dutiful daughter of the patriarchs nevertheless. Peripherally involved, marginally connected, not all entirely in agreement with what she could see, and yet sufficiently close to the common cause of humanity to actually take responsibility for the gruelling mess and dare speak the words: "that's not it, that's not the way to do it all."

For there is no outside, no absolute purity or uncontamination from patriarchal practices of the material or discursive kind. Although the non-mixity of the women's movement is a powerful political strategy, a device prompting a woman-centered mode of analysis, it cannot be conceptually allowed to conceal our implication in a system which has actively discriminated against us, in a culture which has assigned us to a depreciated set of values. Born free, we lived at a discount. We have no choice but staying IN, with one foot out—split twice over, and over.

There is also a separatism of the mind. My speaking stance as a feminist has accustomed me to address women as my privileged interlocutors—I can only view the prospect of addressing Pheminist men with a touch of benevolent fatigue. The feminist in me is a fighter, a winner, a (re)vindicator, an activist, a social figure. She is fully involved with patriarchy through rejection; anger, rebellion, and passion for justice keep her IN, tied to a death-and-life struggle with her

main enemy. Consciously phallic, she wants to get IN—she is politically reformist: wanting to put women IN, all the way.

However, the feminist is not all of me; she is directly and intimately
related to my being-a-woman-alongside-other-women-in-the-world.
There exists a common world of women, as A. Rich put it, a *continuum*
in the woman-centered vision of the world: my subjectivity is attached
to the presence of the other woman. The woman-in-me is not a full-
time member of patriarchy, neither by rejection nor by acceptance;
she is elsewhere—on the margin, in the periphery, in the shade (to
the delight of Lacanian psychoanalysts)—she cannot be contained in
one sentence. Contrary to Lacan, I maintain that my ex-centricity vis-
à-vis the system of representation points to another logic, another
way of "making sense": the woman-in-me is not silent, she is part
of a symbolic referential system by and of women themselves. She
just speaks an-other language; radically different (Irigaray). Whereas
Monique Wittig in her article on "The Straight Mind[13] claims that the
margin of non-involvement by women with the patriarchal system
has to do with lesbian identity, I think that the patterns of symbolic
female homosexuality transcend the mere choice of women as erotic
objects. Choosing to love a woman is not a sufficient (though it may
be necessary) condition to escape from the logic of patriarchy. Language and sexuality are not spatial structures that one can just avoid,
by-pass, and eventually step out of.

The woman-in-me is IN language but in process within it; directly
connected to the feminist I chose to be, the woman-in-me has taken
her distance from compulsory heterosexuality while remaining involved with men—though not necessarily Pheminist men. The
project of redefining the content of the woman-in-me so as to disengage her from the trappings of a "feminine" defined as dark continent, or of "femininity" as the eternal masquerade, will take my
life-time, all the time I have. The woman-in-me is developing, alongside other women but not exclusively on their behalf, a redefinition
of what it means to be human. Being-a-woman is always-already there
as the ontological pre-condition for my existential becoming as a subject: one has to start with the body and the bodily roots of subjectivity
(A. Rich).

This is why feminism matters: it carries ethical and transcendental
values that simply cannot be reduced to yet another ideology or theory—a doxa or a dogma for general consumption. Feminism is also
the liberation of women's ontological desire to be female subjects: to
transcend the traditional vision of subjectivity as gender-free, to inscribe the subject back into her/his corporeal reality. To make sexual
difference operative at last.

Feminism as the theoretical project aimed at affirming female subjectivity acts as the threshold through which the fundamental dis-

symetry between the sexes turns at last into the question of sexual difference. As Irigaray puts it: this is the utopia of our century.

So as to avoid the pitfalls of ready-made essentialism, of positing woman as originally and constitutionally other; so as to avoid that her plural lips repeat a certain uniformity, we feminists need a political project, a practice, a movement. Difference, to be operative, has to be acted ON and acted OUT, collectively, in the *here and now* of our common world.

Beyond the principle of envy—the ethics of sexual difference. And if love means, as Lacan put it, giving what you haven't got to someone who doesn't want it anyway, then I guess love is what I have been thinking about, after all.

24.
A Conversation
Alice Jardine and Paul Smith

Side One

AJ: To begin in a somewhat confessional mode. Basically there's never been anything further from my mind than to isolate the question of "men in feminism" . . . . But in a sense, I think about it all the time. My book, *Gynesis,* is about going after what I think is a male *fantasme*—not going after it to kill it but rather to look at where it opens up or where it connects (after all it's everyone's *fantasme,* and not just a male thing). So I work on male theorists and in the rest of my life it's a constant nagging question: men are definitely an issue in my personal, political, intellectual, and professional feminist life. So it's all around me and I think about it, am engaged in it all the time, but the thought of positing it as a question *per se* would never have entered my mind.

PS: Why not, do you know? Is there a theoretical reason?

AJ: Yes, I'd have trouble saying what we mean by all three terms: "men," "in," "feminism." It would be that basic. For me, right now, I'm not post-feminist in any measure, but I do feel the urgent thing is to think through what we know from feminism and make that part of a larger interrogation—though it is important to avoid the male leftist thing of saying: now let's move along to the bigger issues. It's just about not always focussing

---

The following conversation, the result of our first face-to-face meeting as editors, was taped on September 9th, 1986, as we were in the process of compiling the final manuscript of the book. Not all contributions had been received, and we didn't in any case set out to discuss even all those we had. Our idea was to talk generally about some of the problems which the various articles had brought up. In no sense did we manage or intend to construct an overview of the work in the book, but rather we simply wanted to touch upon issues which were particularly on our minds. Thus we offer the following not as an editorial, but rather as one more contribution to the book's dialogues. Accordingly we have tried to reproduce as closely as possible the actual tone and content, as well as the conversational texture, of our discussion. We have resisted the urge to edit ourselves, even where we have felt ourselves vulnerable. Where it seemed appropriate we have added page references to other essays in the book; a list of other references we make is appended.

on questions like "French feminist theory" or "men and . . . ,"
or "woman and . . . ." It's more about changing the object of
study. For example, I'm working now on machines, and people
often don't see the connections, but it has . . . it's all interconnected. I would never have thought to put feminism and men
or women or anything else at the center. But that's also one of
my limitations—I'm not always capable of thinking through
those nitty-gritty things. I tend to do it on a personal, inter-
subjective level, pre-theoretically, whatever that means.

PS: For me the assumption that this could be abstracted as a topic
from a whole set of other practices and discourses was more or
less equivalent to your saying we can talk about machines. It
wasn't to suggest that this was to be taken as a really central
problem. I was assuming that the work being done by feminists
crossed a certain kind of "topic" of which this was just *one*. I,
in any case, didn't want to put it forward as a central question,
as especially crucial. It's one of many possible topics which
might be able to contribute in the way that talking about, say,
"women and pornography" might contribute, or talking about
"women and the work force." Not necessarily more or less important than anything else. Though I am a little surprised by
the dimensions it has taken on, and the interest it has provoked.

AJ: Do you think a woman (feminist) would have proposed it?

PS: Probably not as a topic for discussion. But certainly women have
already written about it, mostly with a negative perspective on
it. In the back of my mind at the beginning were a number of
pieces of writing, like some of Christine Delphy's work in *Close
to Home*, and Elaine Showalter's "Critical Cross-Dressing" [pp.
116–32], where men in feminism is clearly an issue. It's surely
something women think about, and it produces reactions readily
enough.

AJ: That's how *Gynesis* got started . . . in the back of my mind was
going to Paris and hearing all those men talk about *le féminin.
Et j'en avais marre.* Slowly I realized that it wasn't just male intellectuals in Paris being paranoid, but something more than
that was going on. It took me a long time . . . . Maybe it's that
I wouldn't have posited it as a topic at the MLA! All of that
aside, "men in feminism" struck me at the time as possibly
something only a man would have proposed. That's not just a
critique. In my *imaginaire*, I experienced—this is confessional—
intense amusement about this topic from the very beginning.
Then the mood-swings set in as I considered it more seriously.
One minute I worried about its (perhaps) inevitable hetero-
centrism, its (potential) elitism, and wanted to forget about it
. . . . The next minute, I worried about the real political con-

sequences of ignoring or dismissing the question . . . . And I still swing from intense amusement to real worry and even something close to engagement with the knots of the problem. But when first asked to be on the panel I thought: what a riot!

PS: I wish you'd told me that!

AJ: Yes, when I first started thinking about it I felt a mixture of amusement and anger—that's my MLA paper [pp. 54–61]. Then when you asked me to do the book I was taken aback, and from there it became an anecdotal situation where I mentioned it to a few women—feminists—who said we shouldn't do it. The more I was told I shouldn't do it, the more I wanted to. I thought: what is this about? Because most of the reactions were strictly theoretical and professional—though some were personal. It seemed that the real issue was about power, about men who wanted to be feminists in the academy . . . who were perhaps exploring new modes of seduction.

So I began thinking about how that mode was working in my *imaginaire*, a perhaps female imaginary, and about the place of the institutionally recognized feminist theoretician in your *imaginaire*, a perhaps male imaginary . . . and decided that doing this book together is a very strange thing and will be perceived as strange. I had a feeling that men in feminism was absolutely impossible, but I was interested in thinking about where that impossibility comes from, at least right now.

PS: I suppose I agree in a sense about the impossibility, but think it's a very limited impossibility (almost a common-sense one, which is that men can't be in the place that women experience). But I don't know how useful it is to stress the impossibility, especially because currently there are a lot of men approaching feminist discourses—not only approaching them (miming them, appropriating them, or genuinely trying to understand them) but also publishing in "feminist" journals, teaching in women's studies programs, and so on. There's certainly something to talk about in all that.

AJ: Would you say it's mainly straight men?

PS: I'm not sure—a lot of those who've become successful are straight.

AJ: A lot of the women I've talked to realize that it's easier if the man is gay. I don't always understand why that is. I guess it's because we don't then worry about being penetrated; we worry less about being invaded, fooled, penetrated . . . This is also some kind of *imaginaire*.

PS: Obviously I see that whole issue from another side. I came in for a lot of criticism from feminist colleagues for doing the panel. It seemed to me—and this partly explains my tone in my MLA paper [pp. 33–40]—that the criticism relied too heavily on this scenario of seduction: personal and professional techniques, manners, desires, etc. It seemed to me very strange . . .

AJ: People did make that explicit, didn't they?

PS: But it still seemed odd. I thought that, even if there was a point to the seduction stuff, other things still needed to be taken into account. One of those factors, which Andrew Ross pointed out, is education [p. 86]. He and I were educated in the same place at roughly the same time; for us, part of what we were given as our education was feminism. Andrew and I did our graduate work at the University of Kent where some of the *Screen* people were working and where there were strong feminist voices. The discourse was in place; the interest was there. There wasn't any question but that we could "assimilate" these discourses. No one said, so far as I recall, that there's a problem with us as biological men learning these discourses . . .

AJ: But that was while you were still students. It's different isn't it? You had less power. Did you come over to the "other side," i.e., become a professor, in the USA? And did that coincide with the criticisms about your feminism?

PS: More or less. And I can see how that might produce a problem for feminists, where they see an area or a discourse picked up by men whose qualifications . . . It's still pretty unusual in America that men should be educated in that way.

AJ: That's a good point. That's why I was wondering about the student/professor, Britain/USA boundaries because there just aren't . . . After all, a lot of American male ventures into feminism haven't exactly bowled anyone over . . . They often talked about things that women feminists had been talking about for years . . . Interestingly enough, one of the first incursions by a male theorist that really upset a lot of feminists was Terry Eagleton's. So there may be a national boundary problem here, combined with the power issue.

PS: That's something important, obviously. It's true there are some male colleagues who put on the mantel of feminism and make themselves some kind of institutional reputation and power. In most cases there's good reason to be distrustful of that. In other cases there may not be. I was trying to say in my MLA paper that you have to listen in order to decide. I don't think it's right to assume (and I felt it had been assumed) that a man could have only bad motives.

AJ: Conscious motives.

PS: But one can consciously adapt to, compensate for, or even fight against unconscious motives. And those gestures need to be counted . . .

AJ: So, clearly, in terms of the initiation of the project, there were several agendas, several *imaginaires*. In any case I guess my reasoning remains the same. Gender is one of the pieces we've used to construct this world. And we've got some major problems to face in this world . . . So, if men want to take gender into account in order to attack these larger problems, I'm all for it; that was never an issue. The problem for me is when men just automatically do feminist literary criticism, feminist theory, or anything feminist recognized by the institution, instead of using their reading and their knowledge about gender to attack the problems the university *doesn't* want to recognize . . . It's something about focussing on feminism in a way that various institutions can recognize—that a press would publish for instance—this is where I begin to question . . .

Side Two

PS: At least one of our contributors, Stephen Heath, might be said to be institutionally recognized and also recognized by many women as an actual contributor to feminist theory. Just the same, I was quite surprised by how sympathetic the women's reaction to his "Male Feminism" (q.v.) was: it was perceived as more or less OK. To me, and I think to some of its other male readers, the article seems rather to be full of a kind of penitence, a kind of abjection in regard to feminism. I know that you value struggle and I think you're right to, and for men that's what a large part of their dealing with feminism has to consist in, but penitence can be a way of transcending struggle. In other words, I see few signs of political struggle in this paper. Why did you for one seem so sympathetic to it? What is it about the piece? What does it do that you think is both acceptable and useful?

AJ: First of all, I don't think it was universally perceived as "OK." It was received—by me anyway—as a text, and not an isolated text. I had, of course, read other things of his and this was an intertext or, rather, a hiatus in his super-theoretical work . . . Perhaps he was indulging himself a bit, being self-reflective, etc. But it's complicated. There's a certain seductive power to that for any feminist theorist who's had to separate so radically her "soul-searching" from her theoretical activity (not out of choice, but because of institutional arrangements). I think there was a kind of recognition: this man has to do it, too. Certainly one of the strongest feminist myths, if not insights, is that very rarely do men do any self-analysis in regard to what they're feeling.

So my criteria were different. Heath didn't immediately throw up the theory flag. The paper was explicitly about him, autobiographical in a sense, and therefore I didn't immediately come to it as a theorist. Dare I say I listened to it as a woman who was fascinated by this man making public his soul-searching? But it wasn't totally well received because of course I knew I was doing this (and other women who had positive reactions knew they were doing it too). And as a theorist, I suppose I would have to go on about how the paper is at least partially "guilty as charged."

Except that it was a question of a different *écoute* . . . at least initially. The problem came at the end where he evokes his hospitalized mother [p. 30]. I was shaken out of my passive, perhaps seduced state by that image. It was almost as if he purposely took us to the point where we could no longer remain fascinated because suddenly there was the mother in a hospital ward and . . . "admiration," precisely. It shook you up and awake. This text did not threaten me in any way. It didn't ask of me . . . Perhaps it's still an artificial activity for women today to engage in theory; perhaps it's still something that you do after you've dealt with all the emotional, affective, personal relationships to texts . . . to . . . (I'm only speaking for myself; there *are* feminist theorists who'd find that an appalling statement—myself included, sometimes). Historically, though, it is a double process for women; and there's still something very seductive about a man putting down his theoretical weapons, giving up in a sense, indulging in a narcissism which historically has been available only to women or to certain feminized sectors of the culture which have been devalorised as popular culture or . . . .

PS: I don't think I mean it's narcissistic, but indulgent in the sense that one might indulge a child. I suspect that feminists are being *played to* here: you women are right and I (Heath) am going to please you.

AJ: He does bring up the Barthes—love me, love me, accept me as modestly and ingloriously marginal—which coming from Heath the theoretician was very seductive.

PS: I can see that. But I'm suspicious of his indulging feminists. It sounds as if you're interested in it as a spectacle, as an entertainment; but from what you're saying about the ending, it isn't something you can finally be drawn into. The question then would be: what does this constitute as a contribution; is there any firm or useful political effect to this if it seduces the feminist but does not finally draw her in?

AJ: Tough one. Pragmatically, it covers a lot of different territories, a whole range of issues (pornography, psychoanalysis, women

on male sexuality, poststructuralism, etc.) that were to be part
of the discussions; and at that level it's helpful to have this seductive, sympathetic, "unarmed" male take on these different
fields.

In terms of the more difficult question you're asking about
spectacle . . . I don't know. I'd never seen Heath perform before.
Yet, I read his paper in print the same way . . . And I had the
same kind of reaction to his "Difference" article several years
ago: here is a man who has clearly read everything that's relevant and who has put together a piece of writing which has a
pedagogical function. It will educate. So what if he is repeating
what other feminists have said in obscure places . . . ? He gets
it "right." So "Difference" was in the back of my mind. That
article educated, became mandatory secondary reading. I wasn't
necessarily seduced as a theorist; I was seduced as a feminist
reader and listener.

PS: Andrew pointed out in "No Question of Silence" (q.v.) that
there is what Elizabeth Weed calls a "bad feminism" [p. 87]
beneath Stephen's article: psychoanalytical feminism. Psychoanalytical thinking is one of the things that his article most
defends itself against, and so it becomes a target. But it seems
to me there's a certain contradiction here. That stuff at the end
about admiration, where you stopped: despite Stephen's finding
all that fetishism in my article, there doesn't seem anything non-
fetishistic about this notion of "admiration." I was suspicious,
not really because admiration is itself fetishistic but because fetishism is something that Stephen clearly thinks is at the base
of what's "wrong" with men; it's the thing which for him seems
to prevent men being feminists or makes the relation impossible.

AJ: Which is ironic in some ways. At least since Sarah Kofman's
notion (in "Ça Cloche") that a certain kind of *female* fetishism
might be the strongest theoretical tool that women have.

PS: That's something Naomi Schor mentions in her article (q.v.).
The contradiction in Heath is that he doesn't really want feminist
psychoanalysis, but on the other hand the psychoanalytical concept of fetishism is right at the base of his thinking about the
impossibility of men in feminism. That's an almost overdetermined way to construct for yourself impasses and knots. Maybe
that's what's seductive about it—maybe what you're reading as
struggle is a willed and willful complication of the difficulties in
an almost defensive way. And where you stop following him,
around the admiration bit, is where he let's go the difficulty.

AJ: The complication becomes passive?

PS: And what more overdetermined object for a man to return to
than his mother?

AJ: It's true that when his mother comes into it . . . The notion of willful complication is an interesting idea, if we haven't ourselves willfully complicated his piece.

PS: I'm putting it forward as part of a more general chain of thought about the way this notion of the impossibility of men's relation to feminism is posed by various contributors. It occurred to me, for instance, that those who were most offended by *my* rhetoric, but who liked Stephen's, seemed the ones who were most unwilling to actually think a place or a strategy for men in or around feminism.

AJ: Men and women?

PS: Not just the men. I mean those who wanted to say, like Stephen, that it's impossible; like Cary Nelson, that it's superfluous; like Elizabeth Weed, that it's a tired issue; like Meaghan Morris, that it's *a priori* a ridiculous idea. That comes back to my original question about what Stephen's piece actually does. One thing it does is to preclude the possibility of thinking through a male feminism.

AJ: I myself am incapable of thinking it through. I know that. That may be a symptom of what's going on here. It's true that when you put it down . . . .

PS: So what do you think of the new ending where Stephen admits to a problem with this notion of admiration, but basically says he's not going to deal with it [pp. 30–32]?

AJ: It's true that admiration was one of the things he seemed to feel strongly about in the bulk of the paper, and then he ties that into a knot in his new ending. You may have something, but I still, also, have a suspicion that *you* are willfully complicating *his* gesture . . .

PS: Can you say that as a theorist or as a . . .

AJ: This is the knot: there's the theory, the theorist, the subject and the object of theory, and then there's something else—tone or whatever. With students I talk about how women theorists and writers sometimes feel that they have to work at two speeds. Perhaps whatever it is that we haven't been able to theorize has been picked up by Naomi's paper as "doubling." It's also a form of fetishism, wanting both.

PS: I'd locate some of the drive towards that in deconstructive thinking. Elizabeth Weed quotes Derrida on doing the radical and the conservative gesture at once, for instance [p. 74]. I myself am now skeptical enough about the political use of deconstruction to want to say that, if that's where this notion comes from, I'm suspicious.

AJ: Someone suggested to me recently that some of the men involved in feminist theory are actually "using" it to plug into other quarrels with other male theorists. That came up in some of our letters to each other, about Derrida "getting to you," but not to me.

PS: I was saying that in general Derrida annoys me; but I found it interesting that he was saying things in his interview that I was saying too—about the law and its other. I wondered what to make of that. I think perhaps I'd want to do something different with those ideas. He says that when the law is established, when women become the law, that's inevitable and it needs to be deconstructed—and on we go in a continual deconstruction. I'd say that under current conditions there's not much possibility of there being anything else, there'd just be the law. My difference with Derrida is that he would make a virtue out of the continual, revolving, tropical turning stuff, and I wouldn't. I'd say we need some more trenchant political action; otherwise we all become quiet observers at a tropological carnival.

AJ: But do you think it's just a *fantasme* or is there any validity to this notion that some men might be making a connection with male theorists in a safe fashion through feminism?

PS: But it wouldn't be safe just because it's involved with feminism, surely?

AJ: But because men theorists who engage with other men theorists in public usually have to do it directly, with the phallus . . . . With Derrida, in particular, you can't do that. There's no access to Derrida in the male mode. So if it's filtered through feminism, through women . . . . I'm wondering about it in terms of unconscious strategies, which is after all what matters. If this doubling/fetishism/2-speed thing, having to be double, is a theoretical tool for women, if that is fundamentally plugged into some Derridean mode then perhaps . . . . I do think that one reason I wrote *Gynesis* was because that doubleness (the yes/ but, yes/no, presence/absence thing) has some fundamental, historically specific, but fundamental libidinal connection to women and the way they experience the world.

PS: I agree and that makes sense, but I'm wondering about the Derrida connection, especially in relation to what he does with it in the seminar here, or in some of his recent texts. One of the conclusions, I think, of what he's doing these days is that basically you go on as normal; things don't change. For example, when he says that speaking against apartheid would be "too dialectical," so remain silent. It's the same thing with his article about the nuclear threat, and with this interview we have here.

AJ: That brings up a topic—silence, and I would add, laughter.

PS: Because you've been laughing about our project all along?

AJ: The value of laughter and silence as political tools may be seen by some as a tired topic, but it does come up in a few places . . . .

PS: But how about first making some sort of distinction around Stephen's paper and the question of fetishism—its desire and its bad object—and this doubling process you're pointing to as a fetishism. What are we to make of those two different forms of fetishism in relation to men in feminism?

SJ: Heath doesn't reject psychoanalysis altogether.

PS: Fetishism does seem to be at the root of why he says men in feminism is impossible. And yet he keeps his distance from psychoanalysis.

AJ: It's there, but it might not be there.

PS: He wants to use fetishism . . .

AJ: I was shocked at the end when he says he *watched* his mother [p. 30].

PS: There's part of the irony of his combing through my MLA paper for its fetishism [pp. 41–46]. If what stops men in feminism is male fetishism, and yet he affirms (and demonstrates) the impossibility of avoiding it, and if there's also another sense of fetishism as a procedure of doubling . . . I guess the question is: is it possible for the old manners of male fetishism to be dismantled or transformed, and thus for men to take on this doubling procedure?

AJ: Or some other procedure.

PS: Or doesn't it already happen? The two-speed idea is, I think, a version of something that already happens to anyone in a political situation. You're always working at two speeds—radically *and* conservatively, etc.—and I wonder whether it's possible to critique the claim that this is something specific to feminism.

AJ: This was raised in different ways in other pieces. Elizabeth talks of the sleight of hand [p. 74] . . . . The two pieces of the fetishism for some of the writers are maybe the question of oppression (beyond Derrida: what are we going to do about apartheid), and complex subjectivity (high theory versus whatever this other thing is). I agree that's not specific to feminism, but to any radical, contestatory practice.

But this feeling of doubling/splitting may perhaps be plugging into an intensity, a concentration of intention, to the extent that feminism is made up mostly of women; to the extent that it is plugged into an historically and ideologically constructed way of dealing with the world (as women). It may be about intensity.

PS: Well, then I have a further problem. In Naomi's article the argument for this doubling goes along with a claim for the specificity of women and a critique of male theorists for never having taken seriously the claim to feminine specificity. Naomi says that those male theorists . . . "no feminist theoretician *who is not also a woman* has ever fully espoused the claims to a feminine specificity, an irreducible difference" [p. 109].

AJ: But she also says "those who adopt the masculine position [on difference] press for an end to sexual difference and only grudgingly acknowledge claims for feminine specificity, [and that] those who adopt the feminine position concede the strategic efficacy of undoing sexual oppositions, all the while pursuing the construction of difference [p. 110]. Not to confuse feminine specificity and essence.

PS: They might be confused from her argument.

AJ: There's a translation problem. In the USA the two tend to be equated, whereas for me there's a missing piece—the semiotic working, which if it had been taken into account here would have precluded all the premature accusations against Luce Irigaray as an essentialist, for example.

PS: Yes, outside the USA specificity means cultural and historical specificity as well as . . .

AJ: In France, at least, specificity to a body but a body that's historically constituted.

Side Three

AJ: So you disagree with Naomi's argument that men in feminism refuse to think feminine specificity?

PS: Not exactly. But there's . . .

AJ: There's a difference between all the old French guys talking about the feminine and, say, you and Andrew talking about it?

PS: There's a gap, certainly. We may not be in a position yet to say what it is that we're doing on this side of the gap. But one of the successes of feminism has been to take the old white male (French) masters to task, and it's true that we can only learn from that.

AJ: At the same time I think this other related point that Naomi makes is right. There is a feminist position that doesn't so much take the masters to task as concede (with male allies) that perhaps, politically, it may in fact be more strategically important to undo sexual difference, to break down the binary opposition and work for a radical hetero-sexuality (in Jane Gallop's sense), i.e., to work for multiple sexualities. At the same time, in the kitchen, a lot of us are working at trying to figure out what is specific to women. But we'll concede with our male allies that in the public sphere it's more important to emphasise *hetero-sexualities*, whereas . . .

PS: That's to already assume that male allies could not or do not accept the notion of female specificity (specificity understood in the historicized way we just mentioned). But at this point it would be absurd for us not to accept that and I think many of us do (even if some of us certainly *have* been absurd in that regard!). The question is then, who is "us"—and I'm not quite sure. There are the older theorists and then there's a gap, and then "us."

AJ: Do you think there's a filial thing going on there, too? Or do you think this has anything to do with the question of feminist *écoute?* You keep saying, "we're different."

PS: It's true that something has to happen after the "old" theory, because of where it now is and how it's institutionalized itself and so on. If that something involves emptying the authority of the fathers, that's not only inevitable, but acceptable. But, importantly, one of the ways of getting to that next step is joining with one's siblings rather than *simply* rejecting the fathers.

AJ: What about feminism and poststructuralism? Don't you think it's important not just to go on to the "next step" but also to step back and re-radicalize poststructuralism (almost in Adrienne Rich's sense of re-visioning) in spite of how impatient we might be . . . to step back and remember what was so exciting about so-called poststructuralism before its massive institutionalization?

PS: I agree absolutely. And perhaps because of the momentum of poststructuralism and its institutionalization we've forgotten some of the radical moments and oppositional tendencies of *structuralism*. This is something I suggest in *Discerning the Subject*. And I think that in some measure feminism gives us an example of how to go about recovering some of that from the institutionalization of poststructuralism.

AJ: In a way, the institution has been very helpful in the way it has indicated what in poststructuralism could be effortlessly and quickly recuperated and what couldn't. We could have never thought our way through that . . . and now we do . . .

One of those forgotten radical moments was when we understood the importance of not bypassing or over-passing sexual difference and the necessity of constantly complicating it. This still seems a valid strategy.

PS: In that regard, something I was trying to do in what Cary Nelson calls (quite unconsciously, I suspect) my "opening" paragraph [p. 170] . . . I was trying to suggest that one approach to that re-visioning is through enunciation. That's why I was upset by what you were saying about tone, intonation, etc. What I *thought* I was doing there was saying that the overdetermined history of this kind of masculinist language is still mutable and that, depending on context and speaker, it can mean something different, a distance can be marked. It's maybe possible to get from there to realising that work can be done on *masculine* specificity.

AJ: How would you describe what you were doing, rhetorically? Was it irony?

PS: Yes, but not irony, as Meaghan thought, that intended to be amusing to anyone. Irony as distanciation perhaps.

AJ: Since we're there, I wanted to talk about Cary's and Meaghan's readings of that paragraph. Because the name you give to the rhetorical figure you were employing is important. You can't be too careful here. There are different rhetorical devices, with specific histories, and it would be difficult simply to make one up on the spot. I'm not sure I understand what figure you were using, because I don't think it really was irony. Let's say I take your word for it and totally "trust" you (that you were consciously employing a figure), then the point becomes to figure out how this rhetorical figure failed or was misread.

PS: Cary misread it, in my view, because he didn't think it was self-consciously produced.

AJ: Was he being a very literal reader? This, of course, has gender implications since women are often accused of being "literal" and men "figurative" . . . In any case, women are supposed always to make a mistake, to confuse the two (cf. Claudine Herrmann's *Les Voleuses de langue*). So, in a sense, if Cary read it wrong and so did Meaghan (i.e., literally instead of figuratively), what was the difference between the misreadings? Is it that Meaghan's mis-reading is more "sophisticated"?

PS: Meaghan seemed to me to read it as irony in an old sense—she seemed to see here someone standing apart from their language and almost cynically letting the language say what they dare not say.

AJ: That's been gendered as a male figure.

PS: Yes, and its usual function has been satire, humor, etc. That's precisely what I didn't intend. Even though I now have to recognize the "failure" of the utterance, I can still say that I intended it in a way those two readers didn't want to hear.

AJ: But it's a question somewhere between intentionality and reading. It's not just about reading, or about vindicating you or your intentions; there's something else going on there.

PS: In any context there are two sets of intentions, and two sets of readings involved. My objection to Meaghan's reading is that she intended already that men in feminism not work out. It's her prejudice. My problem with myself there was that I think I had the right political intentions but read myself wrongly.

AJ: So Meaghan had the intention wrong and the reading right, and you had the intention right and the reading wrong!

PS: But on another hand, it would all seem to be so obvious. There's the question of context, too. Here I am a male wanting to speak (whatever you might think about wanting there) to/with feminism, to ask the question of how men can usefully interact with women feminists. What would I be doing using that kind of language if I weren't trying to do something different with it?

AJ: But I think Meaghan gets it . . . she gives it an interesting twist. She understands . . .

PS: In Meaghan's paper, she calls my strategy "good-humoured, perhaps well-meant" [p. 174], but she still wants to read it as innuendo, as a sleazy male way of constructing a coherence between sex and property and so on. I actually thought I was trying to say that those kinds of coherences, those familiar metonymic coherences between the components of male language, must clearly fall apart when uttered in a particular context, addressing a particular issue and with a particular audience. Perhaps I need to make an argument around the idea of specificity here, but I think I can only fall back again on intention and context.

AJ: I'm not sure that's enough.

PS: That's where I recognize a failure. It seems to have been a misjudged strategy, because it produced an effect I still don't understand too well. But, to paraphrase Gayatri Spivak, maybe it's time to take the risk of intentionality.

AJ: In a recent public lecture I played with feminism "penetrating the institution." Everybody laughed. It's OK for me because I can't penetrate anything.

PS: So it's partly a question of presence and, as Meaghan says, of hearing. What makes me uncomfortable about her paper is that it deliberately assumes the worst. In order to make that reading it has to ignore context. What would I have been thinking of to write what she says I wrote? I'd have to be a rapist.

AJ: Or just a straight white male academic.

PS: That's the problem. I am a straight white male academic, but . . .

AJ: But what? *That's* the problem.

PS: My argument would be that, for pragmatically political reasons, you can't *a priori* load every subject with such an historical weight. This might be something that I've learned from feminism, in fact—from seeing women fight against patriarchal attitudes. You can't assume that a woman in 1986 is necessarily going to be a feminist, any more than you can assume that a straight white male academic is going to be a rapist. But that's the assumption, the decision that Meaghan has made. It's a preconstituted condemnation.

I don't think it's very useful to go on trying to defend myself in this way. Maybe I'll just say that I don't quite understand why, in the whole collection (apart perhaps from you in your "practical agenda" [pp. 60–61]), none of the contributors has really tried to think this issue in a positive way. So maybe I'm just disappointed at the way in which the very question of men in feminism is foreclosed upon, stalemated.

AJ: Isn't that what almost everyone in the collection does?

PS: I don't think with the same determination as Meaghan, who seemed to me to be the most reluctant to deal with the whole question. Her paper says: as soon as you open your mouth, I'm going to ask you to withdraw . . .

AJ: That brings us back to question of silence. Why do you even think it's necessary to try to find a way to say this? What's wrong with withdrawing? What *is* this desire to play the rhetorical field?

It reminds me of a time I was working in a feminist seminar on black feminist theory, with the white feminists simply saying, "Please tell us what we can do. How can we say it differently? How can we write differently?" It ended in a stalemate. And I felt there was very little place there, if any, and rightly so, for me as a white feminist to play with the rhetorical field. The inclusion/exclusion question was clearly different, but the rhetorical bind was similar.

PS: Why do you want to say to black feminists, come on in, and to male ones, present your credentials?

AJ: Because black women haven't done anything to me . . .

PS: That's obviously the only answer, but the question still remains . . . Isn't it feasible to stop thinking in these terms? Are there no variations in this group, "black women," or the group "men"? Does every subject have to be slaughtered on the bench of history . . . ? A lot of my own energy around this question of men and feminism comes from my objection to being regarded as the subject of a history that's *not necessarily* mine, but is the history of a group into which I'm placed.

AJ: I, as a woman, could have said that, too. Now *that* was said with the right intonation!

PS: Thank you!

AJ: I'm being ironic here. OK. What I mean is that your statement need not necessarily be about what Naomi calls a male strategy of *clinamen*. Your statement does not necessarily imply that we're no longer going to talk about men and women but about a certain subjectivity that doesn't want to be slaughtered on the bench of history . . . that we're going to create a mode of enunciation that could be either male or female. Your mode of enunciation was not that of a *clinamen*. It did not posit a discursive situation where you're no longer a man and I'm no longer a woman and so we can just talk about subjectivity with the right intonation—it's just not about that (although it helps in a way, that enunciation).

PS: What it leads to for me (a step only possible because of feminism) is a recognition. Through the fact that women have been making the theoretical steps necessary for "proving" their own specificity, men have to do something of the same thing. But I don't think that currently that can be done except through feminism—the place for men in feminism might in that sense be *through* it. This is maybe what we have to do to make our next step. I *am* on Naomi's side in that I can see no use for the poststructuralism of indifference—there's no reason to imagine that sexuality will wither away. It's just that there are only certain kinds of recognizable implements at any given moment—in this case a certain discursive technology which is being developed by feminism. Not by men, but I think men can use it.

AJ: I do think of one implement—the Deleuzian molar/molecular/ *ligne de fuite* topology (even with its problems)—which might help to get us out of the dialectical mode . . . . If there were some way for a man—he who has a body constructed as male today—to not exactly go *through* feminism (which feminism, at which level in any case?), but rather . . . Deleuze does talk about feminism at the molar level . . . so it would be about moving through feminism at the molar level, the level at which the strongest block comes from feminists. But it would be more at the molecular level where something new could happen, where there would be *seuils*, thresholds—like what you just did moving over the question of subjectivity, not to "clinamen your way out of it," but to put us in the same space of enunciation, if only for a few moments. So there would be more local strategies, possibly even very rapid ones (*lignes de fuite*), that would not involve penetrating or breaking and entering at the molar level (because property and *le propre* exist only at the molar level).

So it may be that there are actually implements in male thinkers—poststructuralist thinkers. Maybe what we *won't* be able to go back and sort out is that, if in fact a lot of poststructuralist theory is about a certain form of male anxiety, then all the emphasis on the feminine and the female may have been a diversion. If one could ever go back through and trace that anxiety, there probably are a lot of implements in male poststructuralist

theory for men to think about, for finding new modes of enunciation and subjectivities, etc., without necessarily going *through*
feminism.

PS: I think I'd still disagree with that—if only because I don't see
any easy way of neatly extricating current academic feminist
theory from poststructuralist theory . . . the critiques of and re-
finements on poststructuralist theory, which have both formed
and been formed by feminism, are *right* and now have to be
dealt with and used.

AJ: So do you see *any* efficacy in a politics of silence? The topic of
silence came up in places, as a kind of thematic (for example,
in Andrew's paper). Perhaps the fundamental feminist political
argument is that "we will not be silenced" . . . and I've often
felt very rebellious about that politics of saying everything,
speaking explicitly in prose. So what do you think about silence
like the silence of "poetry," as opposed to the explicitness of
"prose"?

PS: If you're recommending "silence" as a kind of equivalent to
what Meaghan calls "strategic withdrawal," I wonder whether
it's even a possible strategy at this point, simply because the
"penetration" has already been made.

But beyond that, there is in another sense no such thing as
silence. If, as a male, one followed through on even just one of
the items you put on your pragmatic agenda, that would constitute a non-silence, in that all those items are signifiying acts.
And I'd add that, so far as I'm concerned, all the things on your
agenda are not just options; they're necessities for us to do.
Maybe you mean to suggest a relative silence and perhaps it
would be a good idea if men stopped writing and publishing
"in" feminism (I'm intrigued by Cary's idea about publishing
under female pseudonyms—though I wonder whether women
might not be just as suspicious of our motives there as elsewhere). But in any case it certainly wouldn't be a good idea to
stop fighting, stop working along the pragmatic lines you yourself have suggested.

AJ: I'm just thinking about . . . like in the 60s when we stuffed
marshmallows into guns; about silence as passivity and how it
was perceived then as a strong political tool; and about the 70s
in France where a preconservative Duras advocated silence—
she said we needed to *silencer la machine* (the theoretical machine). I'm not suggesting this as something only for men; in
fact it's something that I'm increasingly drawn to as a strategy
for myself . . . there's something about the drive to say all and
know all, the drive to get everyone a position from which to
speak, etc., that makes me very suspicious. And there is a desire

to pull back and be silent, not to stop fighting at all, but to stay quiet long enough at least to see what's going on.

PS: You seem to be repeating some of Meaghan's argument. Even if I recognize some of the power of that, I still keep feeling that being silent is not being silent, is still signifying.

AJ: You mean like the Silent Majority?

PS: Yes, and that becomes an intractable, abysmal kind of question.

AJ: It does. I was struck, though, by a sentence in Andrew's paper where he devalorizes, as political strategy, the women in the movie having recourse to silence and laughter [pp. 89–90]. He says that we may well get a lot of affective or emotional satisfaction out of that at this moment, but that this is not enough . . . Well. Since when does one say no to affective and emotional . . . ? It's a question of context. Given that film, I couldn't figure out what his investment would be in saying: don't be a sucker, don't get pulled into that . . .

Side Four

He doesn't seem to value their reducing to nonsense the male game of question and answer (for example, in a courtroom) whereas I do. He does, however, admit that it may be "nothing more than a symptom of my litigious male mind that thoughts of 'men in feminism' should invoke discussion of trials, defenses, prosecutions, diminished capacities, criminal liabilities, justifications, excuses, verdicts, and various murderous acts" [p. 91]. Well . . . I must say . . .

PS: But at one level isn't that what we're all talking about: the question of inclusion/exclusion?

AJ: But I don't think you use legal language *per se* in your paper, do you?

PS: To an extent.

AJ: But in the collection itself others like Andrew, Denis Donoghue and Derrida use it explicitly in terms of inclusion/exclusion . . . For me feminist theory is just too heterogeneous (sometimes I'm not even included in it myself).

PS: But we could talk, as we did earlier, about particular discourses and implements, and the right to use them.

AJ: To have access to them.

PS: Access, yes. We come back to . . . you prefaced one of the bits of the dialogue by saying: let's assume that I trust you, etc. Maybe the question isn't inclusion/exclusion, rights/nonrights, but simply trust. Then we go back to the question of being slaughtered on the bench of history. Who are you going to trust and why? One glib answer might be that a preoccupation with intonation and tone and so on, and using that as a guideline to deciding questions of access, is maybe not enough—especially if someone, a male, *is* following that pragmatic agenda of yours.

But what do you think is the correlation: if someone is doing the agenda, does that, or can that produce the right intonation?

AJ: I hope so. Some kind of combination of following the agenda . . . using what we know about gender to attack other problems; somehow the combination would produce a situation where it would no longer feel as if you had to ask the question of trust . . . worrying about whether I had to slaughter you or be slaughtered by you before we could talk . . . The question of access or of law and access isn't accidental, after all. When we talk about trust here, we're not talking about trust for life; we're talking about editing a book in a certain institutional context, about two people coming together in the law, next to the law; about two people working theoretically together in the institution or next to it. This is not a private discussion . . . this is about access to a body, but a body of work. What kind of access and in view of what? . . . *Devant qui?* Who is the judge? If I'm not judging you and you're not judging me but we both have a sense of being judged then, who is doing it?

I have very informal theories about that, about the institution as phallic mother (not paternal at all—the school taking the place of the mother in our culture) . . . there is something very frightening about that particular phallic maternal *regard* which would place us, male and female feminists, in the position of . . . what I don't know.

PS: There are no guarantees. I think of Cary writing about the various atrocities that he sees women doing to other women in the academy. Yet nonetheless those women might be trusted by feminists.

AJ: I recognize that problem but I think feminists in the institution are a lot savvier about that than they used to be a few years ago . . .

PS: If men are in the institution doing the things you recommend, they inevitably come into conflict with other men, most of whom are probably more powerful (precisely because they're *not* doing that agenda). So they conflict with the law in a way possibly more pointedly than women do.

AJ: Must be horrendous . . .

PS: Well, even so . . . one of the things that didn't get explicitly asked in any of the papers, and which I think is a basic question: what is it that would motivate someone to be so suspicious when, just by looking (rather than hearing), one could see that the institutional stakes are very threatening to men who announce themselves as allies of feminism?

Side Five

AJ: But what about Dick Ohmann's paper in that regard?

PS: It's true that his paper doesn't seem to register any of the threat that I was talking about. I like the honesty with which he approaches his predicament. He probably wouldn't want to formally theorize his experience in between, as it were, the women's studies program and the white male administration at his university. But that's probably not a problem. Everyone involved seems to be able to accept his role, and everyone benefits in one way or another. In fact, given that the situation is not threatening to him, maybe I'd have liked him to talk more—along with the other men, me included—about what actual pleasure or benefit we get from our work with feminism.

AJ: The question of pleasure does rarely come up in the collection. I was taken to task by Cary on that issue: that feminism is not only about suffering and struggle. And of course he's right. I've emphasized the pleasure and camaraderie elsewhere, but it's true that in this particular project I've emphasized the struggle . . .

PS: It's obviously an important question. Perhaps it can be related to an issue that I thought might well have been mentioned by someone—the question of men making alliances amongst themselves in order to contest sexism and support feminism. I mean, it seems that often pleasure for women feminists is a product of solidarity and alliance.

AJ: If that's absent for men, what kind of pleasure *do* you get from being a feminist?

PS: Well, actually very little . . .

At one point Dick wonders about himself as he sits, the older authoritative male, in a room of young women [p. 186]. My own pleasure in similar sorts of situations to that (including actually teaching feminism and feminist theory) is obviously to some degree narcissistic. But it's a pleasure that you fight against or learn to think of as peripheral, since it gets in the way of the politically invested reasons for teaching in the first place. Maybe I would claim that in any case this is less a pleasure of being a male feminist, and more like a part of the job. *Any* student-teacher relation is eroticized, of course. Though I'd like to think that we'd all still be teaching even in the hypothetical case where that narcissistic pleasure wasn't there, because teaching has fun-

damentally political effects (both beyond any of its personal per-
quisites and beyond any lack of them!).

AJ: About pleasure. In the beginning, for me, it was a major moment
when I experienced the pleasure of being in an all-female en-
vironment, being able to talk about your "private" life in relation
to the "public" sphere, although that pleasure is less present
now for me . . .

PS: That's a pleasure for me as well. But perhaps one of the best
aspects of teaching about feminism is seeing women with little
interest in feminist matters become interested and even
committed.

AJ: Yes, but for me now that's a kind of melancholic pleasure, because many of the students now learn it just for pleasure without
living it in its emotional complexity, and so once again . . . And
yet the whole issue of pleasure is important, I think, in terms
of the inclusion/exclusion problem because for most women in
feminism I know there's an enormous pleasure involved in
working together . . . collective pleasure, the pleasure of collectivity, and a lot of that comes from the mixing of levels . . .
talking about your lover and the College of Arts and Sciences
on the same continuum . . . it's *fun*. But what about men in
feminism? Because there's certainly no collectivity there.

PS: That's why I thought someone might have spoken about male
alliances. But for me personally one of the great pleasures is to
be working with women. Even though it's not actually a taboo,
there's currently something automatically subversive about that
and so there's a pleasure of subversion, and of course it makes
the male establishment quite uncomfortable to see. But importantly the pleasure isn't any longer a function of the old male
systems of rivalry for the women (women as the objects of exchange), but is the function of a political act based on friendships, commonality of aims, and so on.

But are you asking this question about pleasure in order to
relate it to the notion of women's specificity?

AJ: Perhaps rather because of the desire to practice politically differently . . . I'm just back from Europe where a lot of younger
women are resisting intellectual and political stagnation by refusing to be killed libidinally either by the Institution or by the
Political Struggle. That's why I mention laughter . . . There's an
insistence on remaining radical, paying the price for that, and
then laughing about it. But at the moment it's not necessarily
about "female specificity."

PS: I was thinking about one of your letters where you said that
women "network" but men just "globulate."

AJ: I was laughing about something very serious: (female) merging and (male) separation . . . As I said before, for me feminism can no longer be *only* about women or men as objects of study, but needs to be also about forming, encouraging, and protecting a certain shape of subjectivity that will be able to address the massive and urgent issues facing the entire planet. And so, for me, the issue of *alliance* between men and women to these ends is clearly on the agenda. And yet there are still very few men in my opinion who have nurtured that subjectivity in themselves— even if they have theorized it ad nauseam.

PS: So you mean we can talk about the issue of inclusion/exclusion, for example, but not in the terms we've been using—of men *in* or *out* of feminism . . . Otherwise women are going to be simply "loved and left," as it were.

AJ: Right, the problem needs to be articulated in some other mode. And so merging/fusion and separation/division become an issue for me . . . And even if it's not specific to female and male bodies, this is an historical construction of sexuality that has to be dealt with. And even our "collaboration" here (a word which implies capitulation, hypocrisy, occupation) needs to be rethought with labor (co-labor) to bring to birth a new, non-paranoid, non-male, non-heterocentric, form of alliance between men and women for the future . . . .

Notes

Introduction

[1] In *Notebooks in Cultural Analysis*, N. Cantor and N. King, eds., vol. 1 (Durham, N.C.: Duke Univ. Press, 1984), pp. 81–102.

1. Male Feminism

[1] Claire Pajaczkowska, "The Heterosexual Presumption: A Contribution to the Debate on Pornography," *Screen* vol. 22, no. 1 (1981), p. 92.

[2] B. Ruby Rich, "Anti-Porn: Soft Issue, Hard World," *Feminist Review* no. 13 (Spring 1983), p. 66.

[3] Elizabeth Wilson, *What Is To Be Done About Violence Against Women?* (Harmondsworth: Penguin, 1983), pp. 135–68.

[4] Stephen Heath, *The Sexual Fix* (London: Macmillan, 1982) p. 163.

[5] Sigmund Freud, "Analysis Terminable and Interminable," *The Standard Edition of the Complete Psychological Works of Sigmund Freud* (London: Hogarth, 1953–74) vol. XXIII, p. 252.

[6] Jacques Derrida, "La Question du style," *Nietzsche aujourd'hui?* (Paris: Union Générale d'Editions, 1973) vol. I, pp. 299, 244.

[7] Rosalind Coward, *Female Desire: Women's Sexuality Today* (London: Paladin, 1984), p. 227.

[8] William Thackeray, *Vanity Fair* (1848) [Harmondsworth: Penguin, 1982]), p. 659.

[9] Jacques Lacan, *Le Séminaire livre XX Encore* (Paris: Seuil, 1975) p. 75. Freud's question occurs in a letter to Marie Bonaparte, cit. Ernest Jones, *Sigmund Freud: Life and Work* vol. 2 (London: Hogarth, 1955), p. 468. Lacan's 1932 thesis containing the Aimée case and the 1933 essay on the Papin sisters published in the Surrealist review *Le Minotaure* can be found in Lacan, *De la psychose paranoïaque dans ses rapports avec la personnalité* (Paris: Seuil, 1975).

[10] Lacan, seminar 16 November 1976, *Ornicar?* no. 12/13 (1977), p. 12.

[11] Eugénie Lemoine-Luccioni, *La Robe* (Paris: Seuil, 1983), p. 25.

[12] Juliet Mitchell, 'Feminine Sexuality: Interview with Juliet Mitchell and Jacqueline Rose,' *m/f* no. 8 (1983), p. 15.

[13] Michèle Montrelay, intervention, Journées de l'Ecole Freudienne de Paris, Lille 1977, *Lettres de l'Ecole Freudienne* no. 22 (March 1978), p. 144.

[14] Stephen Heath, "Difference," *Screen* vol. 19, no. 3 (Autumn 1978), pp. 51–112.

[15] Millicent Garrett Fawcett, *Women's Suffrage: A Short History of a Great Movement* (London: Jack, 1912), p. 16.

[16] Terry Eagleton, *Walter Benjamin: or Towards a Revolutionary Criticism* (London: New Left Books, 1981), all quotations from pp. 99–100.

[17] The translator of the Penguin Classics *Symposium* notes that "It is almost universally and no doubt rightly held that Diotima is a fictitious personage, in spite of the apparently historical statements made about her by Socrates," Plato, *The Symposium* trans. William Hamilton (Harmondsworth: Penguin, 1975), p. 19. No doubt rightly since the voice-off is always anyway theory's fiction for itself.

[18] See particularly Luce Irigaray, *Speculum, de l'autre femme* (Paris: Minuit, 1974).

[19] Lacan, *Le Séminaire livre XX Encore*, p. 69.

[20] Ann Snitow, Christine Stansell and Sharon Thompson eds., *Desire: The Politics of Sexuality* (London: Virago, 1984).

[21] Irène Roublef, intervention, Journées des Cartels de l'Ecole Freudienne de Paris, Paris 1975, *Lettres de l'Ecole Freudienne*, no. 18 (April 1976), p. 211.

[22] Paul Brown and Carolyn Faulder, *Treat Yourself to Sex* (Harmondsworth: Penguin, 1979) p. 81.

[23] Montrelay, *L'Ombre et son nom* (Paris: Minuit, 1977), p. 151; subsequent quotation, p. 142.

[24] Gayatri Spivak, cit. Elaine Showalter, "Critical Cross-Dressing: Male Feminists and The Woman of the Year", *Raritan* vol. III no. 2 (1983/4) p. 133. (See this volume, p. 118.)

[25] Barthes, "Digressions," *Promesse*, no. 29 (1971), p. 27; Tillie Olsen, *Silences* (London: Virago, 1980), p. 255.

[26] Lacan, *Le Séminaire livre XI, Les quatre concepts fondamentaux de la psychanalyse* (Paris: Seuil, 1973) p. 240; trans. Alan Sheridan, *The Four*

Fundamental Concepts of Psycho-Analysis (Harmondsworth: Penguin, 1979), p. 266.

27 Freud, "Female Sexuality," *Standard Edition*, vol. XX1, p. 226; *New Introductory Lectures on Psycho-Analysis, Standard Edition*, vol. XX11, p. 134.

28 Lacan, "L'Etourdit," *Scilicet*, no. 4 (1973), p. 47.

29 Lacan, seminar 15 March 1977, *Ornicar?*, no. 17/18 (1979), p. 9.

30 Barthes, *Le Plaisir du texte* (Paris: Seuil, 1973) pp. 92–3; trans. Richard Miller, *A Barthes Reader* ed. Susan Sontag (London: Jonathan Cape, 1982) p. 412; Laura Mulvey, "Visual Pleasure and Narrative Cinema," *Screen*, vol. 16, no. 3 (Autumn 1975), p. 6; Juliet Mitchell, *Women: The Longest Revolution* (London: Virago, 1984), p. 221.

31 Editorial, *Feminist Review*, no. 14 (Summer 1983), p. 1.

32 Jacqueline Rose, "Femininity and its Discontents," *Feminist Review*, no. 14 (Summer 1983), p. 5.

33 Jeanne Favret-Saada, "Excusez-moi, je ne faisais que passer," *Les Temps modernes*, no. 371 (June 1977), pp. 2089–103.

34 Barthes, "La Crise du désir," *Le Nouvel Observateur*, 20 April 1980, p. 87.

35 Olsen, *Silences*, p. 255.

36 Peggy Kamuf, "Writing like a Woman," *Women and Language in Literature and Society*, ed. Sally McConnell-Ginet, Ruth Borker & Nelly Furman (New York: Praeger, 1980), p. 298.

37 Showalter, "Critical Cross-Dressing: Male Feminists and The Woman of the Year", p. 143; subsequent quotations, pp. 133, 147. (See this volume, pp. 116–32.) Showalter's article has been very much part of the writing of the present essay.

38 Quotations here are from: Adrienne Rich, *Driving into the Wreck* (New York: Norton, 1973)—DW: *The Dream of a Common Language* (New York: Norton, 1978)—CL: *A Wild Patience Has Taken Me This Far* (New York: Norton, 1981)—WP.

39 Irigaray, *Ethique de la différence sexuelle* (Paris: Minuit, 1984), p. 20.

40 Descartes, *Les Passions de l'Ame* (1649), *Oeuvres et lettres* (Paris: Gallimard "Pléiade," 1953), p. 729.

41 Irigaray, *Ethique de la différence sexuelle*, pp. 19–20.

42 Letters from a number of people in response to the original pub-

lication of "Male Feminism" have helped me think further about the issues it raises. I am specifically indebted to Paul Willemen for comments on its final paragraph and to Rosalind Delmar for sustained discussion.

2. *Men in Feminism: Men in Feminist Theory (Smith)*

[1] I have made a good number of changes to the text which appeared in *Critical Exchange,* 18, pp. 1–18. On the other hand, some phrases, statements, and sentiments which I might otherwise have changed have been left mostly intact since other essays in this volume make quotation from the original version. This is a pragmatic option and it doesn't at all mean that I haven't learned from ensuing discussions.

[2] These phrases caused a number of misunderstandings in subsequent discussions. I'm referring here to what is known in the academic vernacular as feminist theory (the structuralist/poststructuralist variety). I don't mean to suggest that feminist practice in other of its aspects isn't guided by theory—nor even would I wish in general to separate out theory and practice.

[3] This is a criticism I would make particularly of my own "A Question of Feminine Identity," the article which provoked the first dialogue between Alice Jardine and myself. See *Notebooks in Cultural Analysis,* N. Cantor and N. King, eds., vol. 1 (Durham, N.C.: Duke Univ. Press, 1984), pp. 81–102.

[4] One of the "champions" I'm thinking of here is Julia Kristeva. See my *Discerning the Subject* (Minneapolis: Univ. of Minnesota Press, 1987).

3. *Men in Feminism: Men and Feminist Theory (Heath)*

[1] Paul Smith, "Men in Feminism: Men and Feminist Theory"; some quotations here are from the draft distributed to the MLA panel speakers.

[2] Sigmund Freud, *The Standard Edition of the Complete Psychological Works of Sigmund Freud* (London: Hogarth Press, 1953–74), vol. XX1, p. 157; vol. XIX, p. 142.

[3] Jacques Derrida, "Choreographies" (interview with Christie V. McDonald), *Diacritics,* Summer 1982, p. 69.

[4] Ibid., p. 68.

[5] Ibid., p. 76.

[6] Dorothy Richardson, "About Punctuation," *The Adelphi*, April, vol. I no. 11, p. 990.

[7] Dorothy Richardson, *Revolving Lights* (London: Duckworth & Co., 1923), p. 87.

4. Demonstrating Sexual Difference

[1] See Hilary Allen, "At the Mercy of Her Hormones: Premenstrual Tension and the Law," *m/f*, 9 (1984), pp. 19–44. Allen argues against recognizing premenstrual tension as grounds for pleading diminished responsibility. If premenstrual tension were considered as a potentially universal condition for women, and if these biological facts were consequently held to directly determine social cases in the case of "all women," then the danger is that all women who menstruate would be held by the law to be "close to madness and prone to crime" periodically in their lives. Allen's concluding point is that biology is a *necessary* but never *sufficient* ground for explaining social behavior.

[2] My paper generally draws upon media accounts of Sutcliffe's trial, journalists' discussions of his personal history, and Nicole Ward Jouve's remarkable reflections on the whole case, published by Editions de Femmes, under the title, *Un Homme Nommé Zapolski* (Paris, 1983).

[3] A fascinating account of one particular episode in their history can be found in Judith Walkowitz, *Prostitution and Victorian Society: Women, Class and State* (Cambridge Univ. Press, 1980), which examines the attempted state regulation of prostitutes in Britain under the Contagious Diseases Acts of 1864, 1866, and 1869, and the ensuing alliance of prostitutes and feminists against the medical and police authorities. In the course of the legal, social, and political upheaval that sprang up around the crusade on both sides, the difficulty of defining what it was to be a prostitute became a crucial factor. The "ideological" pathology of medical opinion was frequently called upon to support the state case; presented with the argument that "all women," prostitutes and non-prostitutes alike, could both contract and communicate gonorrhea, Inspector Slogget and Dr. Moore of the Royal Albert disagreed. They vehemently denied that the two categories of women could be medically confused. Instead, they argued that "in a prostitute there is a [purulent] discharge from the uterus which is never or seldom present in a virtuous woman . . ." (p. 228). However, the polemical insistence on the case for "all women" generated equally undesirable consequences: "The vaginal discharge of

virtuous women could also generate 'disease' in men, thereby contradicting the ideological association of disease and sinful habits. This virtuous source of infection also challenged the sexual-moral code that rigidly segregated 'pure' women from the 'impure'. By designating all women as potential pollutants of men and reservoirs of infection, it evoked instead a more general hostility and dread of females and female 'nature'" (p. 56).

4 In her close analysis of the Ripper case, Bland goes on to argue that both defense and prosecution "'met in a common 'understanding' of Sutcliffe's acts, in terms of *female precipitation*. . . . despite different objectives (the one to establish Sutcliffe's 'reason,' the other to establish 'diminished responsibility'), [both] took the actions of certain women in Sutcliffe's life as the key to understanding and explaining his behaviour" (p. 198). "The Case of the Yorkshire Ripper," in *Causes for Concern: British Criminal Justice on Trial?* ed. Phil Scraton and Paul Gordon (Harmondsworth: Penguin, 1984).

5 Wendy Holloway has argued that the plea for diminished responsibility was a way of avoiding "'uncomfortable questions about male violence" in general: "No one seemed to point out what to me was the obvious loophole in the psychiatric argument: the explanation that it was a delusion does not show *why* the voice told Sutcliffe to kill women. Whether it was God's voice, the Devil's, or the projected voice of Sutcliffe's own hatred makes no difference: the content derives from a generalized, taken-for-granted misogyny" (p. 35). "'I Wanted to Kill a Woman.' Why? The Ripper and Male Sexuality," in *Feminist Review*, 9 (Fall 1981).

6 Quoted by David Yallop in *Deliver Us From Evil* (New York: Coward, McCann & Geoghegan, 1982), a book written by a muckraking dramatist-cum-journalist, which unremittingly charges the South Yorkshire police with gross incompetence and criminal negligence, but otherwise assumes the staple form of a follow-in-the-footsteps-of-the-Ripper narrative.

7 Jouve's virtuoso discussion of the cemetery "revelation" rests upon an analysis of the operative S/Z distinction in the names Sutcliffe/Zapolski (Zapolski is the name on the tombstone), an analysis which extends into her interpretation of other linguistic details of Sutcliffe's case history. Indeed, in view of the abject failure of psychiatric opinion under the pressure of court circumstances, her interpretation might stand as cogent alternative testimony to the nature of Sutcliffe's "schizophrenia." See in particular, the chapter "S/Z: le cimetière sur la colline," pp. 103–21.

6. *Walking the Tightrope* of Feminism and Male Desire

[1] Research for this essay was made possible by a grant from the Ohio Arts Council.

[2] J. Hoberman, "Double Indemnity," *The Village Voice*, August 28, 1984, p. 46.

[3] B. Ruby Rich, "Anti-Porn: Soft Issue, Hard World," *Feminist Review*, no. 13 (Spring 1983), p. 66.

7. *A Man's Place*

[1] "Semiotics and Experience" in *Alice Doesn't: Feminism, Semiotics, Cinema* (Bloomington: Indiana Univ. Press, 1984).

9. *No Question of Silence*

[1] As for the historical universal "Man," *that* calls for an entirely different critique, a critique that is similar and increasingly relevant in the West to the categorical distinctions between "all Americans" and the cultural universal described as "American"—and these are distinctions that are increasingly difficult to hold in place as each new wave of anti-Americanism chooses its targets, polemical or otherwise.

[2] Hasse concludes that a "political" defense is not a winning one: in fact, "the lawyer is more likely to keep her client out of jail if she constructs an excuse for that client by appealing to sexist notions that jurors are likely to harbor about the weak will, moral frailty, immaturity, mental instability, hysterical unpredictability, and other incapacities of the weaker sex. The strength of the individual battered wife's excuse for her act lies in the failure of the female collectivity's justification of the rationality of that act and, perhaps, shows why a feminist and a trial lawyer cannot be, at once, a feminist and a trial lawyer." See Lisbeth Hasse, "Killing Husbands" in *University Publishing*, 12 (Winter 1984), pp. 30–32.

10. *A Double Life (Femmeninism II)*

[1] *Louise Labé: Oeuvres complètes*, Critical Edition by Enzo Giudici (Geneva: Droz, 1981), p. 58. The entire sonnet reads:

Baise m'encore, rebaise moy et baise:

Donne m'en un de tes plus savoureus,
Donne m'en un de tes plus amoureus:
Je t'en rendray quatre plus chaus que braise.

Las, te pleins tu? ça que ce mal j'apaise,
En t'en donnant dix autres doucereus.
Ainsi meslans nos baisers tant heureus
Jouissons nous l'un de l'autre à notre aise.

Lors double vie à chacun en suivra.
Chacun en soy et son ami vivra.
Permets m'Amour penser quelque folie:

Tousjours suis mal, vivant discrettement,
Et ne me puis donner quelque contentement,
Si hors de moy ne fay quelque saillie.

So as not to burden the text quotations in both French and English, the reader may refer to the following translation, more than ever inadequate:

Kiss me again, and again, and again:
Give me one of your most delicious ones,
Give me one of your most loving ones:
I will give you back four hotter than coals.

Alas, are you suffering? That is the ill I shall soothe
By giving you ten more, sweeter still.
Thus mingling our happy kisses
Let us enjoy one another at our leisure.

From there will follow a double life for each.
Each will live in self and in the beloved.
Permit (me) my Love to think a certain madness:

I am always unwell, living discreetly,
And can give myself no contentment,
If I do not go outside myself.

[2] For a superb discussion of the Cartesian subject as fable, see Jean-Luc Nancy, *Ego sum*, in particular the chapter "Mundus est fabula" (Paris: Aubier-Flammarion, 1979).

[3] Dorothy O'Connor, *Louise Labé: sa vie et son oeuvre* (Paris: 1926), p. 146; cited approvingly by Enzo Giudici (op. cit.), p. 188, n. 112.

[4] A less selective reading of this sonnet would have to consider that the "suis mal" echoes the lover's "mal" of line 6: "Las, te pleins tu? ça que ce mal j'apaise." The question would not be whether to

discern one "mal" from the other, but rather whether the "mal" in question can be discerned from discernibility or discretion in general.

5 "A Man's Place," q.v., pp. 71–77

6 "Men In Feminism: Odor di uomo or Compagnons de route?" q.v., pp. 54–61

11. Dreaming Dissymmetry: Barthes, Foucault, and Sexual Difference

1 Ann Snitow, Christine Stansell, and Sharon Thompson, eds., *Powers of Desire: The Politics of Sexuality* (New York: Monthly Review Press, 1983), p. 9.

2 Ibid, p. 10.

3 Ibid. As valuable as this point is, Biddy Martin reminds us, in her article "Feminism, Criticism, and Foucault" (*New German Critique* [Fall 1982], 27:3–30), that "Foucault's deconstructive methodology provides an immanent critique of such a search for *the* authentic female voice or *the* sexuality, a warning against the commitment to any confessional mode as necessarily liberating, and a challenge to the notion that simply speaking or writing frees us in any simple way from patriarchy or phallocentrism" (p. 15).

4 Roland Barthes, *Roland Barthes*, trans. Richard Howard (New York: Hill and Wang, 1977), p. 74.

5 I am thinking of Claudine Herrmann who in her book *Les voleuses de langue* (Paris: des femmes, 1976) catches out Barthes's subtle reinscription of cultrual stereotypes of femininity, see pp. 16–18.

6 On the question of the relationship between feminist jouissance and Barthes, see Jane Gallop, "Beyond the *jouissance* Principle," *Representations* (1984), 7:110–15.

7 Stephen Heath, "Barthes on Love," *Sub-Stance* (1983), 37–38: 105. Not all readers of *A Lover's Discourse* share Heath's view that discourse operates in a sexual limbo. Writing in *Christopher Street*, Richard Sennett asserts: "I do not wish to leave you with the impression that *A Lover's Discourse* is a neutered book. It is clearly about love between men" (p. 27).

8 Jane Gallop, "Feminist Criticism and the Pleasure of the Text," *North Dakota Quarterly*, forthcoming.

9 John Sturrock, "Roland Barthes" in John Sturrock, ed., *Structuralism and Since: From Levi-Strauss to Derrida* (Oxford: Oxford Univ.

Press, 1979), p. 73. See also p. 53 where Sturrock traces Barthes's lifelong crusade against essentialism to the origins of his thought in Sartrean existentialism, which may indeed be the original modern French philosophical discourse of indifference.

[10] Sarrasine's misprision relies on a triad on "enthymemes" or "imperfect syllogisms," what Barthes calls "the three proofs": narcissistic, psychological, aesthetic. Example: "all women are timid; La Zambinella is timid; therefore La Zambinella is a woman." Roland Barthes, *S/Z*, trans. Richard Miller (New York: Hill and Wang, 1974), p. 148.

[11] Stephen Heath, *Vertige du déplacement* (Paris: Fayard, 1974), p. 20. All translations mine except where otherwise noted.

[12] *S/Z*, p. 36. Cf. the almost identical analysis Barthes offers of the dramatis personae in *Sur Racine*. "The division of the Racinian world into strong and weak, into tyrants and captives, covers in a sense the division of the sexes: it is their situation in the relation of force that orchestrates [*verse*] some characters as virile and others as feminine, without concern for their biological sexes . . . Here we find a sketch of Racinian fatality: a simple relation, in origin purely circumstantial (captivity or tyranny), is converted into a biological datum; situation is converted into sex, chance into essence." From *On Racine*, trans. Richard Howard, in *A Barthes Reader*, Susan Sontag, ed. (New York: Hill and Wang, 1982), p. 180. Here sexual difference is not primary, not a given; it is the consequence of the position a subject occupies in a configuration of power. Masculinity does not guarantee power; it is the possession of power that produces masculinity. Femininity, by the same token, is the sex of the powerless, irrespective of their biological sense.

[13] Kaja Silverman, *The Subject of Semiotics* (New York: Oxford Univ. Press, 1983), p. 272.

[14] In her brilliant reading of Barthes's reading of Balzac's *Sarrasine*, Barbara Johnson has shown how by fetishizing castration, Barthes, unlike Balzac, reduces the tale to a mere "reversal" of the readerly/writerly paradigm, failing to account for Balzac's more radical deconstruction of the difference within the readerly: "Balzac's text does not operate a simple *reversal* of the readerly hierachy: Balzac does not proclaim castration as the truth behind the readerly's blindness in as unequivocal a way as Barthes's own unequivocality would lead us to believe," "The Critical Difference," *Diacritics* (June 1978), p. 8.

[15] Roland Barthes, "Masculin, Féminin, Neutre," in *Echanges et Communications: Mélanges offerts à Claude Lévi-Strauss à l'occasion de son*

60ème anniversaire, Jean Pouillon and Pierre Maranda, eds.; 2 vols. (The Hague: Mouton, 1970), 2:899.

[16] In his *De Rerum Natura,* Lucretius writes: "While the first bodies are being carried downwards by their own weight in a straight line through the void, at times quite uncertain and uncertain places [sic], they swerve a little from their course, just so much as you might call a change of motion. For if they were not apt to incline, all would fall downwards like raindrops through the profound void, no collision would take place and no blow would be caused among the first-beginnings: thus nature would never have produced anything." trans. W.H.D. Rouse, Loeb Classical Library (Cambridge: Harvard Univ. Press, 1975) p. 113, as quoted by Joan de Jean in her article, "*La Nouvelle Héloise,* or the Case for Pedagogical Deviation," *Yale French Studies* (1982), 63:98–116. Bloom's appropriation of the term in *The Anxiety of Influence* (New York: Oxford Univ. Press, 1973) is typical of its recent usage: for him it is synonymous with "misprision," the felicitious misreading by the poet of his strong predecessor. Cf. Shoshana Felman, "De la nature des choses ou de l'écart à l'équilibre," *Critique* (January 1979), 380:3–15.

[17] Roland Barthes, *The Fashion System,* trans. Matthew Ward and Richard Howard (New York: Hill and Wang, 1983), p. ix.

[18] Michel Foucault, *Power/Knowledge: Selected Interviews and Other Writings 1972–1977,* Colin Gordon, ed., Colin Gordon, et al., trs. (New York; Pantheon Books, 1980), pp. 219–20. Foucault goes on to contrast the desexualization of the women's movement with the fixation of sexuality in the gay rights movement.

[19] Michel Foucault, *Herculine Barbin,* trans. Richard McDougall (New York: Pantheon Books, 1980), p. xiii.

[20] But is this the only way to read Herculine's story? Herculine, Foucault notes, did not write her memoirs as a man because she never adjusted to her belated masculine identity. Rather like a wild child who cannot acquire human speech, Herculine-Abel could not learn to speak like a man, because, of course, masculinity is not just an anatomical fact: it is also the product of socialization. Nevertheless there are places in the memoirs where the narrator grapples with his dilemma by focusing on the signs of his difference from his fellow students, and in so doing Herculine-Abel reinscribes one of the most stereotypical cultural differences between the sexes. He writes of his early school days:

> My progress was rapid, and more than once it aroused the astonishment of my excellent teachers.

It was not the same for handicrafts, for which I showed the deepest aversion and greatest incapacity.

The times my companions employed in making those little masterpieces intended to decorate a drawing room or dress up a younger brother, I myself spent reading. History, ancient and modern, was my favorite passion. (p. 8)

According to the dominant cultural code, women are naturally drawn to that lower order of the arts, handicrafts; patience, meticulous attention to details are some of woman's most time-honored virtues. The products of women's artistic endeavors are destined to brightening up the home and pleasing the family. To men belongs the world of public adventure and bold actions, even if only in the realm of fantasy. In short, what I am suggesting is that despite her sexual indeterminancy Herculine Barbin was what we would call an essentialist.

[21] Michel Foucault, *The Use of Pleasure*, trans. Robert Hurley (New York: Pantheon Books 1985), pp. 5–6.

[22] Michel Foucault, *Le souci de soi* (Paris: Gallimard, 1984), p. 175. Translations mine.

[23] Myra Jehlen, "Against Human Wholeness: A Suggestion for a Feminist Epistemology," unpublished paper presented to the Columbia University Seminar on Women and Society.

[24] The references here are to: Luce Irigaray, *Ce Sexe qui n'en est pas un* (Paris: Minuit, 1977), pp. 73–74; Annette Kolodny, "Dancing through the Minefield: Some Observations on the Theory, Practice, and Politics of a Feminist Literary Criticism," *Feminist Studies* (Spring 1980), 6:1–25; Laura Mulvey, "Visual Pleasure and Narrative Cinema," *Screen* (Autumn 1975), 6:6—18; Mary Ann Doane, "Film and Masquerade: Theorizing the Female Spectator," *Screen* (September/October 1982), 23:74–87; Teresa de Lauretis, *Alice Doesn't: Feminism, Semiotics, Cinema* (Bloomington: Indiana Univ. Press, 1984) especially pp. 142–44; Sandra Gilbert and Susan Gubar, *The Madwoman in the Attic* (New Haven: Yale Univ. Press, 1979), pp. 75 passim (interestingly, "palimpsest" is indexed under "duplicity"); Sarah Kofman, *The Enigma of Woman: Woman in Freud's Writings*, trans. Catherine Porter (Ithaca: Cornell University Press, 1985); Elisabeth Berg, "The Third Woman," *Diacritics* (Summer 1982), 12:11–20; Naomi Schor, "Female Fetishism: The Case of George Sand," *Poetics Today* (1985), 6:301–10, and "Reading Double: Sand's Difference," *The Poetics of Gender*, Nancy Miller, ed., (New York: Columbia Univ. Press, 1986); Jane Gallop, "Annie Leclerc Writing a Letter, with Vermeer (La Lettre d'A-

mour)," *October* (1985), 33:103–18; Biddy Martin, "Feminism, Criticism, and Foucault," *New German Critique* (Fall 1982), 27:13.

[25] Simone de Beauvoir, *The Second Sex*, trans. H.M. Parshley (New York: Knopf, 1971).

[26] Hélène Cixous, "Sorties," trans. Ann Liddle in *New French Feminisms*, Elaine Marks and Isabelle de Courtivron, eds. (Amherst: The Univ. of Massachusetts Press, 1980), p. 97.

15. Elaine Showalter Replies

[1] Pamela Fishman, "What Do Couples Talk About When They're Alone?" in *Women's Language and Style*, ed. Douglass Butturff and Edmund L. Epstein (Akron, Ohio, 1978), p. 21.

16. Miller: Man on Feminism: A Criticism of His Own

[1] For his part, Donoghue never mentions Gilbert's and Gubar's names; he refers to them as the editors.

[2] The thinking that informs Naomi Schor's essays in *Breaking the Chain*, cited by Donoghue in passing, articulates a working relation with Derrida's and Irigaray's problematics; my own essay in the Showalter anthology refers to Irigarary's analysis of mimeticism; but these are exceptions to the vast body of feminist criticism evoked by the titles under review, and hardly constitute a dominant agenda. We have to see how much of what is going on here is a displacement of Donoghue's (always?) already constituted problems with Derrida.

[3] As in, for instance, his earlier hostile account of the subject, "Deconstructing Deconstruction," *The New York Review of Books*. June 12, 1980; pp. 37–41.

[4] The term seems to be a kind of negative buzzword in his lexicon of conservative doxa. In "The Promiscuous Cool of Postmodernism," *The New York Times Book Review*, June 22, 1986, Donoghue opposes "man-made" to an "artist's desire for spontaneity or an original relation to the world"; "man-made" images are "quotations from quotations" (37). In her provocative study of American literature, *Sensational Designs: The Cultural Work of American Fiction, 1790–1860* (New York: Oxford Univ. Press, 1985), Jane Tompkins underlines the implications at the heart of the feminist argument Donoghue has so much trouble with: "To question the standard definition of the classic, and thus the canon as it is presently constituted, is also to question

the way of thinking about literature on which the canon is based. . . . The following attempt to describe the man-made, historically produced nature of a single author's reputation, therefore, is likely to arouse a host of objections because it challenges, all at once, an entire range of assumptions on which literary criticism has traditionally operated. The strength of these assumptions does not stem from their being grounded in the truth about literature, however, but from the pervasiveness of one particular mode of constructing literature—namely, the one that assigns to literary greatness an ahistorical, transcedental ground" (5).

5 Perhaps he is attracted to Robinson's position because it provides an insider's critique of feminist criticism; or is it just woman on woman, like his choice of Godwin on Gilbert and Gubar; and closer to home for him, Brigid Brophy.

6 In this report card on feminist criticism, Carroll Smith-Rosenberg's new book gets high marks for its "exemplary" attention to "forgotten or ignored moments in the past." Donoghue is impressed and interested by her methodology (unlike the regressive work evoked earlier) and her "documentary materials." He is interested in what she has to say about "mothers and daughters, friendship between women, marriage, menstruation, menopause, the New Woman, androgyny." This study of women's experience, values, etc.—as opposed to its documentation in the *Norton*—that constitutes a real contribution to American studies would not have occurred without the "context of feminist criticism." But here's the rub: Smith-Rosenberg is a *historian*, not a literary critic.

7 Feminists who work with and through Bakhtin, for example, like Patricia S. Yaeger. See her '"Because a Fire Was in My Head': Eudora Welty and the Dialogic Imagination," *PMLA*, 99, 5 (October 1985), 955–73.

8 The anxiety about "separatist difference" seems to haunt the texts of male critics who want nevertheless to take on feminist criticism; see, for example, K. K. Ruthven's *Feminist Literary Studies: An Introduction* (1984), reviewed by Naomi Schor in the journal *Paragraph*, Autumn 1986; and Mary Jacobus's remarks on his case in *Reading Woman: Essays in Feminist Criticism* (New York: Columbia Univ. Press, 1986), 283–85.

I am indebted to thank Alice Y. Kaplan for her generous, witty and helpful reading of the first draft of this piece.

17. Men, Feminism: The Materiality of Discourse

1 Traditional sexism itself of course continues in university life. In 1984 I read a letter of recommendation (written by a male faculty

member on behalf of a woman who had just received her Ph.D.) that included the following: "Her flaming red hair will remind you of the young Greer Garson."

² See Mary Daly, *Gyn/Ecology: The Metaethics of Radical Feminism* (Boston: Beacon Press, 1978).

³ As early as 1981, Carolyn Heilbrun was able to observe insights in new books by male literary critics that would not have been possible without feminism. See her "Women, Men, Theories, and Literature," *Profession* (1981), pp. 25–29.

⁴ See my "Envoys of Otherness: Difference and Continuity in Feminist Criticism," in Paula A. Treichler, et al., eds. *For Alma Mater: Theory and Practice in Feminist Scholarship* (Urbana: Univ. of Illinois Press, 1985).

⁵ See Toril Moi, *Sexual/Textual Politics: Feminist Literary Theory* (New York: Methuen, 1985); K. K. Ruthven, *Feminist Literary Studies: An Introduction* (Cambridge: Cambridge Univ. Press, 1984); and Paula A. Treichler, "Teaching Feminist Theory," in Cary Nelson, ed., *Theory in the Classroom*, (Urbana: Univ. of Illinois Press, 1986).

⁶ See John Stoltenberg, "Refusing to be a Man," in Jon Snodgrass, ed. *For Men Against Sexism* (San Rafel, Calif.: Times Change Press, 1977), reprinted in *Women's Studies International Forum*, 7:1 (1984), pp. 25–27.

⁷ For a dialogue between Catharine MacKinnon and Ellen Willis see Cary Nelson and Lawrence Grossberg, eds. *Marxism and the Interpretation of Culture (Urbana: Univ. of Illinois Press, 1987).*

⁸ *Luce Irigaray, This Sex Which Is Not One*, trans. Catherine Porter with Carolyn Burke (Ithaca: Cornell Univ. Press, 1985), p. 197.

⁹ Jacques Derrida and Christie V. McDonald, "Choreographies: Interview," *Diacritics*, 12:2 (1982), p. 69.

¹⁰ Jacques Derrida with Geoff Bennington, "On Colleges and Philosophy: Interview," *ICA Documents No. 5* (London: Institute of Contemporary Arts, 1986), 10. On the function of the image of woman within philosophy see Derrida, *Spurs: Nietzsche's Styles*, trans. Barbara Harlow (Chicago: Univ. of Chicago Press, 1979). For his analysis of the figure of the hymen see Derrida's *Dissemination*, trans. Barbara Johnson (Chicago: Univ. of Chicago Press, 1981). Invagination is discussed in "Living On: Border Lines," *Deconstruction and Criticism*, ed. Harold Bloom et al. (New York: Seabury Press, 1979) and in "The Law of Genre," *Glyph* no. 7 (1980).

18. *in any event* . . .

[1] Michèle Le Doeuff, *L'imaginaire philosophique* (Paris; Payot, 1980), p. 150. My translation.

[2] Barbara Johnson, *The Critical Difference* (Baltimore: The Johns Hopkins Univ. Press, 1980), p. 5.

[3] One history of the function of such representation in a particular culture is Ann Summers, *Damned Whores and God's Police: The Colonization of Women in Australia* (Victoria: Penguin), 1975.

[4] The papers by Alice Jardine, Elizabeth Weed, and Judith Mayne have commented on this process in the MLA seminar as a whole.

[5] Helen Grace, "'For all her shouting, she was as if mute' . . . ," paper delivered to The Women's Studies Conference, The Women's College, University of Sydney, September 1985.

[6] Gayatri Chakrovorty Spivak, "The Politics of Interpretation," *Critical Inquiry*, 9 (1), 267.

20. *Women in the Beehive*

[1] Gayatri Spivak, "Love Me, Love My Ombre, Elle," *Diacritics* (Winter 1984), pp. 19–36.

[2] Jacques Derrida, *La Carte Postale: de Socrate à Freud et au-delà*, (Paris: Flammarion, 1980).

[3] Jacques Derrida and Christie V. McDonald, "Choreographies," *Diacritics* 12 (Summer 1982), pp. 66–76.

[4] Jacques Derrida, "The Law of Genre," *Critical Inquiry* 7 (Autumn 1980), pp. 55–82.

22. *Outlaws: Gay Men in Feminism*

[1] "Displacement and the Discourse of Women," in *Displacement: Derrida and After*, ed. Mark Krupnick (Bloomington: Indiana University Press, 1983), p. 177.

[2] *Between Men: English Literature and Male Homosocial Desire* (New York: Columbia University Press, 1985), p. 20.

[3] Ibid.

[4] These words do appear in a letter addressed to the publisher of

The Anti-Aesthetic (Port Towsend, Wash.: Bay Press, 1983); they are reprinted here with the permission of Linda Nochlin. I agree with her that the absence of women writing about feminism is a serious problem with the collection; the original text of "The Discourse of Others" made a similar accusation, which was cut. My primary concern in this essay, however, is to differentiate the monolithic "men" in "men and feminism".

⁵ Sedgwick, pp. 88–89; 87.

⁶ "Critical Cross-Dressing," see pp. 116–32 above.

⁷ Robert Stoller, *Presentations of Gender* (New Haven: Yale University Press, 1983). See in particular Stoller's list of "gender disorders" beginning on p. 18.

⁸ Spivak, p. 176.

⁹ Maria Antonietta Macciocchi, quoted in Sedgwick, p. 220, n27. This frequently quoted homophobic formulation is especially surprising in light of Macciocchi's eloquent defense of Pasolini's feminism. See "Quatre Hérésies Cardinales pour Pasolini," in *Pasolini, seminare dirigé par Maria Antonietta Macciocchi* (Paris: Grasset, 1980), pp. 127–58.

¹⁰ Luce Irigaray, "Women on the Market," in *This Sex Which Is Not One,* trans. Catherine Porter (Ithaca: Cornell University Press, 1985), p. 180.

¹¹ *Ibid.,* p. 171; and "Commodities among Themselves," pp. 192–93.

¹² See Jeffrey Weeks, preface to Guy Hocquenghem, *Homosexual Desire,* trans. Daniella Dangoor (London: Allison & Busby, 1978), p. 11.

¹³ Irigaray, "Commodities," p. 193.

¹⁴ In *Toward an Anthropology of Women,* ed. Rayna R. Reiter (New York and London: Monthly Review Press, 1975), pp. 179–80.

¹⁵ Ibid., pp. 180; 182.

¹⁶ Supreme Court of the United States, *Bowers v. Hardwick,* no. 85–140 (1986), n.p.

¹⁷ Bernard Knox, "Subversive Activities," *The New York Review of Books* XXXII, 20 (1985), p. 7.

¹⁸ Georgia statute 16–6–2 was actually rewritten in 1968 because it had been interpreted as inapplicable to heterosexual and lesbian sodomy. However, the legal history of homosexuality makes it im-

possible to regard ours as a "progressive" society: Under the Napoleonic code, homosexuality was not subject to legal sanctions in France until 1942; the Gaullist regime intensified legal sanctions in the 1960s. Although Britain repealed the death penalty for sodomy in 1861, it was only thereafter that the persecution of homosexual men began in earnest. In fact, the "liberalization" of laws criminalizing homosexuality has almost always been followed by an increase in prosecutions. See Weeks, pp. 11, 25.

[19] From *Bowers v. Hardwick*.

[20] Michel Foucault, *The History of Sexuality* I, trans. Robert Hurley (New York: Pantheon, 1978), p. 43.

[21] *Psychoanalysis and Feminism* (New York: Vintage, 1975), pp. 375–76.

[22] Ibid.

[23] Cited by Lévi-Strauss in *The Elementary Structures of Kinship* (Boston: Beacon Press, 1969), p. 485.

[24] Obviously, when we attribute "homosexuality" to non-Western cultures, we are exporting Western sexual ideology (as Foucault remarks, the term *homosexuality* itself dates to 1870), just as the tendency to regard the Greeks as "homosexual" (and Plato and Sappho as gay ancestors), or Michelangelo as a "gay" artist, is anachronistic, at best. However, I retain these terms here as indications of the historical limits of a society that can regard homosexual behavior only as a manifestation of homosexual identity.

[25] See *Ritualized Homosexuality in Melanesia*, ed. Gilbert H. Herdt (Berkeley: University of California Press, 1984).

[26] Lévi-Strauss is in Porto Esperanca, Brazil, which he describes as "the weirdest spot one could hope to find on the face of the earth, with the possible exception of Fire Island in New York State." Here is the conclusion of his account of the strange rituals practiced by the inhabitants: "To complete the picture I must add that Cherry Grove is chiefly inhabited by male couples, attracted no doubt by the general pattern of inversion. Since nothing grows in the sand, apart from broad patches of poisonous ivy, provisions are collected once a day from the one and only shop, at the end of the landing-stage. In the tiny streets, on higher ground more stable than the dunes, the sterile couples can be seen returning to their chalets pushing prams (the only vehicles suitable for the narrow paths) containing little but the weekend bottles of milk that no baby will consume." *Tristes Tropiques*, trans. J. and D. Weightman (New York: Washington Square Press, 1977), pp. 168–69. I should perhaps add that only once does Lévi-

Strauss mention that his wife accompanied him on the travels chron-
icled in *Tristes Tropiques.*

27 Ibid., p. 354.

28 Irigaray, "Women," p. 171. Lévi-Strauss's remark appears in
Elementary Structures, p. 38.

29 *Ritualized Homosexuality in Melanesia.*

30 Although Lévi-Strauss insists that the avunculate has disappeared in modern Western societies, some attention to male homosexual experience suggests that it has not disappeared *entirely.* As
James Saslow writes at the conclusion of the Acknowledgments in
his recent book *Ganymede in the Renaissance: Homosexuality in Art and
Society* (New Haven and London: Yale University Press, 1986), "For
those who, in Plato's words, are 'better equipped for offspring of the
soul than for those of the body,' the birth of a nephew is perhaps the
most immediate experience of the continuity of life and the value of
working for future generations" (p. xvi).

31 In *Ecrits: A Selection,* trans. Alan Sheridan (London: Tavistock,
1977).

32 In *Lacan and Narration: The Psychoanalytic Difference in Narrative
Theory,* ed. Robert Con Davis (Baltimore and London: Johns Hopkins
University Press, 1983), pp. 943–44; 960.

33 Ibid., p. 944.

34 See Sarah Kofman's excellent treatment of the problem women's
"inaccessibility" posed for Freud. *The Enigma of Woman: Woman in the
Writings of Freud* trans. Catherine Porter (Ithaca: Cornell University
Press, 1985).

35 Consider the following, from *France-Dimanche* in 1962, purport-
ing to tell "The Truth About Homosexuality": "A Swiss psychiatrist
goes straight to the point: according to him, in seventy per cent of
cases, it is the parents who are responsible for their children's homosexuality, and particularly the mother! . . . *Stress the mother's responsibility, however astounding it may seem. Too many mothers wish in
their heart of hearts for their sons to be homosexual*" (italics original). Cited
in Hocquenghem, p. 69.

36 In *Sexuality and the Psychology of Love,* ed. Philip Reiff (New York:
Collier, 1963), p. 187.

37 Here is one statement of this theory, from the Schreber case:
"After the stage of heterosexual object-choice has been reached, the
homosexual tendencies are not, as might be supposed, done away

with or brought to a stop; they are merely deflected from their sexual aim and applied to fresh uses. They now combine with portions of the ego-instincts and, as 'anaclitic' components, help to constitute the social instincts, thus contributing an erotic factor to friendship and comradeship, to *esprit de corps* and to the love of mankind in general. How large a contribution is in fact derived from erotic sources (though with the sexual aim inhibited) could scarcely be guessed from the normal social relations of mankind." "Psychoanalytic Notes upon an Autobiographical Account of a Case of Paranoia (Dementia Paranoides)," in *Three Case Histories*, ed. Philip Rieff (New York: Collier, 1963), p. 164.

[38] Bob Gallagher and Alexander Wilson, "Michel Foucault: An Interview," *Edinburgh Review* (1986), p. 58.

[39] Sedgwick, p. 87.

[40] Gallagher and Wilson, p. 58.

[41] Sedgwick, p. 89.

[42] Hocquenghem, p. 35.

[43] Sedgwick, pp. 89–90.

[44] René Girard, *The Scapegoat*, trans. Yvonne Freccero (Baltimore: Johns Hopkins University Press, 1986), pp. 2–3.

23. Envy: or With Your Brains and My Looks

[1] See C. Duchen, *Feminism in France* (London: Routledge & Kegan Paul, 1986).

[2] Especially in *Of Woman Born* (New York: Bantam Books, 1977).

[3] See J. Lloyd, *The Man of Reason* (London: Methuen, 1985). Also, J. Benjamin, "The Bonds of Love: Rational Violence and Erotic Domination," in H. Eisenstein & A. Jardine, eds., *The Future of Difference* (Boston: G. K. Hall, 1980)

4. This is the line I try to argue in my doctoral dissertation, *Féminisme et Philosophie* (Université Paris I, Panthéon-Sorbonne, 1981), and in the following articles: "Femmes et philosophie, questions à suivre," *La Révue d'En Face*, no. 13, 1982; "Modelli di dissonanza," in P. Magli, ed., *Le Donne e i Segni* (Urbino, 1983); and "Ethics Revisited: Women and/in Philosophy," in L. Gross & C. Pateman, eds., *Feminist Challenges* (Sydney: Unwin & Allen, 1986).

[5] See *Le Séminaire XX—Encore* (Paris: Seuil, 1977).

[6] See *Eperons* (Paris: Flammarion, 1978).

[7] See *L'Usage des plaisirs* and *Le Souci de soi* (Paris: Gallimard, 1984).

[8] See G. Deleuze and F. Guattari, *L'Anti-Oedipe* (Paris: Minuit, 1972); also, *Mille Plateaux* (Paris: Minuit, 1980).

[9] This is the line pursued by Irigaray, especially in *Ce Sexe qui n'en est pas un* (Paris: Minuit, 1977), as well as by the Italian A. Bocchetti, "L'Indecente indifferenza" (Edizioni del Centro Culturale V. Woolf, Rome, 1983), and by A. Cavarero, "Somiglianza e differenza, "forthcoming in *Il Pensiero della differenza sessuale.*

[10] See E. Badinter, *Le Même est l'autre* (Paris, 1986); and G. Lipovetsky, *L'Ere du vide* (Paris: Gallimard, 1983).

[11] See *Man-Made Women* (London: Hutchinson, 1986).

[12] See A. Rich, "Compulsory Heterosexuality and the Lesbian Experience," *Signs*, vol. 5, no. 4, 1980.

[13] See M. Wittig, "La Pensée straight," *Questions Féministes*, no. 7, 1980.

24. A Conversation

References

Roland Barthes. *A Lover's Discourse.* New York: Hill & Wang, 1978).

Gilles Deleuze and Claire Parnet. *Dialogues.* Paris: Flammarion, 1977).

Christine Delphy, *Close to Home: A Materialist Analysis of Women's Oppression,* (Amherst: Univ. of Massachusetts Press, 1984).

Jacques Derrida, "No Apocalypse, Not Now," *Diacritics*, vol. 14, no. 2.

Marguerite Duras, *Les Parleuses* (Paris: Minuit, 1974). Forthcoming in translation from Univ. of Nebraska Press.

Terry Eagleton, *The Rape of Clarissa* (Minneapolis: Univ. of Minnesota Press, 1982).

Jane Gallop, *The Daughter's Seduction* (Ithaca: Cornell Univ. Press, 1982).

Stephen Heath, "Difference," Screen, vol. 19, no. 3.

Claudine Herrmann, *Les Voleuses de langue* (Paris: Des femmes, 1976).

Alice Jardine, *Gynesis* (Ithaca: Cornell Univ. Press, 1985).

Sarah Kofman, "Ça cloche," in *Les Fins de l'homme*, eds. P. Lacoue-Labarthe & J.-L. Nancy (Paris: Galilée, 1974).

Adrienne Rich, *On Lies, Secrets, and Silence* (New York: Norton, 1979).

Paul Smith, *Discerning the Subject* (Minneapolis: Univ. of Minnesota Press, 1987).

Jacques Derrida has objected to my characterization of his work in these few remarks, and has asked for some explanation. I certainly regret that he should have been personally offended by what I said, especially since I have been intrigued by his work for many years and find much to admire in it. Nonetheless (and even if I hereby demonstrate my own limited understanding), I can only repeat my unease with what I take to be one of the upshots of deconstruction: its undermining of the very possibility of adopting or developing an active political *position*. Indeed, I often feel frustrated by the perception that, in the particular academic context to whose constitution deconstruction has contributed so much, an insistence on vindicating the need for such positions is somewhat retrogressive. And yet I do insist. Thus, I'm happy that M. Derrida claims himself to be personally opposed to apartheid: one needs perhaps only refer for corroboration to the book on Nelson Mandela which he recently helped edit. At the same time, I myself can't understand that deconstructive work such as I refer to in this conversation can directly entail, cause, or subvent M. Derrida's personal political stances or opinions.

Paul Smith

Reply

I am grateful to Paul Smith for having agreed to clarify his point. But the argument thus opened up deserves more than a single note. At present I would only add this: my *position* toward—that is, my unconditional *opposition* to—apartheid was declared without the slightest equivocation even before *For Nelson Mandela* (which I coedited and to which I contributed) and as early as the texts cited here ("Racism's Last Word," translated by Peggy Kamuf, Critical Inquiry, autumn 1985, 12:1, reprinted in *'Race,' Writing and Difference*, ed. H. L. Gates, Jr., University of Chicago Press, 1986). Not only did I never write that "Speaking against apartheid would be 'too dialectical,' so remain silent" (and I wonder what might justify the inverted commas around 'too dialectical'?); on the contrary, I have said that one must oppose certain overly conciliatory dialectics, and oppose them "very loudly and in a single breath." *I have also written that, contrary to "good conscience or denegation," "it was, it will have to be, it is necessary to appeal unconditionally to the future of another law and another force..."* ('Race,' Writing and Difference, p. 337 of the book, p. 298 of the journal issue and passim). Is this remaining silent? Is it a call to remain silent? Who has spoken so clearly on apartheid that he should give me a lesson on the subject? Who wants to reduce whom to silence?

Jacques Derrida

Contributors

Rosi Braidotti teaches at the Collège International de Philosophie and in the Columbia University Programs in Paris. She is a member of the editorial board of the feminist journal, *Cahiers du Grif* and has published articles in both English and French on questions related to contemporary French philosophy, women, and feminism.

Jacques Derrida is among the most well-known and celebrated of contemporary philosophers. Among his works of deconstruction that have been translated into English are *Dissemination, The Margins of Philosophy, Of Grammatology, Positions, Spurs, Writing and Difference,* as well as many other books and articles.

Terry Eagleton is a Fellow of Wadham College, Oxford, and author of many books on Marxism, literature, and contemporary theory, including *Marxism and Literary Criticism, Walter Benjamin: Towards a Revolutionary Criticism, Literary Theory,* and the recent collection, *Against the Grain.* He is also general editor of Blackwell's "Rereading Literature" series.

Jane Gallop is Professor of Humanities at Rice University and is the author of *Intersections: A Reading of Sade with Bataille, Blanchot and Klossowski, The Daughter's Seduction: Feminism and Psychoanalysis,* and *Reading Lacan.*

Alice Jardine is Associate Professor of Romance Languages and Literatures at Harvard University. She has coedited *The Future of Difference* (with Hester Eisenstein), and has translated many of Julia Kristeva's writings. She is author of *Gynesis: Configurations of Woman and Modernity.*

Stephen Heath is a Fellow of Jesus College, Cambridge. He is the author of *The Nouveau Roman, Le Vertige du déplacement* (on Roland Barthes), *Questions of Cinema, The Sexual Fix,* and of many articles on contemporary cultural theory and film.

Peggy Kamuf teaches French at Miami University, Ohio. She has published many articles on feminism, deconstruction, and French literature, and a book, *Fictions of Feminine Desire.*

Judith Mayne is an Associate Professor with a joint appointment in French and in the Women's Studies program at Ohio State University, Columbus. She is author of many articles on feminism and on film in such journals as *Signs, New German Critique,* and *Wide Angle.*

Nancy Miller is Professor of Women Studies and Director of the Women's Studies Program at Barnard College. She is author of *The Heroine's Text: Readings in the French and English Novel, 1722–1782,* and editor of *The Poetics of Gender.*

Meaghan Morris is a former lecturer in semiotics and a film critic in Australia; she now writes full-time. She has coedited two collections: *Language, Sexuality and Subversion,* and *Michel Foucault: Power, Truth, and Strategy* and is currently finishing a book of essays in feminist criticism.

Cary Nelson is Professor of English and founding Director of the Unit for Criticism and Interpretive Theory at the University of Illinois. He is the author of *The Incarnate Word: Literature as Verbal Space* and *Our last First Poets: Vision and History in Contemporary American Poetry;* the editor of *Theory in the Classroom;* and the coeditor of, among other books, *Marxism and the Interpretation of Culture.* He is currently completing *Reading Criticism: The Literary and Institutional Status of Critical Discourse.*

Richard Ohmann, Professor of English at Wesleyan University, is an editor of *Radical Teacher* and has published many articles on twentieth century literature and culture, as well as the important study, *English in America.*

Craig Owens is a senior editor for *Art in America* and publishes widely on issues in the contemporary arts and the theory of the visual arts.

Andrew Ross teaches English at Princeton University and has published widely on cultural theory and sexual politics. He is author of *The Failure of Modernism: Symptoms of American Poetry* and cotranslator of Jacques Aumont's *Montage Eisenstein.*

Robert Scholes is Alumni-Alumnae Professor of English at Brown University and a prolific author of work on modern literature, literary theory, and pedagogical issues. His books include *Structuralism in Literature, Semiotics and Interpretation,* and most recently *Textual Power.*

Naomi Schor is Nancy Duke Lewis Professor of French at Brown

University and author of many articles and books on feminism, literary theory and French literature, including *Breaking the Chain: Women, Theory, and French Realist Fiction* and, most recently, *Reading in Detail: Aesthetics and the Feminine.*

Elaine Showalter teaches English at Princeton University and is author of many important writings on women and literature, including *A Literature of Their Own*, and the recent *The Female Malady.* She has also edited a collection of essays called *The New Feminist Criticism.*

Paul Smith is Associate Professor of Literary and Cultural Studies at Carnegie Mellon University. He is author of many articles on literary and cultural theory, and of *Pound Revised* and *Discerning the Subject.*

Elizabeth Weed is the Assistant Director of Brown University's Pembroke Center for Teaching and Research on Women.